A-Level

Mathematics

for Edexcel Statistics 1

CGP
- books
like no others!

CGP

The Complete Course for Edexcel S1

Contents

About this book

In this book you'll find...

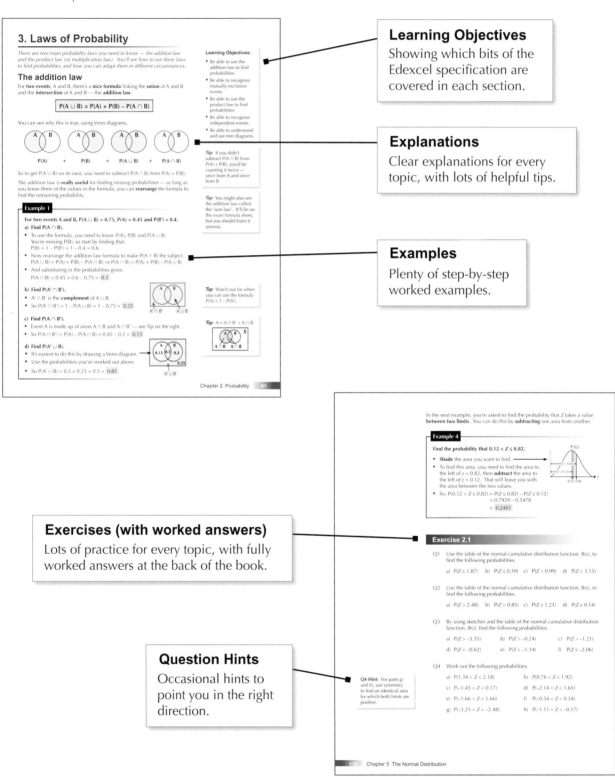

Learning Objectives
Showing which bits of the Edexcel specification are covered in each section.

Explanations
Clear explanations for every topic, with lots of helpful tips.

Examples
Plenty of step-by-step worked examples.

Exercises (with worked answers)
Lots of practice for every topic, with fully worked answers at the back of the book.

Question Hints
Occasional hints to point you in the right direction.

Review Exercise — Chapter 1

Q1 The stem and leaf diagram on the right represents the lengths (in cm) of 15 bananas. Write down the original data as a list.

```
12 | 8
13 | 2  5
14 | 3  3  6  8
15 | 2  9
16 | 1  1  2  3
17 | 0  2
```
Key 12|8 means 12.8 cm

Q2 Twenty phone calls were made by a householder one evening. The lengths of the calls (in minutes to the nearest minute) are recorded below. Draw a histogram of the data.

Length of calls	0 - 2	3 - 5	6 - 8	9 - 15
Number of calls	10	6	3	1

Q3 Calculate the mean, median and mode of the data in the table on the right.

x	0	1	2	3	4
f	5	4	4	2	1

Q4 The speeds of 60 cars travelling in a 40 mph speed limit area were measured to the nearest mph. The data is summarised in this table. Calculate estimates of the mean and median, and state the modal class.

Speed (mph)	30 - 34	35 - 39	40 - 44	45 - 50
Frequency	12	37	9	2

Q5 Find the mean and standard deviation of the following numbers: 11, 12, 14, 17, 21, 23, 27.

Q6 The scores in an IQ test for 50 people are recorded in the table below.

Score	100 - 106	107 - 113	114 - 120	121 - 127	128 - 134
Frequency	6	11	22	9	2

Estimate the mean and variance of the distribution.

Q7 For a set of data, $n = 100$, $\sum(x - 20) = 125$, and $\sum(x - 20)^2 = 221$. Find the mean and standard deviation of x.

Review Exercises
Mixed questions covering the whole chapter, with fully worked answers.

Exam-Style Questions — Chapter 1

1 The profits of 100 businesses are given in the table.

Profit, $£x$ million	Number of businesses
$4.0 \leqslant x < 5.0$	24
$5.0 \leqslant x < 5.5$	26
$5.5 \leqslant x < 6.0$	21
$6.0 \leqslant x < 6.5$	19
$6.5 \leqslant x < 8.0$	10

  a) Represent the data in a histogram. *(3 marks)*

  b) Comment on the distribution of the profits of the businesses. *(2 marks)*

2 A group of 19 people played a game. The scores, x, that the people achieved are summarised by:
$$\sum(x - 30) = 228 \text{ and } \sum(x - 30)^2 = 3040$$

  a) Calculate the mean and the standard deviation of the 19 scores. *(3 marks)*

  b) Show that $\sum x = 798$ and $\sum x^2 = 33\,820$. *(3 marks)*

  c) Another student played the game. Her score was 32. Find the new mean and standard deviation of all 20 scores. *(4 marks)*

3 In a supermarket two types of chocolate drops were compared. The masses, a grams, of 20 chocolate drops of brand A are summarised by:
$$\sum a = 60.3 \qquad \sum a^2 = 219$$
The mean mass of 30 chocolate drops of brand B was 2.95 g, and the standard deviation was 1 g.

  a) Find the mean mass of a brand A chocolate drop. *(1 mark)*

  b) Find the standard deviation of the masses of the brand A chocolate drops. *(3 marks)*

  c) Compare brands A and B. *(2 marks)*

  d) Find the standard deviation of the masses of all 50 chocolate drops. *(4 marks)*

Exam-Style Questions
Questions in the same style as the ones you'll get in the exam, with worked solutions and mark schemes.

Formula Sheet and Statistical Tables
Containing all the formulas and statistical tables you'll be given in the S1 exam.

Glossary
All the definitions you need to know for the exam, plus other useful words.

Practice Exam Papers (on CD-ROM)
Two printable exam papers, with fully worked answers and mark schemes.

A-Level
Mathematics
for Edexcel

S1

Exam Practice Papers
& Worked Answers
CGP

Published by CGP

Editors:
Ali Palin, Andy Park, Charlotte Whiteley.

Contributors:
Katharine Brown, George Davies, Alastair Duncombe, Anna Gainey,
Claire Jackson, James Nicholson, Gary Rowlands.

ISBN: 978 1 84762 807 7

With thanks to Mona Allen and Glenn Rogers for the proofreading.
With thanks to Alastair Duncombe for the reviewing.

Groovy website: www.cgpbooks.co.uk

Printed by Elanders Ltd, Newcastle upon Tyne.
Jolly bits of clipart from CorelDRAW®

1. Mathematical Models in Probability and Statistics

Mathematical models are basically descriptions of things in the real world, and are usually written to help solve some kind of problem. They're usually much simpler than the real-world situations they describe, but are still useful.

Learning Objectives:
- Be able to explain the mathematical modelling process
- Be able to describe some of the reasons for carrying out mathematical modelling

The benefits of mathematical models

Understanding real-world problems

- A technology company is going to launch a new product — the USB-Penguin.
  The company's managers would like to **maximise profits** from USB-Penguin sales. (At the very least, they need to sell enough USB-Penguins to recover the money spent on development.)

- They are trying to decide what would be the best **price** to charge for the USB-Penguin. They realise that the variables '**price**', '**sales**', and '**profit**' are linked.
  For example:
  - If the **price** is low, then **sales** should be higher.
    - (i) However, if sales aren't as high as expected, the low price may mean that the company will not be able to recover the development costs.
    - (ii) But if the low price encourages lots of people to buy the USB-Penguin, then **profits** could be high.
  - If the **price** is high, then they can expect to **sell fewer** USB-Penguins.
    - (i) However, if sales turn out to be higher than expected, then the company will make a very big **profit**.
    - (ii) But if the high price puts people off buying, then the company won't recover the development costs.

- The managers need to answer the following question:

  What is the best price to charge for the USB-Penguin to maximise profits (or to have the best chance of recovering the development costs)?

Saving money and reducing risk

They decide to try and answer the question using a **mathematical model**.

- This is a mathematical description of the situation using **equations**.

- Because real-life situations can be so complicated, some **assumptions** and **simplifications** are usually made — basically, to make the maths easier.

- The model allows possible prices to be **tried out** (in the model) and the sales and profits to be **predicted**.

- Using a model to test what might happen in various scenarios means there is less **risk** of something going **expensively wrong** in real life (such as the company losing so much money it goes out of business).

The modelling process

There are **seven** important steps in creating a mathematical model.

(1) *Recognising a real-world problem*

The managers' pricing dilemma, for example.

(2) *Making the mathematical model*

- This will involve writing down one or more **equations**.
- For example, there might be an equation describing how the **retail price** (r) affects **sales** (s). There might also be another equation describing how the price and sales affect **profit** (P).
- Writing these equations might involve making a number of **assumptions** and **simplifications**.
  - For example, the managers might have to make their 'best guess' at the effect on sales of reducing the price.
  - And they might not take into account factors such as how increased sales might lead to more competition (as other firms make products similar to the USB-Penguin).

Tip: Linear regression is a form of mathematical modelling — see Chapter 4.

(3) *Use the model to make some predictions*

The equations can then be used to **predict** how many USB-Penguin sales are expected at various prices, and the effect this would have on profits.

(4) *Collect some real-world data*

When the USB-Penguin goes on sale, the company will be able to collect some **real-life data** — by recording the actual sales of the USB-Penguin at the price they choose.

(5) *Compare the predictions with the real-world data*

The predicted number of sales and the actual number of sales can then be **compared**.

Tip: You won't be expected to carry out any statistical tests in S1.

(6) *Test whether the model 'works'*

Statistical tests can be carried out to test **how well** the model describes the real-world situation.

Tip: When you update the model, you need to go through steps 3 to 6 again.

(7) *Improve the model*

If necessary, the model can be **improved** by changing some of the equations (or adding some new ones) so that it makes predictions that are closer to what is observed in real life. This might allow the company to adapt its prices in the future so that sales and profits improve.

1. Representing Data

Data is to statistics what fuel is to a car — without data, all the statistics knowledge in the world won't be much use. This chapter covers the essentials about data — from graphs, through to location, dispersion and skewness.

Learning Objectives:

- Be able to recognise different types of variables.
- Be able to interpret frequency tables and grouped frequency tables.
- Be able to draw and interpret histograms, and stem and leaf diagrams.

Data basics

A lot of the subject of **statistics** involves analysing **data**.

Data consists of a number of **observations** (or **measurements**). Each of these observations records the value of a particular **variable**.

There are different kinds of variables.

- Variables that take **non-numerical** values (i.e. they're not numbers) — these are called **qualitative** variables.

- Variables that take **numerical** values (i.e. they're numbers) — these are called **quantitative** variables.

There are then two different types of **quantitative** variables.

- A **discrete** variable can only take **certain values** within a particular range (e.g. shoe sizes) — this means there are 'gaps' between possible values (you can't take size 9.664 shoes, for example).

- A **continuous** variable can take **any value** within a particular range (e.g. lengths or masses) — there are no gaps between possible values.

Tip: Or you can think of a discrete variable changing 'in steps'.

Example 1

An employer collects information about the computers in his office. He gathers observations of the 5 variables shown in this table.

1. Manufacturer	Bell	Banana	Deucer	Deucer	a
2. Processor speed (in GHz)	2.6	2.1	1.8	2.2	b
3. Year of purchase	2009	2010	2011	2009	b
4. Memory (in MB)	2	3	3.1	4.8	b
5. Colour	Grey	Grey	Grey	Black	a

Which of the five variables are:

a) qualitative?
- The variables 'Manufacturer' and 'Colour' take values that are not numbers.
- So there are two qualitative variables: 'Manufacturer' and 'Colour'.

b) quantitative?
- The variables 'Processor speed', 'Year of purchase' and 'Memory' take values that are numbers.
- So there are three quantitative variables: 'Processor speed', 'Year of purchase' and 'Memory'.

Example 2

The variables below are all quantitative.
(i) length, (ii) weight, (iii) number of brothers, (iv) time,
(v) total value of 6 coins from down the back of my sofa

a) Which of these 5 quantitative variables are continuous?
- 'Length', 'weight' and 'time' can all take any value in a range.
- So the continuous variables are: 'length' , 'weight' and 'time' .

b) Which of these 5 quantitative variables are discrete?
- 'Number of brothers' and 'total value of 6 coins' can only take certain values.
- So there are two discrete variables — these are: 'number of brothers' and 'total value of 6 coins' .

Tip: 'Number of brothers' can only take whole-number values.

'Total value of 6 coins' can only take particular values. For example, they could be worth 12p or 13p, but not 12.8p.

Data is often shown in the form of a **table**.
There are two types you need to be really familiar with.

Tip: Frequency just means 'the number of times something happens'.

- **Frequency tables** show the number of observations of various values.

  For example, this frequency table shows the number of bananas in thirty 1.5 kg bags.

Number of bananas	8	9	10	11	12
Frequency	3	7	10	6	4

Tip: Frequency tables and grouped frequency tables can also be drawn 'vertically', like this:

Number of bananas	Frequency
8	3
9	7
10	10
11	6
12	4

- **Grouped frequency tables** show the number of observations whose values fall within certain **classes** (i.e. **ranges** or **groups of values**). They're often used when there is a large range of possible values.

  For example, this grouped frequency table shows the number of potatoes in thirty 25 kg sacks.

Number of potatoes	50-55	56-60	61-65	66-70	71-75
Frequency	1	8	12	7	2

  - Notice how grouped frequency tables **don't** tell you the **exact** value of the observations — just the most and the least they **could** be.
  - And notice how the different classes **don't overlap**. In fact, there are 'gaps' between the classes because this is **discrete** data.

Grouped frequency tables are also used for **continuous** data. Since there are no 'gaps' between possible data values for continuous variables, there can be no gaps between classes in their grouped frequency tables either.

For example, this grouped frequency table shows the masses of 50 potatoes.

Tip: You don't always need to leave the top and bottom classes without a lower and upper limit — e.g. if you know for a fact that very small or very large data values are impossible.

- **Inequalities** have been used to define the **class boundaries** (the upper and lower limits of each class). There are no 'gaps' and no overlaps between classes.
- The smallest class doesn't have a lower limit — so very small potatoes can still be put into one of the classes. Similarly, the largest class doesn't have an upper limit.

Mass of potato (m, in g)	Frequency
$m < 100$	7
$100 \leq m < 200$	8
$200 \leq m < 300$	16
$300 \leq m < 400$	14
$m \geq 400$	5

This grouped frequency table shows the lengths (to the nearest cm) of the same 50 potatoes.

Length of potato (*l*, in cm)	Frequency
4-5	5
6-7	11
8-9	15
10-11	16
12-13	3

- The shortest potato that could go in the 6-7 class would actually have a length of 5.5 cm (since 5.5 cm would be rounded up to 6 cm when measuring to the nearest cm).

  So the **lower class boundary** of the 6-7 class is 5.5 cm.

- The **upper class boundary** of the 6-7 class is the same as the lower class boundary of the 8-9 class — this is 7.5 cm. This means there are never any **gaps** between classes.

- For each class, you can find the **class width** using this formula:

  $$\text{class width} = \text{upper class boundary} - \text{lower class boundary}$$

- And you can find the **mid-point** of a class using this formula:

  $$\text{mid-point} = \frac{\text{lower class boundary} + \text{upper class boundary}}{2}$$

Tip: Even though a potato of length 7.5 cm would go in the 8-9 class, this is still the upper class boundary of the 6-7 class.

Tip: The upper class boundary of the 12-13 class will be 13.5 cm.

Tip: A class with a lower class boundary of 50 g and upper class boundary of 250 g can be written in different ways.

So you might see:

- '100 – 200, to the nearest 100 g'

- '50 ≤ mass < 250'

- '50–', followed by '250–' for the next class, and so on.

They all mean the same.

Example 1

A researcher measures the length (to the nearest 10 cm) of 40 cars. Her results are shown in the table.
Add four columns to the table to show:

Length (cm)	Frequency
250-350	5
360-410	11
420-450	17
460-500	7

(i)   **the lower class boundaries**
(ii) **the upper class boundaries**
(iii) **the class widths**
(iv) **the class mid-points**

- The shortest car that measures 250 cm (to the nearest 10 cm) is 245 cm long. So the lower class boundary of the 250-350 class is 245 cm.

- The upper class boundary of the 250-350 class is 355 cm (even though a car measuring 355 cm would actually go into the 360-410 class).

- Once you have the class boundaries, use the above formulas to find the class widths and the mid-points.

Length (cm)	Frequency	lower class boundary (cm)	upper class boundary (cm)	class width (cm)	mid-point (cm)
250-350	5	245	355	110	300
360-410	11	355	415	60	385
420-450	17	415	455	40	435
460-500	7	455	505	50	480

Tip: 355 cm must be the upper class boundary for the 250-350 class, because no number less than this would work.

For example, the upper class boundary can't be 354.99 cm, because then a car of length 354.999 cm wouldn't fit into any of the classes. And the upper class boundary can't be 354.999 cm, because then a car of length 354.9999 cm wouldn't fit into any of the classes. And so on.

Example 2

A researcher measures the (nose-to-tip-of-tail) length of 40 cats.
His results are shown in the table.
Add two columns to the table to show:
(i)   the lower class boundaries
(ii) the upper class boundaries

Length, l (mm)	Frequency
$250 \leq l < 350$	3
$350 \leq l < 410$	15
$410 \leq l < 450$	17
$450 \leq l < 500$	5

- The classes are written using inequalities this time. That makes it easy to tell where the class boundaries are.
- The shortest cat that can go in the $250 \leq l < 350$ class measures 250 mm. The length of a cat any shorter than 250 mm wouldn't satisfy the inequality.
- Similarly, the upper class boundary of the $250 \leq l < 350$ class is 350 mm.

Tip: Even though a cat of length 350 mm wouldn't go into the $250 \leq l < 350$ class, the upper class boundary of this class is still 350 mm (since no number smaller than 350 mm is suitable — see page 5 for more information).

Length, l (mm)	Frequency	lower class boundary (mm)	upper class boundary (mm)
$250 \leq l < 350$	3	250	350
$350 \leq l < 410$	15	350	410
$410 \leq l < 450$	17	410	450
$450 \leq l < 500$	5	450	500

Exercise 1.1

Q1   A mechanic collects the following information about cars he services:

  Make, Mileage, Colour, Number of doors, Cost of service

  Write down all the variables from this list that are:
  a) qualitative
  b) quantitative

Q2   Amy is an athletics coach. She records the following information about each of the athletes she trains:

  Number of medals won last season, Height, Mass, Shoe size

  Write down all the variables from this list that are examples of:
  a) discrete quantitative variables
  b) continuous quantitative variables

Q3   The heights of the members of a history society are shown in the table.
  a) Explain why 'height' is a continuous variable.
  b) For each class, write down the:
    (i)   lower class boundary
    (ii) upper class boundary
    (iii) class width
    (iv) class mid-point

Height, h (cm)	Number of members
$140 \leq h < 150$	3
$150 \leq h < 160$	9
$160 \leq h < 170$	17
$170 \leq h < 180$	12
$180 \leq h < 190$	5
$190 \leq h < 200$	1

Histograms

Histograms look like bar charts. However, because they're used to show frequencies of **continuous variables**, there are **no gaps** between the bars.

To plot a histogram, you plot the **frequency density** rather than the frequency (as you would in a bar chart). Use this formula to find frequency density:

$$\text{Frequency density} = \frac{\text{frequency}}{\text{class width}}$$

Tip: The formula for frequency density (f.d.) can actually be written:

$$\text{f.d.} = \frac{1}{k} \times \frac{\text{frequency}}{\text{class width}},$$

where k can be any number.

However, it usually makes sense to use $k = 1$ when drawing your own histograms.

You'll see on the next page how to interpret histograms where different values for k have been used.

- Here's some data showing the heights of 24 people.

Height (cm)	lower class boundary (cm)	upper class boundary (cm)	class width (cm)	Frequency	Frequency density
$130 \leq h < 150$	130	150	20	3	0.15
$150 \leq h < 160$	150	160	10	4	0.4
$160 \leq h < 165$	160	165	5	5	1
$165 \leq h < 170$	165	170	5	6	1.2
$170 \leq h < 190$	170	190	20	6	0.3

- Here's the same data plotted as a histogram.

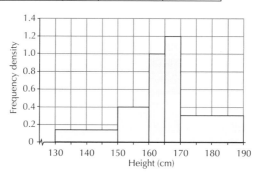

Tip: If you just plotted the **frequency** (rather than the frequency density), then your graph would look like this:

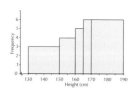

It looks like there are lots of tall people but this is just an illusion created by the width of the final class. If this data was split into classes all the same width, then the graph would look a lot more like the histogram on the left.

Notice how:

(i) The vertical axis shows **frequency density**.

(ii) The horizontal axis has a **continuous** scale like an ordinary graph, and there are **no gaps** between the columns.

(iii) A bar's left-hand edge corresponds to the **lower class boundary**. A bar's right-hand edge corresponds to the **upper class boundary**.

Example 1

Draw a histogram to represent the data below, showing the masses of parcels (given to the nearest 100 g).

Mass of parcel (to nearest 100 g)	100 - 200	300 - 400	500 - 700	800 - 1100
Number of parcels	100	250	600	50

- First draw a table showing the upper and lower class boundaries, plus the frequency density:

Mass of parcel	Lower class boundary	Upper class boundary	Class width	Frequency	Frequency density
100 - 200	50	250	200	100	0.5
300 - 400	250	450	200	250	1.25
500 - 700	450	750	300	600	2
800 - 1100	750	1150	400	50	0.125

- Now you can draw the histogram.

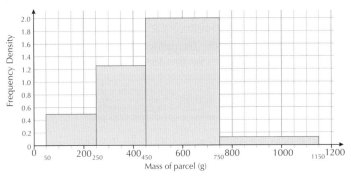

Tip: In a bar chart, it's the **height** of a bar that represents the frequency.

On a histogram, the frequency in a class is proportional to the **area** of its bar. In other words, frequency = k × area of bar (where k is a number).

Example 2

This histogram shows the heights of a group of people.

There were 6 people between 155 and 160 cm tall.

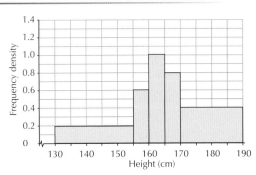

Tip: You always need to go through an initial stage of working out how area and frequency are related — basically, you're working out the value of k that's been used. (See the 'Tip' about the frequency density formula on the previous page.)

Tip: Or you can say that 1 square unit represents 2 people.

a) How many people in the group are between 130 cm and 155 cm tall?

Before looking at the 130-155 class, you need to use the information you have about the 155-160 class.

- Work out the area of the bar for 155 cm to 160 cm to find how area and frequency are related.

  Width of bar = 160 − 155 = 5
  Height of bar = 0.6
  So area of bar = 5 × 0.6 = 3

- An area of 3 represents a frequency of 6 — so '**frequency = 2 × area**'.

- Now you need to find the area of the bar from 130 cm to 155 cm.

  Width of bar = 155 − 130 = 25
  Height of bar = 0.2
  So area of bar = 25 × 0.2 = 5

- Remember...
  frequency = 2 × area.

  So 10 people are between 130 cm and 155 cm tall.

b) How many people in the group are over 165 cm tall?

- There are two bars representing people over 165 cm tall. You need to find the frequencies represented by both of them.

  165-170 cm:
  Area of bar = 5 × 0.8 = 4
  This represents 8 people.
  170-190 cm:
  Area of bar = 20 × 0.4 = 8
  This represents 16 people.

- Add the individual frequencies to find the total frequency.

  So 8 + 16 = 24 people are over 165 cm tall.

Example 3

The histogram below shows the speeds of cars along a stretch of road. There were 26 cars travelling between 50 and 60 mph.

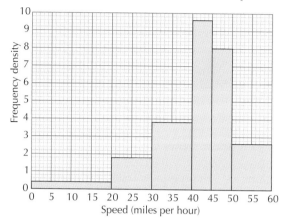

Estimate the number of cars travelling at 25 mph or less.

- Work out the area of the bar from 50 mph to 60 mph to find how area and frequency are related.

  Width of bar = 60 − 50 = 10
  Height of bar = 2.6
  So area of bar = 10 × 2.6 = 26

- An area of 26 represents a frequency of 26 — so '**frequency = area**'.

You now need to find the area of the bars to the **left** of 25 mph on the horizontal axis (because you need the frequency of cars travelling at 25 mph or **less**).

- First, find the area of the 0-20 mph bar.

  Width of bar = 20 − 0 = 20
  Height of bar = 0.4
  So area of bar = 20 × 0.4 = 8
  This represents 8 cars.

- Now find **half** the area of the 20-30 mph bar — this represents speeds from 20 mph up to 25 mph.

  Width of bar = 30 − 20 = 10
  Height of bar = 1.8
  Total area of bar = 10 × 1.8 = 18
  So half the bar's area = 18 ÷ 2 = 9
  This represents 9 cars.

- Add these figures together to estimate the total number travelling at 25 mph or less.

  Total travelling at 25 mph or less
  = 8 + 9 = 17 cars

Tip: You can only **estimate** the number of cars travelling at 25 mph or less because you don't know exactly what the speeds in the group 20-30 mph were.

Tip: Or you can say that 1 square unit represents 1 person.

Tip: Finding half of the area under the 20-30 bar makes an **assumption** that half the cars travelling at 20-30 mph were going 25 mph or less while the other half were travelling faster than 25 mph.

Q1 A pet shop records the mass (m, in g) of their adult hamsters.
The results are shown in the table.

Draw a histogram to show the masses of the hamsters.

Mass (m, in g)	Frequency
$100 \le m < 110$	6
$110 \le m < 120$	9
$120 \le m < 130$	11
$130 \le m < 140$	14
$140 \le m < 150$	10

Q2 The histogram below shows the audition times (in seconds) for contestants applying for a place on a television talent show.
The auditions for 54 contestants lasted between 30 and 45 seconds.

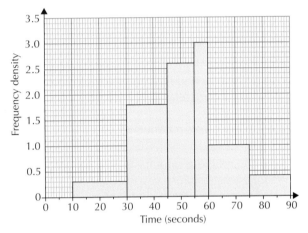

a) Work out the number of contestants whose auditions lasted less than 30 seconds.

b) Work out the total number of contestants who auditioned.

Q3 A butterfly enthusiast measures the wingspans (w, in mm), to the nearest millimetre, of a sample of tortoiseshell butterflies. She groups her measurements and displays the data in a histogram.

The group containing butterflies with $44.5 \le w < 47.5$ has a frequency of 12. This group is represented on the histogram by a bar of width 1.5 cm and height 9 cm.

a) Show that each butterfly is represented on the histogram by an area of 1.125 cm².

b) The bar representing the butterflies with $51.5 \le w < 53.5$ has an area of 22.5 cm². Work out the frequency for this group.

c) The frequency for butterflies with $53.5 \le w < 58.5$ is 14. Work out the width and the height of the bar used to represent this group.

Stem and leaf diagrams

Stem and leaf diagrams are another way to represent data.
In fact, the data values themselves appear in a stem and leaf diagram.

- Each data value is split into a '**stem**' and a '**leaf**'.

- A complete stem and leaf diagram looks something like this:

These are the stems. →
```
1 | 1 3 7
2 | 4 5 5 7 8
3 | 0 0 1 9
4 | 3 3
```
← These are the leaves.

Key: 2 | 8 means 28

> **Tip:** The stem represents a much bigger part of the value than the leaf. For example, if you had the data value 28, the stem might be 2 (which represents 20), while the leaf might be 8 (which represents 8).
>
> Or with the data value 3.7, the stem might be 3 (representing 3), while the leaf might be 7 (representing 0.7).

- A stem and leaf diagram always needs a **key** to tell you how to read it.

  So in the above stem and leaf diagram, the first row represents the values 11, 13 and 17, while the second row represents the values 24, 25, 25, 27 and 28. You can read the other two rows in a similar way.

> **Tip:** The leaves in each row are usually sorted into the correct order, from lowest to highest.

Example 1

The lengths in metres of cars in a car park were measured to the nearest 10 cm. The results were: 2.9, 3.5, 4.0, 2.8, 4.1, 2.7, 3.1, 3.6, 3.8 and 3.7. Draw a stem and leaf diagram to show the data.

- Use the numbers before the decimal point as the stems. So the stems will look like this: →
```
2 |
3 |
4 |
```

- Use the numbers after the decimal point as the leaves. Add them to the correct row of the diagram one at a time. It's a good idea to cross out the numbers in the list (in pencil) as you add them to your diagram.
```
2 | 9 8 7
3 | 5 1 6 8 7
4 | 0 1
```

- Then put the digits after the decimal point in order. →
- And finally, add a key. Key 2|9 means 2.9 m
```
2 | 7 8 9
3 | 1 5 6 7 8
4 | 0 1
```

> **Tip:** It's best to do a rough version first, and then put the leaves in order afterwards.

Example 2

The results of a survey of people's heights are shown below in the form of a stem and leaf diagram.

a) **How many people's heights were measured?**
   Count the leaves — this will be the number of people who had their height recorded. This is 22 people .

```
14 | 1 3 7 7 9    (5)
15 | 2 2 2 5      (4)
16 | 0 0 1 1 4    (5)
17 | 5 6 8 9      (4)
18 | 1 1 2 3      (4)
```
Key 15|2 means 152 cm

b) **What was the:**
   (i) **minimum height recorded?**
       The minimum height recorded was 141 cm .
   (ii) **maximum height recorded?**
       The maximum height recorded was 183 cm .

> **Tip:** The numbers in brackets are the number of data values in each row. These aren't always shown though.

A **back-to-back stem and leaf diagram** is basically two normal stem and leaf diagrams drawn either side of the same stems.

For example, this back-to-back stem and leaf diagram shows the ages of two sets of newspaper readers — for the Daily Rant and the Daily Pry. The stems are the numbers in the middle, between the two vertical lines.

Daily Rant		Daily Pry
9 4 2 1	2	2 3 4 7 7 8
8 8 7 7 3 3	3	0 0 2 5 6
7 5 3 2 2 1 1 0	4	1 3 3 3 8 9
6 6 2 1	5	2 7 7 8 8 9 9

Key: 1 | 2 | 3 means 21 for Daily Rant and 23 for Daily Pry

The stem and leaf diagram for the Daily Rant is read 'backwards' — because the stems are on the right of the leaves. Make sure you understand the key.

Tip: Also, since smaller leaves are shown nearer the stem, the leaves for the Daily Rant decrease in size as you read from left to right.

Example 1

The heights of boys and girls in a year 11 class are given to the nearest cm in the back-to-back stem and leaf diagram on the right.

Write out the data in full.

Boys		Girls
	15	9
8	16	1 5 9
9 8 1	17	0 2 3 5
5 2	18	0
1	19	

Key 1 | 17 | 0 means 171 for Boys and 170 for Girls

- Remember, the boys' heights are read backwards.
  So the first boy, 8|16|, has height 168 cm.

- So the heights in cm of the boys are: 168, 171, 178, 179, 182, 185, 191

- The first girl, |15|9, has height 159 cm.

- So the heights in cm of the girls are: 159, 161, 165, 169, 170, 172, 173, 175, 180

Example 2

Construct a back-to-back stem and leaf diagram to represent the following data:

Boys' test marks: 34, 27, 15, 39, 20, 26, 32, 37, 19, 22
Girls' test marks: 21, 38, 37, 12, 27, 28, 39, 29, 25, 24, 31, 36

- Use the tens digits as the stems.
  So the stems will look like this:

Boys		Girls
	1	
	2	
	3	

- Add the units digits one at a time as the leaves.

Boys		Girls
9 5	1	2
2 6 0 7	2	1 7 8 9 5 4
7 2 9 4	3	8 7 9 1 6

- Then put the leaves in order, and add a key.

Boys		Girls
9 5	1	2
7 6 2 0	2	1 4 5 7 8 9
9 7 4 2	3	1 6 7 8 9

Key 0|2|1 means 20 for Boys and 21 for Girls

Tip: The smallest leaf should be the one **nearest the stem**. So the leaves for the boys are in **descending** order (getting smaller from left to right), while the leaves for the girls are in **ascending** order (getting bigger from left to right).

12 Chapter 1 Data

Q1 The stem and leaf diagram
    shows the number of members
    in each of the choirs taking
    part in a choir competition.

1	2 6 7 9	(4)
2	1 2 2 2 5 6 7 8	(8)
3	0 3 6 7 9	(5)
4	1 4 5 5 7 8	(6)
5	0 1 3 3 9	(5)
6		(0)
7	1 3	(2)

Key: 1 | 2 = 12 members

a) How many choirs were competing in this competition altogether?

b) How many choirs had 45 members?

c) How many choirs had more than 52 members?

d) What was the size of the largest choir?

Q2 The stem and leaf diagram shows the
    minimum recorded temperature (to
    the nearest 0.1 °C) in 24 towns one
    June night.

8	2 5	(2)
9	4 7 8 9 9	(5)
10	1 3 7 7 7 9	(6)
11	0 4 5 8	(4)
12	1 3 6 8	(4)
13	2 6 7	(3)

Key: 8 | 2 = 8.2 °C

a) How many towns had a minimum temperature below 10 °C?

b) Which temperature was recorded most frequently?

c) What was the difference between the highest and lowest
    temperatures recorded in these towns?

Q3 Sixteen children belong to an orchestra. The distances (in kilometres)
    that the children live from the practice hall are shown below.

2.4	4.3	1.5	0.8	2.7	5.6	1.6	1.2
3.7	2.6	3.5	2.9	2.1	4.0	2.5	6.4

a) Draw a stem and leaf diagram to show this information.

b) Use your stem and leaf diagram to find:
    (i)   the furthest distance that a child lives from the practice hall.
    (ii) how many children live less than 2 km from the practice hall.

Q4 Freddie has a collection of films on DVD. He has 24 comedies and
    20 dramas. This back-to-back stem and leaf diagram shows the
    running times (to the nearest minute) of these films.

	Comedies			Dramas	
(5)	7 5 3 1 0	6			(0)
(6)	9 6 5 4 2 2	7	6		(1)
(6)	8 8 7 4 1 1	8	7 9		(2)
(4)	8 6 5 0	9	1 2 4 7		(4)
(2)	4 2	10	2 4 4 5 5 7 8		(7)
(1)	4	11	1 1 4 5 6 7		(6)

Key: 1 | 8 | 7 means 81 minutes for comedies and 87 minutes for dramas

a) What is the running time of Freddie's shortest comedy?

b) How many of his dramas last more than 90 minutes?

c) How many of his comedies last between 70 and 80 minutes?

- Be able to calculate the mean, median and mode for a data set.
- Be able to estimate values for the mean and median for a grouped data set, and to find a modal class.
- Be able to recognise when each measure of location is most suitable.

2. Location: Mean, Median and Mode

*The mean, median and mode are measures of **location** — this means they are a summary of where the 'centre' of the data lies. Measures of location are sometimes called **averages**. You'll have met the mean before, for sure.*

The mean

The most common measure of location is called the **mean** (and is often just called 'the average'... though not while you're doing A-level Maths).

The formula for the mean ($\overline{x}$, pronounced 'x-bar') is:

$$\text{Mean} = \overline{x} = \frac{\sum x}{n} \text{ or } \frac{\sum fx}{\sum f}$$

where each x is a data value, f is the frequency of each x (the number of times it occurs), and n is the total number of data values.

Tip: The Σ (sigma) just means you add things together — so Σx means you add up all the values of x.

Tip: $n = \sum f$

Tip: Instead of Σx (which means 'add up all the values of x'), you sometimes see Σx_i.

Here, you have to imagine there are x-values $x_1, x_2, x_3...$ — then Σx_i means 'add up the values of x_i for all the different values of i' (which is just another way of telling someone to add up all the different values of x).

So Σx and Σx_i mean exactly the same thing.

Example 1

Find the mean of the following list of data: 2, 3, 6, 2, 5, 9, 3, 8, 7, 2

- First, find $\sum x = 2 + 3 + 6 + 2 + 5 + 9 + 3 + 8 + 7 + 2 = 47$

- Then divide by $n = 10$ (since there are 10 values).

  This gives: $\overline{x} = \frac{\sum x}{n} = \frac{47}{10} = 4.7$

Example 2

A scientist counts the number of eggs in some song thrush nests. His data is shown in this table.

Number of eggs, x	2	3	4	5	6
Number of nests, f	4	9	16	8	3

Calculate the mean number of eggs in these nests.

- This time you have frequencies. It's best to add to the table:
  (i) a row showing the values of fx,
  (ii) a column showing the totals $\sum f$ and $\sum fx$.

Number of eggs, x	2	3	4	5	6	Total
Number of nests, f	4	9	16	8	3	40
fx	8	27	64	40	18	157

- Now use the formula for the mean: $\overline{x} = \frac{\sum fx}{\sum f} = \frac{157}{40} = 3.925$ eggs

If you have **two** sets of data and then **combine** them, you can find the mean of the combined set of data in the following way.

Example 3

Tip: Here, $\overline{x}_1$ is the mean of one data set, and $\overline{x}_2$ is the mean of another data set.

a) Find the mean ($\overline{x}_1$) of the data values 2, 3, 4, 5, 6.

The mean of this data is $\overline{x}_1 = \frac{\sum x}{n} = \frac{2 + 3 + 4 + 5 + 6}{5} = \frac{20}{5} = 4$

b) **Find the mean ($\overline{x}_2$) of the data values 10, 12, 14.**

The mean of this data is $\overline{x}_2 = \dfrac{\sum x}{n} = \dfrac{10 + 12 + 14}{3} = \dfrac{36}{3} = \boxed{12}$

c) **Find the mean ($\overline{x}$) of the combined data set 2, 3, 4, 5, 6, 10, 12, 14.**

The mean of the combined data set is

$$\overline{x} = \frac{\sum x}{n} = \frac{2 + 3 + 4 + 5 + 6 + 10 + 12 + 14}{8} = \frac{56}{8} = \boxed{7}$$

Tip: You **can't** just add $\overline{x}_1$ and $\overline{x}_2$ together.

And you **can't** just find the mean of $\overline{x}_1$ and $\overline{x}_2$.

If you know a data set of size n_1 has mean $\overline{x}_1$ and another data set of size n_2 has mean $\overline{x}_2$, then the combined mean is $\overline{x}$, where:

$$\overline{x} = \frac{n_1\overline{x}_1 + n_2\overline{x}_2}{n_1 + n_2}$$

Example 4

A data set consisting of 5 values has mean $\overline{x}_1$ = 4.
A second data set consisting of 3 values has mean $\overline{x}_2$ = 12.
Find the mean ($\overline{x}$) of the combined data set.

- Here, n_1 = 5 and n_2 = 3.

- Using the formula: $\overline{x} = \dfrac{n_1\overline{x}_1 + n_2\overline{x}_2}{n_1 + n_2} = \dfrac{(5 \times 4) + (3 \times 12)}{5 + 3} = \dfrac{56}{8} = \boxed{7}$

Tip: This is the same problem as in Example 3, only it's been solved using the formula.

Exercise 2.1

Q1 Katia visits 12 shops and records the price of a loaf of bread. Her results are shown in the table below.

£1.08	£1.15	£1.25	£1.19	£1.26	£1.24
£1.15	£1.09	£1.16	£1.20	£1.05	£1.10

Work out the mean price of a loaf of bread in these shops.

Q2 Twenty students sit a maths exam. The teacher records their marks $\{x_1, ..., x_{20}\}$ and calculates that $\sum x = 1672$.
Work out the mean mark for these students.

Q3 The numbers of goals scored by 20 football teams in their most recent match are shown in the table.

Number of goals, x	0	1	2	3	4
Frequency, f	5	7	4	3	1

Calculate the mean number of goals scored by these teams in their most recent match.

Q4 A drama group has 15 members.
The mean age of the members is 47.4 years.
a) Work out the total of the ages of all members of the drama group.
b) A person aged 17 joins the drama group. Find the new mean age.

The mode and the median

There are two other important measures of location you need to know about — the **mode** and the **median**.

Tip: The mode is often called the **modal value**.

> **Mode** = most frequently occurring data value.

Examples

Find the modes of the following data sets.

a) **2, 3, 6, 2, 5, 9, 3, 8, 7, 2**

The most frequent data value is 2, appearing three times.

So the mode = 2 .

Tip: If a data set has two modes, then it is called **bimodal**.

b) **4, 3, 6, 4, 5, 9, 2, 8, 7, 5**

This time there are two modes — the values 4 and 5 both appear twice.

So the modes = 4 and 5 .

c) **4, 3, 6, 11, 5, 9, 2, 8, 7, 12**

This time there are no modes — each value appears just once.

The median is slightly trickier to find than the mode.

> **Median** = value in the middle of the data set when all the data values are placed in order of size.

First put your n data values **in order**, then find the **position** of the median in the ordered list. There are two possibilities:

(i) if $\frac{n}{2}$ is a **whole number** (i.e. n is even), then the median is halfway between the values in this position and the position above.

(ii) if $\frac{n}{2}$ is **not** a **whole number** (i.e. n is odd), **round it up** to find the position of the median.

Examples

Find the medians of the following data sets.

a) **2, 3, 6, 2, 6, 9, 3, 8, 7**

- Put the values in order first: 2, 2, 3, 3, 6, 6, 7, 8, 9

- There are 9 values, and $\frac{n}{2} = \frac{9}{2} = 4.5$. Rounding this up to 5 means that the median is the 5th value in the ordered list — median = 6 .

b) **4, 3, 11, 4, 10, 9, 3, 8, 7, 8**

- Put the values in order first: 3, 3, 4, 4, 7, 8, 8, 9, 10, 11

- There are 10 values, and $\frac{n}{2} = \frac{10}{2} = 5$.

Tip: The value halfway between two numbers is their mean.

- So the median is halfway between the 5th value in the ordered list (= 7) and the 6th value (= 8). So the median = 7.5 .

If your data is in a **frequency table**, then the mode and the median are still easy to find as long as the data **isn't grouped**.

Example

The number of letters received one day in a sample of houses is shown in this table.

Number of letters	Number of houses
0	11
1	25
2	27
3	21
4	9
5	7

Tip: Frequency means the number of times a data value occurs.

Here, the data values are the 'numbers of letters' they received. So the frequencies are the 'numbers of houses' (that received that many letters).

a) **Find the modal number of letters.**
- The modal number of letters just means the mode.
- The highest frequency is for 2 letters — so the mode = 2 letters .

b) **Find the median number of letters.**
- It's useful to add a column to show the **cumulative frequency** — this is just a **running total** of the frequency column.

No. of letters	No. of houses (frequency)	Cumulative frequency
0	11	11
1	25	36
2	27	63
3	21	84
4	9	93
5	7	100

- The total number of houses is the final cumulative frequency, so $n = 100$.
- Since $\frac{n}{2} = \frac{100}{2} = 50$, the median is halfway between the 50th and 51st data values.
- Using the cumulative frequency, you can see that the data values in positions 37 to 63 all equal 2. This means the data values at positions 50 and 51 are both 2. So the median = 2 letters .

Finding the median and mode from a **stem and leaf diagram** also shouldn't cause too many problems.

Example

Some people's heights are shown in this stem and leaf diagram.

```
14 | 1 3 7 7 9      (5)
15 | 2 2 2 5        (4)
16 | 0 0 1 1 4      (5)
17 | 5 6 8 9        (4)
18 | 1 1 2 3        (4)
```
Key 15 | 2 means 152 cm

Tip: It's easy to find the mode and the median from a stem and leaf diagram, because the data values are in order.

a) **Find the modal height.**
Look for the number that appears consecutively most often in one of the rows of leaves. Here, there are three 2's in the second row, representing 152 cm. So the mode = 152 cm .

b) **Find the median height.**
Find the total frequency — here you've been given the number of values in each row, so you can just add them up to find that $n = 22$.
Since $\frac{n}{2} = \frac{22}{2} = 11$, the median is halfway between the 11th data value (= 160 cm) and the 12th data value (= 161 cm).
So the median = 160.5 cm .

Q1 Seventeen friends took part in a charity fun run.
    The amount of money that each friend raised is shown below.

£250	£19	£500	£123	£185	£101
£45	£67	£194	£77	£108	£110
£187	£216	£84	£98	£140	

a) Find the median amount of money raised by these friends.

b) Explain why it is not possible to find the mode for this data.

Q2 A financial adviser records the interest rates charged by 12 different
    banks to customers taking out a loan. His findings are below.

6.2%   6.9%   6.9%   8.8%   6.3%   7.4%

6.5%   6.4%   9.9%   6.2%   6.4%   6.9%

a) Write down the mode of these interest rates.

b) Find the median interest rate charged by these banks.

Q3 An online seller has received
    the ratings shown in this table.

a) Write down the modal
   customer rating.

b) Work out the median
   customer rating.

Rating	Number of customers
1	7
2	5
3	25
4	67
5	72

Q4 A theatre stages 35 performances of its
    pantomime one year.

    This stem and leaf diagram
    shows the number of empty
    seats for each performance.

a) Write down the value
   of the mode.

b) Work out the median
   number of empty seats.

```
0 | 0 3 5 5 5 6 6 8 9 9    (10)
1 | 1 2 2 3 5 7 8          (7)
2 | 0 2 3 4 4 5            (6)
3 | 1 4 5 6 8 8 9          (7)
4 | 3 5 5 7                (4)
5 | 7                      (1)
```

Key: 3 | 1 = 31 empty seats

Q5 Kwasi and Ben each check the download speeds on their computers
    on a number of different occasions.
    Their results are shown in this back-to-back stem and leaf diagram.

```
        Kwasi        Ben
                 | 3 | 5 7 8              (3)
(6)    7 4 2 1 0 0 | 4 | 0 2 6 6 8        (5)
(5)        8 8 4 3 0 | 5 | 1 3 5 9        (4)
(6)      9 9 8 7 6 1 | 6 | 1 2 2 2 4 5 7  (7)
(2)            9 2 | 7 | 4 7 8            (3)
```

Key: 3 | 5 | 9 represents a speed of 5.3 Mbit/s for Kwasi
      and a speed of 5.9 Mbit/s for Ben.

a) Write down the modal download speed(s) for: (i) Kwasi (ii) Ben

b) Find the median download speed for: (i) Kwasi (ii) Ben

Averages of grouped data

If you have **grouped data**, you can only **estimate** the mean and median.
This is because the grouping means you no longer have the exact data values.
And instead of a mode, you can only find a **modal class**.

Modal class

- To find a **modal class**, you need to find the class with the **highest frequency density**.

- If all the classes are the same width, then this will just be the class with the **highest frequency**.

Tip: See p7 for more about frequency density.

Example

Find the modal class for this data showing the heights of various shrubs.

Height of shrub to nearest cm	11-20	21-30	31-40	41-50
Number of shrubs	11	22	29	16

- In this example, all the classes are the same width (= 10 cm).
- So the modal class is the class with the highest frequency.
- This means the modal class is 31-40 cm .

Mean

- To find an estimate of the **mean**, you assume that every reading in a class takes the value of the class **mid-point**.

- Then you can use the formula $\overline{x} = \dfrac{\sum fx}{\sum f}$.

Tip: This is the formula from page 14.

Example

The heights of a number of trees were recorded.
The data collected is shown in this table.

Height of tree to nearest m	0-5	6-10	11-15	16-20
Number of trees	26	17	11	6

Find an estimate of the mean height of the trees.

- It's best to make another table. Include extra rows showing:
  (i) the class mid-points (x),
  (ii) the values of fx, where f is the frequency.

- And add an extra column for the totals $\sum f$ and $\sum fx$.

Tip: The frequency (f) is the 'Number of trees'.

Height of tree to nearest m	0-5	6-10	11-15	16-20	**Total**
Class mid-point, x	2.75	8	13	18	
Number of trees, f	26	17	11	6	60 (= Σf)
fx	71.5	136	143	108	458.5 (= Σfx)

Tip: For the first class:

Lower class boundary = 0

Upper class boundary = 5.5

So the class mid-point = $(0 + 5.5) \div 2 = 2.75$

(See p4-5 for more information.)

- Now you can use the formula for the mean given above.

$$\text{Mean} = \overline{x} = \frac{\sum fx}{\sum f} = \frac{458.5}{60} = 7.64 \text{ m (to 2 d.p.)}$$

Median

To find an estimate for the median, use **linear interpolation**.

This table shows the 'tree data' from the second example on the previous page. I've also added a row showing the **cumulative frequency**.

Height of tree to nearest m	0-5	6-10	11-15	16-20
Number of trees	26	17	11	6
Cumulative frequency	26	43	54	60

Tip: 'Linear interpolation' is sometimes just called 'interpolation'.

- First, find **which class** the median is in.

  Since $\frac{n}{2} = \frac{60}{2} = 30$, there are 30 values less than or equal to the median.

  This means the median must be in the 6-10 class.

- Now, the idea behind **linear interpolation** is to **assume** that all the readings in this class are evenly spread. So divide the class (whose width is 5) into 17 equally wide intervals (one interval for each of the data values in the class), and assume there's a reading in the middle of each interval, like this.

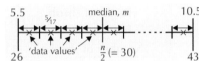

Tip: The red crosses in the diagram aren't the **actual** data values — they're **interpolated** data values (we've made an **assumption** about them being at these points).

- The numbers **on the top** of the scale are **heights** (measured in metres). The **upper and lower class boundaries** are shown, and the **median** (m) is also marked (but you don't know its value yet).

- The numbers **underneath** the scale are **cumulative frequencies**. The cumulative frequency at the lower class boundary is 26, while the cumulative frequency at the upper class boundary is 43.

Tip: In this method, you **only** need to find $\frac{n}{2}$ — you **don't** then need to follow the rules described on page 16.

However, the two ways of using $\frac{n}{2}$ turn out to be **equivalent**.

For example... here, using the rules on p16, you'd expect the median to be between the 30th and 31st values. And if you look at the picture, that's where it is.

The difference is that we're now using $\frac{n}{2}$ to decide how many of those 'mini-intervals' to count along, whereas on p16 we were using $\frac{n}{2}$ to decide the position of a term in a sequence of numbers.

- In fact, you don't need to draw the small intervals and the data points every time — a simplified version like the one on the right is enough to find a median.

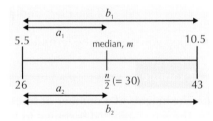

- To find the **median**, m, you need to solve: $\dfrac{a_1}{b_1} = \dfrac{a_2}{b_2}$

Example 1

Tip: This is the same data as in the explanation above — so you already know which class contains the median.

Estimate the median height for the trees recorded in this table.

Height of tree to nearest m	0-5	6-10	11-15	16-20
Number of trees	26	17	11	6

- First draw the picture of the class containing the median (m) — just show the important numbers you're going to need.

Tip: Work out the values of a_1, b_1, a_2, b_2 from the diagram:
$a_1 = m - 5.5$
$b_1 = 10.5 - 5.5$
$a_2 = 30 - 26$
$b_2 = 43 - 26$ (b_2 is just the class frequency from the original table).

- Then solve the equation $\dfrac{a_1}{b_1} = \dfrac{a_2}{b_2}$.

- Substituting in the numbers gives: $\dfrac{m - 5.5}{10.5 - 5.5} = \dfrac{30 - 26}{43 - 26}$

- And so $\dfrac{m - 5.5}{5} = \dfrac{4}{17}$, or $m = 5 \times \dfrac{4}{17} + 5.5 = \boxed{6.68 \, \text{m (to 2 d.p.)}}$

Example 2

Estimate the median length of the newts described in this table.

Length (to nearest cm)	0-2	3-5	6-8	9-11
Number of newts	3	18	12	4

- There are $n = 3 + 18 + 12 + 4 = 37$ data values in total.

  So $\frac{n}{2} = 18.5$ — meaning the median will be in the 3-5 class.

- Now draw the picture of the class containing the median.

- So you need to solve:
  $$\frac{m - 2.5}{5.5 - 2.5} = \frac{18.5 - 3}{21 - 3}$$

- This gives $\frac{m - 2.5}{3} = \frac{15.5}{18}$, or $m = 3 \times \frac{15.5}{18} + 2.5 = \boxed{5.1\,\text{cm (to 1 d.p.)}}$

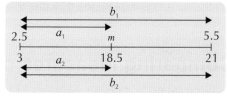

Tip: You don't always need to add a row to the table to show cumulative frequency. Here, the numbers are small enough that you can quickly tell which class the median lies in.

You can see that $\frac{n}{2}$ is greater than the cumulative frequency of the first class, but less than the cumulative frequency of the second — so the median is in the second class.

Exercise 2.3

Q1 The time that 60 students took to change after PE is shown below.

Time (t, mins)	Frequency, f	Mid-point, x	fx
$3 \leq t < 4$	7	3.5	24.5
$4 \leq t < 5$	14	4.5	
$5 \leq t < 6$	24		
$6 \leq t < 8$	10		
$8 \leq t < 10$	5		

Q1 Hint: Don't give your answers to too many decimal places when you're estimating something.

a) Copy and complete the table.

b) Use the table to work out an estimate of the mean time it took these children to change.

Q2 A postman records the number of letters delivered to each of 50 houses one day. The results are shown in this table.

Number of letters	Number of houses
0-2	20
3-5	16
6-8	7
9-11	5
12-14	2

a) State the modal class.

b) Estimate the mean number of letters delivered to these houses.

c) Write down the interval containing the median.

Q3 The table shows the amount of rainfall (r, in mm) recorded at some weather stations one March.

Use linear interpolation to estimate the median rainfall at the weather stations.

Rainfall (r, mm)	Frequency
$20 \leq r < 40$	5
$40 \leq r < 50$	7
$50 \leq r < 60$	9
$60 \leq r < 80$	15
$80 \leq r < 100$	8
$100 \leq r < 120$	2

Q4 The table below shows the times that a random sample of 60 runners took to complete a marathon.

a) Estimate the mean time of these runners. (You may use $\sum fx = 16\,740$, where x is the mid-point of a class.)

b) Calculate an estimate for the median time it took these runners to complete the marathon.

Time (t, mins)	Frequency, f
$180 \leq t < 240$	8
$240 \leq t < 270$	19
$270 \leq t < 300$	21
$300 \leq t < 360$	9
$360 \leq t < 480$	3

Comparing measures of location

You've seen three different measures of location — the mean, the median and the mode. Each of them is useful for different kinds of data.

Tip: There's more about **outliers** on page 28.

Mean

- The mean's a good average because you use **all** your data in working it out.
- But it can be heavily affected by **extreme values / outliers** and by distributions of data values that are **not symmetric**.
- And it can only be used with **quantitative** data (i.e. numbers).

Tip: A **symmetric** data set is one where the distribution of data values **above** the mean is the mirror image of the distribution of values **below** the mean.

See page 41 for more about symmetry of data sets.

Median

- The median is **not** affected by extreme values — so this is a good average to use when you have **outliers**.
- This also makes it a good average to use when then data set is **not symmetric**.

Tip: You saw a **bimodal** data set (with two modes) on p16.

Other data sets may have more than two modes.

Mode

- The mode can be used with **qualitative** (non-numerical) data.
- But some data sets can have **more than one** mode (and if every value in a data set occurs just once, then the mode isn't very helpful at all).

Exercise 2.4

Q1 Explain whether the mean, median or mode would be most suitable as a summary of each of the following data sets.

a) Salaries of each employee at a company.

b) Length of adult female adder snakes.

c) Make of cars parked in a car park.

d) Weight of all newborn full-term babies born one year at a hospital.

e) Distance a firm's employees travel to work each morning.

Q1 Hint: Think about the shape of the histogram you might expect for each data set. For example, in part a), think about how many people you might expect to earn quite a low salary, and how many you might expect to earn a very high salary.

Q2 Hosi records the number of bedrooms in the houses lived in by a sample of 10 adults. His results are shown in the table.

Number of bedrooms	1	2	3	4	5	6	7	8
Frequency	1	2	4	2	0	0	0	1

Explain why the mean may not be the most suitable measure of location for the data.

3. Dispersion and Skewness

A measure of location tells you roughly where the centre of the data lies. Dispersion, on the other hand, tells you how spread out the data values are. And skewness tells you how symmetrically distributed they are.

Range, interquartile range and interpercentile range

Range

The **range** is about the simplest measure of dispersion you can imagine.

> Range = highest value − lowest value

But the range is heavily affected by **extreme values**, so it isn't really the most useful way to measure dispersion.

Interquartile range

A more useful way to measure dispersion is to use the **interquartile range** — but first you have to find the **quartiles**. You've already seen how the median divides a data set into two halves. The quartiles are similar — there are three quartiles altogether (usually labelled Q_1, Q_2 and Q_3) and they divide the data into **four parts**.

- Q_1 is the **lower quartile** — 25% of the data is less than or equal to the lower quartile.
- Q_2 is the **median** — 50% of the data is less than or equal to the median.
- Q_3 is the **upper quartile** — 75% of the data is less than or equal to the upper quartile.

For example, the values in the data set below have been sorted so that they're in numerical order, starting with the smallest. The three quartiles are shown.

$$1 \quad 2 \quad 3 \quad \overset{|}{4} \quad 4 \quad 4 \quad 5 \Big| 5 \quad 5 \quad 6 \quad \overset{|}{6} \quad 7 \quad 7 \quad 9$$

$$\begin{array}{ccc} Q_1 & Q_2 & Q_3 \end{array}$$

$Q_1 = 4$
$Q_2 = 5$
$Q_3 = 6$

The quartiles are worked out in a similar way to the median — by first finding their **position** in the ordered list of data values.

> To find the position of the **lower quartile** (Q_1), first work out $\frac{n}{4}$.
>
> - if $\frac{n}{4}$ is a **whole number**, then the **lower quartile** is halfway between the values in this position and the position above.
> - if $\frac{n}{4}$ is **not** a whole number, **round it up** to find the position of the lower quartile.

> To find the position of the **upper quartile** (Q_3), first work out $\frac{3n}{4}$.
>
> - if $\frac{3n}{4}$ is a **whole number**, then the **upper quartile** is halfway between the values in this position and the position above.
> - if $\frac{3n}{4}$ is **not** a whole number, **round it up** to find the position of the upper quartile.

Learning Objectives:

- Be able to calculate the range, interquartile range, and interpercentile range.
- Be able to determine whether a reading is an outlier.
- Be able to draw and interpret box plots.
- Be able to calculate and interpret variance and standard deviation (including with the use of coding).
- Be able to calculate and interpret coefficients of skewness.

Tip: There are various ways you can find the quartiles, and they sometimes give different results. But if you use the methods below, you'll be fine.

Tip: This is the same as the method used on page 16 for finding the median, only with $\frac{n}{2}$ replaced by $\frac{n}{4}$.

Tip: This is the same as the method used on page 16 for finding the median, only with $\frac{n}{2}$ replaced by $\frac{3n}{4}$.

Once you've found the upper and lower quartiles, you can find the **interquartile range** (IQR).

> Interquartile range (IQR) = upper quartile (Q_3) – lower quartile (Q_1)

- The interquartile range is a measure of **dispersion**.
- It actually shows the range of the 'middle 50%' of the data.
- This means it's not affected by **extreme values**, but it still tells you something about how spread out the data values are.

Example

a) Find the median and quartiles of the following data set:
2, 5, 3, 11, 6, 8, 3, 8, 1, 6, 2, 23, 9, 11, 18, 19, 22, 7

- First put the list in order:
  1, 2, 2, 3, 3, 5, 6, 6, 7, 8, 8, 9, 11, 11, 18, 19, 22, 23

- You need Q_1, Q_2 and Q_3, so find $\frac{n}{4}$, $\frac{n}{2}$ and $\frac{3n}{4}$, where $n = 18$.

- $\frac{n}{4} = \frac{18}{4} = 4.5$. This is **not** a whole number, so round up to 5. This means the lower quartile is equal to the 5th term: $Q_1 = 3$

- $\frac{n}{2} = \frac{18}{2} = 9$ is a **whole number**. The median is halfway between the 9th term (= 7) and the 10th term (= 8). So $Q_2 = 7.5$

- $\frac{3n}{4} = \frac{54}{4} = 13.5$ is **not** a whole number, so round up to 14. This means the upper quartile is equal to the 14th term: $Q_3 = 11$

b) Find the interquartile range for the above data.
- Interquartile range = $Q_3 - Q_1 = 11 - 3 = 8$

When your data is **grouped**, you'll need to use **linear interpolation** to find an **estimate** for the lower and upper quartiles.

Example

a) Estimate the lower and upper quartiles for the tree heights in this table.

Height of tree to nearest m	0-5	6-10	11-15	16-20
Number of trees	26	17	11	6

- First add a row to the table showing cumulative frequency.

Height of tree to nearest m	0-5	6-10	11-15	16-20
Number of trees	26	17	11	6
Cumulative frequency	26	43	54	60

Now to find the quartiles, starting with the **lower quartile** (Q_1).

- First calculate $\frac{n}{4} = \frac{60}{4} = 15$.
- Using the cumulative frequency, you can see that Q_1 is in the class 0-5.

- Now draw a picture of the class containing Q_1 — just show the important numbers you're going to need.

Put heights one side of the line (I've put them on top) and cumulative frequencies on the other side.

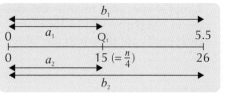

Tip: Remember... b_2 should match the class frequency from the original frequency table.

- Then solve the equation $\frac{a_1}{b_1} = \frac{a_2}{b_2}$.

- Substituting in the numbers gives: $\dfrac{Q_1 - 0}{5.5 - 0} = \dfrac{15 - 0}{26 - 0}$

- And so $\dfrac{Q_1}{5.5} = \dfrac{15}{26}$, or $Q_1 = 5.5 \times \dfrac{15}{26} = \boxed{3.2\,\text{m (to 1 d.p.)}}$

Find the **upper quartile** (Q_3) in the same way.

- First, calculate $\dfrac{3n}{4} = \dfrac{3 \times 60}{4} = 45$.

- So Q_3 is in the class 11-15.

- Now draw your picture of the class containing Q_3.

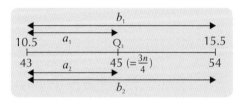

- Substituting numbers into $\frac{a_1}{b_1} = \frac{a_2}{b_2}$ gives: $\dfrac{Q_3 - 10.5}{15.5 - 10.5} = \dfrac{45 - 43}{54 - 43}$

- And so $\dfrac{Q_3 - 10.5}{5} = \dfrac{2}{11}$, or $Q_3 = 10.5 + 5 \times \dfrac{2}{11} = \boxed{11.4\,\text{m (to 1 d.p.)}}$

b) Estimate the interquartile range for this data.

- Interquartile range (IQR) = $Q_3 - Q_1$
  $= 11.4 - 3.2 = \boxed{8.2\text{ m (to 1 d.p.)}}$

Interpercentile range

You've seen how the quartiles divide the data into four parts, where each part contains the same number of data values. **Percentiles** are similar, but they divide the data into **100 parts**.

> The **position** of the xth percentile (P_x) is $\dfrac{x}{100} \times$ total frequency (n).

Tip: The median is the 50th percentile and Q_1 is the 25th percentile, and so on.

For example, to find the 11th percentile in a data set containing a total of 200 values:

- Calculate $\dfrac{11}{100} \times 200 = 22$.

- Use linear interpolation to estimate the value in this position in the **ordered** list of data values.

Tip: When you're finding percentiles, the data set is usually large, and will probably be grouped.

You can find **interpercentile ranges** by subtracting two percentiles.

> The $a\%$ to $b\%$ interpercentile range is $P_b - P_a$.

- For example, the 20% to 80% interpercentile range is $P_{80} - P_{20}$.

Example

A reptile specialist records the mass (m, in kilograms) of 150 tortoises. Her results are shown in the table.

Mass (kg)	Frequency
$0.2 \leq m < 0.6$	27
$0.6 \leq m < 1.0$	43
$1.0 \leq m < 1.4$	35
$1.4 \leq m < 1.8$	31
$1.8 \leq m < 2.2$	14

a) Estimate the 10th percentile for this data.

- It'll help to add a column showing cumulative frequency.

- Now calculate $\frac{10}{100} \times 150 = 15$.

- Using the cumulative frequency, you can see that this will be in the '$0.2 \leq m < 0.6$' class.

Mass (kg)	Frequency	Cumulative frequency
$0.2 \leq m < 0.6$	27	27
$0.6 \leq m < 1.0$	43	70
$1.0 \leq m < 1.4$	35	105
$1.4 \leq m < 1.8$	31	136
$1.8 \leq m < 2.2$	14	150

Tip: As always with linear interpolation, solve $\frac{a_1}{b_1} = \frac{a_2}{b_2}$.

- So draw a picture of this class showing the important masses and cumulative frequencies.

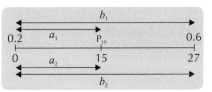

- The equation $\frac{a_1}{b_1} = \frac{a_2}{b_2}$ gives $\frac{P_{10} - 0.2}{0.6 - 0.2} = \frac{15 - 0}{27 - 0}$, which means:

$$P_{10} = 0.2 + 0.4 \times \frac{15}{27} = \boxed{0.42 \, \text{kg (to 2 d.p.)}}$$

b) Estimate the 90th percentile for this data.

- $\frac{90}{100} \times 150 = 135$

- So the 90th percentile will be in the class '$1.4 \leq m < 1.8$'.

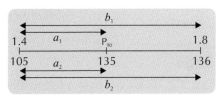

- The equation $\frac{a_1}{b_1} = \frac{a_2}{b_2}$ gives $\frac{P_{90} - 1.4}{1.8 - 1.4} = \frac{135 - 105}{136 - 105}$.

This means: $P_{90} = 1.4 + 0.4 \times \frac{30}{31} = \boxed{1.79 \, \text{kg (to 2 d.p.)}}$

c) Find the 10% to 90% interpercentile range for this data.

- 10% to 90% interpercentile range = $P_{90} - P_{10}$
  = $1.79 - 0.42 = \boxed{1.37 \, \text{kg (to 2 d.p.)}}$

Q1 The diameters (in miles) of the eight planets in the Solar System are given below:

3032, 7521, 7926, 4222, 88846, 74898, 31763, 30778

For this data set, calculate:

a) the range

b) (i)   the lower quartile (Q_1)
   (ii) the upper quartile (Q_3)
   (iii) the interquartile range (IQR)

Q2 Each of the three data sets below shows the speeds (in mph) of 18 different cars observed at a certain time and place.

In town at 8:45 am:
14, 16, 15, 18, 15, 17, 16, 16, 18, 16, 15, 13, 15, 14, 16, 17, 18, 15

In town at 10:45 am:
34, 29, 36, 32, 31, 38, 30, 35, 39, 31, 29, 30, 25, 29, 33, 34, 36, 31

On the motorway at 1 pm:
67, 76, 78, 71, 73, 88, 74, 69, 75, 76, 95, 71, 69, 78, 73, 76, 75, 74

For each set of data, calculate:

a) the range

b) the interquartile range (IQR)

Q3 The weights (w, in kg) of the items of baggage checked in on a flight from Manchester to New York are shown in the table.

For this data, estimate:

a) the lower quartile (Q_1)

b) the upper quartile (Q_3)

c) the interquartile range (IQR)

Weight of baggage (w)	Number of items
$0 < w < 10$	22
$10 \le w < 14$	75
$14 \le w < 18$	102
$18 \le w < 25$	53

Q4 The lengths of a zoo's beetles measured to the nearest mm (l) are shown in this table.

For this data, estimate:

a) the 20th percentile

b) the 80th percentile

c) the 20% to 80% interpercentile range.

Length (l)	Number of beetles
0-5	82
6-10	28
11-15	44
16-30	30
31-50	16

Outliers and box plots

Outliers

Tip: There are various ways to calculate the values of the fences, but in an exam you will always be told what method to use.

An **outlier** is a freak piece of data that lies a long way from the majority of the readings in a data set.

To decide whether a reading is an outlier, you have to **test** whether it falls **outside** certain limits, called **fences**.

A very common way to test for outliers is to use the following values for the fences:

- for the **lower fence**, use the value $Q_1 - (1.5 \times IQR)$
- for the **upper fence**, use the value $Q_3 + (1.5 \times IQR)$

So using these fences, x is an outlier if:

either: $x < Q_1 - (1.5 \times IQR)$

or: $x > Q_3 + (1.5 \times IQR)$

Example

The lower and upper quartiles of a data set are 70 and 100. Use the fences $Q_1 - (1.5 \times IQR)$ and $Q_3 + (1.5 \times IQR)$ to decide whether the data values 30 and 210 are outliers.

- First work out the IQR: $Q_3 - Q_1 = 100 - 70 = 30$
- Then you can find where your **fences** are.

   Lower fence: $Q_1 - (1.5 \times IQR) = 70 - (1.5 \times 30) = 25$

   Upper fence: $Q_3 + (1.5 \times IQR) = 100 + (1.5 \times 30) = 145$

- 30 is **inside** the lower fence, so it is **not** an outlier.

   210 is **outside** the upper fence, so it **is** an outlier.

Box plots

Tip: Box plots are sometimes called 'box and whisker diagrams' (where the whiskers are the horizontal lines at either end of the box).

A **box plot** is a kind of 'visual summary' of a set of data. Box plots show the **median**, **quartiles** and **outliers** in an easy-to-look-at kind of way.

They look like this:

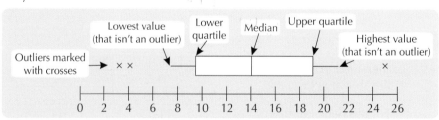

- The **scale** is really important — always include one.
- The box extends from the **lower quartile** to the **upper quartile**. (So the box shows the 'middle 50%' of the data.)
- A vertical line drawn on the box marks the **median**.
- A horizontal line is drawn from each end of the box. These lines extend in each direction as far as the last data value that **isn't** an outlier.
- **Outliers** are marked with **crosses**.

Example

The back-to-back stem and leaf diagram below shows the IQs of year 11 students at two schools, Vale Academy and Cherry Comprehensive.

	Vale Academy										Cherry Comprehensive								
(1)									8	**9**	3								(1)
(8)	9	8	7	6	6	5	3	1		**10**	5	8	9						(3)
(5)					8	6	4	2	1	**11**	0	2	3	5	6	8	9		(7)
(3)							7	4	2	**12**	0	0	1	3	4	6	8		(7)
(2)								6	1	**13**	2	4							(2)
(1)									0	**14**	4								(1)

> **Key: 1 | 10 | 5** represents an IQ of 101 at Vale Academy and an IQ of 105 at Cherry Comprehensive

a) Draw a box plot to represent the data from Cherry Comprehensive. Use $Q_1 - 1.5 \times IQR$ and $Q_3 + 1.5 \times IQR$ as your fences for identifying outliers.

- First work out the quartiles (Q_1, Q_2 and Q_3) and the fences.
    - Find the number of data values (n) for Cherry Comprehensive. Here, $n = 21$.
    - Since $\frac{n}{2} = 10.5$, the median is the 11th data value. So the **median (Q_2) = 119**.
    - Since $\frac{n}{4} = 5.25$, the lower quartile is the 6th data value. So Q_1 **= 112**.
    - Since $\frac{3n}{4} = 15.75$, the upper quartile is the 16th data value. So Q_3 **= 124**.
    - The interquartile range is IQR = $Q_3 - Q_1 = 124 - 112 = $ **12**.
    - This gives a **lower fence** of $Q_1 - (1.5 \times IQR) = 112 - (1.5 \times 12) = $ **94**.
    - And an **upper fence** of $Q_3 + (1.5 \times IQR) = 124 + (1.5 \times 12) = $ **142**.
- Now you can decide if you have any outliers.
    - The value 93 is **outside** the lower fence (94), so 93 is an outlier.
    - And the value 144 is **outside** the upper fence (142), so 144 is also an outlier, but there are no other outliers.

Tip: Remember... only extend a line as far as the biggest or smallest data value that **isn't** an outlier.

- Now you can draw the box plot itself.

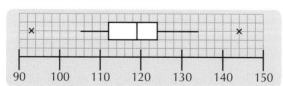

b) Draw a box plot to represent the data from Vale Academy.

- For Vale Academy:
    - $n = 20$.
    - $\frac{n}{2} = 10$, so the median is halfway between the 10th and 11th data values — **median (Q_2) = 111.5**.

Tip: Remember... when you're counting along the values for the left-hand part of a back-to-back stem and leaf diagram, you have to count along the leaves from right to left.

- $\frac{n}{4} = 5$, so the lower quartile is halfway between the 5th and 6th data values — $Q_1 = 106$.

- $\frac{3n}{4} = 15$, so the upper quartile is halfway between the 15th and 16th data values — $Q_3 = 123$.

- The interquartile range, IQR is $Q_3 - Q_1 = 123 - 106 = 17$.

■ This gives a **lower fence** of $Q_1 - (1.5 \times IQR) = 106 - (1.5 \times 17) = 80.5$. And an **upper fence** of $Q_3 + (1.5 \times IQR) = 123 + (1.5 \times 17) = 148.5$. This means there are **no outliers** at Vale Academy.

■ So the box plot for Vale Academy looks like this:

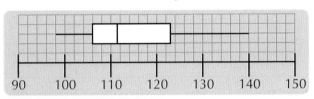

Exercise 3.2

Q1 The lower and upper quartiles of a data set are 19 and 31. Use the fences $Q_1 - (1.5 \times IQR)$ and $Q_3 + (1.5 \times IQR)$ to decide whether the data values 4 and 52 are outliers.

Q2 A set of data was analysed and the following values were found.
minimum value = 4, maximum value = 49
$Q_1 = 16$, median = 24, $Q_3 = 37$

a) Find the interquartile range.

b) Are there any outliers in this data set?
Use the values $Q_1 - (1.5 \times IQR)$ and $Q_3 + (1.5 \times IQR)$ as fences.

c) Draw a box plot to illustrate the data set.

Q3 A traffic officer counted the number of cars using a town centre car park on different occasions. His results are in the stem and leaf diagram.

Key: 1 | 7 = 17 cars

0	1									(1)
1	0	2	7							(3)
2	0	1	3							(3)
3	1	4	4	5	7	8	8	8	9	(9)
4	1	3	5	6	6	7	8	8	9	(9)
5	0	1	3	5	5	6	7	9	9	(9)
6	2	4								(2)
7	2	5								(2)
8	0									(1)
9	1	9								(2)

a) Use the stem and leaf diagram to calculate:
(i) the median
(ii) the lower quartile (Q_1)
(iii) the upper quartile (Q_3)
(iv) the interquartile range (IQR)
(v) the lower fence, $Q_1 - (1.5 \times IQR)$
(vi) the upper fence, $Q_3 + (1.5 \times IQR)$

b) Are any of the data values outliers? If so, which ones?

c) Draw a box plot to illustrate the data.

Q4 The numbers of items of junk mail received in a day by people living in the towns of Goossea and Pigham are shown in this back-to-back stem and leaf diagram.

Goossea					Pigham					
(3)			6 2 0	0						
(4)	9	7 5	3	1	4 7					(2)
(4)	8	8 7	4	2	0 0 3 6					(4)
(3)		5 2	1	3	2 3 5 5 9					(5)
(2)			4 1	4	1 2 6 8					(4)
(1)			0	5	2 4 5					(3)
				6						
(1)			5	7						

Key: 4 | 2 | 0 represents 24 items of junk mail in Goossea
and 20 items of junk mail in Pigham

a) For the data from Pigham, calculate the following:
   (i)   the median
   (ii) the lower quartile
   (iii) the upper quartile
   (iv) the interquartile range
   (v)   the lower fence, $Q_1 - 1.5 \times IQR$
   (vi) the upper fence, $Q_3 + 1.5 \times IQR$

b) Are any of the data values from Pigham outliers? Explain your answer.

c) Draw a box plot to illustrate the data from Pigham.

d) Draw a box plot to illustrate the data from Goossea. (Use the same rules to find the fences as you used for Pigham.)

Variance and standard deviation

Variance and standard deviation are two (very closely related) measures of **dispersion** — they give you an idea of **how spread out** the data values are from the mean. The bigger the variance (or standard deviation), the more spread out your readings are.

Variance

- There are two ways to write the formula for the **variance**. The second one in the box below is usually much easier to use.

$$\text{variance} = \frac{\sum(x - \bar{x})^2}{n} \quad \text{or} \quad \text{variance} = \frac{\sum x^2}{n} - \bar{x}^2$$

- Here, the x-values are the data, $\bar{x}$ is the mean, and n is the total number of data values.

- The two formulas above are equivalent to each other — you can rearrange one to get the other (although you **won't** be asked to do this in the exam).

$$\frac{\sum(x - \bar{x})^2}{n} = \frac{1}{n}\sum(x^2 - 2x\bar{x} + \bar{x}^2) \quad \text{(multiplying out brackets)}$$

$$= \frac{1}{n}\sum x^2 - 2 \cdot \frac{1}{n} \cdot \bar{x}\sum x + \frac{1}{n}\sum \bar{x}^2 \quad \text{(writing as 3 summations)}$$

$$= \frac{1}{n}\sum x^2 - 2 \cdot \frac{1}{n} \cdot n\bar{x}^2 + \frac{1}{n}\sum \bar{x}^2 \quad \text{(since } \sum x = n\bar{x})$$

$$= \frac{1}{n}\sum x^2 - 2 \cdot \frac{1}{n} \cdot n\bar{x}^2 + \frac{1}{n} \cdot n\bar{x}^2 \quad \text{(since } \sum \bar{x}^2 = n\bar{x}^2)$$

$$= \frac{1}{n}\sum x^2 - \bar{x}^2 = \frac{\sum x^2}{n} - \bar{x}^2 \quad \text{(combining the 2nd and 3rd terms)}$$

Tip: You can think of the formula on the right as saying:

'The variance is equal to the mean of the squares $(\frac{\sum x^2}{n})$ minus the square of the mean $(\bar{x}^2)$.'

Tip: Although the formula on the right is easier to use, the one on the left makes it easier to understand what the variance actually is — it's 'the average of the squared deviations from the mean'.

Tip: Remember... $\bar{x}$ is just a number, so you can 'take it outside the summation' — i.e. $\sum x\bar{x} = \bar{x}\sum x$.

Standard deviation

Tip: The variance is measured in squared units. For example, if the data values are measured in metres (m), then the variance is measured in m².

The **standard deviation** is equal to the **square root** of the variance.

$$\text{Standard deviation} = \sqrt{\text{variance}}$$

The standard deviation is measured in the same units as the data values themselves — this sometimes makes it a more useful measure of dispersion than the variance.

Tip: The alternative formula for the variance is $\text{variance} = \dfrac{\sum(x - \bar{x})^2}{n}$.

But it's more fiddly to use this formula than the one used in the example. This is because once you've worked out the mean, you then have to **subtract it from each individual data** value, before squaring and adding the results, and then dividing by n.

The formula used on the right involves only a **single subtraction**.

Example

Find the variance and standard deviation of the following data set:
$$2, 3, 4, 4, 6, 11, 12$$

- Find the **sum of** the numbers first: $\sum x = 2 + 3 + 4 + 4 + 6 + 11 + 12 = 42$

- Then finding the **mean** is easy: $\bar{x} = \dfrac{\sum x}{n} = \dfrac{42}{7} = 6$

- Next find the **sum of the squares**: $\sum x^2 = 4 + 9 + 16 + 16 + 36 + 121 + 144 = 346$

- Now finding the 'mean of the squares' is easy: $\dfrac{\sum x^2}{n} = \dfrac{346}{7}$

- The **variance** is the 'mean of the squares minus the square of the mean':
$$\text{Variance} = \frac{\sum x^2}{n} - \bar{x}^2 = \frac{346}{7} - 6^2 = 13.428... = \boxed{13.4 \text{ (to 3 s.f.)}}$$

- Take the **square root** of the variance to find the **standard deviation**:
$$\text{Standard deviation} = \sqrt{13.428...} = \boxed{3.66 \text{ (to 3 s.f.)}}$$

If your data is given in a **frequency table**, then the variance formula can be written like this, where f is the frequency of each x.

$$\text{variance} = \frac{\sum fx^2}{\sum f} - \bar{x}^2, \quad \text{where } \bar{x} = \frac{\sum fx}{\sum f}$$

Tip: Here, $n = \sum f$.

Tip: Remember...
fx^2 means $f \times (x^2)$
— not $(fx)^2$.

Tip: You could also write this formula as
$\text{variance} = \dfrac{\sum f(x - \bar{x})^2}{\sum f}$
But it's trickier to use than the formula in the blue box — again, because of all the extra subtracting you need to do.

Example

Find the variance and standard deviation of the data in this table.

x	2	3	4	5	6	7
frequency, f	2	5	5	4	1	1

- It's best to start by adding an extra row to the table showing the values of fx.

x	2	3	4	5	6	7
frequency, f	2	5	5	4	1	1
fx	4	15	20	20	6	7

- The **number** of values is: $\sum f = 2 + 5 + 5 + 4 + 1 + 1 = 18$

- The **sum** of the values is: $\sum fx = 4 + 15 + 20 + 20 + 6 + 7 = 72$

- So the **mean** of the values is: $\bar{x} = \dfrac{\sum fx}{\sum f} = \dfrac{72}{18} = 4$

- Now add two more rows to your table showing x^2 and fx^2.

x^2	4	9	16	25	36	49
fx^2	8	45	80	100	36	49

- Now you can work out $\sum fx^2$.

$$\sum fx^2 = 8 + 45 + 80 + 100 + 36 + 49 = 318$$

- And now you can find the variance.

$$\text{Variance} = \frac{\sum fx^2}{\sum f} - \bar{x}^2 = \frac{318}{18} - 4^2 = 1.666... = \boxed{1.67 \text{ (to 3 s.f.)}}$$

- Then take the **square root** of the variance to find the **standard deviation**:

$$\text{Standard deviation} = \sqrt{1.666...} = \boxed{1.29 \text{ (to 3 s.f.)}}$$

If your data is **grouped**, then you can only **estimate** the variance and standard deviation (because you don't know the actual data values — see p19).

In this case, assume that each data value is equal to the **class mid-point**. Then go through the same steps as in the example above.

Tip: This is the same assumption you used when you found the **mean** of grouped data on p19.

Example

The heights of sunflowers in a garden were measured, and are recorded in the table below.

Height of sunflower, h (cm)	$150 \le h < 170$	$170 \le h < 190$	$190 \le h < 210$	$210 \le h < 230$
Frequency, f	5	10	12	3

Estimate the variance and the standard deviation of the heights.

- Start by adding extra rows for the class mid-points x, as well as fx, x^2 and fx^2:

Height of sunflower, h (cm)	$150 \le h < 170$	$170 \le h < 190$	$190 \le h < 210$	$210 \le h < 230$
Frequency, f	5	10	12	3
Class mid-point, x	160	180	200	220
fx	800	1800	2400	660
x^2	25 600	32 400	40 000	48 400
fx^2	128 000	324 000	480 000	145 200

- The **number** of values is: $\sum f = 5 + 10 + 12 + 3 = 30$

- The **sum** of the values is: $\sum fx = 800 + 1800 + 2400 + 660 = 5660$

- So the **mean** of the values is: $\bar{x} = \dfrac{\sum fx}{\sum f} = \dfrac{5660}{30}$

- $\sum fx^2 = 128\,000 + 324\,000 + 480\,000 + 145\,200 = 1\,077\,200$

- So variance $= \dfrac{\sum fx^2}{\sum f} - \bar{x}^2 = \dfrac{1\,077\,200}{30} - \left(\dfrac{5660}{30}\right)^2 = 311.5555...$

$$= \boxed{312 \text{ cm}^2 \text{ (to 3 sig.fig.)}}$$

- And standard deviation $= \sqrt{311.5555...} = \boxed{17.7 \text{ cm (to 3 sig. fig.)}}$

Tip: The variance is sometimes labelled σ^2 (where σ is the Greek letter 'sigma'), and sometimes s^2. There is a difference, although you **don't** need to know about it for S1.

But if you're curious... The symbol σ^2 is used when you have information about an entire **population**, and the symbol s^2 is used when you only have information about a **sample**.

σ^2 and s^2 are actually worked out slightly differently too. (The method in this book is the one for working out σ^2.)

Tip: Remember... variance takes 'squared' units.

You can use the variances (or standard deviations) of two small data sets to find the overall variance (or standard deviation) of the larger, combined set of data. But it's a bit fiddly, and so you need to do this very carefully.

Example

The mean of 10 boys' heights is 180 cm, with a standard deviation of 10 cm. The mean height of 9 girls is 165 cm, with a standard deviation of 8 cm.

Find the variance and standard deviation of the combined group of 19 heights.

You need to know the mean of the combined set of heights to be able to work out the variance. So find that first.

- Call the boys' heights x and the girls' heights y.

- First, write down the formula for the mean, and substitute in the mean for the boys ($\bar{x}$) and the total number of values (n). This gives you the **sum** of all the boys' heights, $\sum x$.

$$\bar{x} = \frac{\sum x}{n} \Rightarrow 180 = \frac{\sum x}{10}$$
$$\Rightarrow \sum x = 1800$$

- Do the same to find the sum of the girls' heights, $\sum y$.

$$\bar{y} = \frac{\sum y}{n} \Rightarrow 165 = \frac{\sum y}{9} \Rightarrow \sum y = 1485$$

- So the sum of the heights of the combined group of boys and girls is:

$$\sum x + \sum y = 1800 + 1485 = 3285$$

- The total number of boys and girls is 10 + 9 = 19. So the mean height of the combined group is:

$$\frac{3285}{19} = \textbf{172.9 cm}$$

Now you need to go through a very similar process to find the sum of the squares of the combined set of heights.

- The standard deviation for the boys is 10, so the variance = 10^2 = 100. The standard deviation for the girls is 8, so the variance = 8^2 = 64.

- Substitute the boys' variance into the formula for the variance. This will give you the sum of the squares of their heights, $\sum x^2$.

$$\text{variance}_x = \frac{\sum x^2}{n} - \bar{x}^2 = \frac{\sum x^2}{10} - 180^2 = 100$$
$$\text{So } \sum x^2 = 10 \times (180^2 + 100) = 325\,000$$

- Now do the same for the girls to find $\sum y^2$.

$$\text{variance}_y = \frac{\sum y^2}{n} - \bar{y}^2 = \frac{\sum y^2}{9} - 165^2 = 64$$
$$\text{So } \sum y^2 = 9 \times (165^2 + 64) = 245\,601$$

- So the sum of the squares for the combined group of boys and girls is:

$$\sum x^2 + \sum y^2 = 325\,000 + 245\,601 = \textbf{570\,601}$$

Tip: You could use the formula from p15 to find the combined mean:
$$\bar{x} = \frac{n_1\bar{x}_1 + n_2\bar{x}_2}{n_1 + n_2}$$

Tip: Round the fraction to 1 d.p. to give your answer. But when you use the mean in more calculations, use the fraction (or your calculator's memory) so you don't lose accuracy.

Tip: Here, variance$_x$ is the variance of the boys' heights, and variance$_y$ is the variance of the girls' heights.

- You now have all the information you need to find the variance for the combined group.

$$\text{variance} = \frac{570\,601}{19} - \left(\frac{3285}{19}\right)^2 = 139.0415... = \boxed{139.0\,\text{cm}^2\,\text{(to 1 d.p.)}}$$

Tip: Don't use the rounded mean (172.9) — you'll lose accuracy.

- And finally the standard deviation of the boys and the girls is:

$$\text{standard deviation} = \sqrt{139.0415...} = \boxed{11.8\,\text{cm}\,\text{(to 1 d.p.)}}$$

You've seen that different measures of **location** are useful in different ways (see page 22). The same is true of measures of **dispersion** — the range, interquartile range, variance and standard deviation all have pros and cons.

Range
- The range is the **easiest** measure of dispersion to calculate.
- But it's heavily affected by even a **single** extreme value / outlier. And it depends on only **two** data values — it **doesn't** tell you anything about how spread out the rest of the values are.

Interquartile range
- It's **not** affected by **extreme values** — so if your data contains **outliers**, then the interquartile range is a good measure of dispersion to use.
- It's fairly **tricky** to work out.

Variance
- The variance depends on **all** the data values — so no values are 'ignored'.
- But it's **tricky** to work out, and is affected by **extreme values / outliers** (meaning that 'freak' values have more influence than they deserve).
- It's also expressed in **different units** from the actual data values, so it can be difficult to interpret.

Standard deviation
- Like the variance, the standard deviation depends on **all** the data values — so no values are 'ignored'.
- It has the **same units** as the data values themselves, and so is easier to understand and interpret.
- But it is also **tricky** to work out, and affected by **extreme values / outliers**.

Exercise 3.3

Q1 The attendance figures (x) for Wessex Football Club's first six matches of the season were: 756, 755, 764, 778, 754, 759.
  a) Find the mean ($\overline{x}$) of these attendance figures.
  b) Calculate the sum of the squares of the attendance figures, $\sum x^2$.
  c) Use your answers to find the variance of the attendance figures.
  d) Hence find the standard deviation of the attendance figures.
  e) Explain why the standard deviation is a reasonable measure of dispersion to use with this data.

Q2 The number of runners in the first eight Broughton marathons were:
32, 21, 75, 22, 88, 98, 71, 73

a) Calculate the variance for these figures.

b) Find the standard deviation of the number of runners.

Q3 The figures for the number of TVs (x) in the households of 20 students are shown in the table below.

x	1	2	3	4
frequency, f	7	8	4	1

a) Find the mean number of TVs $(\overline{x})$ in the 20 households.

b) By adding rows showing x^2 and fx^2 to the table, find $\sum fx^2$.

c) Calculate the variance for the data above.

d) Hence find the standard deviation.

Q4 Find the variance of the data in this frequency table.

x	7	8	9	10	11	12
frequency, f	2	3	5	7	4	2

Q5 The pulse rates while resting of a number of students were measured. They are shown in the grouped frequency table below.
(You can assume that a pulse rate is always a whole number.)

Pulse rate	56-60	61-65	66-70	71-75	76-80
frequency, f	1	2	4	8	5

a) Add four extra rows to the table showing:
   (i) the class mid-points (x)
   (ii) fx (iii) x^2 (iv) fx^2

b) Use your table to find: (i) $\sum f$ (ii) $\sum fx$ (iii) $\sum fx^2$

c) Use your answers to estimate the variance of the pulse rates.

Q6 The yields $(w$, in kg$)$ of potatoes from a number of allotments is shown in the grouped frequency table on the right.

a) Estimate the variance for this data.

b) Estimate the standard deviation.

Yield, w (kg)	Frequency
$50 \leq w < 60$	23
$60 \leq w < 70$	12
$70 \leq w < 80$	15
$80 \leq w < 90$	6
$90 \leq w < 100$	2

Q7 Su and Ellen are collecting data on the durations of the eruptions of the volcano in their garden. Between them, they have recorded the duration of the last 60 eruptions.
  • Su has timed 23 eruptions, with an average duration of 3.42 minutes and a standard deviation of 1.07 minutes.
  • Ellen has timed 37 eruptions, with an average duration of 3.92 minutes and a standard deviation of 0.97 minutes.

They decide to combine their observations into one large data set.

a) Calculate the mean duration of all the observed eruptions.

b) Find the variance of the set of 60 durations.

c) Find the standard deviation of the set of 60 durations.

Coding

Coding means doing something to all the readings in your data set to make the numbers easier to work with. That could mean:

- **adding** a number to (or **subtracting** a number from) all your readings,
- **multiplying** (or **dividing**) all your readings by a number,
- **both** of the above.

For example, finding the mean of 1831, 1832 and 1836 looks complicated. But if you subtract 1830 from each number, then finding the mean of what's left (1, 2 and 6) is much easier — it's 3. So the mean of the original numbers must be 1833 (once you've 'undone' the coding). That's coding in a nutshell.

Tip: Choose what to add/subtract and multiply/divide by based on what makes your data easiest to work with.

- You have to change your original variable, x, to a different one, such as y (so in the example above, if $x = 1831$, then $y = 1$).
- An **original** data value x will be related to a **coded** data value y by an equation of this form: → $\boxed{y = \dfrac{x - a}{b}}$ where a and b are numbers you choose.
- The mean and standard deviation of the **original** data values will then be related to the mean and standard deviation of the **coded** data values by the following equations:

  - $\bar{y} = \dfrac{\bar{x} - a}{b}$, where $\bar{x}$ and $\bar{y}$ are the means of variables x and y
  - standard deviation of $y = \dfrac{\text{standard deviation of } x}{b}$

Tip: Note that if you **don't multiply or divide** your readings by anything (i.e. if b = 1), then the dispersion isn't changed.

Example

Find the mean and standard deviation of: 1 862 020, 1 862 040, 1 862 010 and 1 862 050.

- All the **original** data values (call them x) start with the same four digits (1862) — so start by subtracting 1 862 000 from every reading to leave 20, 40, 10 and 50.
- You can then make life even simpler by dividing by 10 — giving 2, 4, 1 and 5. These are the **coded** data values (call them y).
- So putting those steps together, each x-value is related to a corresponding y-value by the equation: $y = \dfrac{x - 1862\,000}{10}$
- Now work out the **mean** and **standard deviation** of the (easy-to-use) coded values.

$$\bar{y} = \frac{2 + 4 + 1 + 5}{4} = \frac{12}{4} = 3$$

Tip: This means a = 1 862 000 and b = 10.

$$\text{standard deviation of } y = \sqrt{\frac{2^2 + 4^2 + 1^2 + 5^2}{4} - 3^2}$$
$$= \sqrt{\frac{46}{4} - 9} = \sqrt{2.5} = 1.58 \text{ to 3 sig. fig.}$$

Tip: Remember... standard deviation $= \sqrt{\dfrac{\sum x^2}{n} - \bar{x}^2}$

- Then find the mean and standard deviation of the original values using the formulas above.
- $\bar{y} = \dfrac{\bar{x} - a}{b}$, so $\bar{x} = a + b\bar{y}$. This means: $\bar{x} = 1862\,000 + 10\bar{y}$

$$= 1862\,000 + (10 \times 3)$$
$$= 1862\,030$$

- And standard deviation of $y = \dfrac{\text{standard deviation of } x}{b}$

  So standard deviation of x = b × standard deviation of y
  $$= 10 \times 1.58 = 15.8 \text{ (to 3 sig. fig.)}$$

Carry out the method in exactly the same way with **grouped** data. Remember, with grouped data, you assume that all the readings equal the **class mid-point**, and so this is the x-value that you use with the coding equation $y = \dfrac{x - a}{b}$.

Tip: So here, a = 15.5 and b = 10.

Example

Estimate the mean and standard deviation of this data concerning job interviews using the coding $y = \dfrac{x - 15.5}{10}$.

Length of interview, to nearest minute	11-20	21-30	31-40	41-50
Frequency, f	17	21	27	15

- Make a new table showing the class mid-points (x) of the original data, and the coded class mid-points (y). Also include rows for fy, y^2 and fy^2.

Length of interview, to nearest minute	11-20	21-30	31-40	41-50
Frequency, f	17	21	27	15
Class mid-point, x	15.5	25.5	35.5	45.5
Coded value, y	0	1	2	3
fy	0	21	54	45
y^2	0	1	4	9
fy^2	0	21	108	135

Now use your table to find the mean of the **coded** values ($\overline{y}$).
- The **number** of coded values is: $\sum f = 17 + 21 + 27 + 15 = 80$
- The **sum** of the coded values is: $\sum fy = 0 + 21 + 54 + 45 = 120$
- So the **mean** of the coded values is: $\overline{y} = \dfrac{\sum fy}{\sum f} = \dfrac{120}{80} = \mathbf{1.5}$

Now for the standard deviation...
- $\sum fy^2 = 0 + 21 + 108 + 135 = 264$
- So variance $= \dfrac{\sum fy^2}{\sum f} - \overline{y}^2 = \dfrac{264}{80} - 1.5^2 = 1.05$

- This gives a standard deviation for the **coded** data of:
  standard deviation of $y = \sqrt{1.05} = \mathbf{1.02}$ (to 3 sig. fig.).

And now you can use these figures to find the mean and standard deviation of the **original** data.

- $\overline{y} = \dfrac{\overline{x} - a}{b}$, so $\overline{x} = a + b\overline{y} = 15.5 + 10 \times 1.5 = 30.5 \text{ minutes}$

- And standard deviation of $y = \dfrac{\text{standard deviation of } x}{b}$.

  So standard deviation of x = b × standard deviation of y
  $$= 10 \times 1.02 = 10.2 \text{ minutes (to 3 sig. fig.)}$$

- This means the standard deviation of the interview lengths is 10.2 minutes (to 3 sig. fig.) .

Sometimes, you won't have the data itself — just some **summations**.

Example

A travel guide employee collects some data on the cost (c, in £) of a night's stay in 10 hotels in a particular town. He codes his data using $d = 10(c - 93.5)$, and calculates the summations below.

$$\sum d = 0 \text{ and } \sum d^2 = 998\,250$$

Calculate the mean and standard deviation of the original costs.

First find the **mean** of the coded values:
- The **number** of values (n) is 10.
- So the **mean** of the coded values is: $\bar{d} = \dfrac{\sum d}{n} = \dfrac{0}{10} = \mathbf{0}$

Tip: The variables aren't x and y this time, but you can still go through exactly the same steps as before.

Now for the **standard deviation** of the coded values:
- variance $= \dfrac{\sum d^2}{n} - \bar{d}^2 = \dfrac{998\,250}{10} - 0^2 = 99\,825$

- This gives a standard deviation for the **coded** data of:
  standard deviation $= \sqrt{99\,825} = \mathbf{316.0}$ (to 4 sig. fig.).

Now you can find the mean and standard deviation of the **original** data.
- $\bar{d} = 10(\bar{c} - 93.5)$, so $\bar{c} = 93.5 + \dfrac{\bar{d}}{10} = 93.5$, i.e. $\boxed{\bar{c} = £93.50}$

- standard deviation of $d = 10 \times$ standard deviation of c,
  so standard deviation of $c = \dfrac{\text{standard deviation of } d}{10} = \dfrac{316.0}{10} = 31.60$

  That is, $\boxed{\text{standard deviation of } c = £31.60 \text{ (to the nearest penny)}}$.

There are lots of different ways to ask questions about this topic.

Example

A set of 10 numbers (x-values) can be summarised as shown below:

$$\sum(x - 10) = 15 \text{ and } \sum(x - 10)^2 = 100$$

Find the mean and standard deviation of the numbers.

- You can simplify those summations if you write $y = x - 10$.
  This is the same as **coding** the x-values.
- Rewriting the summations means: $\sum y = 15$ and $\sum y^2 = 100$
- Now you can work out the mean and standard deviation of the coded data in the normal way.

- Mean, $\bar{y} = \dfrac{\sum y}{n} = \dfrac{15}{10} = 1.5$

- Variance of coded data $= \dfrac{\sum y^2}{n} - \bar{y}^2 = \dfrac{100}{10} - 1.5^2 = 10 - 2.25 = 7.75$

  So standard deviation of coded data $= \sqrt{7.75} = 2.78$ to 3 sig. fig.

- Now finding the mean and standard deviation of the x-values is easy:
  $\bar{y} = \bar{x} - 10$, so $\bar{x} = \bar{y} + 10 = 1.5 + 10 = \boxed{11.5}$

  Standard deviation of $x = $ standard deviation of y
  $= \boxed{2.78 \text{ (to 3 sig. fig.)}}$

Tip: The dispersion (i.e. the standard deviation) of x is the same as the dispersion of y since you've only subtracted 10 from every number — you've not done anything to change how spread out or tightly packed they are.

Q1 In each case below, find the mean and standard deviation of the original data sets.

a) A set of data values (x) are coded using $y = x - 500$.
The mean of the coded data ($\bar{y}$) is 12, and the standard deviation of the coded data is 4.22.

b) A set of data values (x) are coded using $y = 4x$.
The mean of the coded data ($\bar{y}$) is 6, and the standard deviation of the coded data is 2.14.

c) A set of data values (x) are coded using $y = \dfrac{x - 20\,000}{15}$.
The mean of the coded data ($\bar{y}$) is 12.4, and the standard deviation of the coded data is 1.34.

Q1 Hint: In part b),
$b = \dfrac{1}{4}$.

Q2 In each case use the given coding to find the mean and standard deviation of the given data.

a) 2003, 2007, 2008   Use the coding: $y = x - 2000$

b) 0.02, 0.17, 0.03, 0.11, 0.07   Use the coding: $y = 100x$

c) 353.5, 351, 360, 357.5   Use the coding: $y = 2(x - 350)$

d) −7900, −7930, −7960, −8000, −7940

     Use the coding: $y = \dfrac{x + 8000}{10}$

Q3 The widths (in cm) of 10 sunflower seeds in a packet are given below.
0.61, 0.67, 0.63, 0.63, 0.66, 0.65, 0.64, 0.68, 0.64, 0.62

a) Code the data values above (x) to form a new data set consisting of integer values (y) between 1 and 10.

b) Find the mean and standard deviation of your coded values (y).

c) Use your answers to find the mean and standard deviation of the original values (x).

Q4 The table below displays the weight (x, to the nearest gram) of 12 items on a production line.

Weight (to nearest g)	100-104	105-109	110-114	115-119
Frequency	2	6	3	1

Use the coding $y = x - 102$ to estimate the mean and standard deviation of the items' weights.

Q5 Twenty pieces of data (x) have been summarised as follows:
$$\sum(x + 2) = 7 \quad \text{and} \quad \sum(x + 2)^2 = 80.$$
Calculate the mean and standard deviation of the data.

Skewness

Skewness tells you how **symmetrical** or **asymmetrical** (lopsided) the distribution of your data is.

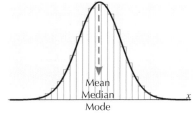

- This is a typical **symmetrical** distribution.
- Notice: mean = median = mode

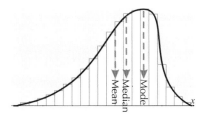

- A **negatively skewed** distribution has a 'tail' on the left.
- This means most data values are relatively high, but there are some 'extreme' low values.
- Notice: mean < median < mode

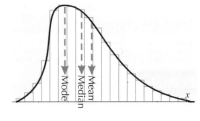

- A **positively skewed** distribution has a 'tail' on the right.
- This means most data values are relatively low, but there are some 'extreme' high values.
- Notice: mode < median < mean

Tip: It's these 'extreme' low (or high) values that reduce (or increase) the mean and make it an unsuitable measure of location for a data set that isn't symmetrical — see p22.

For nearly **all** distributions, the following is **approximately** true:

$$\boxed{\text{mean} - \text{mode} = 3 \times (\text{mean} - \text{median})}$$

Example

A primate keeper at a zoo records the mass (in kilograms) of fruit eaten by 50 monkeys and apes in one morning. Her results are shown in the table.

Mass (kg)	0.2-0.6	0.6-1.0	1.0-1.4	1.4-1.8	1.8-2.2	2.2-2.6	2.6-3.0
Frequency	10	14	11	8	4	2	1

Draw a histogram of the data, and state the type of skewness present.

- Draw the histogram.
- This has a '**tail**' on the **right-hand** side.
- Most of the values are relatively **low**.
- So this distribution is **positively skewed**.

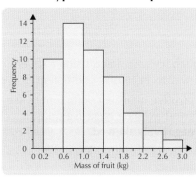

Tip: All the classes are the same width, so I've plotted the frequency, rather than the frequency density.

Plotting the frequency density wouldn't change the **shape** of the graph at all.

You don't always have to judge skewness by eye, though.
You can use a **coefficient of skewness** to measure how 'all-up-one-end' your data is. There are a couple of important coefficients of skewness — the first of these is **Pearson's coefficient of skewness**.

Tip: These two definitions should give approximately the same answer, because for nearly all distributions, 'mean – mode' and '3 × (mean – median)' are approximately equal (see p41).

(In the exam, you'll be told what formula to use.)

$$\text{Pearson's coefficient of skewness} = \frac{3(\text{mean} - \text{median})}{\text{standard deviation}}$$

$$\approx \frac{\text{mean} - \text{mode}}{\text{standard deviation}}$$

Pearson's coefficient of skewness usually lies **between –3 and +3**.

- **Positive values** mean that your data is **positively skewed**.
- **Negative values** mean that your data is **negatively skewed**.
- A **symmetrical** distribution would give a skewness coefficient of **zero**.
- The more highly skewed your data is, the **closer to 3 or –3** Pearson's coefficient of skewness will be.

So a coefficient of 2.7 would mean your data is very heavily positively skewed — with a lot of low values but a long tail on the right.
But if Pearson's coefficient of skewness is –0.1, then the distribution is **slightly** negatively skewed.

Tip: You have to use the formula involving the median, because you don't have a figure for the mode.

Tip: Pearson's coefficient of skewness is positive and not too large — just as you'd expect it to be from the histogram on the previous page.

Example

For the 'primate' data in the previous example, the mean = 1.136, the median = 1.036 and the standard deviation = 0.60.
Find Pearson's coefficient of skewness for the data.

- Pearson's coefficient of skewness $= \dfrac{3(\text{mean} - \text{median})}{\text{standard deviation}}$

$$= \frac{3 \times (1.136 - 1.036)}{0.60} = 0.5$$

The **quartile coefficient of skewness** is another coefficient of skewness.

Tip: Remember that Q_1 is the lower quartile, Q_3 is the upper quartile, and Q_2 is the median.

$$\text{Quartile coefficient of skewness} = \frac{(Q_3 - Q_2) - (Q_2 - Q_1)}{Q_3 - Q_1} = \frac{Q_3 - 2Q_2 + Q_1}{Q_3 - Q_1}$$

Although it's calculated using a different formula, you interpret it in much the same way as Pearson's coefficient of skewness.

- A **positive** quartile coefficient of skewness means your data is **positively skewed**, while a **negative** quartile coefficient of skewness means your data is **negatively skewed**.
- The **larger** the quartile coefficient of skewness, the **more highly skewed** your data is.
- A value of **zero** means your data is **symmetrically distributed**.

A **box plot** can quickly tell you the skew of a data set. Each of these three histograms has its corresponding box plot shown underneath.

- If $Q_3 - Q_2 = Q_2 - Q_1$ then the quartile coefficient of skewness will be **zero**.
- This corresponds to a **symmetrical** distribution of data and a **symmetrical** box plot.

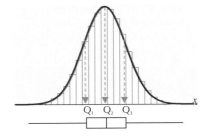

- If $Q_3 - Q_2 > Q_2 - Q_1$ then the quartile coefficient of skewness will be **positive**, showing that the distribution is **positively skewed**.
- This corresponds to a long tail on the right-hand side of the histogram, and to Q_2 (the median) being closer to Q_1 than to Q_3 on the box plot.

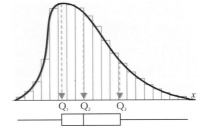

- If $Q_3 - Q_2 < Q_2 - Q_1$ then the quartile coefficient of skewness will be **negative**, showing that the distribution is **negatively skewed**.
- This corresponds to a long tail on the left-hand side of the histogram, and to Q_2 (the median) being closer to Q_3 than to Q_1 on the box plot.

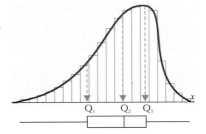

Example

The masses (in kilograms) of fruit eaten by 50 monkeys and apes in a zoo one morning have $Q_1 = 0.671$, $Q_2 = 1.036$, and $Q_3 = 1.525$.

Find the quartile coefficient of skewness for this data.

- Quartile coefficient of skewness $= \dfrac{Q_3 - 2Q_2 + Q_1}{Q_3 - Q_1}$

$$= \frac{1.525 - 2 \times 1.036 + 0.671}{1.525 - 0.671}$$

$$= 0.145 \text{ (to 3 d.p.)}$$

Tip: These figures describe the 'primate' data in the example on page 41.

Tip: Again, this is positive but not too large (which is what you'd expect from the histogram on page 41).

Example

The ages of 15 lottery winners are given in this stem and leaf diagram.

1	9	(1)
2	2 3 7	(3)
3	8 8 9	(3)
4	1 4 7 9	(4)
5	1 2 3 7	(4)

Key 3|8 means 38 years of age

a) Calculate Pearson's coefficient of skewness using $\dfrac{3(\text{mean} - \text{median})}{\text{standard deviation}}$.

- The sum of the ages is $\sum x = 600$. So the **mean** age is $\dfrac{600}{15} = 40$.

- The sum of the squares is $\sum x^2 = 26\,102$.
  So the **standard deviation** is $\sqrt{\dfrac{26\,102}{15} - 40^2} = \mathbf{11.84}$ (to 2 d.p.).

- There are 15 values, so the median is the 8th value in the ordered list. This means the **median** = **41**.

- So Pearson's coefficient of skewness is $\dfrac{3(40 - 41)}{11.84} = -0.253$ (to 3 d.p.)

Tip: These two answers are similar, but not identical.

b) **Calculate the quartile coefficient of skewness.**

- As there are 15 values, the lower quartile is the 4th value in the list. So $\mathbf{Q_1 = 27}$.

- The upper quartile is the 12th value in the list. So $\mathbf{Q_3 = 51}$.

- The quartile coefficient of skewness is $\dfrac{51 - 2 \times 41 + 27}{51 - 27}$

  $= -0.167$ (to 3 d.p.)

Tip: This small, negative coefficient of skewness corresponds to the slight negative skew you can see on the stem and leaf diagram (though you have to imagine it rotated 90° anticlockwise).

c) **Use your answers to describe the skewness of the data.**

- These skewness coefficients are both small and negative, so the data is **slightly negatively skewed**.

Exercise 3.5

Q1 Match each diagram below to one of the descriptions in the box:

positively skewed   negatively skewed   symmetrical

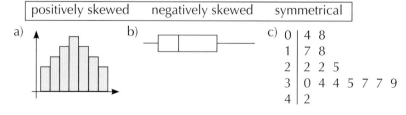

a)

b)

c)

0	4 8
1	7 8
2	2 2 5
3	0 4 4 5 7 7 9
4	2

Q2 Find Pearson's coefficient of skewness for each distribution below, and use your answer to say whether the distribution is positively skewed, negatively skewed or symmetrical.

a) mean = 7   mode = 5   standard deviation = 1.6

b) mean = 12   median = 13.5   standard deviation = 1.8

c) mean = 14   mode = 14   standard deviation = 2.37

d) mean = –9   median = –8   standard deviation = 2.5

Q3 Find the quartile coefficient of skewness for each distribution below, and use your answer to say whether the distribution is positively skewed, negatively skewed or symmetrical.

a) $Q_1 = 3$ $Q_2 = 8$ $Q_3 = 15$

b) $Q_1 = 35$ $Q_2 = 119$ $Q_3 = 194$

c) lower quartile = –28   median = –23   upper quartile = –10

d) lower quartile = 2.4   median = 5.3   upper quartile = 8.2

Q4 The following data shows the winnings (in pounds) of a bingo player one summer: 1, 6, 9, 10, 10, 10, 11, 11

a) Find the mean, median and standard deviation of the data.

b) Find Pearson's coefficient of skewness using $\dfrac{3(\text{mean} - \text{median})}{\text{standard deviation}}$.

c) Use your answer to describe the skewness of the distribution.

Q5 The salaries (in thousands of pounds) of a small firm's ten employees are shown below.

12, 18, 18, 22, 22, 22, 24, 24, 27, 60

a) Calculate Pearson's coefficient of skewness using $\dfrac{\text{mean} - \text{mode}}{\text{standard deviation}}$.

b) Use your answer to describe the skewness of the distribution.

Comparing distributions

It's really common in the exam to be asked to **compare** two distributions.

To do this, there are different kinds of things you can say, depending on what information you have about the distributions. You can:

- Compare measures of **location**, such as the mean, median or mode.
  - You'll need to say which distribution has the higher mean/median/mode, and by how much.
  - Then say what this means **in the context of the question**.
- Compare measures of **dispersion**, such as variance, standard deviation, range, interquartile range, or interpercentile range.
  - You'll need to say which distribution's data values are more 'tightly packed', or which distribution's values are more spread out.
  - Then say what this means **in the context of the question**.
- Compare measures of **skewness** — such as Pearson's coefficient of skewness or the quartile coefficient of skewness.
  - For each distribution, say whether it is symmetrical, positively skewed, or negatively skewed, and whether it is highly skewed, or just slightly.
  - Then say what this means **in the context of the question**.

Tip: '...in the context of the question' means you need to use the same 'setting' in your answer as the question uses.

For example, if the question is all about the weights of tigers in a zoo, then you need to talk about the weights of tigers in the zoo in your answer as well.

Example 1

This table summarises the marks obtained by a group of students in Maths 'Calculator' and 'Non-calculator' papers.

a) **Comment on the location and dispersion of the distributions.**

Calculator paper		Non-calculator paper
40	Lower quartile, Q_1	35
58	Median, Q_2	42
70	Upper quartile, Q_3	56
55	Mean	46.1
21.2	Standard deviation	17.8

Location:
- The mean and the median are both higher for the Calculator paper (the mean is approximately 9 marks higher, while the median is 16 marks higher).
- This means that scores were generally higher on the Calculator paper.

Dispersion:
- The interquartile range (IQR) for the Calculator paper is $Q_3 - Q_1 = 70 - 40 = 30$.
- The interquartile range (IQR) for the Non-calculator paper is $Q_3 - Q_1 = 56 - 35 = 21$.
- So the IQR and the standard deviation are both higher for the Calculator paper.
- This means the scores on the Calculator paper are more spread out than those for the Non-calculator paper.

b) **Calculate Pearson's coefficient of skewness for each paper, using $\dfrac{3(\text{mean} - \text{median})}{\text{standard deviation}}$.**
   Comment on your answers.

For the **Calculator** paper:
- Pearson's coefficient of skewness $= \dfrac{3 \times (55 - 58)}{21.2} = -0.425$ (to 3 d.p.)

For the **Non-calculator** paper:
- Pearson's coefficient of skewness $= \dfrac{3 \times (46.1 - 42)}{17.8} = 0.691$ (to 3 d.p.)

- The Calculator paper scores are negatively skewed. This means that most scores were relatively high, but there was a 'tail' of low scores.
- The Non-calculator paper scores are positively skewed. This means that most scores were relatively low, but there was a 'tail' of high scores.

Tip: Don't forget to give your answer in the context of the question, so here you need to talk about scores on Calculator and Non-calculator papers.

You may have to base your comparison on a **graph** instead of numbers.

Example 2

The box plots on the right show how the masses (in g) of the tomatoes in two harvests were distributed.

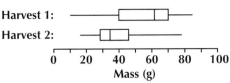

Compare the distributions of the two harvests.

Location:
- The median is more than 25 g higher for Harvest 1.
- This shows that the tomatoes in Harvest 1 were generally heavier.

Dispersion:
- The interquartile range (IQR) and the range for Harvest 1 are higher than those for Harvest 2.
- This shows that the masses of the tomatoes in Harvest 1 were more varied than the masses of the tomatoes in Harvest 2.

Skewness:
- The distribution of the tomatoes' masses in Harvest 1 is negatively skewed, showing that there is a tail on the left of this distribution.
- This means the masses of the tomatoes were generally relatively high, but there were some much lighter tomatoes as well.
- Harvest 2 is very different — for this harvest, the distribution of the tomatoes' masses is positively skewed, showing that there is a tail on the right of this distribution.
- This means the masses of the tomatoes were generally relatively low, but there were some much heavier tomatoes as well.

Tip: This question is to do with harvests of tomatoes, so you need to mention these in your answer.

Exercise 3.6

Q1 The box plots below represent the prices of shoes (in £) from two different shops.

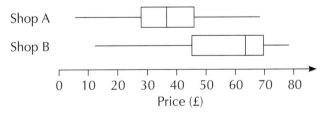

Use the box plots to compare:
a) the location of the two shops' prices
b) the dispersion of the two shops' prices
c) the skewness of the two shops' prices

Q2 This back-to-back stem and leaf diagram shows the daily sales of two competing small cafés over a 14-day period.

							Café A			Café B			
(0)								5	3 4 9				(3)
(1)							8	6	1 2				(2)
(6)		8 6 5 2 1					1	7	0 7				(2)
(7)	9 7 5 4 4 4						2	8	6 6 7				(3)
(0)								9	0 5				(2)
(0)								10	8				(1)
(0)								11	8				(1)

> Key: 8 | 6 | 1 represents £68 of sales in Café A
> and £61 of sales in Café B

a) (i) Calculate the mean sales and the median sales for both cafés.

   (ii) Use your answers to compare the locations of the two data sets.

b) (i) Calculate the standard deviation for both cafés' sales.

   (ii) Use your answers to compare the dispersion of the two data sets.

c) (i) Find the quartiles for both cafés.
Hence find the quartile coefficient of skewness of each data set.

   (ii) Use your answers to compare the skewness of the two data sets.

Q3 10 men and 10 women were asked how many hours of sleep they got on a typical night. The results are shown below.

Men: 6, 7, 9, 8, 8, 6, 7, 7, 10, 5

Women: 9, 9, 7, 8, 5, 11, 10, 8, 10, 8

a) (i) Calculate the mean and median of the individual data sets.

   (ii) Use your answers to compare the locations of the two data sets.

b) (i) Calculate the standard deviation of the individual data sets.

   (ii) Use your answers to compare the dispersion of the two data sets.

c) (i) Find Pearson's coefficient of skewness

for each data set, using $\dfrac{3(\text{mean} - \text{median})}{\text{standard deviation}}$.

   (ii) Use your answers to compare the skewness of the two data sets.

Review Exercise — Chapter 1

Q1 The stem and leaf diagram on the right represents the lengths (in cm) of 15 bananas. Write down the original data as a list.

12	8
13	2 5
14	3 3 6 8
15	2 9
16	1 1 2 3
17	0 2

Key 12|8 means 12.8 cm

Q2 Twenty phone calls were made by a householder one evening. The lengths of the calls (in minutes to the nearest minute) are recorded below. Draw a histogram of the data.

Length of calls	0 - 2	3 - 5	6 - 8	9 - 15
Number of calls	10	6	3	1

Q3 Calculate the mean, median and mode of the data in the table on the right.

x	0	1	2	3	4
f	5	4	4	2	1

Q4 The speeds of 60 cars travelling in a 40 mph speed limit area were measured to the nearest mph. The data is summarised in this table. Calculate estimates of the mean and median, and state the modal class.

Speed (mph)	30 - 34	35 - 39	40 - 44	45 - 50
Frequency	12	37	9	2

Q5 Find the mean and standard deviation of the following numbers: 11, 12, 14, 17, 21, 23, 27.

Q6 The scores in an IQ test for 50 people are recorded in the table below.

Score	100 - 106	107 - 113	114 - 120	121 - 127	128 - 134
Frequency	6	11	22	9	2

Estimate the mean and variance of the distribution.

Q7 For a set of data, $n = 100$, $\sum(x - 20) = 125$, and $\sum(x - 20)^2 = 221$. Find the mean and standard deviation of x.

Q8   The time taken (to the nearest minute) for a commuter to travel to work on 20 consecutive work days is recorded in the table.

Use the coding $y = x - 35.5$ to estimate the mean and standard deviation of the times, where x is the class mid-point.

Time to nearest minute	30 - 33	34 - 37	38 - 41	42 - 45
Frequency, f	3	6	7	4

Q9   A data value is considered an outlier if it's more than 1.5 times the IQR above the upper quartile or more than 1.5 times the IQR below the lower quartile. If the lower and upper quartiles of a data set are 62 and 88, decide which of the following data values are outliers:

a) 124   b) 131   c) 28

Q10 a) Find the median and quartiles of the data below.

Amount of pocket money (in £) received per week by twenty 15-year-olds:
10, 5, 20, 50, 5, 1, 6, 5, 15, 20, 5, 7, 5, 10, 12, 4, 8, 6, 7, 30.

b) Using the values $Q_1 - 1.5 \times IQR$ and $Q_3 + 1.5 \times IQR$ as fences, determine whether any of these values are outliers.

c) Draw a box plot to illustrate the data and use it to comment on any skewness.

Q11 A set of data has a median of 132, a lower quartile of 86 and an upper quartile of 150. Calculate the quartile coefficient of skewness, and draw a possible sketch of the distribution.

Q12 Two workers iron clothes. Each irons 10 items, and records the time it takes for each, to the nearest minute:

Worker A: 3 5 2 7 10 4 5 5 4 12
Worker B: 4 4 8 6 7 8 9 10 11 9

a) For worker A's times. Find:
(i)   the median
(ii)   the lower and upper quartiles
(iii) whether any of these values are outliers, using the values
      $Q_1 - 1.5 \times IQR$ and $Q_3 + 1.5 \times IQR$ as fences.

b) On graph paper draw, using the same scale, two box plots to represent the times of each worker.

c) Make one statement comparing the two sets of data.

d) Which worker would be better to employ? Give a reason for your answer.

Exam-Style Questions — Chapter 1

1   The profits of 100 businesses are given in the table.

Profit, £x million	Number of businesses
$4.0 \leqslant x < 5.0$	24
$5.0 \leqslant x < 5.5$	26
$5.5 \leqslant x < 6.0$	21
$6.0 \leqslant x < 6.5$	19
$6.5 \leqslant x < 8.0$	10

   a)   Represent the data in a histogram.

   (3 marks)

   b)   Comment on the distribution of the profits of the businesses.

   (2 marks)

2   A group of 19 people played a game. The scores, x, that the people achieved are summarised by:
$$\sum(x - 30) = 228 \text{ and } \sum(x - 30)^2 = 3040$$

   a)   Calculate the mean and the standard deviation of the 19 scores.

   (3 marks)

   b)   Show that $\sum x = 798$ and $\sum x^2 = 33\,820$.

   (3 marks)

   c)   Another student played the game. Her score was 32.
        Find the new mean and standard deviation of all 20 scores.

   (4 marks)

3   In a supermarket two types of chocolate drops were compared.
    The masses, a grams, of 20 chocolate drops of brand A are summarised by:
$$\sum a = 60.3 \qquad\qquad \sum a^2 = 219$$
    The mean mass of 30 chocolate drops of brand B was 2.95 g,
    and the standard deviation was 1 g.

   a)   Find the mean mass of a brand A chocolate drop.

   (1 mark)

   b)   Find the standard deviation of the masses of the brand A chocolate drops.

   (3 marks)

   c)   Compare brands A and B.

   (2 marks)

   d)   Find the standard deviation of the masses of all 50 chocolate drops.

   (4 marks)

4 The stem and leaf diagram shows the test marks for 30 male students and 16 female students.

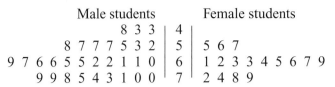

Male students   Female students
               8 3 3 | 4 |
       8 7 7 7 5 3 2 | 5 | 5 6 7
9 7 6 6 5 5 2 2 1 1 0 | 6 | 1 2 3 3 4 5 6 7 9
     9 9 8 5 4 3 1 0 0 | 7 | 2 4 8 9

Key 5|6|2 means Male student test mark 65
              and Female student test mark 62

a) Find the median test mark of the male students.

(1 mark)

b) Compare the distribution of the male and female marks.

(2 marks)

5 The table shows the number of hits received by people at a paint ball party.

No. of hits	12	13	14	15	16	17	18	19	20	21	22	23	24	25
Frequency	2	4	6	7	6	4	4	2	1	1	0	0	0	1

a) Find the median and mode number of hits.

(3 marks)

b) An outlier is a data value which is more than $1.5 \times (Q_3 - Q_1)$ above Q_3 or more than $1.5 \times (Q_3 - Q_1)$ below Q_1. Is 25 an outlier? Show your working.

(2 marks)

c) Sketch a box plot of the distribution and comment on any skewness.

(2 marks)

d) How would the shape of the distribution be affected if the value of 25 was removed?

(1 mark)

6 The histogram shows the nose-to-tail lengths of 50 lions in a game reserve.

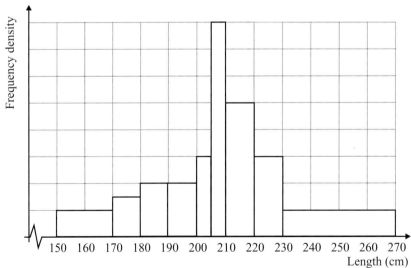

Use the histogram to find the number of lions who measured over 220 cm from nose to tail.

(5 marks)

1. Elementary Probability

Probability is a measure of how likely events are to happen. We're starting with a reminder of the basics, which you'll have seen before. But it's all important stuff as you'll be using it throughout the rest of the chapter.

The basics of probability

- In a **trial** (or experiment), the things that can happen are called **outcomes**. For example, if you roll a six-sided dice, the numbers 1-6 are the outcomes.

- **Events** are 'groups' of one or more outcomes. So a possible event for the dice roll is that 'you roll an odd number' (corresponding to the outcomes 1, 3 and 5). If any outcome corresponding to an event happens, then you can say that the event has also happened.

- When all the possible outcomes are **equally likely**, you can work out the **probability** of an event using this formula:

$$P(\text{event}) = \frac{\text{Number of outcomes where event happens}}{\text{Total number of possible outcomes}}$$

- Remember, the probability of any event has to be **between 0** (the event is impossible) **and 1** (the event is certain to happen).

Learning Objectives:

- Understand the meanings of the terms used in probability.
- Be able to calculate probabilities of events when all the outcomes are equally likely.
- Be able to identify sample spaces.

Tip: 'P(event)' is short for 'the probability of an event'.

Tip: Remember, you can write probabilities as fractions, decimals or percentages.

Examples

A bag contains 15 balls — 5 are red, 6 are blue and 4 are green. If one ball is selected from the bag at random, find the probability that:

a) the ball is red

- The **event** is 'a red ball is selected'.
- There are 5 red balls, so there are **5 outcomes** where the event happens and **15 possible outcomes** altogether.

- So: P(red ball) = $\frac{5}{15} = \frac{1}{3}$ ← It's usually best to simplify your answer as much as possible.

b) the ball is blue

- The **event** is 'a blue ball is selected'.
- There are 6 blue balls, so there are **6 outcomes** where the event happens and **15 possible outcomes** altogether.

- So: P(blue ball) = $\frac{6}{15} = \frac{2}{5}$

c) the ball is red or green

- The **event** is 'a red ball or a green ball is selected'.
- There are 5 red balls and 4 green balls, so there are **9 outcomes** where the event happens and **15 possible outcomes** altogether.

- So: P(red or green ball) = $\frac{9}{15} = \frac{3}{5}$

Tip: Always check that your probability is between 0 and 1.

The sample space

The **sample space** (called S) is the set of **all possible outcomes** of a trial. Drawing a **diagram** of the sample space can help you to count the outcomes you're interested in. Then it's an easy task to find probabilities using the formula on the previous page.

If a trial consists of two separate activities, then a good way to draw your sample space is as a grid.

Example 1

> **Tip:** Because the dice is being rolled twice, the outcomes here are a **combination** of the score on the first roll and the score on the second roll.

A six-sided dice is rolled twice.

a) Draw a sample-space diagram to show all the possible outcomes.

- Draw a pair of axes, with the outcomes for the first roll on one axis and the outcomes for the second roll on the other axis.

- Mark the intersection of each pair of numbers to show every possible outcome for the two rolls combined.

  e.g. 1 then 1

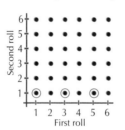

$6 \times 6 = 36$ outcomes altogether

> **Tip:** When there are two completely separate parts to an experiment, like the two dice rolls here, the total number of outcomes equals the number of outcomes for one part × the number of outcomes for the other part.

b) Find the probability of rolling an odd number, followed by a 1.

- Circle the outcomes corresponding to the event 'odd number, then 1'.

- All of the outcomes are equally likely. There are **3** outcomes where the event happens and **36** outcomes in total.

So, P(odd number, then 1) = $\frac{3}{36} = \frac{1}{12}$

Sometimes, the outcomes you're interested in aren't the numbers themselves, but are calculated from them...

Example 2

> **Tip:** A sample-space diagram can also be drawn as a table — with the outcomes for one activity along the top and the outcomes for the other activity down the left-hand side. E.g:
>
> | | | Bag A | | | |
> |---|---|---|---|---|---|
> | + | 1 | 3 | 3 | 4 | 5 |
> | 1 | 2 | 4 | 4 | 5 | 6 |
> | 2 | 3 | 5 | 5 | 6 | 7 |
> | 4 | 5 | 7 | 7 | 8 | 9 |
> | 4 | 5 | 7 | 7 | 8 | 9 |
> | 5 | 6 | 8 | 8 | 9 | 10 |
>
> (Bag B down the left-hand side)

Two bags each contain five cards. Bag A contains cards numbered 1, 3, 3, 4 and 5, and bag B contains cards numbered 1, 2, 4, 4 and 5. A card is selected at random from each bag and the numbers on the two cards are added together to give a total score.

Use a sample-space diagram to find the probability that the total score is no more than 6.

- Start by drawing a sample-space diagram showing all the possible **total scores**.

- This time you need to show the total score for each pair of numbers at each intersection.

  e.g. 1 + 2 = 3

- Circle all the scores of 6 or less.

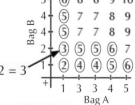

$5 \times 5 = 25$ outcomes altogether

- So now you can use the probability formula. There are **12** outcomes where the event 'total score is no more than 6' happens and **25** outcomes altogether.

So, P(total score is no more than 6) = $\frac{12}{25}$

Exercise 1.1

Q1   One card is selected at random from a standard pack of 52 playing cards. Find the probability of selecting each of the following:

    a)   the 7 of diamonds   b)   the queen of spades

    c)   a 9 of any suit   d)   a heart or a diamond

Q1 Hint: A pack of cards is split into 4 suits — hearts, diamonds, spades and clubs.

Q2   The following sample-space diagram represents a dice game where two dice are rolled and the product of the two scores is calculated:

×	1	2	3	4	5	6
1	1	2	3	4	5	6
2	2	4	6	8	10	12
3	3	6	9	12	15	18
4	4	8	12	16	20	24
5	5	10	15	20	25	30
6	6	12	18	24	30	36

    a)   Find the probability that the product is a prime number.

    b)   Find the probability that the product is less than 7.

    c)   Find the probability that the product is a multiple of 10.

Q3   A game involves picking a card at random from 10 cards, numbered 1 to 10, and tossing a coin.

    a)   Draw a sample-space diagram to show all the possible outcomes.

    b)   Find the probability that the card selected shows an even number and the coin shows 'tails'.

Q4   Martha rolls two fair six-sided dice and calculates a score by subtracting the smaller result from the larger.

    a)   Draw a sample-space diagram to show all the possible outcomes.

    b)   Find P(the score is zero).

    c)   Find P(the score is greater than 5).

    d)   What is the most likely score? And what is its probability?

Q5   Spinner 1 has five equal sections, labelled 2, 3, 5, 7 and 11, and spinner 2 has five equal sections, labelled 2, 4, 6, 8 and 10.

If each spinner is spun once, find the probability that the number on spinner 2 is greater than the number on spinner 1.

2. Venn Diagrams

Learning Objectives:

- Be able to draw Venn diagrams for two or three events.
- Use the correct notation to describe the different areas of a Venn diagram.
- Use Venn diagrams to find probabilities.
- Understand and use complementary events.

Venn diagrams are a really useful tool for solving probability problems. Here you'll see how to draw them to represent two or three events, and how to use them to find probabilities.

Using Venn diagrams

A **Venn diagram** shows how a collection of **objects** is split up into different **groups**, where everything in a group has something in common.

- Here, for example, the objects are **outcomes** and the groups are **events**. So the collection of objects, represented by the **rectangle**, is the **sample space** (**S**). Inside the rectangle are two **circles** representing **two events**, **A** and **B**.

- The **circle A** represents all the outcomes corresponding to event A, and the **circle B** represents all the outcomes corresponding to event B.

- The diagram is usually labelled with the **number of outcomes** (or the **probabilities**) represented by each area.

- Since **S** is the set of **all possible outcomes**, the **total probability** in S equals **1**.

So that's the basic idea of Venn diagrams. To describe the different areas of the diagram, you can use **set notation**.

Tip: If events don't have any outcomes in common, then the circles won't overlap. These events are called **mutually exclusive** — and they're covered in detail on pages 63-64.

- The area where the circles overlap represents all the outcomes corresponding to **both event A and event B** happening.
- This area is called the **intersection** of A and B — written **A ∩ B**.

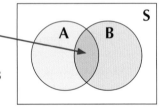

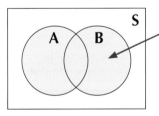

- The shaded area represents all the outcomes corresponding to **either event A or event B or both** happening.
- This area is called the **union** of A and B — written **A ∪ B**.

Tip: This is because if there are *n* outcomes altogether in S, and *p* of these are in event A, then *n* − *p* must be in A'.
$P(A) = \frac{p}{n}$, $P(A') = \frac{n-p}{n}$, which means that $P(A) + P(A') = 1$.

- The shaded area represents all the outcomes corresponding to **event A not** happening.
- These outcomes make up an event called the **complement of A** — written **A'** (and sometimes read as '**not A**').
- Since an event A must either happen or not happen, and since P(S) = 1:

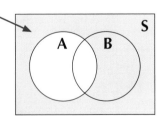

$$P(A) + P(A') = 1 \quad \Rightarrow \quad P(A') = 1 - P(A)$$

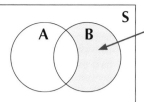

The shaded area represents all the outcomes corresponding to **event B** happening **and event A not** happening. This area is written **A′ ∩ B**.

The shaded area represents all the outcomes corresponding to **event A not** happening **and event B not** happening. This area is written **A′ ∩ B′**.

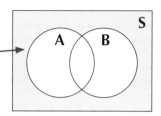

Here's an example where the **objects** are **people**, and they're divided into groups based on whether they have **certain characteristics** in common.

Example 1

There are 30 pupils in a class. 14 of the pupils are girls and 11 of the pupils have brown hair. Of the pupils with brown hair, 6 are boys.

a) Show this information on a Venn diagram.

- OK, so first you need to identify the **groups**. Let **G** be the group of **girls** and **BH** be the group of **pupils** with **brown hair**.

- **Draw** a Venn diagram to represent the groups G and BH.

- Now you need to **label** it with the numbers of **pupils** in each part of the diagram.

- You're told that there are 6 boys with brown hair, which means there are **6 pupils** who **have brown hair and aren't girls**.
  So label the area **BH ∩ G′** with 6 pupils.

- There are 11 pupils in total with brown hair, so there are **11 − 6 = 5 girls with brown hair**.
  So label the area **G ∩ BH** with **5** pupils.

- Now, there are 14 girls in total, so the number who **don't have brown hair** = 14 − 5 = 9. So label the area **G ∩ BH′** with 9 pupils.

- Finally, don't forget the pupils that **aren't in G or BH**. There are 30 pupils altogether, so the number of **boys** who **don't have brown hair** = 30 − (9 + 5 + 6) = **10**. So label the area **G′ ∩ BH′** with 10 pupils.

> **Tip:** Each of the groups needs to be based on a characteristic that a person either has or doesn't have. Then if a person **has** that characteristic, they're included **inside** the circle. If they don't have the characteristic, they're outside the circle. E.g. all the girls are included in circle G, and all the boys ('not girls') are outside G.

> **Tip:** Remember, '∩' means 'and', so the area G ∩ BH is the area 'girls **and** brown hair'.

b) A pupil is selected at random from the class. Find the probability that the pupil is a girl who doesn't have brown hair.

Using the Venn diagram, there are **9** girls who don't have brown hair, out of the **30** pupils in the class.

So, P(girl who doesn't have brown hair) = $\frac{9}{30} = \frac{3}{10}$

> **Tip:** All the outcomes are equally likely, so you can use the probability formula on page 53.

c) A girl is selected at random from the class. Find the probability that she has brown hair.

Using the Venn diagram, there are **5** girls who have brown hair, out of the **14** girls in the class.

So, P(the girl selected has brown hair) = $\frac{5}{14}$

> You already know that the pupil is a girl, so you're only looking at the outcomes in circle G, not the whole class.

Example 2

The Venn diagram below represents two events, A and B. The numbers show how many outcomes correspond to each of the two events.

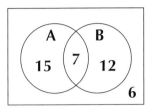

Use the diagram to find the following probabilities:

a) P(A ∩ B)

- This is the probability of event **A and** event **B both** happening.

> **Tip:** Remember... A ∩ B includes all the outcomes in **both A and B**.

- Use the Venn diagram to **find** the number of outcomes in A ∩ B and the number of outcomes in total.

    There are **7** outcomes in **A ∩ B**,
    and 15 + 7 + 12 + 6 = **40** outcomes in **total**. ◄——— Just add all the numbers.

- So using the formula, P(A ∩ B) = $\frac{7}{40}$

b) P(B)

- Use the Venn diagram to **work out** the number of outcomes in B.

    There are 7 + 12 = **19** outcomes in **B**, and **40** outcomes in **total**.

- So using the formula, P(B) = $\frac{19}{40}$

c) P(A′)

> **Tip:** Remember... A′ includes all the outcomes that are **not** in **A**.

- Use the Venn diagram to **work out** the number of outcomes in A′.

    There are 12 + 6 = **18** outcomes in **A′**, and **40** outcomes in **total**.

- So using the formula, P(A′) = $\frac{18}{40} = \frac{9}{20}$

d) P(A ∪ B′)

- P(A ∪ B′) is the probability of **either** event **A** happening **or** event **B not** happening or **both** of the above.

> **Tip:** A ∪ B′ includes all the outcomes that are **either** in A, **or** not in B, **or** both of the above (i.e. in A but not in B).

- Use the Venn diagram to **work out** the number of outcomes in A ∪ B′. There are 15 + 7 = 22 outcomes in A, plus another 6 outcomes that aren't in B. So that's 22 + 6 = **28** outcomes in **A ∪ B′**, and **40** outcomes in **total**.

- So using the formula, P(A ∪ B′) = $\frac{28}{40} = \frac{7}{10}$

You also need to be able to draw and use Venn diagrams for **three overlapping groups** (or events). There's an example on the next page. Instead of showing the 'number of objects' (or outcomes), the numbers show **proportions**, but the ideas are exactly the same.

A survey was carried out to find out what pets people like.

The proportion who like dogs is 0.6, the proportion who like cats is 0.5, and the proportion who like gerbils is 0.4. The proportion who like dogs and cats is 0.4, the proportion who like cats and gerbils is 0.1, and the proportion who like gerbils and dogs is 0.2. Finally, the proportion who like all three kinds of animal is 0.1.

a) Draw a Venn diagram to represent this information.

- First, identify the **groups**. Let **C** be the group 'likes **cats**', **D** be the group 'likes **dogs**' and **G** be the group 'likes **gerbils**'.
- **Draw** a Venn diagram to represent the groups C, D and G.

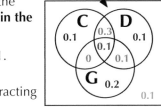

- Now you need to **label** it — this time with the **proportions** for each area. It's best to **start in the middle** and work outwards...

  The proportion who like all 3 animals is 0.1. So label the area $C \cap D \cap G$ with **0.1**.

- Next do the 'likes 2 animals' areas, by subtracting 0.1 from each of the given proportions.
  So $C \cap D \cap G' = 0.3$, $C \cap G \cap D' = 0$, and $D \cap G \cap C' = 0.1$.

- Then complete each circle by making sure that the proportions add up to the proportion given in the question for each animal.
  $C \cap D' \cap G' = 0.5 - (0.3 + 0.1 + 0) = \mathbf{0.1}$,
  $D \cap C' \cap G' = 0.6 - (0.3 + 0.1 + 0.1) = \mathbf{0.1}$, and
  $G \cap C' \cap D' = 0.4 - (0.1 + 0.1 + 0) = \mathbf{0.2}$.

- Finally, subtract all the proportions from 1 to find the proportion who like none of these animals: $C' \cap D' \cap G' = 1 - 0.9 = \mathbf{0.1}$.

Tip: Label the diagram with proportions this time, because that's the information you're given in the question.

Tip: If they like 3 animals, they'll also be in the 'likes 2 animals' bits. So subtracting this proportion gives us the proportions of liking **just 2** of the animals.

One person who completed the survey is chosen at random.

b) Find the probability that this person likes dogs or cats (or both).

This is represented by the shaded area. The **probability** of the person being in this area is **equal** to the **proportion** of people in the area. So you just need to add up the numbers.

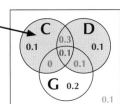

So, P(likes dogs, cats or both)
= 0.1 + 0.3 + 0 + 0.1 + 0.1 + 0.1 = 0.7

Tip: When you select a person at random, the above proportions equal the probabilities of that person being in each area of the diagram.

Tip: You could also do this by subtracting the probabilities outside circles C and D from 1.

c) Find the probability that this person likes gerbils, but not dogs.

This is represented by the shaded area. So add up all the probabilities in this area.

So, P(likes gerbils, but not dogs)

= 0 + 0.2 = 0.2

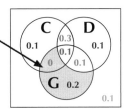

d) Find the probability that a dog-lover also likes cats.

Tip: You can also think of this as 'the probability that the person likes cats, **given** that they like dogs'. This is an example of a **conditional** probability. Conditional probabilities are covered in detail on pages 65-67.

- This is the proportion of dog-lovers who also like cats.
- D ∩ C is represented by the shaded area, which forms a proportion of 0.3 + 0.1 = **0.4** of the whole group of people.
- But we're only interested in the '**likes dogs**' circle, not the whole group, so that means we need to **divide** by **0.6**.
- So, P(dog-lover also likes cats) = $\dfrac{0.4}{0.6} = \dfrac{4}{6} = \dfrac{2}{3}$

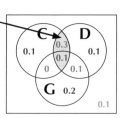

Exercise 2.1

Q1 Hint: You're given the information as probabilities, rather than numbers of outcomes corresponding to each event. So label your diagram with probabilities.

Q1 For events A and B, P(A) = 0.4, P(B) = 0.5 and P(A ∩ B) = 0.15.
    a) Draw a Venn diagram to represent events A and B.
    b) What is P(A' ∩ B')?

Q2 A sixth form college has 144 students — 46 of the students study maths, 38 study physics and 19 study both.
    a) Represent the information given above using a Venn diagram.
    b) Find the probability that a randomly selected student from the college studies at least one of either maths or physics.
    c) Given that a student studies maths, what is the probability that they also study physics?

Q3 Hint: If two circles don't overlap, it means the events can't both happen.

Q3 Use the Venn diagram to find the following probabilities:
    a) P(L ∩ M)   b) P(L ∩ N)
    c) P(L' ∩ N)   d) P(L' ∩ M' ∩ N')
    e) P(L ∪ M)   f) P(M')

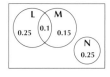

Q4 Two hundred people were asked which of the countries Spain, France and Germany they have visited. The results are shown in the diagram.

Find the probability that a randomly selected person has been to:
    a) none of the three countries
    b) Germany, given that they have been to France
    c) Spain, but not France

Q5 Hint: It doesn't tell you to draw a Venn diagram, but that's the easiest way to answer the question.

Q5 1000 football supporters were asked if they go to home league matches, away league matches, or cup matches. 560 go to home matches, 420 go to away matches, and 120 go to cup matches. 240 go to home and away matches, 80 go to home and cup matches, and 60 go to away and cup matches. 40 go to all 3 types of match.
Find the probability that a randomly selected supporter goes to:
    a) exactly two types of match   b) at least one type of match

3. Laws of Probability

There are two main probability laws you need to know — the addition law and the product law (or multiplication law). You'll see how to use these laws to find probabilities, and how you can adapt them in different circumstances.

The addition law

For **two events**, A and B, there's a **nice formula** linking the **union** of A and B and the **intersection** of A and B — the **addition law**:

$$P(A \cup B) = P(A) + P(B) - P(A \cap B)$$

You can see why this is true, using Venn diagrams.

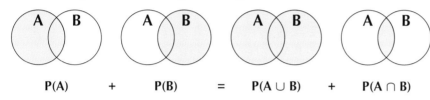

P(A)　　+　　P(B)　　=　　P(A ∪ B)　　+　　P(A ∩ B)

So to get P(A ∪ B) on its own, you need to subtract P(A ∩ B) from P(A) + P(B).

The addition law is **really useful** for finding missing probabilities — as long as you know three of the values in the formula, you can **rearrange** the formula to find the remaining probability.

Example 1

For two events A and B, P(A ∪ B) = 0.75, P(A) = 0.45 and P(B′) = 0.4.

a) Find P(A ∩ B).

- To use the formula, you need to know P(A), P(B) and P(A ∪ B). You're missing P(B), so start by finding that.
  P(B) = 1 − P(B′) = 1 − 0.4 = 0.6.
- Now rearrange the addition law formula to make P(A ∩ B) the subject.
  P(A ∪ B) = P(A) + P(B) − P(A ∩ B) ⇒ P(A ∩ B) = P(A) + P(B) − P(A ∪ B)
- And substituting in the probabilities gives:
  P(A ∩ B) = 0.45 + 0.6 − 0.75 = $\boxed{0.3}$

b) Find P(A′ ∩ B′).

- A′ ∩ B′ is the **complement** of A ∪ B.
- So P(A′ ∩ B′) = 1 − P(A ∪ B) = 1 − 0.75 = $\boxed{0.25}$

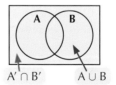

c) Find P(A ∩ B′).

- Event A is made up of areas A ∩ B and A ∩ B′ — see Tip on the right.
- So P(A ∩ B′) = P(A) − P(A ∩ B) = 0.45 − 0.3 = $\boxed{0.15}$

d) Find P(A′ ∪ B).

- It's easiest to do this by drawing a Venn diagram.
- Use the probabilities you've worked out above.
- So P(A′ ∪ B) = 0.3 + 0.25 + 0.3 = $\boxed{0.85}$

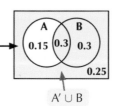

A′ ∪ B

Learning Objectives:

- Be able to use the addition law to find probabilities.
- Be able to recognise mutually exclusive events.
- Be able to use the product law to find probabilities.
- Be able to recognise independent events.
- Be able to understand and use tree diagrams.

Tip: If you didn't subtract P(A ∩ B) from P(A) + P(B), you'd be counting it twice — once from A and once from B.

Tip: You might also see the addition law called the 'sum law'. It'll be on the exam formula sheet, but you should learn it anyway.

Tip: Watch out for when you can use the formula P(A) = 1 − P(A′).

Tip: A = A ∩ B′ + A ∩ B

Example 2

On any given day, the probability that Jason eats an apple is 0.6, the probability that he eats a banana is 0.3, and the probability that he eats both an apple and a banana is 0.2.

a) Find the probability that he eats an apple or a banana (or both).

- Let **A** be the event 'eats an apple' and **B** be the event 'eats a banana'.
- You want to find **P(A ∪ B)**, so use the addition law:
  P(A ∪ B) = P(A) + P(B) − P(A ∩ B) = 0.6 + 0.3 − 0.2 = 0.7
- So P(he eats an apple or a banana, or both) = $\boxed{0.7}$

b) Find the probability that he either doesn't eat an apple, or doesn't eat a banana.

- You want to find **P(A' ∪ B')**. You can either do this using a Venn diagram, or you can use the addition law by replacing A with A' and B with B'. Like this:
- P(A' ∪ B') = P(A') + P(B') − P(A' ∩ B')
            = [1 − P(A)] + [1 − P(B)] − [1 − P(A ∪ B)]
            = (1 − 0.6) + (1 − 0.3) − (1 − 0.7) = 0.4 + 0.7 − 0.3 = 0.8
- So P(he either doesn't eat an apple, or doesn't eat a banana) = $\boxed{0.8}$

Tip: A' ∪ B' is also the complement of A ∩ B, so you could work out:

P(A' ∪ B') = 1 − P(A ∩ B)
           = 1 − 0.2
           = 0.8

Exercise 3.1

Hint: Remember, you can always draw a Venn diagram to help you.

Q1 If P(A) = 0.3, P(B) = 0.5 and P(A ∩ B) = 0.15, find:
   a) P(A')   b) P(A ∪ B)   c) P(A' ∩ B')

Q2 If P(A') = 0.36, P(B) = 0.44 and P(A ∩ B) = 0.27, find:
   a) P(B')   b) P(A ∪ B)   c) P(A ∩ B')   d) P(A ∪ B')

Q2 d) Hint: You have all the information you need to use the addition law, replacing B with B'.

Q3 A car is selected at random from a car park. The probability of the car being blue is 0.25 and the probability of it being an estate is 0.15. The probability of the car being a blue estate is 0.08.
   a) What is the probability of the car not being blue?
   b) What is the probability of the car being blue or being an estate?
   c) What is the probability of the car being neither blue nor an estate?

Q4 If P(X ∪ Y) = 0.77, P(X) = 0.43 and P(Y) = 0.56, find:
   a) P(Y')   b) P(X ∩ Y)   c) P(X' ∩ Y')   d) P(X' ∪ Y')

Q5 If P(C' ∪ D) = 0.65, P(C) = 0.53 and P(D) = 0.44, find:
   a) P(C' ∩ D)   b) P(C' ∩ D')   c) P(C' ∪ D')   d) P(C ∩ D)

Q6 The probability that a student has read 'To Kill a Mockingbird' is 0.62. The probability that a student hasn't read 'Animal Farm' is 0.66. The probability that a student has read at least one of these two books is 0.79. Find:
   a) The probability that a student has read both the books.
   b) The probability that a student has read 'Animal Farm' but hasn't read 'To Kill a Mockingbird'.
   c) The probability that a student has read neither of the books.

Mutually exclusive events

Events can happen at the same time when they have one or more outcomes in common. For example, the events 'I roll a 3' and 'I roll an odd number', both happen if the outcome of my dice roll is a '3'. Events which have **no outcomes** in **common**, **can't happen** at the same time. These events are called **mutually exclusive** (or just 'exclusive').

- If A and B are mutually exclusive events, then **P(A ∩ B) = 0**.
- And since the **intersection** is **zero**, a Venn diagram would show the events as non-overlapping circles.

We defined the addition law on page 61 as $P(A \cup B) = P(A) + P(B) - P(A \cap B)$. When A and B are mutually exclusive, we can substitute $P(A \cap B) = 0$, to give a slightly simpler version.

For two events, A and B, where A and B are **mutually exclusive**:

$$\boxed{\mathbf{P(A \cup B) = P(A) + P(B)}}$$

And you can write a general form of this for *n* exclusive events.
For exclusive events $A_1, A_2, ..., A_n$:

$$\mathbf{P(A_1 \cup A_2 \cup ... \cup A_n) = P(A_1) + P(A_2) + ... + P(A_n)}$$

Tip: A Venn diagram for mutually exclusive events A and B might look like this.

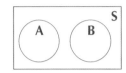

Tip: With *n* exclusive events, $A_1, ..., A_n$, none of the events can happen at the same time as **any** of the others.

In other words, **only one** out of $A_1, ..., A_n$ can happen at a time.

Example

A card is selected at random from a standard pack of 52 cards. Find the probability that the card is either a picture card (a Jack, Queen or King), or the 7, 8 or 9 of clubs.

- Start by defining the two events. Let A be the event 'select a picture card' and B be the event 'select the 7, 8 or 9 of clubs'.
- You want to find the probability of A or B, $P(A \cup B)$. The card **can't** be both a picture card **and** the 7, 8, or 9 of clubs, so A and B are mutually exclusive, which means that $P(A \cup B) = P(A) + P(B)$.
- Using the formula for equally likely outcomes:

$$P(A) = \frac{12}{52} \quad \text{and} \quad P(B) = \frac{3}{52}$$

12 outcomes where event happens out of a total of 52

3 outcomes where event happens out of a total of 52

- So the probability of A or B is $P(A \cup B) = P(A) + P(B)$

$$= \frac{12}{52} + \frac{3}{52} = \frac{15}{52}$$

- This means P(card is either a picture card or the 7, 8 or 9 of clubs) $= \frac{15}{52}$

To show whether or not events A and B are mutually exclusive, you just need to show whether the intersection of A and B is zero or non-zero — i.e. whether $P(A \cap B) = 0$ or $P(A \cap B) \neq 0$.

Tip: You could also show that
$P(A \cup B) \neq P(A) + P(B)$ — that's the same as showing that
$P(A \cap B) \neq 0$.

Tip: Drawing a Venn diagram can be helpful to see areas.

Examples

a) **For two events, A and B, P(A) = 0.38, P(B) = 0.24 and P(A ∪ B) = 0.6.**
   Show whether events A and B are mutually exclusive.

- The easiest way to do this is to use the addition law to find $P(A \cap B)$.
  $P(A \cup B) = P(A) + P(B) - P(A \cap B)$
  $\Rightarrow P(A \cap B) = P(A) + P(B) - P(A \cup B) = 0.38 + 0.24 - 0.6 = 0.02$
- So, $P(A \cap B) \neq 0$, which means that A and B are **not mutually exclusive**.

b) **For two events, A and B, P(A) = 0.75 and P(A ∩ B′) = 0.75.**
   Show whether events A and B are mutually exclusive.

- This one looks a bit trickier, but you just need to think about the different areas that make up event A.
  $P(A) = P(A \cap B) + P(A \cap B')$
  $\Rightarrow P(A \cap B) = P(A) - P(A \cap B') = 0.75 - 0.75 = 0$
- So, $P(A \cap B) = 0$, which means that A and B **are mutually exclusive**.

Exercise 3.2

Q1 If X and Y are mutually exclusive events,
   with P(X) = 0.48 and P(Y) = 0.37, find:
   a) $P(X \cap Y)$ b) $P(X \cup Y)$ c) $P(X' \cap Y')$

Q2 P(L) = 0.28, P(M) = 0.42 and P(N) = 0.33. If the pairs
   of events (L and M) and (L and N) are mutually exclusive,
   and P(M ∩ N) = 0.16, find:
   a) $P(L \cup M)$ b) $P(L \cup N)$ c) $P(M \cup N)$ d) $P(L \cap M \cap N)$
   e) Draw and label a Venn diagram to show events L, M and N.

Q3 Dave is planning his evening. The probabilities that he will go
   bowling, to the cinema and out for dinner are 0.17, 0.43 and 0.22
   respectively. Given that he only has time to do one activity, find:
   a) The probability that he either goes bowling or to the cinema.
   b) The probability that he doesn't do any of the 3 activities.

Q4 For events A, B and C, P(A) = 0.28, P(B) = 0.66, P(C) = 0.49,
   P(A ∪ B) = 0.86, P(A ∪ C) = 0.77 and P(B ∪ C) = 0.92.

   Find each of the probabilities below and say whether each pair of
   events is mutually exclusive.
   a) $P(A \cap B)$ b) $P(A \cap C)$ c) $P(B \cap C)$

Q5 For events C and D, P(C′) = 0.6, P(D) = 0.25 and P(C ∩ D′) = 0.4.
   a) Show that C and D are mutually exclusive.   b) Find P(C ∪ D)

Q6 A box contains 50 biscuits. Of the biscuits, 20 are chocolate-coated
   and the rest are plain. Half of all the biscuits are in wrappers.
   One biscuit is selected at random from the box.

   If P is the event 'the biscuit is plain', and W is the event 'the biscuit is
   in a wrapper', show that the events P and W are not exclusive.

The product law — conditional probability

A probability is conditional if it **depends** on what has already happened.

The probability that an event B happens, **given** that an event A has already happened, is called the conditional probability of 'B given A', written **P(B | A)**.

You can work out the probability of **B given A**, using this formula:

$$P(B \mid A) = \frac{P(A \cap B)}{P(A)}$$

Here's an explanation of where this formula comes from...

Tip: Events A and B might be occurring at the **same time** — i.e. P(B|A) is the probability of B occurring, given that A occurs.

Tip: The probability of A given B is:

$$P(A \mid B) = \frac{P(A \cap B)}{P(B)}$$

Event A has happened and for B|A to happen, B will also happen.

- If you know that A has already happened, then the only remaining possible outcomes must be the ones corresponding to A.

- And the only remaining possible outcomes corresponding to B also happening must be the ones in A ∩ B.

- Using the **probability formula** (and assuming event **A** has **already happened**):

$$P(B \mid A) = \frac{\text{number of possible outcomes corresponding to B}}{\text{total number of possible outcomes}}$$

$$= \frac{\text{number of outcomes in } A \cap B}{\text{number of outcomes in A}}$$

- So if $n(A \cap B)$ = number of outcomes in A ∩ B, and $n(A)$ = number of outcomes in A:

$$P(B \mid A) = \frac{n(A \cap B)}{n(A)}$$

- Now, if we divide the top and bottom of the fraction by $n(S)$ (the total number of outcomes in S), its value doesn't change, but we can write it in a different way:

$$\mathbf{P(B \mid A)} = \frac{n(A \cap B)}{n(A)} = \frac{n(A \cap B) \big/ n(S)}{n(A) \big/ n(S)} = \frac{\mathbf{P(A \cap B)}}{\mathbf{P(A)}} \quad \leftarrow \text{the formula in the box above}$$

And if we rearrange this formula for conditional probabilities, we get our second important probability law, called the **product law**. For events A and B:

$$\boxed{\mathbf{P(A \cap B) = P(A)P(B \mid A)}}$$

- So this law says that to find the probability that A **and** B **both** happen, you multiply the probability of A by the probability of B given that A has happened.

- Or you can write this the other way around, by swapping A and B:

  P(A ∩ B) = P(B)P(A | B).

Tip: The product law is given in this form on your exam formula sheet. But you can easily rearrange it into the form given above to find conditional probabilities.

Example 1

For events A and B: $P(A) = 0.6$, $P(B) = 0.5$, $P(A \cap B) = 0.3$, $P(B' \,|\, A) = 0.5$.

a) **Find $P(A \,|\, B)$.**

Using the formula for conditional probability:

$$P(A \,|\, B) = \frac{P(A \cap B)}{P(B)} = \frac{0.3}{0.5} = \boxed{0.6}$$

b) **Find $P(A \cap B')$.**

Tip: Just replace B with B′ in the product law.

Using the product law: $P(A \cap B') = P(A)P(B' \,|\, A)$
$$= 0.6 \times 0.5$$
$$= \boxed{0.3}$$

Example 2

The Venn diagram below represents two events, C and D. The numbers of equally likely outcomes corresponding to the events are shown.

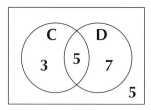

a) **Find $P(C \,|\, D)$.**

- Here you're given the numbers of outcomes, so you can find the probability by using the original probability formula from page 53.

- Once event **D has happened**, there are **5** possible outcomes corresponding to event **C** happening ⟵ 5 outcomes in C ∩ D and **12** possible remaining outcomes in **total**.

Tip: Doing it this way is a bit simpler than using the conditional probability formula. But if you did use the formula, you'd work out:

$P(C \cap D) = \frac{5}{20}$ and $P(D) = \frac{12}{20}$

And so, $P(C \,|\, D) =$

$\frac{P(C \cap D)}{P(D)} = \frac{\frac{5}{20}}{\frac{12}{20}} = \frac{5}{12}$

- So, $P(C \,|\, D) = \dfrac{\text{number of outcomes corresponding to C}}{\text{total number of possible outcomes}} = \boxed{\dfrac{5}{12}}$

b) **Find $P(D \,|\, C')$.**

- Once event **C hasn't happened**, there are **7** possible outcomes corresponding to event **D** happening ⟵ 7 outcomes in D ∩ C′ and **12** possible remaining outcomes in **total**.

- So, $P(D \,|\, C') = \dfrac{\text{number of outcomes corresponding to D}}{\text{total number of possible outcomes}} = \boxed{\dfrac{7}{12}}$

Example 3

Vikram either walks or runs to the bus stop. The probability that he walks is 0.4. The probability that he catches the bus is 0.54. If he walks to the bus stop, the probability that he catches the bus is 0.3.

a) **Draw a Venn diagram representing the events W, 'Vikram walks to the bus stop', and C, 'Vikram catches the bus'.**

- Okay, this one looks a bit scary, but it'll make more sense when you write down the probabilities you know:

    $P(W) = 0.4$, $P(C) = 0.54$ and $P(C|W) = 0.3$

- To draw the Venn diagram, you need to find the intersection $C \cap W$. And you can do that using the **product law**:

    $P(C \cap W) = P(C|W)P(W) = 0.3 \times 0.4 = 0.12$

- Now you can draw the Venn diagram:

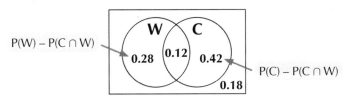

> **Tip:** The probability that Vikram catches the bus, given that he walks to the bus stop, is 0.3.

b) **Find the probability that Vikram catches the bus, given that he runs to the bus stop.**

- This is the probability, $P(C|W')$.

- Using the formula for conditional probability: $P(C|W') = \dfrac{P(C \cap W')}{P(W')}$

- $P(C \cap W') = 0.42$ and $P(W') = 1 - 0.4 = 0.6$

- So, $P(C|W') = \dfrac{P(C \cap W')}{P(W')} = \dfrac{0.42}{0.6} = 0.7$

- So P(Vikram catches the bus, given that he runs to the bus stop) = $\boxed{0.7}$

> **Tip:** He either walks or runs to the bus stop, so P(runs) = P(W').

Exercise 3.3

Q1   If $P(G) = 0.7$, $P(H) = 0.63$ and $P(G \cap H) = 0.24$, find:
   a) $P(G|H)$ b) $P(H|G)$

Q2 $P(A) = 0.68$, $P(B') = 0.44$, $P(C) = 0.44$, $P(A \cap B) = 0.34$,
   $P(A \cap C) = 0.16$ and $P(B \cap C') = 0.49$. Find:
   a) $P(B|A)$ b) $P(A|C)$ c) $P(C'|B)$

Q3   In a group of eleven footballers, five are over 6 feet tall.
   Two of the three players who can play in goal are over 6 feet tall.
   One of the players is selected at random.
   a) If the player is over 6 feet tall, what is the probability that they can play in goal?
   b) If the player can play in goal, what is the probability that they are over 6 feet tall?

Q4 The Venn diagram below shows the numbers of students studying Maths, English and Art, from a group of 100 students. One of the students is selected at random.

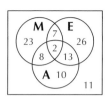

a) If the student is studying Art, what is the probability that they are also studying Maths?

b) If the student is studying English and Maths, what is the probability that they are also studying Art?

c) If the student is not studying Maths, what is the probability that they are studying English?

d) Find $P(A \mid E')$.

e) Find $P(M \mid A \cap E)$.

Q5 Given that $P(X) = 0.44$, $P(Y') = 0.72$, $P(Z) = 0.61$, $P(X \mid Y) = 0.75$, $P(Z \mid X) = 0.25$, $P(Y \cap Z') = 0.2$ and $P(X \cap Y \mid Z) = \frac{7}{61}$, find:

a) $P(Y)$ b) $P(X \cap Y)$ c) $P(X \cap Z)$

d) $P(Y \mid Z')$ e) $P(X \cap Y \cap Z)$

Independent events

If the probability of an event B happening **doesn't depend** on whether an event A has happened or not, events A and B are **independent**.

- For example, if a dice is rolled twice, the events A = 'first roll is a 4' and B = 'second roll is a 4', are independent, because the number rolled on the second roll doesn't depend on the number rolled on the first roll.

- Or, suppose a card is selected at random from a pack of cards, then replaced, then a second card is selected at random. The events A = 'first card is a 7' and B = 'second card is a 7', are independent because P(B) is unaffected by what was selected on the first pick.

Tip: If the first card **isn't** replaced, then A and B are not independent (B is conditional on A).
If A happens, $P(B) = \frac{3}{51}$, but if A doesn't happen, $P(B) = \frac{4}{51}$.

If A and B are **independent**, then P(B) is the same, whether A happens or not. And that means you have the following results:

- $P(B \mid A) = P(B \mid A') = P(B)$. Similarly, $P(A \mid B) = P(A \mid B') = P(A)$.

- The **conditional probability** formula becomes: $P(B \mid A) = P(B) = \dfrac{P(A \cap B)}{P(A)}$

- The **product law** becomes: $P(A \cap B) = P(A)P(B \mid A) = P(A)P(B)$

So, for two events, A and B, where A and B are **independent**:

$$\boxed{P(A \cap B) = P(A)P(B)}$$

Example

V and W are independent events, where P(V) = 0.2 and P(W) = 0.6.

a) Find P(V ∩ W).

Just put these probabilities into the **product law** for independent events:

P(V ∩ W) = P(V)P(W) = 0.2 × 0.6 = 0.12

b) Find P(V ∪ W).

You know the probability of each event and the probability of the intersection, so you can use the **addition law** to find the union:

P(V ∪ W) = P(V) + P(W) − P(V ∩ W) = 0.2 + 0.6 − 0.12 = 0.68

To show that events A and B are independent, you just need to show that **one** of the following statements is true:

- P(B | A) = P(B) [or P(A | B) = P(A)]
- P(A) × P(B) = P(A ∩ B)

Tip: If one of these is true, then the other one will also be true.

Example 1

A scientist is investigating the likelihood that a person will catch two infectious diseases, after being exposed to one and then the other. The probability of catching the first disease is 0.25, the probability of catching the second disease is 0.5, and the probability of catching both diseases is 0.2.

Show that the events 'catch first disease' and 'catch second disease' are not independent.

- Let A = 'catch first disease' and B = 'catch second disease'.
- There are several different ways to show the result, but it's probably easiest to compare P(A) × P(B) with P(A ∩ B).
- P(A) = 0.25, P(B) = 0.5 and P(A ∩ B) = 0.2
  P(A) × P(B) = 0.25 × 0.5 = 0.125 ≠ 0.2

  So, since P(A) × P(B) ≠ P(A ∩ B), the events 'catch first disease' and 'catch second disease' are not independent.

Tip: You could also show that:

$P(B|A) =$

$\dfrac{P(A \cap B)}{P(A)} = \dfrac{0.2}{0.25} = 0.8$

$\neq P(B) = 0.5,$

or $P(A|B) =$

$\dfrac{P(A \cap B)}{P(B)} = \dfrac{0.2}{0.5} = 0.4$

$\neq P(A) = 0.25.$

Example 2

For events A and B, P(A) = 0.4, P(B | A) = 0.25 and P(A' ∩ B) = 0.2.

a) Find: (i) P(A ∩ B),   (ii) P(A'),   (iii) P(B' | A),
**   (iv) (B | A'),   (v) P(B),   (vi) P(A | B).**

(i) Using the **product law**: **P(A ∩ B)** = P(A)P(B | A) = 0.4 × 0.25 = 0.1

(ii) **P(A')** = 1 − P(A) = 1 − 0.4 = 0.6

Now at this stage, things are starting to get a bit trickier. It'll help a lot if you draw a **Venn diagram** showing what you know so far.

- You know from the question that:
  P(A) = 0.4, P(B | A) = 0.25 and P(A′ ∩ B) = 0.2
- And you've found:
  P(A ∩ B) = 0.1 and P(A′) = 0.6   P(A) – P(A ∩ B) →

(iii) Using the **conditional probability** formula:

$$P(B' \mid A) = \frac{P(B' \cap A)}{P(A)}$$

You can see from the Venn diagram that P(B′ ∩ A) = 0.3, so:

$$\mathbf{P(B' \mid A)} = \frac{P(B' \cap A)}{P(A)} = \frac{0.3}{0.4} = \boxed{0.75}$$

(iv) Using the **conditional probability** formula:

$$\mathbf{P(B \mid A')} = \frac{P(B \cap A')}{P(A')} = \frac{0.2}{0.6} = \boxed{\frac{1}{3}}$$

(v) You can see from the Venn diagram that:
   $\mathbf{P(B)} = P(B \cap A) + P(B \cap A') = 0.1 + 0.2 = \boxed{0.3}$

And finally...

(vi) $\mathbf{P(A \mid B)} = \dfrac{P(A \cap B)}{P(B)} = \dfrac{0.1}{0.3} = \boxed{\dfrac{1}{3}}$

Tip: Another way of getting P(B′|A) is to do 1 – P(B|A), since B|A is the complement of B′|A.

Tip: You can also find P(B) by doing:
P(B|A)P(A) + P(B|A′)P(A′)

That's because...
P(B|A)P(A) = P(B ∩ A),
P(B|A′)P(A′) = P(B ∩ A′)

And...
P(B∩A) + P(B∩A′) = P(B)

b) **Say whether or not A and B are independent.**

Again, there are different ways you can do this. For example, if you compare the values of P(B|A) and P(B), you can see that:

P(B|A) = 0.25 ≠ P(B) = 0.3, so A and B are **not independent**.

Tip: Or you can show:
P(A|B) ≠ P(A), or
P(A) × P(B) ≠ P(A ∩ B).

Exercise 3.4

Q1   If X and Y are independent events, with P(X) = 0.62 and P(Y) = 0.32, calculate P(X ∩ Y).

Q2   P(A ∩ B) = 0.45 and P(B′) = 0.25. If A and B are independent events, what is P(A)?

Q3   Events M and N are independent, with P(M) = 0.4 and P(N) = 0.7. Calculate the following probabilities:
     a) P(M ∩ N)   b) P(M ∪ N)   c) P(M ∩ N′)

Q3 Hint: If M and N are independent, then M and N′ are also independent.

Q4   A card is picked at random from a standard pack of 52 cards. The card is replaced and the pack is shuffled, before a second card is picked at random.
     a) What is the probability that both cards picked are 'hearts'?
     b) Find the probability that the 'ace of hearts' is chosen both times.

Q5　For events A, B and C: $P(A) = \frac{3}{11}$, $P(B) = \frac{1}{3}$, $P(C) = \frac{15}{28}$,

$P(A \cap B) = \frac{1}{11}$, $P(A \cap C) = \frac{2}{15}$ and $P(B \cap C) = \frac{5}{28}$.

Show whether or not each of the pairs of events, (A and B), (A and C) and (B and C) are independent.

Q6　X, Y and Z are independent events, with $P(X) = 0.84$, $P(Y) = 0.68$ and $P(Z) = 0.48$. Find the following probabilities:

a) $P(X \cap Y)$　b) $P(Y' \cap Z')$　c) $P(Y|Z)$　d) $P(Z'|Y')$　e) $P(Y|X')$

Q7　Jess, Keisha and Lucy go shopping independently. The probabilities that they will buy a DVD are 0.66, 0.5 and 0.3 respectively.

a) What is the probability that all three of them buy a DVD?

b) What is the probability that at least two of them buy a DVD?

Q7 Hint: The product law for independent events applies for any number of events.

Tree diagrams

Tree diagrams show probabilities for **sequences** of two or more events.

Here's a tree diagram representing two trials. There are two possible results for the first trial — events A and A', and there are two possible results for the second trial — events B and B'.

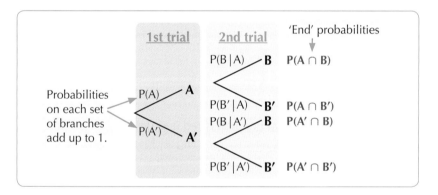

Tip: The 'end' probabilities are the probabilities of the different sequences of events.

Answers to questions are often found by adding the relevant 'end' probabilities.

- Each '**chunk**' of the diagram represents one **trial**.
- Each **branch** of a 'chunk' is a **possible result** of the trial.
- To find the **probability** of a sequence of events, you **multiply along the branches** representing those events.
- The **total** of the 'end' probabilities is always **1**.

Tree diagrams for independent events

Tree diagrams for **independent** events look a bit simpler than the one above.

- Events A and B have no effect on each other, so $P(B|A) = P(B)$, and so on.
- So for the diagram above, the second set of branches would look slightly different:

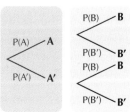

Example

A bag contains 10 balls, 6 of which are red and 4 of which are purple. One ball is selected from the bag at random, then replaced. A second ball is then selected at random.

a) Draw a tree diagram to show this information.

- There are **two trials** — '1st ball selection' and '2nd ball selection'.
- Each trial has **two possible results** — 'red' and 'purple'.
- The **probability** of selecting a **red** ball on each pick is **0.6** and the probability of selecting a **purple** ball on each pick is **0.4**.
- So you can draw a **tree diagram** like this:

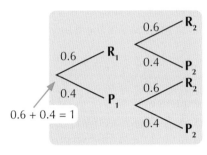

R_1 = 'first ball is red'
R_2 = 'second ball is red'
P_1 = 'first ball is purple'
P_2 = 'second ball is purple'

b) Find the probability that both balls are red.

- There is **1 'path'** along the branches that gives the result 'red and red'.
- Multiply along the branches R_1 and R_2 to give:
  $P(R_1 \cap R_2) = 0.6 \times 0.6 = \boxed{0.36}$

c) Find the probability that one ball is red and the other is purple.

- There are **2 'paths'** along the branches that give the result 'red and purple' — (R_1 and P_2) and (P_1 and R_2).
- Multiply along these pairs of branches to give:
  $\mathbf{P(R_1 \cap P_2)} = 0.6 \times 0.4 = \mathbf{0.24}$ and $\mathbf{P(P_1 \cap R_2)} = 0.4 \times 0.6 = \mathbf{0.24}$
- Now, you want to find the probability of (R_1 and P_2) **or** (P_1 and R_2), so you **add** these two probabilities together:
  $P(1 \text{ red and 1 purple}) = P(R_1 \cap P_2) + P(P_1 \cap R_2) = 0.24 + 0.24 = \boxed{0.48}$

Tip: Here, the selection is done 'with **replacement**' — so the result of the second selection is independent of the result of the first.

Tip: You can answer questions like b) and c) without using a tree diagram, but very often if you draw one, it helps to make things clearer.

Tip: This is the same as using the product rule for independent events R_1 and R_2.

Tip: This is the same as using the product rule for independent events twice, followed by the addition rule for mutually exclusive events.

Tree diagrams for dependent events

When you're dealing with events that **depend** on each other, the probabilities on the second set of branches are **conditional** on those on the first set of branches (see the diagram on the previous page).

This means you have to be a bit more careful when you're labelling your tree diagram.

Example 1

A box of 6 biscuits contains 5 chocolate biscuits and 1 lemon biscuit. George takes out a biscuit at random and eats it. He then takes out another biscuit at random.

a) Draw a tree diagram to show this information.

- There are **two trials** — '1st biscuit selection' and '2nd biscuit selection'. Let C_i = 'biscuit i is chocolate' and L_i = 'biscuit i is lemon', for $i = 1, 2$.

- The **probability** of selecting a **chocolate** biscuit on the first pick is $\frac{5}{6}$ and the probability of selecting a **lemon** biscuit on the first pick is $\frac{1}{6}$.

Tip: Here, the selection is done '**without replacement**' — so the result of the second selection is conditional on the result of the first.

- The probabilities for the **second** biscuit are **conditional**:
  - If the first pick is **chocolate**, then: $P(\text{choc}) = \frac{4}{5}$ — i.e. $P(C_2 \mid C_1) = \frac{4}{5}$, and $P(\text{lemon}) = \frac{1}{5}$ — i.e. $P(L_2 \mid C_1) = \frac{1}{5}$.
  - If the first pick is **lemon**, then there are no lemon biscuits left, so: $P(\text{choc}) = 1$ — i.e. $P(C_2 \mid L_1) = 1$ and $P(\text{lemon}) = 0$ — i.e. $P(L_2 \mid L_1) = 0$.

- So you can draw a **tree diagram** like this:

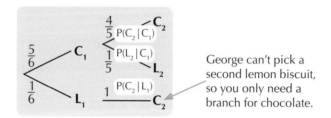

George can't pick a second lemon biscuit, so you only need a branch for chocolate.

Tip: If George took out a third biscuit, you'd get a third set of branches, looking like this:

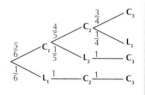

b) Find the probability that George takes out two chocolate biscuits.

- There is **1 'path'** along the branches that gives this result.
- Multiply along the branches C_1 and C_2 to give:

$$P(C_1 \cap C_2) = P(C_1)P(C_2 \mid C_1) = \frac{5}{6} \times \frac{4}{5} = \frac{20}{30} = \frac{2}{3}$$

- So P(George takes out two chocolate biscuits) = $\frac{2}{3}$

c) Find the probability that the second biscuit he takes is chocolate.

- There are **2 'paths'** along the branches that give the result 'second biscuit is chocolate' — (C_1 and C_2) and (L_1 and C_2).
- You've already found $P(C_1 \cap C_2)$, so find $P(L_1 \cap C_2)$ in the same way:

$$P(L_1 \cap C_2) = P(L_1)P(C_2 \mid L_1) = \frac{1}{6} \times 1 = \frac{1}{6}$$

- Now **add** the probabilities for the two 'paths' together:

$$P(\text{2nd biscuit is chocolate}) = P(C_1 \cap C_2) + P(L_1 \cap C_2) = \frac{2}{3} + \frac{1}{6} = \frac{5}{6}$$

Tip: Another way to find P(2nd biscuit is choc) is to find P(2nd biscuit is lemon) and subtract this probability from 1. Sometimes finding the complement and subtracting it from 1 is an easier way to find a probability.

Example 2

Horace is either late for school or on time for school, and when he gets to school he is either shouted at or not shouted at. The probability that he's late for school is 0.4. If he's late, the probability that he's shouted at is 0.7. If he's on time, the probability that he's shouted at is 0.2.

Given that Horace is shouted at, what is the probability that he was late?

- It's best to take complicated questions like this step by step.
  You're given information about two events:
  Let **L** = 'Horace is late' and let **S** = 'Horace is shouted at'.

- Start by writing down the probability you want to find: that's **P(L | S)**.

  Using the conditional probability formula: $P(L \mid S) = \dfrac{P(L \cap S)}{P(S)}$

- So you need to find $P(L \cap S)$ and $P(S)$ — and the easiest way is by drawing a **tree diagram** using the information in the question:

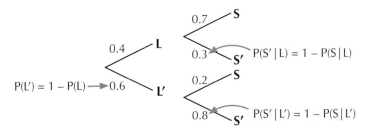

- Using the tree diagram:
  $\mathbf{P(L \cap S)} = P(L)P(S \mid L) = 0.4 \times 0.7 = \mathbf{0.28}$
  $\mathbf{P(S)} = P(L \cap S) + P(L' \cap S) = 0.28 + P(L')(S \mid L')$
  $\qquad\qquad = 0.28 + 0.6 \times 0.2$
  $\qquad\qquad = \mathbf{0.4}$

- So, $P(L \mid S) = \dfrac{P(L \cap S)}{P(S)} = \dfrac{0.28}{0.4} = 0.7$

- This means P(Horace was late, given he is shouted at) = 0.7

Tip: Be careful with questions like this... The question tells you the probability of S conditional on L (and L'). But you need to think of the situation the 'other way round' — with L conditional on S. So don't just rush in.

Tip: In general, if B depends on A, then A depends on B.

Here, S depends on L, so L depends on S.

Example 3

For events M and N: P(M) = 0.2, P(N | M) = 0.4 and P(N' | M') = 0.7.

a) Draw a tree diagram representing events M and N.

- You need **two** sets of branches — one for event M and one for event N. Since you're told the probability of M, but not that of N, show **M** on the **first** set and N on the second set.

  Each pair of branches will either show **M** and its complement **M'**, or **N** and its complement **N'**.

- Draw the tree diagram and write on as much as you know so far:

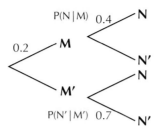

- Now use this information to find the **remaining probabilities**:

  P(M′) = 1 − P(M) = 1 − 0.2 = **0.8**

  P(N′ | M) = 1 − P(N | M) = 1 − 0.4 = **0.6**

  P(N | M′) = 1 − P(N′ | M′) = 1 − 0.7 = **0.3**

> **Tip:** This is just using the fact that the probabilities on each set of branches add up to 1 — see p71.

- Finally, add these probabilities to the tree diagram:

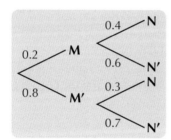

b) Find P(N).

$$P(N) = P(M \cap N) + P(M' \cap N) = P(M)P(N|M) + P(M')P(N|M')$$
$$= 0.2 \times 0.4 + 0.8 \times 0.3$$
$$= \boxed{0.32}$$

> **Tip:** There are 2 'paths' giving N, so find the probability of each, then add them together.

c) Find P(M′ | N′).

- Remember, If N′ is conditional on M′, then M′ is conditional on N′.
- Using the conditional probability formula: $P(M' | N') = \dfrac{P(M' \cap N')}{P(N')}$
- Using the probabilities you found above:

  P(N′) = 1 − P(N) = **0.68**

  P(M′ ∩ N′) = P(M′)P(N′ | M′) = 0.8 × 0.7 = **0.56**

- So, $P(M' | N') = \dfrac{P(M' \cap N')}{P(N')} = \dfrac{0.56}{0.68} = \dfrac{56}{68} = \boxed{\dfrac{14}{17}}$

Q1   The probability that Jake will win two consecutive darts matches is shown on the tree diagram.

a) Explain whether the events 'wins 1st match' and 'wins 2nd match' are independent?

b) Find the probability that Jake will win:

(i) both matches   (ii) at least one match

Q2   A game involves rolling a fair, six-sided dice and tossing a fair coin. A player wins if they roll a '6' and the coin shows 'tails'.

a) Complete the tree diagram by showing the probability on each branch.

b) Find the probability that a person wins the game.

Q3   The probability that a randomly selected Year 13 student has passed their driving test is 0.3. The probability that they intend to go to university, given that they have passed their driving test, is 0.75.

a) Assuming that 'passed driving test' and 'intend to go to university' are independent, draw a tree diagram to show this information.

b) Find the probability that a randomly selected student hasn't passed their driving test and does not intend to go to university.

c) What is the probability that a student picked at random does not intend to go to university?

Q4   A restaurant has found that if a diner orders a roast dinner, the probability that they order apple pie for pudding is 0.72. If they order a different main course, they order apple pie with probability 0.33. The probability that a diner orders a roast dinner is 0.56.

By drawing a tree diagram, find the probability that a randomly selected diner will order apple pie for pudding.

Q5   A group of people were asked about their mobile phones. 62% of them own a smartphone and 53.9% of them have a contract costing more than £25 a month. Of the people with a smartphone, 29% have a contract costing £25 a month or less.

Use a tree diagram to find the probability that a person from the group owns a smartphone, given that their contract costs more than £25 a month.

Q6   A game involves picking two balls at random from a bag containing 12 balls — 5 red, 4 yellow and 3 green — where the first ball isn't replaced. A player wins if they pick two balls of the same colour.

a) Draw a tree diagram to show the possible results of each pick.

b) Find the probability that a player wins the game.

c) The game is changed so that the first ball is replaced before the second one is picked. Is a player more or less likely to win now?

Review Exercise — Chapter 2

Q1   A fair, six-sided dice and a fair coin are thrown and a score is recorded.
If a head is thrown, the score is double the number on the dice.
If a tail is thrown, the score is the number on the dice plus 4.

    a) Draw a sample-space diagram to represent all the possible outcomes.

    b) What is the probability of scoring more than 5?

    c) If a tail is thrown, what is the probability that the score is an even number?

Q2   Half the students in a sixth-form college eat sausages for dinner and 20% eat chips.
2% eat sausages and chips together.

    a) Draw a Venn diagram to show this information.

    b) Find the percentage of students who eat chips but not sausages.

    c) Find the percentage of students who eat either chips or sausages but not both.

Q3   Arabella rolls two fair, six-sided dice and calculates her score by adding
the two results together.

    a) What is the probability that her score is a prime number?

    b) What is the probability that her score is a square number?

    Let P be the event 'Arabella's score is a prime number' and S be the event
'Arabella's score is a square number'.

    c) Explain whether or not the events P and S are mutually exclusive.

    d) Find $P(P \cup S)$.

    Arabella carries out the experiment twice. Let S_1 be the event 'score from first pair of rolls is
a square number' and S_2 be the event 'score from second pair of rolls is a square number'.

    e) Explain whether or not the events S_1 and S_2 are independent.

    f) Find $P(S_1 \cap S_2)$.

Q4   A school orchestra is made up of pupils in either the upper or the lower school.
40% of the musicians are boys. Of the boys, 30% are in the upper school.
Of the girls in the orchestra, 50% are in the upper school.

    a) Draw a tree diagram to show this information.

    b) A musician is chosen at random. Find the probability that the musician is:

        (i)   in the lower school, given that they are a boy

        (ii)   a girl in the lower school

        (iii) in the upper school

1   A soap company asked 120 people about the types of soap (from Brands A, B and C) they
    bought. Brand A was bought by 40 people, Brand B by 30 people and Brand C by 25.
    Both Brands A and B (and possibly C as well) were bought by 8 people,
    B and C (and maybe A) were bought by 10 people, and A and C (and maybe B) by 7 people.
    All three brands were bought by 3 people.

   a)   Represent this information in a Venn diagram.

        (5 marks)

   b)   If a person is selected at random, find the probability that:

        (i)   they buy at least one of the soaps

              (2 marks)

        (ii) they buy at least two of the soaps

              (2 marks)

        (iii) they buy soap B, given that they buy only one of the soaps

              (3 marks)

2   A jar contains counters of 3 different colours. There are 3 red counters, 4 white counters
    and 5 green counters. Two random counters are removed from the jar one at a time.
    Once removed, the colour of the counter is noted. The first counter is not replaced before
    the second one is drawn.

   a)   Draw a tree diagram to represent this situation.

        (3 marks)

   b)   Find the probability that the second counter is green.

        (2 marks)

   c)   Find the probability that both the counters are red.

        (2 marks)

   d)   Find the probability that the two counters are not both the same colour.

        (3 marks)

3   Event J and Event K are independent events, where $P(J) = 0.7$ and $P(K) = 0.1$.

   a)   Find:
        (i) $P(J \cap K)$

              (1 mark)

        (ii) $P(J \cup K)$

              (2 marks)

   b)   If L is the event that neither J or K occurs, find $P(L|K')$.

        (3 marks)

4 When Albert eats in a certain restaurant, he always eats either chicken or beef for his main course. And he always eats either sponge pudding or ice cream for his dessert.

The probability that he eats chicken is $\frac{1}{3}$, the probability that he eats ice cream given that he eats chicken is $\frac{2}{5}$, and the probability that he eats ice cream given that he eats beef is $\frac{3}{4}$.

   a) Find the probability that he eats either chicken or ice cream, but not both.

(3 marks)

   b) Find the probability that he eats ice cream.

(3 marks)

   c) Find the probability that he has eaten chicken,
       given that he is eating ice cream.

(3 marks)

5 A film club with 20 members meets once a week. 14 of the members go every week and 13 plan to renew their membership for another year. Of those planning to renew their membership, 10 go every week.

One member of the club is selected at random.

   a) Find the probability that the person selected plans to renew their membership
       and goes to the club every week.

(3 marks)

   b) Find the probability that the person selected goes to the club every week,
       but doesn't plan to renew their membership.

(2 marks)

   c) Show whether or not going to the club every week and renewing membership
       are independent.

(2 marks)

6 For a particular biased dice, the event 'roll a 6' is called event B. $P(B) = 0.2$.
This biased dice and a fair, six-sided dice are rolled together.

   a) Write down the probability that the biased dice doesn't show a 6.

(1 mark)

   b) Find the probability that at least one of the dice shows a 6.

(2 marks)

   c) Find the probability that exactly one of the dice shows a 6,
       given that at least one of them shows a 6.

(4 marks)

1. Probability Distributions

Probability distributions show the probability of a discrete random variable taking certain values. They can be used to make predictions about the outcomes of random experiments.

Discrete random variables

First things first, you'll need to know what a discrete random variable is:

- A **variable** is just something that can take a variety of values — its value isn't fixed.
- A **random variable** is a variable that takes different values with different probabilities.
- A **discrete random variable** is a random variable which can only take a certain number of values.

A **discrete random variable** is usually represented by an **upper case letter** such as X. The **particular values** that X can take are represented by the lower case letter x.

Tip: Remember that **discrete data** can only take **certain** values (unlike continuous data which can take all the values in a certain range). See page 3.

These examples should help you to get used to the difference between x and X.

> Rolling a fair dice and recording the score:
> - X is the name of the random variable. Here it's '**score on dice**'.
> - x is a particular value that X can take. Here x could be **1**, **2**, **3**, **4**, **5** or **6**.

> Tossing a fair coin twice and counting the number of heads:
> - X is '**number of heads**'.
> - x could be **0**, **1** or **2**.

Tip: Notice that in these two examples, the discrete random variable can only take a few different values. The possible values are all whole numbers — but they don't have to be.

Probability distributions and functions

A **probability distribution** is a **table** showing all the possible values a discrete random variable can take, plus the **probability** that it'll take each value.

> **Example**
>
> **Draw the probability distribution table for X, where X is the score on a fair, six-sided dice.**
>
> X can take the values 1, 2, 3, 4, 5 and 6, each with probability $\frac{1}{6}$.
>
> > List all the possible values that X can take here.
>
> | x | 1 | 2 | 3 | 4 | 5 | 6 |
> |---|---|---|---|---|---|---|
> | $P(X = x)$ | $\frac{1}{6}$ | $\frac{1}{6}$ | $\frac{1}{6}$ | $\frac{1}{6}$ | $\frac{1}{6}$ | $\frac{1}{6}$ |
>
> > This notation means 'the probability that X takes the value x'.
>
> > The probability of each number being rolled on a fair dice is $\frac{1}{6}$.

A **probability function** is a formula that generates the probability of X taking the value x, for every possible x. It is written **P($X = x$)** or sometimes just **p(x)**. A probability function is really just another way of representing the information in the probability distribution table.

Tip: Even though it's described as a 'formula', the probability function can just be a number — you'll see ones like this in the examples.

Examples

a) **A fair coin is tossed once and the number of tails, X, is counted. Write down the probability function of X.**

- To write down the probability function, you need to work out the **possible values**, x, that X can take and the **probability** of each value.

  The outcome can either be heads or tails, so X can either take the value **0** (if it lands on heads) or **1** (if it lands on tails).

  The probability of each outcome is $\frac{1}{2}$.

- Now you can write down the probability function:

$$P(X = x) = \frac{1}{2} \quad x = 0, 1$$

List the possible values of x after the 'formula'.

Tip: The probability of x being any value other than 0 or 1 is zero — it's impossible.

b) **A biased coin, for which the probability of heads is $\frac{3}{4}$ and tails is $\frac{1}{4}$, is tossed once and the number of tails, X, is counted. Write down the probability function of X.**

- Again, the outcome can either be heads or tails, so X can either be **0** or **1**. The probability of heads, P($X = 0$), is $\frac{3}{4}$ and the probability of tails, P($X = 1$), is $\frac{1}{4}$.

- This time, the probabilities are **different** for different values of x — so it's best to use two 'formulas', one for each x value. Write the probability function as a bracket like this:

$$P(X = x) = \begin{cases} \frac{3}{4} & x = 0 \\ \frac{1}{4} & x = 1 \end{cases}$$

Put each value of x next to the 'formula' which gives its probability.

There's an important rule about probabilities that you'll use in solving lots of discrete random variable problems:

> The **probabilities** of **all** the possible values that a discrete random variable can take **add up to 1**.

For a **discrete random variable** X:

$$\sum_{\text{all } x} P(X = x) = 1$$

We can check this works for the **fair coin** in **Example a)** above:

$$\sum_{\text{all } x} P(X = x) = \sum_{x=0,1} P(X = x) = P(X = 0) + P(X = 1) = \frac{1}{2} + \frac{1}{2} = 1 \checkmark$$

The only values of x are 0 and 1.

The probability of each outcome is $\frac{1}{2}$.

Chapter 3 Discrete Random Variables   81

You can use the fact that all the probabilities add up to 1 to solve problems where **probabilities** are **unknown** or contain unknown factors.

Example

The random variable X has probability function
$P(X = x) = kx \quad x = 1, 2, 3$. Find the value of k.

So X has three possible values ($x = 1$, 2 and 3), and the probability of each is kx (where you need to find the unknown k).

It's easier to understand if you write out the probability distribution:

Tip: It'll often help to write down the probability distribution table when solving problems like these — that way you won't miss out any values.

x	1	2	3
$P(X = x)$	$k \times 1 = k$	$k \times 2 = 2k$	$k \times 3 = 3k$

Now just use the rule: $\sum_{\text{all } x} P(X = x) = 1$

Here, this means: $k + 2k + 3k = 6k = 1$

$$\Rightarrow k = \frac{1}{6}$$

You may be asked to find the probability that X is **greater** or **less** than a value, or **lies between** two values. You just need to identify all the values that X can now take and then it's a simple case of **adding up** all their **probabilities**.

Example

The discrete random variable X has the following probability distribution:

x	0	1	2	3	4
$P(X = x)$	0.1	0.2	0.3	0.2	a

Find: a) the value of a,   b) $P(2 \le X < 4)$,   c) the mode

a) Use $\sum_{\text{all } x} P(X = x) = 1$ again.

From the table: $0.1 + 0.2 + 0.3 + 0.2 + a = 1$

$$\Rightarrow 0.8 + a = 1$$
$$\Rightarrow a = 0.2$$

Tip: Careful with the inequality signs — you need to include $X = 2$ but not $X = 4$.

b) This is asking for the probability that
'X is greater than or equal to 2, but less than 4'.
In other words the probability that $X = 2$ or $X = 3$.

Just add up the probabilities:
$P(2 \le X < 4) = P(X = 2 \text{ or } 3)$
$= P(X = 2) + P(X = 3)$
$= 0.3 + 0.2 = 0.5$

The events $X = 2$ and $X = 3$ are mutually exclusive so you can add the probabilities. See p63.

Tip: The mode of a **random variable** is the value you'd **expect** to occur most if you repeated the experiment lots of times — the most likely value.

c) The **mode** is the most likely value — so it's the value with the highest probability. The highest probability in the table is 0.3 when $X = 2$, so the mode = 2 .

When it's not clear what the probability distribution or function should be, it can be helpful to draw a **sample-space diagram** of all the **possible outcomes** and work it out from that. For more on sample-space diagrams, see page 54.

Example 1

An unbiased six-sided dice has faces marked 1, 1, 1, 2, 2, 3.
The dice is rolled twice.
Let X be the random variable 'sum of the two scores on the dice'.
a) Find the probability distribution of X.

- To find the probability distribution, you need to identify all the possible values, x, that X could take and the probability of each.

  The easiest way to do this is to draw a sample-space diagram showing the 36 possible outcomes of the dice rolls:

				Score on roll 1		
+	1	1	1	2	2	3
1	2	2	2	3	3	4
1	2	2	2	3	3	4
1	2	2	2	3	3	4
2	3	3	3	4	4	5
2	3	3	3	4	4	5
3	4	4	4	5	5	6

(Score on roll 2 labels the left column: 1, 1, 1, 2, 2, 3)

- From the diagram you can see that there are only five values that X can take: x = 2, 3, 4, 5, 6.

- Since all 36 outcomes are equally likely, you can find the probability of each value by counting how many times it occurs in the diagram and dividing by 36.

  9 out of the 36 outcomes give a score of 2.
  So $P(X = 2) = \frac{9}{36} = \frac{1}{4}$

  12 out of the 36 outcomes give a score of 3.
  So $P(X = 3) = \frac{12}{36} = \frac{1}{3}$

  Similarly,
  $P(X = 4) = \frac{10}{36} = \frac{5}{18}$, $P(X = 5) = \frac{4}{36} = \frac{1}{9}$, $P(X = 6) = \frac{1}{36}$

- So the probability distribution is:

x	2	3	4	5	6
$P(X = x)$	$\frac{1}{4}$	$\frac{1}{3}$	$\frac{5}{18}$	$\frac{1}{9}$	$\frac{1}{36}$

b) Find $P(X < 5)$.

This is asking for the probability that X is strictly less than 5, in other words X takes values 2, 3 or 4. Just add the probabilities together.

$P(X < 5) = P(X = 2) + P(X = 3) + P(X = 4) = \frac{1}{4} + \frac{1}{3} + \frac{5}{18} = \frac{31}{36}$

Tip: See p53 for the equally likely outcomes formula.

Tip: Don't forget to change the fractions into their simplest form.

Tip: You should always check that all the probabilities in your table add up to 1 — if they don't you've done something wrong.

Example 2

A game involves rolling two fair dice. If the sum of the scores is greater than 10 then the player wins 50p. If the sum is between 8 and 10 (inclusive) then they win 20p. Otherwise they get nothing.

a) If X is the random variable 'amount player wins', find the probability distribution of X.

- There are three possible amounts of money to be won, so there are three possible values that X can take: 0, 20 and 50.

- For each x value, you need to find the probability of getting a sum of scores which results in that value of x.

$$P(X = 0) = P(\text{Sum of scores} < 8)$$
$$P(X = 20) = P(8 \leq \text{Sum of scores} \leq 10)$$
$$P(X = 50) = P(\text{Sum of scores} > 10)$$

- To find these probabilities, draw a sample-space diagram showing the 36 possible outcomes of the dice rolls.
  Mark on your diagram all the outcomes that give each value of x.

Score on dice 1

+	1	2	3	4	5	6
1	2	3	4	5	6	7
2	3	4	5	6	7	8
3	4	5	6	7	8	9
4	5	6	7	8	9	10
5	6	7	8	9	10	11
6	7	8	9	10	11	12

Score on dice 2

- 21 out of 36 outcomes give a sum of scores which is strictly less than 8, so $P(X = 0) = P(\text{Sum of scores} < 8) = \frac{21}{36} = \frac{7}{12}$

- 12 out of 36 outcomes give a sum of scores between 8 and 10 inclusive, so $P(X = 20) = P(8 \leq \text{Sum of scores} \leq 10) = \frac{12}{36} = \frac{1}{3}$

- 3 out of 36 outcomes give a sum of scores strictly greater than 10, so $P(X = 50) = P(\text{Sum of scores} > 10) = \frac{3}{36} = \frac{1}{12}$

- Using this information, draw the probability distribution:

x	0	20	50
$P(X = x)$	$\frac{7}{12}$	$\frac{1}{3}$	$\frac{1}{12}$

b) The game costs 15p to play. Find the probability of making a profit.

- A player will make a profit if they win more than 15p — so if they win 20p or 50p.

- So the probability of making a profit is
$$P(X > 15) = P(X = 20) + P(X = 50) = \frac{1}{3} + \frac{1}{12} = \frac{5}{12}$$

Q1 For each of the following random experiments, identify:
    (i)   The discrete random variable, X.
    (ii) All possible values, x, that X can take.
a) Tossing a fair coin 4 times and recording the number of tails.
b) Picking 4 balls from this bag without replacement and recording the number of orange balls selected.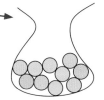
c) Rolling a fair four-sided dice twice and recording the sum of the scores.

Q2 A fair six-sided dice is rolled. Write down the probability distribution for the following random variables:
a) A = 'score rolled on the dice'.
b) B = '1 if the score is even, 0 otherwise'.
c) C = '5 times the score rolled on the dice'.

Q3 a) The random variable X has probability distribution:

x	1	2	3	4
$P(X = x)$	0.2	0.4	0.1	a

    (i) Find a (ii) Find $P(X \geq 2)$

b) The random variable X has probability distribution:

x	1	4	9	16	25	36
$P(X = x)$	k	k	k	k	k	k

    (i)   Find k (ii)   Find $P(X \geq 5)$
    (iii) Find $P(X \geq 10)$ (iv) Find $P(3 \leq X \leq 15)$
    (v) Find $P(X$ is divisible by three)

Q4 For each of the probability functions in a) to c) below:
    (i) Find k.   (ii) Write down the probability distribution of X.

a) $P(X = x) = kx^2$ $x = 1, 2, 3$

b) $P(X = x) = \dfrac{k}{x}$ $x = 1, 2, 3$

c) $P(X = x) = \begin{cases} kx & x = 1, 2, 3, 4 \\ k(8-x) & x = 5, 6, 7 \end{cases}$

> **Q4 Hint:** Remember that when a probability function is written in brackets, different values of x have probabilities given by different formulas.

Q5 An unbiased four-sided dice with possible scores 1, 2, 3 and 4 is rolled twice.
Let X be the random variable 'product of the two scores on the dice'.
a) Write the probability distribution of X.
b) Write the probability function of X.
c) Find $P(3 < X \leq 10)$

The cumulative distribution function

The **cumulative distribution function**, written **F(x)**, gives the probability that X will be **less than or equal to** a particular value, x. It's like a **running total** of probabilities.

To find $F(x_0)$, for a given value x_0, you **add up** all of the probabilities of the values X can take which are less than or equal to x_0.

Tip: You'll sometimes see this written as
$$F(x_0) = \sum_{x \leq x_0} p(x).$$

Remember that p(x) is just the same as writing $P(X = x)$.

$$F(x_0) = P(X \leq x_0) = \sum_{x \leq x_0} P(X = x)$$

Example 1

The probability distribution of the discrete random variable H is shown in the table:

h	0.1	0.2	0.3	0.4
$P(H = h)$	$\frac{1}{4}$	$\frac{1}{4}$	$\frac{1}{3}$	$\frac{1}{6}$

Draw up a table to show the cumulative distribution function F(h).

- There are 4 values of h, so you have to find the probability that H is less than or equal to each of them in turn.

   It sounds trickier than it actually is — you only have to add up a few probabilities...

- Start with the smallest value of h:

   $F(0.1) = P(H \leq 0.1)$ — this is the same as $P(H = 0.1)$, since H can't be less than 0.1. So $F(0.1) = \boxed{\frac{1}{4}}$

   $F(0.2) = P(H \leq 0.2)$ — this is the probability that $H = 0.1$ or $H = 0.2$.
   So, $F(0.2) = P(H = 0.1) + P(H = 0.2) = \frac{1}{4} + \frac{1}{4} = \boxed{\frac{1}{2}}$

   $F(0.3) = P(H \leq 0.3)$
   $= P(H = 0.1) + P(H = 0.2) + P(H = 0.3) = \frac{1}{4} + \frac{1}{4} + \frac{1}{3} = \boxed{\frac{5}{6}}$

$$F(0.4) = P(H \leq 0.4)$$
$$= P(H = 0.1) + P(H = 0.2) + P(H = 0.3) + P(H = 0.4)$$
$$= \frac{1}{4} + \frac{1}{4} + \frac{1}{3} + \frac{1}{6} = \boxed{1}$$

This isn't coincidence — $P(X \leq$ largest value of $x)$ is always 1 because it's the sum of all the possible probabilities, which you know is 1.

- Finally, put these values in a table, and you're done...

h	0.1	0.2	0.3	0.4
$F(h) = P(H \leq h)$	$\frac{1}{4}$	$\frac{1}{2}$	$\frac{5}{6}$	1

Sometimes you'll be asked to work backwards — you can work out the **probability function**, given the cumulative distribution function.

The probability that X is **equal** to a certain x value is the same as the probability that X is less than or equal to that x value, but not less than or equal to the next lowest x value.

To describe these x values, it can be useful to use the notation x_i. For example, if X can take the values $x = 2, 4, 6, 9$, then you can label these as $x_1 = 2$, $x_2 = 4$, $x_3 = 6$ and $x_4 = 9$.

Tip: You might have seen this x_i notation in C1 — it's used for sequences and series.

Using this notation, the probability that '$X = x_i$' is the same as the probability that 'X is **less than or equal** to x_i, but **NOT** less than or equal to x_{i-1}'.

This clever trick can be written:

$$P(X = x_i) = P(X \leq x_i) - P(X \leq x_{i-1}) = F(x_i) - F(x_{i-1})$$

Example 2

The formula below gives the cumulative distribution function F(x) for a discrete random variable X:
$$F(x) = kx, \text{ for } x = 1, 2, 3 \text{ and } 4$$
Find k, and the probability function for X.

Questions with an unknown almost always want you to use the fact that all the probabilities must add up to 1.

- To find k, you know that X has to be 4 or less, so:

$$P(X \leq 4) = 1$$
$$F(4) = 1$$

Substitute 4 in for the 'x' in 'kx'.

This is using the fact that all the probabilities must add up to 1.

$$\Rightarrow 4k = 1 \text{ so } k = \frac{1}{4}$$

Now you can use this to work out the probability function:

- First, work out the probabilities of X being **less than or equal** to 1, 2, 3 and 4. This is easy — just substitute $k = \frac{1}{4}$ into $F(x) = kx$ for each x value.

$$F(1) = P(X \leq 1) = 1 \times k = \frac{1}{4}, \qquad F(2) = P(X \leq 2) = 2 \times k = \frac{1}{2},$$

$$F(3) = P(X \leq 3) = 3 \times k = \frac{3}{4}, \qquad F(4) = P(X \leq 4) = 1$$

Tip: In this example $x_1 = 1$, $x_2 = 2$, $x_3 = 3$ and $x_4 = 4$.

- But you need to find the probabilities of X being **equal** to 1, 2, 3 and 4. This is the clever bit, just use: $\boxed{P(X = x_i) = F(x_i) - F(x_{i-1})}$

$$P(X = 4) = P(X \leq 4) - P(X \leq 3) = 1 - \frac{3}{4} = \frac{1}{4}$$

Think about it...
...if it's ≤ 4,
...but not ≤ 3,
...then it has to **be** 4.

$$P(X = 3) = P(X \leq 3) - P(X \leq 2) = \frac{3}{4} - \frac{1}{2} = \frac{1}{4}$$

$$P(X = 2) = P(X \leq 2) - P(X \leq 1) = \frac{1}{2} - \frac{1}{4} = \frac{1}{4}$$

$$P(X = 1) = P(X \leq 1) = \frac{1}{4}$$

Because x doesn't take any values less than 1.

- Draw out the probability distribution using this information, so you can read off the probability function.
  The probability distribution of X is:

x	1	2	3	4
$P(X = x)$	$\frac{1}{4}$	$\frac{1}{4}$	$\frac{1}{4}$	$\frac{1}{4}$

So the probability function is: $P(X = x) = \frac{1}{4}$ for $x = 1, 2, 3, 4$

Exercise 1.2

Q1 Each of a)-d) shows the probability distribution for a discrete random variable, X. Draw up a table to show the cumulative distribution function $F(x)$ for each one.

a)

x	1	2	3	4	5
$p(x)$	0.1	0.2	0.3	0.2	0.2

b)

x	−2	−1	0	1	2
$p(x)$	$\frac{1}{5}$	$\frac{1}{5}$	$\frac{1}{5}$	$\frac{1}{5}$	$\frac{1}{5}$

c)

x	1	2	3	4
$p(x)$	0.3	0.2	0.3	0.2

d)

x	2	4	8	16	32	64
$p(x)$	$\frac{1}{2}$	$\frac{1}{4}$	$\frac{1}{8}$	$\frac{1}{16}$	$\frac{1}{32}$	$\frac{1}{32}$

Q2 Each of a)-b) shows the probability distribution for a discrete random variable, X. For each part, draw up a table showing the cumulative distribution function, $F(x)$, and use it to find the required probabilities.

a)

x	1	2	3	4
$p(x)$	0.3	0.1	0.45	0.15

b)

x	-2	-1	0	1	2
$p(x)$	$\frac{1}{10}$	$\frac{2}{5}$	$\frac{1}{10}$	$\frac{1}{5}$	$\frac{1}{5}$

Find (i) $P(X \leq 3)$
     (ii) $P(1 < X \leq 3)$

Find (i) $P(X \leq 0)$
     (ii) $P(X > 0)$

Q3 The discrete random variable X has probability function:

$$P(X = x) = \frac{1}{8}, \quad x = 1, 2, 3, 4, 5, 6, 7, 8$$

a) Draw up a table showing the cumulative distribution function, $F(x)$.

b) Find (i) $P(X \leq 3)$ (ii) $P(3 < X \leq 7)$

Q3 Hint: This time you've been given the probability function instead of the probability distribution, but the method is just the same.

Q4 Each table shows the cumulative distribution function of a discrete random variable, X. Write down the probability distribution for X.

a)

x	1	2	3	4	5
$F(x)$	0.2	0.3	0.6	0.9	1

b)

x	-2	-1	0	1
$F(x)$	0.1	0.2	0.7	1

c)

x	2	4	8	16	32	64
$F(x)$	$\frac{1}{32}$	$\frac{1}{8}$	$\frac{1}{4}$	$\frac{1}{2}$	$\frac{3}{4}$	1

Q5 The discrete random variable X has the cumulative distribution function:

x	1	2	3	4
$F(x)$	0.3	a	0.8	1

Given that $P(X = 2) = P(X = 3)$, draw a table showing the probability distribution of X.

Q5 Hint: Find the probabilities $P(X = x)$ for each x as a function of a, and then use the fact that $P(X = 2) = P(X = 3)$ to work out the value of a.

Q6 For each cumulative distribution function, find the value of k, and give the probability distribution for the discrete random variable, X.

a) $F(x) = \dfrac{(x + k)^2}{25}, \quad x = 1, 2, 3$

b) $F(x) = \dfrac{(x + k)^3}{64}, \quad x = 1, 2, 3$

c) $F(x) = 2^{(x - k)}, \quad\quad x = 1, 2, 3$

Q7 The discrete random variable X = 'the larger score showing when a pair of fair six-sided dice are rolled'.
a) Show that the cumulative distribution function, $F(x)$, is given by:

$$F(x) = \frac{x^2}{36}, \quad x = 1, 2, 3, 4, 5, 6$$

b) Hence, find the probability distribution for X.

Q7 Hint: You need to find $P(X \leq x)$ — the probability that the largest score shown by the two dice is no more than x. This means that both rolls must score no more than x, so you're looking for the probability that two independent rolls each score no more than x.

2. Expected Values, Mean and Variance

Learning Objectives:

- Be able to calculate the mean and variance of discrete random variables.
- Be able to calculate the expected value and variance of functions of discrete random variables.
- Use the discrete uniform distribution to find the mean and variance of discrete uniform random variables.

You've seen in Chapter 1 how to find the mean and variance of a data set. Here, you'll be finding these measures for discrete random variables. Instead of working them out from observed data, you'll be finding theoretical values for the mean and variance based on the probability distribution.

The expected value

The expected value of X, E(X)

Every **discrete random variable**, X, has an 'expected value' (or **mean**) E(X). In theory, it's what you'd **expect** the mean of the data to be if you took lots of readings. In practice, the mean is unlikely to be exactly E(X), but it should be pretty close.

If the discrete random variable X can take values $x_1, x_2, x_3, \ldots$ then the expected value of X is:

> Mean = Expected Value E(X) $= \sum x_i P(X = x_i) = \sum x_i p_i$

So all you do is **multiply** each **x-value** by its **probability** and **add** them all together.

Tip: Remember that x_i is just notation for all the different x-values, x_1, x_2 etc.

So $\sum x_i P(X = x_i)$
$= x_1 P(X = x_1)$
$\quad + x_2 P(X = x_2) + \ldots$

And p_i is just short for P($X = x_i$).

Tip: The expected value (or mean) of a random variable is sometimes labelled μ.

Example 1

The probability distribution of X, the number of daughters in a family of 3 children, is shown in the table. Find the expected number of daughters.

x_i	0	1	2	3
p_i	$\frac{1}{8}$	$\frac{3}{8}$	$\frac{3}{8}$	$\frac{1}{8}$

Just add up all the $x_i p_i$'s:

$$E(X) = \sum x_i p_i = \left[0 \times \tfrac{1}{8}\right] + \left[1 \times \tfrac{3}{8}\right] + \left[2 \times \tfrac{3}{8}\right] + \left[3 \times \tfrac{1}{8}\right]$$
$$= 0 + \tfrac{3}{8} + \tfrac{6}{8} + \tfrac{3}{8} = \tfrac{12}{8} = 1.5$$

So the expected number of daughters is 1.5.

Tip: It sounds a bit weird to expect 1.5 daughters —
but all it means is that if you check a large number of 3-child families, the mean will be close to 1.5.

Example 2

A discrete random variable, X, has the probability distribution shown in the table. Given that E(X) = 2.7, find a and b.

x_i	1	2	3	4
p_i	0.2	0.3	a	b

- There are two unknowns to find, so you'll need **two** bits of information. The first is given in the question, **E(X) = 2.7**.

$$E(X) = \sum x_i p_i = [1 \times 0.2] + [2 \times 0.3] + 3a + 4b$$
$$\Rightarrow 2.7 = 0.8 + 3a + 4b$$

So $\quad 1.9 = 3a + 4b$

- It might not be obvious what the second bit of information is — nothing else is given in the question. But there is something that is true for every discrete random variable — all the probabilities must add up to 1.

$$\sum p_i = 1$$

So $0.5 + a + b = 1$ so $a + b = 0.5$

- Now you just need to solve the simultaneous equations

① $a + b = 0.5$ and   ② $3a + 4b = 1.9$

① gives $a = 0.5 - b$ and substituting this into ② gives:

$3(0.5 - b) + 4b = 1.9$

$1.5 - 3b + 4b = 1.9$

$1.5 + b = 1.9$

$b = 0.4$

Substituting $b = 0.4$ into ① gives $a = 0.1$

Tip: This is the 'substitution' method of solving simultaneous equations. In general it means isolating one of the variables (getting a or b on its own) and substituting it into the other equation. You can also solve simultaneous equations using the 'elimination' method (which involves adding or subtracting them to get rid of one unknown).

The expected value of X^2, $E(X^2)$

It is sometimes useful to work out the expected value of 'X^2', $E(X^2)$ — for example, when calculating the **variance** of X (see p93). You can work out a **probability distribution** for X^2, just as you can for X, and then calculating the expected value is easy.

Tip: You'll be using $E(X^2)$ to work out the variance a lot in this chapter so make sure you get comfortable with it here.

Example 1

Here's the probability distribution from Example 1 on the previous page:

x_i	0	1	2	3
p_i	$\frac{1}{8}$	$\frac{3}{8}$	$\frac{3}{8}$	$\frac{1}{8}$

Find the probability distribution of X^2.

The probability distribution table for X^2 is similar to the one for X. You just need to square the x_i values and keep the probabilities the same.

The distribution of X^2 is:

These are just the x_i values squared.

x_i^2	0	1	4	9
$P(X^2 = x_i^2)$	$\frac{1}{8}$	$\frac{3}{8}$	$\frac{3}{8}$	$\frac{1}{8}$

The probabilities don't change, which means $P(X^2 = x_i^2) = P(X = x_i) = p_i$.

If the discrete random variable X can take values $x_1, x_2, x_3, ...$ then the expected value of X^2 is:

$$E(X^2) = \sum x_i^2 P(X = x_i) = \sum x_i^2 p_i$$

Example 2

For the discrete random variable defined in Example 1 on the previous page, find the value of E(X^2).

Tip: Notice that E(X^2) is not the same as [E(X)]^2.

Using the formula:

$$E(X^2) = \sum x_i^2 p_i = \left[0 \times \tfrac{1}{8}\right] + \left[1 \times \tfrac{3}{8}\right] + \left[4 \times \tfrac{3}{8}\right] + \left[9 \times \tfrac{1}{8}\right]$$

$$= 0 + \tfrac{3}{8} + \tfrac{12}{8} + \tfrac{9}{8} = \tfrac{24}{8} = \boxed{3}$$

Exercise 2.1

Q1 Hint: You might want to write out the probability distribution to help you find E(X) — but you don't need to.

Q1 Find E(X) for each of the following discrete random variables.

a) $P(X = x) = 0.2$ $x = 0, 1, 2, 3, 4$ b) $P(X = x) = \dfrac{x^2}{14}$ $x = 1, 2, 3$

c) $P(X = x) = \begin{cases} 0.1 & x = 2 \\ 0.4 & x = 3 \\ 0.5 & x = 1 \end{cases}$ d) $P(X = x) = \begin{cases} 0.1 & x = -2 \\ 0.2 & x = -1, 1, 2 \\ 0.3 & x = 0 \end{cases}$

Q1 Hint: For parts e) and f), you'll need to work out the value of k first.

e) $P(X = x) = k(x + 2)$ $x = 1, 2, 3, 4, 5$ f) $P(X = x) = \dfrac{k}{x}$ $x = 1, 2, 3, 4, 5$

Q2 Each table below shows the probability distribution of a discrete random variable, X. Use the information given to find the required values.

a)

x	2	5	6	p
$P(X = x)$	0.2	0.3	0.1	0.4

If E(X) = 6.5 find the value of p.

Q2 b) Hint: Find a first.

b)

x	4	8	p	15
$P(X = x)$	0.5	0.2	a	0.2

If E(X) = 7.5 find the values of a and p.

Q3 Each table below shows the probability distribution of a discrete random variable, X. Use the information given to find a and b for each.

a)

x	1	2	3	4
$P(X = x)$	0.2	a	0.1	b

where E(X) = 2.5

b)

x	3	7	8	12
$P(X = x)$	0.1	a	b	0.1

where E(X) = 7.8

Q4 In parts a)-c), the tables show the probability distribution for a discrete random variable, X. For each part, find: (i) E(X)   (ii) E(X^2)

a)

x	1	2	3	4	5
$P(X = x)$	0.2	0.1	0.25	0.25	0.2

b)

x	−3	−2	−1	0	1
$P(X = x)$	0.2	0.1	0.25	0.25	0.2

c)

x	3	4	5	7	9
$P(X = x)$	0.1	0.25	0.15	0.3	0.2

Variance

Variance is a measure of **dispersion** — it measures how **spread out** values are from the mean.

Just like you can find the **mean** (μ) of a discrete random variable, you can also find its **variance**. This measures the **spread** of the random variable's distribution about its mean. Again, it's a theoretical value — it's the '**expected variance**' of a large number of readings.

The graphs below show the probability distributions of two **discrete random variables**, X and Y:

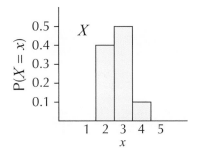
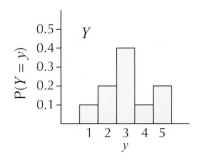

If you were to collect a large number of readings of both X and Y, you'd expect the readings of X to be **less spread out** than the readings of Y.

But... even if you **don't** collect any actual readings of X or Y, you can still work out the variance of X and Y based on their probability distributions. And you'd expect the variance of X to be **smaller** than that of Y.

Now then... suppose a **discrete random variable** X can take values x_1, x_2, x_3,... The variance of X is 'the expected squared deviation from the mean (μ)' — in other words: $\text{Var}(X) = E[(X - \mu)^2] = \sum(x_i - \mu)^2 p_i$ (see Tip above).

But there's a different way to write the formula for the variance that's much **easier to use**:

$$\text{Var}(X) = E(X^2) - [E(X)]^2 = \sum x_i^2 p_i - \left[\sum x_i p_i\right]^2$$

In fact, the formula for the variance can be written in various ways. For example, on the formula sheet you'll get in the exam, it's written as:

$$\text{Var}(X) = \sum(x_i - \mu)^2 P(X = x_i) = \sum x_i^2 P(X = x_i) - \mu^2$$

But these formulas are all **equivalent** — they'll always give the same answers. And you can always take one of these formulas and 'turn it into' any of the others — just by rearranging it, and using the definitions on the right. For example:

$$
\begin{aligned}
\text{Var}(X) &= E[(X - \mu)^2] \\
&= E[X^2 - 2\mu X + \mu^2] &&\text{(multiplying out the brackets)} \\
&= E(X^2) - 2\mu E(X) + \mu^2 &&\text{(see the bottom Tip for more info)} \\
&= E(X^2) - 2[E(X)]^2 + [E(X)]^2 &&\text{(using the definition } \mu = E(X)) \\
&= E(X^2) - [E(X)]^2
\end{aligned}
$$

Tip: The variance of a data set is given by

$$\text{variance} = \frac{\sum(x - \bar{x})^2}{n}$$

— so the variance is 'the average squared deviation from the mean' — see page 31.

Tip: $E[(X - \mu)^2]$
$$= \sum(x_i - \mu)^2 p_i$$
because to work out an expected value, you always:

(i) swap the random variable in the expression for each of its possible values — so here you need to find $(x_i - \mu)^2$ for the various possible values x_i,

(ii) multiply each of those values by the probability (p_i) of x_i,

(iii) sum the results.

Tip: You can remember the variance formula as:

'mean of the square minus the square of the mean.'

Tip: Remember...

(i) $P(X = x_i) = p_i$

(ii) $E(X) = \mu = \sum x_i p_i$

(iii) $E(X^2) = \sum x_i^2 p_i$

Tip: You'll see on p96 that
$E(aX + b) = aE(X) + b$

This tells you that you can 'break apart' an expected value involving addition, or multiplication by a **number** (not by another variable, though). This means you can write
$E[X^2 - 2\mu X + \mu^2]$ as
$E(X^2) - 2\mu E(X) + \mu^2$.

Example 1

**X has the probability function $P(X = x) = k(x + 1)$ $x = 0, 1, 2, 3, 4$.
Find the mean and variance of X.**

- First you need to find k.
  Work out all the probabilities and remember they add up to 1:

  $$P(X = 0) = k \times (0 + 1) = k$$

  Similarly, $P(X = 1) = 2k$
  $$P(X = 2) = 3k$$
  $$P(X = 3) = 4k$$
  $$P(X = 4) = 5k$$

  So $k + 2k + 3k + 4k + 5k = 1$, i.e. $15k = 1$, and so $k = \frac{1}{15}$

- Now use the formulas — find the **mean, E(X),** first:

  $$E(X) = \sum x_i p_i$$
  $$= \left[0 \times \tfrac{1}{15}\right] + \left[1 \times \tfrac{2}{15}\right] + \left[2 \times \tfrac{3}{15}\right] + \left[3 \times \tfrac{4}{15}\right] + \left[4 \times \tfrac{5}{15}\right]$$
  $$= \frac{40}{15} = \boxed{\frac{8}{3}}$$

- For the **variance** you also need **$E(X^2)$**:

  $$E(X^2) = \sum x_i^2 p_i$$
  $$= \left[0^2 \times \tfrac{1}{15}\right] + \left[1^2 \times \tfrac{2}{15}\right] + \left[2^2 \times \tfrac{3}{15}\right] + \left[3^2 \times \tfrac{4}{15}\right] + \left[4^2 \times \tfrac{5}{15}\right]$$
  $$= \frac{130}{15} = \frac{26}{3}$$

Tip: Work out the variance in steps to avoid making mistakes.

You know E(X), so now find E(X²).

Then put them both into the formula for variance.

- And finally:

  $$Var(X) = E(X^2) - [E(X)]^2 = \frac{26}{3} - \left[\frac{8}{3}\right]^2 = \boxed{\frac{14}{9}}$$

Example 2

The discrete random variable X has the following probability distribution:

x	1	4	p	8
$P(X = x)$	0.2	a	0.5	0.2

If E(X) = 5.2, find the values of a and p and the variance of X.

- First find the value of a.
  Use the fact that the sum of the probabilities must be 1:

  $$0.2 + a + 0.5 + 0.2 = 1$$
  $$\Rightarrow 0.9 + a = 1$$
  $$\Rightarrow \boxed{a = 0.1}$$

- Now use $E(X) = 5.2$ to find the value of p:

$$E(X) = [1 \times 0.2] + [4 \times 0.1] + [p \times 0.5] + [8 \times 0.2]$$
$$= 2.2 + 0.5p$$

So $5.2 = 2.2 + 0.5p$

$\Rightarrow \quad 3 = 0.5p$

$\Rightarrow \quad \boxed{p = 6}$

$a = 0.1$

- Now work out $E(X^2)$ so you can calculate the variance.

$$E(X^2) = [1^2 \times 0.2] + [4^2 \times 0.1] + [6^2 \times 0.5] + [8^2 \times 0.2]$$
$$= [1 \times 0.2] + [16 \times 0.1] + [36 \times 0.5] + [64 \times 0.2] = 32.6$$

So $\mathrm{Var}(X) = E(X^2) - [E(X)]^2 = 32.6 - 5.2^2 = 32.6 - 27.04 = \boxed{5.56}$

Exercise 2.2

Q1 For each of the following probability distributions, calculate the mean and variance of X.

a)

x	1	2	3	4	5
$p(x)$	0.2	0.1	0.2	0.1	0.4

b)

x	1	3	6	8	9	10
$p(x)$	$\frac{1}{2}$	$\frac{1}{4}$	$\frac{1}{8}$	$\frac{1}{16}$	$\frac{1}{32}$	$\frac{1}{32}$

c)

x	-2	-1	0	1	2
$p(x)$	0.2	0.1	0.2	0.1	0.4

Q2 Each of the probability functions below defines a discrete random variable, X. Calculate the mean and variance of X.

a) $P(X = x) = \frac{1}{5}$ $x = 1, 2, 3, 4, 5$ b) $P(X = x) = \frac{x^2}{30}$ $x = 1, 2, 3, 4$

Q3 For each of the probability distributions below:
(i) Find a.   (ii) Find the mean and variance of X.

a)

x	1	2	3	4
$P(X = x)$	0.2	a	0.4	0.1

b)

x	-3	-2	-1	0
$P(X = x)$	a	0.3	a	0.1

Q4 Each of the probability distributions below describes a discrete random variable, X.

a)

x	3	4	6	p
$P(X = x)$	0.2	0.3	0.1	0.4

If $E(X) = 5.2$, find the value of p and the variance of X.

b)

x	1	4	p	9
$P(X = x)$	0.2	a	0.4	0.3

If $E(X) = 5.7$, find the values of a and p and the variance of X.

Q5 Each of the probability functions below describes a discrete random variable, X. For each: (i) Find k (ii) Find $E(X)$ (iii) Find $\mathrm{Var}(X)$

a) $P(X = x) = kx^2$ $x = 3, 4, 5$ b) $P(X = x) = \frac{k}{x}$ $x = 3, 4, 5, 6$

Expected value and variance of a function of X

Tip: A function of X is just an expression involving X.

You can find the **expected value** and the **variance** of any function of X, $g(X)$.

If the function of X is **linear** (i.e. of the form $aX + b$, where a and b are any numbers), there are two helpful rules that will speed things up:

Tip: On the exam formula sheet, you're given the formula:
$$E[g(X)]$$
$$= \sum g(x_i)P(X = x_i)$$
for a function of X, $g(X)$.

If you were to put the function $g(X) = aX + b$ into this formula and simplify, you'd get the rule for $E(aX + b)$ shown here.

$$E(aX + b) = aE(X) + b \qquad\qquad Var(aX + b) = a^2Var(X)$$

Example 1

If $E(X) = 3$ and $Var(X) = 7$, find:

a) $E(2X + 5)$ b) $Var(2X + 5)$ c) $E(2 - 4X)$

d) $Var(X - 2)$ e) $Var\left(\dfrac{X}{2}\right)$

Tip: On p91 we were actually finding $E(g(X))$, where $g(X) = X^2$.

a) The function of X is $2X + 5$, so let $a = 2$ and $b = 5$ and use the formula for $E(aX + b)$:
$$E(2X + 5) = 2E(X) + 5 = (2 \times 3) + 5 = \boxed{11}$$
$$E(X) = 3$$

b) The function of X is $2X + 5$, so let $a = 2$ and $b = 5$ and use the formula for $Var(aX + b)$:
$$Var(2X + 5) = 2^2Var(X) = 4 \times 7 = \boxed{28}$$
$$Var(X) = 7$$

c) The function of X is $2 - 4X$. Don't get confused about it being the wrong way round — it's just the same as $-4X + 2$. So let $a = -4$ and $b = 2$:
$$E(2 - 4X) = -4E(X) + 2 = (-4 \times 3) + 2 = \boxed{-10}$$

d) The function of X is $X - 2$, so let $a = 1$ and $b = -2$:
$$Var(X - 2) = 1^2\,Var(X) = \boxed{7}$$

e) The function of X is $\dfrac{X}{2}$. This is just the same as $\dfrac{1}{2}X + 0$, so let $a = \dfrac{1}{2}$ and $b = 0$:
$$Var\left(\frac{X}{2}\right) = \left(\frac{1}{2}\right)^2 Var(X) = \frac{1}{4} \times 7 = \boxed{\frac{7}{4}}$$

Example 2

The discrete random variable X has the following probability distribution:

x	2	3	4	5	6
$P(X = x)$	0.1	0.2	0.3	0.2	k

Find: **a)** k, **b)** $E(X)$, **c)** $Var(X)$, **d)** $E(3X - 1)$, **e)** $Var(3X - 1)$

a) Using the fact that the probabilities add up to 1 —
$0.1 + 0.2 + 0.3 + 0.2 + k = 1$, and so $k = 0.2$

b) Now you can use the formula to find $E(X)$:
$E(X) = \sum x_i p_i$
$= (2 \times 0.1) + (3 \times 0.2) + (4 \times 0.3) + (5 \times 0.2) + (6 \times 0.2) = 4.2$

c) Next work out $E(X^2)$ so you can use it to find the variance:
$E(X^2) = \sum x_i^2 p_i$
$= [2^2 \times 0.1] + [3^2 \times 0.2] + [4^2 \times 0.3]$
$+ [5^2 \times 0.2] + [6^2 \times 0.2]$
$= 19.2$

Then the variance is easy:
$Var(X) = E(X^2) - [E(X)]^2 = 19.2 - 4.2^2 = 1.56$

d) Using the formula for $E(aX + b)$:
$E(3X - 1) = 3E(X) - 1 = 3 \times 4.2 - 1 = 11.6$

e) And finally: $Var(3X - 1) = 3^2 Var(X) = 9 \times 1.56 = 14.04$

Exercise 2.3

Q1 X is a discrete random variable with $E(X) = 4$ and $Var(X) = 3$.
Write down the mean and variance of the following random variables:
a) $Y = X + 3$ b) $Z = 5X$ c) $W = 2X - 7$ d) $V = 7 - 2X$

Q2 X is a discrete random variable with probability distribution:

x	1	2	3	4	5
$P(X = x)$	0.1	0.2	0.3	0.2	0.2

$E(X) = 3.2$ and $Var(X) = 1.56$.

For each of the random variables in a)-d) below, find:
(i)   the probability distribution,
(ii) the mean and variance directly from the probability distribution,
(iii) the mean and variance using the values of $E(X)$ and $Var(X)$ given.
a) $Y = 3X + 4$ b) $Z = 3X - 4$ c) $V = 20 - 3X$ d) $W = 20 + 3X$

Q2 Hint: The probability distribution of a function of X is easy to find — just apply the function to the values of x, but keep the probabilities the same (just like we did with X^2 on p91).

Q3 a) The random variable X is given by the probability distribution:

x	8	10	15	20
$P(X = x)$	0.2	0.3	0.1	0.4

    (i)   Find $E(X)$ and $Var(X)$.

    (ii) $Y = 4X + 3$. Find $E(Y)$ and $Var(Y)$.

    (iii) $Z = 50 - 2X$. Find $E(Z)$ and $Var(Z)$.

b) The random variable X is given by the probability distribution:

x	−4	−1	0	2	5	6
$P(X = x)$	$\frac{1}{2}$	$\frac{1}{4}$	$\frac{1}{8}$	$\frac{1}{16}$	$\frac{1}{32}$	$\frac{1}{32}$

    (i)   Find $E(X)$ and $Var(X)$.

    (ii) $Y = 7 - 2X$. Find $E(Y)$ and $Var(Y)$.

    (iii) $Z = 7 + 2X$. Find $E(Z)$ and $Var(Z)$.

Q4 The random variable X is given by the probability distribution:

x	10	12	13	15	16
$P(X = x)$	0.2	0.3	0.1	0.3	0.1

Q4 Hint: Don't get confused by the letters m and c in this one — just treat them as numbers when working out the expected values.

a) Find $E(X)$ and $Var(X)$.

b) $Y = 26 - mX$. If $E(Y) = 0$, find m and $Var(Y)$.

c) $Z = 3X - c$. If $E(Z) = 30$, find c and $Var(Z)$.

The discrete uniform distribution

Sometimes you'll have a random variable where every value of X is **equally likely** — this is called a **uniform** distribution. For example, rolling a normal, unbiased dice gives you a **discrete uniform distribution**.

The probability distribution of a random variable with a discrete uniform distribution always has the same shape as the one below. This diagram shows the probability distribution for X, where X takes **consecutive whole number** values between a and b with equal probability.

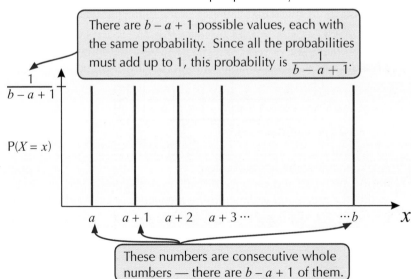

There are $b - a + 1$ possible values, each with the same probability. Since all the probabilities must add up to 1, this probability is $\frac{1}{b - a + 1}$.

These numbers are consecutive whole numbers — there are $b - a + 1$ of them.

You can use the same formulas for **E(X)** and **Var(X)** as you have done for all other discrete random variables throughout the chapter — so you don't **need** to learn any new ones.

But for a discrete uniform distribution X which can take **consecutive whole number** values $a, a + 1, a + 2,..., b$, you get nice simple formulas for the **mean** and **variance**. These will save you some time if you can remember them.

$$\text{Mean} = E(X) = \frac{a + b}{2}$$

$$\text{Variance} = \text{Var}(X) = \frac{(b - a + 1)^2 - 1}{12}$$

Example 1

Find the mean and variance of the score on an unbiased, standard six-sided dice.

If X is the random variable 'score on a dice', then X has the discrete uniform distribution shown in the table:

x	1	2	3	4	5	6
$P(X = x)$	$\frac{1}{6}$	$\frac{1}{6}$	$\frac{1}{6}$	$\frac{1}{6}$	$\frac{1}{6}$	$\frac{1}{6}$

The smallest value of x is 1 and the biggest is 6 — so $a = 1$ and $b = 6$.
Now just substitute these values into the formulas:

$\text{Mean} = \frac{a + b}{2} = \frac{1 + 6}{2} = \frac{7}{2} = \boxed{3.5}$

$\text{Variance} = \frac{(b - a + 1)^2 - 1}{12} = \frac{(6 - 1 + 1)^2 - 1}{12} = \frac{35}{12} = \boxed{2.92 \text{ to 3 s.f.}}$

Tip: The symmetry of the distribution should tell you where the mean is — it has to be halfway between 1 and 6.

Example 2

A lottery involves a ball being picked at random from a box of 30 balls numbered from 11 to 40. The random variable X represents the number on the first ball to be picked. Write down the probability function of X, and find its mean and variance.

Each ball has a probability of $\frac{1}{30}$ of being picked first, so the probability function is:

$$P(X = x) = \frac{1}{30}, \quad x = 11, 12, ..., 40$$

The smallest value is 11 and the largest is 40, so $a = 11$ and $b = 40$.
Using the formulas:

$\text{Mean} = \frac{a + b}{2} = \frac{11 + 40}{2} = \frac{51}{2} = \boxed{25.5}$

$\text{Variance} = \frac{(b - a + 1)^2 - 1}{12} = \frac{(40 - 11 + 1)^2 - 1}{12} = \frac{899}{12} = \boxed{74.9 \text{ to 3 s.f.}}$

Q1 A random variable, X, has a discrete uniform distribution and can take consecutive integer values between 1 and 5 inclusive. Draw a table showing the distribution of X, and find $E(X)$ and $Var(X)$.

Q2 A random variable, Y, has a discrete uniform distribution and can take consecutive integer values between 12 and 15 inclusive. Draw a table showing the distribution of Y, and find $E(Y)$ and $Var(Y)$.

Q3 A random variable, Z, has a discrete uniform distribution given by the probability function:
$$P(Z = z) = \frac{1}{10} \quad z = 11, 12, ..., 20$$
Draw a table showing the distribution of Z, and find the mean and standard deviation of Z.

Q3 Hint: Recall that the **standard deviation** is the square root of the variance.

Q4 A random variable, D, has a discrete uniform distribution given by the probability function:
$$P(D = d) = \frac{1}{6} \quad d = 1, 3, 5, 7, 9, 11$$
Find: a) The mean of D b) The variance of D

Q4 Hint: The values of d aren't consecutive whole numbers.

Q5 A random variable, X, has a discrete uniform distribution given by the probability function:
$$P(X = x) = \frac{1}{8} \quad x = 1, 2, 3, 4, 5, 6, 7, 8$$
a) Find the mean, μ, and variance, σ^2, of X.
b) Calculate $P(|X - \mu| < \sigma)$

Q5 Hint: Part b) may look tricky, but just break down the event $|X - \mu| < \sigma$ into all possible cases and add up the separate probabilities.

Q6 A random variable, Y, has a discrete uniform distribution and can take the value of any single-digit non-negative integer (including zero).
a) Find the mean, μ, and variance, σ^2, of Y.
b) Calculate $P(|Y - \mu| > \sigma)$
c) Calculate $P(|Y - \mu| > 2\sigma)$

Q7 A random variable, Z, has a discrete uniform distribution and can take consecutive integer values from 1 to 7.
a) Find the mean and variance of Z.
b) Calculate the mean and variance of $X = 2 - 2Z$.

Review Exercise — Chapter 3

Q1 The probability distribution of Y is:

y	0	1	2	3
$P(Y = y)$	0.5	k	k	$3k$

 a) Find the value of k. b) Find $P(Y < 2)$.

Q2 The probability distribution for the random variable W is given in the table.
Draw up a table to show the cumulative distribution function.

w	0.2	0.3	0.4	0.5
$P(W = w)$	0.2	0.2	0.3	0.3

Q3 Each probability function below describes a discrete random variable, X.
In each case, draw a table showing the cumulative distribution function,
and use it to find the required probabilities.

 a) $P(X = x) = \dfrac{(x + 2)}{25}$ $x = 1, 2, 3, 4, 5$ Find (i) $P(X \le 3)$ (ii) $P(1 < X \le 3)$

 b) $P(X = x) = \dfrac{1}{8}$ $x = 1, 2, 3, 4, 5, 6, 7, 8$ Find (i) $P(X \le 3)$ (ii) $P(3 < X \le 7)$

Q4 The cumulative distribution function for a random variable R is given in the table.
Work out the probability distribution for R. Find $P(0 \le R \le 1)$.

r	0	1	2
$F(r) = P(R \le r)$	0.1	0.5	1

Q5 The discrete random variable X has a uniform distribution, $P(X = x) = k$ for $x = 0, 1, 2, 3, 4$.
Find the value of k, and then find the mean and variance of X.

Q6 A discrete random variable X has the probability distribution shown in the table,
where k is a constant.

x_i	1	2	3	4
p_i	$\dfrac{1}{6}$	$\dfrac{1}{2}$	k	$\dfrac{5}{24}$

 a) Find k b) Find $E(X)$ and show that $Var(X) = \dfrac{63}{64}$ c) Find $E(2X - 1)$ and $Var(2X - 1)$

Q7 A discrete random variable X has the probability distribution shown in the table.

x_i	1	2	3	4	5	6
p_i	0.1	0.2	0.25	0.2	0.1	0.15

 a) Find $E(X)$ b) Find $Var(X)$

Q8 X is the random variable 'highest score showing when three fair
six-sided dice are rolled'. Find the cumulative distribution function
for X, and then use it to find the probability distribution for X.

Q8 Hint: You're looking for $F(x) = P(X \le x)$. Find the probability that a single fair six-sided dice has a score no more than x and remember that dice rolls are independent.

Exam-Style Questions — Chapter 3

1 In a game a player tosses three fair coins.
If three heads occur then the player gets 20p; if two heads occur then the player gets 10p.
For any other outcome, the player gets nothing.

a) If X is the random variable 'amount received', tabulate the probability distribution of X.

(4 marks)

The player pays 10p to play one game.

b) Use the probability distribution to find the probability that the player wins (i.e. gets more money than they pay to play) in one game.

(2 marks)

2 A discrete random variable X can only take values 0, 1, 2 and 3.
Its probability distribution is shown below.

x	0	1	2	3
$P(X = x)$	$2k$	$3k$	k	k

a) Find the value of k.

(1 mark)

b) Draw up a table to show the cumulative distribution function for X.

(4 marks)

c) Find $P(X > 2)$.

(1 mark)

3 The random variable X takes the following values with equal probability:

0, 1, 2, 3, 4, 5, 6, 7, 8, 9

a) Write down the probability distribution of X.

(1 mark)

b) Find the mean and variance of X.

(3 marks)

c) Calculate the probability that X is less than the mean.

(2 marks)

4   A discrete random variable X has the probability function:
    $P(X = x) = ax$ for $x = 1, 2, 3$, where a is a constant.

    a)   Show that $a = \frac{1}{6}$.

    (1 mark)

    b)   Find E(X).

    (2 marks)

    c)   If Var(X) = $\frac{5}{9}$ find E(X^2).

    (2 marks)

    d)   Find E($3X + 4$) and Var($3X + 4$).

    (3 marks)

5   The number of points awarded to each contestant in a talent competition is given by
    the discrete random variable X with the following probability distribution:

x	0	1	2	3
P($X = x$)	0.4	0.3	0.2	0.1

    a)   Find E(X).

    (2 marks)

    b)   Find E($6X + 8$).

    (2 marks)

    c)   Show that Var(X) = 1.

    (4 marks)

    d)   Find Var($5 - 3X$).

    (2 marks)

6   The discrete random variable X is given by the probability distribution:

x	0	1	2	3
P($X = x$)	a	$5b$	b	0.2

    Given that E(X) = 1.3:

    a)   Find a and b.

    (5 marks)

    b)   Find E($\frac{10}{13}X + 3$).

    (2 marks)

    c)   Show that Var(X) = 1.01.

    (3 marks)

    d)   Find Var($4 - X$).

    (2 marks]

1. Correlation

Correlation is all about how closely two quantities are linked.
For example, as one quantity grows, the other might grow as well.
Or it might shrink. Or there might be no pattern at all to what it does.

Scatter diagrams and correlation

Sometimes variables are measured in **pairs** — maybe because you want to investigate whether they're linked.

These pairs of variables might be things like:

- 'my age' and 'length of my feet',
- 'temperature' and 'number of accidents on a stretch of road'.

Data made up of pairs of values (x, y) is called **bivariate data**. You can plot bivariate data on a **scatter diagram** — where each variable is plotted along one of the axes. The pattern of points on a scatter diagram can tell you something about the data.

- For example, on this scatter diagram, the variables 'my age' and 'length of my feet' seem linked — you can tell because nearly all the points lie **close** to a **straight line**.

- As I got older, my feet got bigger and bigger (though I stopped measuring when I was 10 years old).

- The **line of best fit** on this scatter diagram lies **close** to **most** of the points.

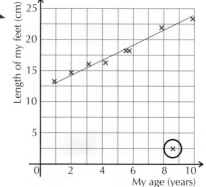

- The circled point doesn't fit the pattern of the rest of the data at all — so the line of best fit doesn't need to pass close to it. A point like this could show a measurement error (like here), or just a 'freak' observation.

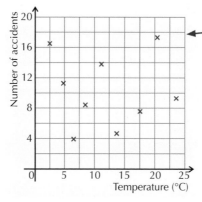

- It's a lot harder to see any connection between the variables 'temperature' and 'number of accidents' on this scatter diagram — the data seems scattered pretty much everywhere.

- You can't draw a line of best fit for this data — there isn't a line that lies close to **most** of the points. (It would be hard to draw a line lying close to more than about half the points.)

Correlation is all about whether points on a scatter diagram lie close to a **straight line**.

- Sometimes, as one variable gets bigger, the other one also gets bigger — in this case, the scatter diagram might look like this.
- Here, a line of best fit would have a **positive gradient**.
- The two variables are **positively correlated**.

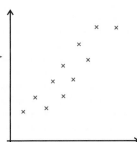

Tip: Or you can say there's a **positive correlation** between them.

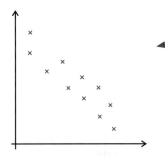

- But if one variable gets smaller as the other one gets bigger, then the scatter diagram would look like this.
- In this case, a line of best fit would have a **negative gradient**.
- The two variables are **negatively correlated**.

Tip: Or you can say there's a **negative correlation** between them.

- And if the two variables are **not** linked at all, you'd expect a **random scattering** of points.
- It's impossible to draw a line of best fit close to most of the points.
- The variables are **not correlated**.

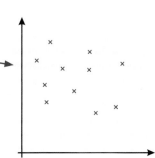

Tip: Or you can say there's **no correlation** between them.

Exercise 1.1

Q1 Owen asked a group of people how far from the town centre they live, and how many visits they made to the cinema in the previous year. The table shows his results.

Distance from centre (km)	0.6	7.0	1.4	16.8	10.4	3.6	9.2
Cinema visits	14	15	21	3	10	18	11

a) Plot a scatter diagram to show this data.

b) Describe the type of correlation shown.

Q2 This table shows the average length and the average circumference of eggs for several species of bird. (All distances are measured in cm.)

Length	6.2	2.1	3.4	5.7	11.9	10	7.2	4.5	6.8
Circumference	14	6.3	7.1	7.4	3.5	24	18.7	11.3	18.4

a) Plot a scatter diagram to show this data.

b) Describe the type of correlation shown.

c) One of the measurements was recorded incorrectly. Use your scatter diagram to determine which one.

S_{xx}, S_{yy} and S_{xy}

Suppose you've got a set of **bivariate** data written as n pairs of values (x, y).

Tip: The formula for variance on page 31 is:
$$\text{variance} = \frac{\sum(x - \overline{x})^2}{n}$$

The formula for the **variance** of the x-values can be written: $\boxed{\text{variance}_x = \dfrac{S_{xx}}{n}}$

where $\boxed{S_{xx} = \sum(x - \overline{x})^2 = \sum x^2 - \dfrac{\left(\sum x\right)^2}{n}}$

Tip: The forms
$$S_{xx} = \sum x^2 - \frac{\left(\sum x\right)^2}{n} \text{ and}$$
$$S_{yy} = \sum y^2 - \frac{\left(\sum y\right)^2}{n}$$
are easier to use.

Similarly, the **variance** of the y-values can be written: $\boxed{\text{variance}_y = \dfrac{S_{yy}}{n}}$

where $\boxed{S_{yy} = \sum(y - \overline{y})^2 = \sum y^2 - \dfrac{\left(\sum y\right)^2}{n}}$

Tip: The form
$$S_{xy} = \sum xy - \frac{\sum x \sum y}{n}$$
is easier to use.

There's also a similar quantity S_{xy} that involves **both** x and y.

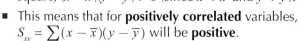
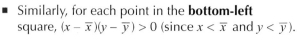

$$S_{xy} = \sum(x - \overline{x})(y - \overline{y}) = \sum xy - \frac{\sum x \sum y}{n}$$

To get a feel for what S_{xy} means, look at the scatter diagrams below. The dotted lines show the value of $\overline{x}$ (the mean of the x-values) and $\overline{y}$ (the mean of the y-values).

Tip: The formulas for S_{xx}, S_{yy} and S_{xy} will be important for the rest of this chapter.

- This scatter diagram shows a pair of variables (x and y) that are **positively correlated** — so most of the values fall in the shaded squares.
- For each point in the **top-right** square, $(x - \overline{x})(y - \overline{y}) > 0$ (since $x > \overline{x}$ and $y > \overline{y}$).
- Similarly, for each point in the **bottom-left** square, $(x - \overline{x})(y - \overline{y}) > 0$ (since $x < \overline{x}$ and $y < \overline{y}$).
- This means that for **positively correlated** variables, $S_{xy} = \sum(x - \overline{x})(y - \overline{y})$ will be **positive**.

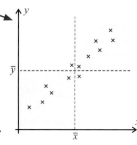

Tip: On the graph, there are two points for which $(x - \overline{x})(y - \overline{y})$ is negative, but there are far more for which $(x - \overline{x})(y - \overline{y})$ is positive.

So overall, S_{xy} is positive.

- In this scatter diagram, x and y are **negatively correlated**. Again, most values fall in the shaded squares.
- For each point in the **top-left** square, $(x - \overline{x})(y - \overline{y}) < 0$ (since $x < \overline{x}$ but $y > \overline{y}$).
- And for each point in the **bottom-right** square, $(x - \overline{x})(y - \overline{y}) < 0$ (since $x > \overline{x}$ but $y < \overline{y}$).
- So for **negatively correlated** variables, $S_{xy} = \sum(x - \overline{x})(y - \overline{y})$ will be **negative**.

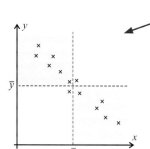

Tip: There are two points for which $(x - \overline{x})(y - \overline{y})$ is positive, but there are far more for which $(x - \overline{x})(y - \overline{y})$ is negative.

Overall, S_{xy} is negative.

Tip: The positive and negative values of $(x - \overline{x})(y - \overline{y})$ largely cancel each other out.

What's left after all this cancelling will be close to zero.

- In this scatter diagram, x and y are **not correlated**.
- In this case, about half the points give a positive value for $(x - \overline{x})(y - \overline{y})$, while the other half give a negative value.
- So $S_{xy} = \sum(x - \overline{x})(y - \overline{y})$ ends up close to zero.

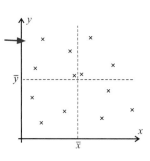

Example 1

Find S_{xy}, S_{xx} and S_{yy} for the data on the right.

x	1.1	1.5	2.3	2.9	3.1	3.8
y	5	8	11	16	17	24

Tip: The formulas for S_{xy}, S_{xx} and S_{yy} are on the formula sheet you'll be given in the exam.

- You're going to need to find $\sum x$, $\sum y$, $\sum x^2$, $\sum y^2$ and $\sum xy$.

  So add rows to the table showing x^2, y^2 and xy.
  And add an extra column to show the total of each row.

x	1.1	1.5	2.3	2.9	3.1	3.8	$\sum x = 14.7$
y	5	8	11	16	17	24	$\sum y = 81$
x^2	1.21	2.25	5.29	8.41	9.61	14.44	$\sum x^2 = 41.21$
y^2	25	64	121	256	289	576	$\sum y^2 = 1331$
xy	5.5	12	25.3	46.4	52.7	91.2	$\sum xy = 233.1$

Tip: Always draw a table — it'll help you avoid mistakes.

- Now you can use the formulas for S_{xy}, S_{xx} and S_{yy}.

$$S_{xy} = \sum xy - \frac{\sum x \sum y}{n} = 233.1 - \frac{14.7 \times 81}{6} = \boxed{34.65}$$

$$S_{xx} = \sum x^2 - \frac{(\sum x)^2}{n} = 41.21 - \frac{14.7^2}{6} = \boxed{5.195}$$

$$S_{yy} = \sum y^2 - \frac{(\sum y)^2}{n} = 1331 - \frac{81^2}{6} = \boxed{237.5}$$

Tip: Remember... n is the number of pairs of data values.

Exam questions won't always use the letters x and y to label bivariate data. But you can still use the formulas for S_{xx}, S_{yy} and S_{xy} by replacing x and y with the letters in the question.

Example 2

Use the following summations to find S_{pq}, S_{pp} and S_{qq}.

$$\sum p = 15.7, \quad \sum q = 36, \quad \sum p^2 = 45.55, \quad \sum q^2 = 278, \quad \sum pq = 93.2, \quad n = 5$$

- To find S_{pq} use the formula for S_{xy} — replacing x with p and y with q.

$$S_{pq} = \sum pq - \frac{\sum p \sum q}{n} = 93.2 - \frac{15.7 \times 36}{5} = \boxed{-19.84}$$

- To find S_{pp} use the formula for S_{xx} — but wherever you see x, write p.

$$S_{pp} = \sum p^2 - \frac{(\sum p)^2}{n} = 45.55 - \frac{15.7^2}{5} = \boxed{-3.748}$$

- Do a similar kind of thing to find S_{qq}.

$$S_{qq} = \sum q^2 - \frac{(\sum q)^2}{n} = 278 - \frac{36^2}{5} = \boxed{18.8}$$

Q1 For the data shown in the table on the right:

x	11	6	9	4	8	2	5
y	24	13	18	5	19	1	12

a) Calculate $\sum x$, $\sum y$, $\sum xy$, $\sum x^2$ and $\sum y^2$.

b) Use your summations to calculate S_{xy}, S_{xx} and S_{yy}.

Q2 Find S_{xy}, S_{xx} and S_{yy} in each case below.

a) $\sum x = 29$ $\sum y = 109$ $\sum x^2 = 167$

  $\sum y^2 = 2031$ $\sum xy = 589$ $n = 5$

b) $\sum x = 206$ $\sum y = 50$ $\sum x^2 = 4504$

  $\sum y^2 = 326$ $\sum xy = 1013$ $n = 10$

Q3 Find S_{pq}, S_{pp} and S_{qq} given the information below.

$\sum p = 115$ $\sum q = 114$ $\sum p^2 = 2383$

$\sum q^2 = 2762$ $\sum pq = 1880$ $n = 6$

Product moment correlation coefficient

The **product moment correlation coefficient** (PMCC, or r for short) measures the strength of the correlation between two variables. It basically tells you how close to a straight line the points on a scatter diagram lie.

The formula for the PMCC involves S_{xy}, S_{xx} and S_{yy}:

$$r = \frac{S_{xy}}{\sqrt{S_{xx}S_{yy}}}$$

Tip: In reality, you'd never expect to get a PMCC of +1 or –1 — your scatter diagram points might lie pretty close to a straight line, but it's unlikely they'd all be on it.

The PMCC is always between +1 and –1.

- If all your points lie **exactly on a straight line** with a **positive** gradient (perfect positive correlation), $r = +1$.
- If all your points lie **exactly on a straight line** with a **negative** gradient (perfect negative correlation), $r = -1$.
- If $r = 0$ (or more likely, pretty close to 0), that would mean the variables **aren't correlated**.

Tip: The closer the value of r to +1 or –1, the stronger the correlation between the two variables. (Values close to +1 mean a strong positive correlation, and values close to –1 mean a strong negative correlation.)

Values of r close to zero mean there is only a weak correlation (but see p113).

These graphs give you an idea of 'what different values of r look like'.

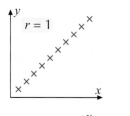

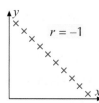

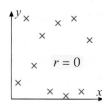

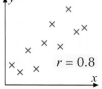

Example 1

The following data show the score (x) of 10 students in a reading test, and the time in seconds (y) it took them to run 40 metres.

x	3.5	5.5	6.1	4.2	2.7	1.9	5.5	3.8	5.1	3.7
y	9.8	4.7	8.4	8.4	5.8	8.4	7.6	8.2	8.9	5.4

Illustrate the data with a scatter diagram, and find the product moment correlation coefficient (r) between the variables x and y.

- The **scatter diagram's** the easy bit — just plot the points.

- Now for the **correlation coefficient**. From the scatter diagram, the points look pretty randomly scattered — so you'd expect a correlation coefficient fairly close to zero.

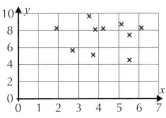

- You need to find S_{xy}, S_{xx} and S_{yy}, so add a few extra rows to your table.

x	3.5	5.5	6.1	4.2	2.7	1.9	5.5	3.8	5.1	3.7	$\sum x = 42$
y	9.8	4.7	8.4	8.4	5.8	8.4	7.6	8.2	8.9	5.4	$\sum y = 75.6$
x^2	12.25	30.25	37.21	17.64	7.29	3.61	30.25	14.44	26.01	13.69	$\sum x^2 = 192.64$
y^2	96.04	22.09	70.56	70.56	33.64	70.56	57.76	67.24	79.21	29.16	$\sum y^2 = 596.82$
xy	34.3	25.85	51.24	35.28	15.66	15.96	41.8	31.16	45.39	19.98	$\sum xy = 316.62$

- This gives:
$$S_{xy} = \sum xy - \frac{\sum x \sum y}{n} = 316.62 - \frac{42 \times 75.6}{10} = -0.9$$

$$S_{xx} = \sum x^2 - \frac{(\sum x)^2}{n} = 192.64 - \frac{42^2}{10} = 16.24$$

$$S_{yy} = \sum y^2 - \frac{(\sum y)^2}{n} = 596.82 - \frac{75.6^2}{10} = 25.284$$

- Now use the formula for r: $\quad r = \dfrac{S_{xy}}{\sqrt{S_{xx}S_{yy}}}$

$$= \frac{-0.9}{\sqrt{16.24 \times 25.284}} = -0.044 \text{ (to 3 d.p.)}$$

Tip: This is very close to zero — there seems to be little (if any) correlation between these two variables.

Example 2

A scientist collects data on the percentage water content (w) of 8 different brands of ham, and its price in pounds (p) per 100 g.
The results are summarised below.

$$\sum w = 152 \quad \sum p = 7.73 \quad \sum w^2 = 3492 \quad \sum p^2 = 8.0169 \quad \sum wp = 130.41$$

a) **Calculate the product moment correlation coefficient (r).**

- Here, $S_{wp} = \sum wp - \dfrac{\sum w \sum p}{n} = 130.41 - \dfrac{152 \times 7.73}{8} = -16.46$

$$S_{ww} = \sum w^2 - \frac{(\sum w)^2}{n} = 3492 - \frac{152^2}{8} = 604$$

$$S_{pp} = \sum p^2 - \frac{(\sum p)^2}{n} = 8.0169 - \frac{7.73^2}{8} = 0.5477875$$

Tip: Don't round your answers yet — you're going to use these values to calculate r.

- So $r = \dfrac{S_{wp}}{\sqrt{S_{ww}S_{pp}}} = \dfrac{-16.46}{\sqrt{604 \times 0.5477875}} = -0.905$ (to 3 d.p.)

b) Give an interpretation of this value of r.

- This is a very high negative value for r (it's very close to -1).
- This means that for the brands of ham tested, a higher percentage water content generally means a lower price.

Exercise 1.3

Q1 Use the information below to find the product moment correlation coefficient (r) between x and y.

$$\sum x = 313 \qquad \sum y = 75 \qquad \sum x^2 = 6875$$

$$\sum y^2 = 473 \qquad \sum xy = 1515 \qquad n = 15$$

Q2 The table below shows the heights and weights of 8 teenage boys.

Height in cm, x	180	171	182	184	166	180	173	167
Weight in kg, y	70	67	66	59	61	75	65	56

a) Calculate the values of S_{xy}, S_{xx} and S_{yy}.

b) Find the value of the product moment correlation coefficient (r) for x and y.

Q3 For the data shown in this table:

p	13	9	15	10	8	11	12	14
q	5	7	2	4	3	8	1	2

a) Calculate $\sum p$, $\sum q$, $\sum p^2$, $\sum q^2$ and $\sum pq$.

b) Use your summations to calculate S_{pq}, S_{pp} and S_{qq}.

c) Find the value of the product moment correlation coefficient (r) for p and q.

Q4 The lengths and widths (in cm) of 8 leaves from a tree were measured. The results are shown below.

Length, l	4.6	7.2	5.1	8.3	2.4	6.4	5.7	3.3
Width, w	3.1	5.2	3.6	5.6	1.7	4.7	4.0	2.5

a) Calculate S_{lw}, S_{ll} and S_{ww}.
(You may use $\sum l^2 = 258$, $\sum w^2 = 128.2$, $\sum lw = 181.75$)

b) Calculate the correlation coefficient r.

c) Give an interpretation of your value for r.

Q5 A nurse at a health centre did a memory test on some patients of different ages. Her results are shown below.

Age in years, a	57	65	94	88	71	62	79	82	52
Test score, s	8.9	4.8	5.4	2.8	7.1	7.5	3.1	6.2	8.4

Calculate the correlation coefficient r and interpret your result.

Q6 A doctor checked the kidney function of some of his patients to see if it was related to their weight. Here, 0 indicates no kidney function at all and 10 indicates that a patient's kidneys are functioning at maximum efficiency.

The table shows the results.

Weight in kg, w	66	74	96	83	79	54	64	71	88
Kidney function, k	7.9	8.2	2.3	7.1	4.8	9.1	8.4	6.8	3.7

a) Find the value of the product moment correlation coefficient (r) for w and k.

b) Interpret the value of this correlation coefficient.

Coded data

You've seen the idea of coding before (see p37). The idea is to make your life easier by making numbers less fiddly to work with.

- The coding you'll be expected to use is of the form:

$$u = \frac{x - a}{b}$$

where x is an **original** data value, u is the corresponding **coded** data value, and a and b are numbers to be chosen.

- This is a **linear transformation** — if you were to draw a graph of u against x, it would be a straight line.

Using a linear transformation to code data values **doesn't affect** the value of the product moment correlation coefficient at all — r for the coded data is **exactly the same** as the value of r for the uncoded data.

Tip: If your data consists of really huge numbers, you could use coding to produce smaller, more manageable numbers.

But if your data values are tiny, you'd code them to produce larger numbers. And so on.

Tip: The reason why the correlation coefficient isn't affected is because coding a set of values in this way doesn't change the pattern of points on a scatter diagram. The effect of coding a variable is the same as relabelling one of the scatter diagram's axes.

Example

The table below shows the annual salaries (s, in £) of six shipping clerks, along with the number of years experience (x) they have.

Experience, x	2	4	5	7	8	10
Salary, s	23 000	24 000	24 500	26 000	26 700	29 000

The values of s are to be coded such that $u = \dfrac{s - 20\,000}{1000}$.

a) **Calculate the value of the product moment correlation coefficient between x and u.**

- Make a new table of values which includes the coded data values u. Also include the values of x^2, u^2 and xu — you'll need them to work out S_{xx}, S_{uu} and S_{xu}.

Experience, x	2	4	5	7	8	10	$\sum x = 36$
Salary, s	23 000	24 000	24 500	26 000	26 700	29 000	
Coded salary, u	3	4	4.5	6	6.7	9	$\sum u = 33.2$
x^2	4	16	25	49	64	100	$\sum x^2 = 258$
u^2	9	16	20.25	36	44.89	81	$\sum u^2 = 207.14$
xu	6	16	22.5	42	53.6	90	$\sum xu = 230.1$

Tip: You can code one or both of the variables.

Tip: The values of 20 000 and 1000 were chosen so that the coded data ended up less than 10. (Dividing by 100 would also have been sensible — the numbers would have been bigger but you wouldn't have any decimals.)

- This gives: $S_{xu} = \sum xu - \dfrac{\sum x \sum u}{n} = 230.1 - \dfrac{36 \times 33.2}{6} = 30.9$

$$S_{xx} = \sum x^2 - \dfrac{(\sum x)^2}{n} = 258 - \dfrac{36^2}{6} = 42$$

$$S_{uu} = \sum u^2 - \dfrac{(\sum u)^2}{n} = 207.14 - \dfrac{33.2^2}{6} = 23.4333...$$

- So $r = \dfrac{S_{xu}}{\sqrt{S_{xx}S_{uu}}} = \dfrac{30.9}{\sqrt{42 \times 23.4333...}} = \boxed{0.985 \text{ (to 3 d.p.)}}$

Tip: This is the correlation coefficient between x and u, but it must also be the correlation coefficient between x and s.

b) Hence write down the value of the product moment correlation coefficient between x and s. Explain your answer.

- Since s and u are related by a linear transformation, the product moment correlation coefficient between x and s must also be $\boxed{0.985 \text{ (to 3 d.p.)}}$.

Q1 Hint: The transformation $u = x - 20$ is of the form $u = \dfrac{x - a}{b}$, but with $b = 1$.

Exercise 1.4

Q1 Find the product moment correlation coefficient for x and y in the table below by using the coding $u = x - 20$ and $v = y - 60$.

x	23	27	22	29	21	25
y	64	61	68	67	63	66

Q2 Hint: The transformation $u = \dfrac{x}{100}$ is of the form $u = \dfrac{x - a}{b}$, but with $a = 0$.

Similarly, the transformation $v = 10y$ is of the form $v = \dfrac{y - a}{b}$, with $a = 0$ and $b = \dfrac{1}{10}$.

Q2 Find the product moment correlation coefficient for x and y in the table below by using the coding $u = \dfrac{x}{100}$ and $v = 10y$.

x	400	600	500	300	200	900	1100	800
y	0.7	2.1	0.9	1.3	1.9	1.5	2	1.6

Q3 Find the product moment correlation coefficient for s and t in the table below by using the coding $u = \dfrac{s - 120}{5}$ and $v = 10(t - 5)$.

s	120	125	130	135	140	145	150	155	160
t	8.2	7.5	7.1	6.7	5.7	6.2	5.8	5.4	5.2

Q3 Hint: The variables won't always be x and y.

Q4 The weights (w) in kg of a number of athletes were recorded, along with the number of seconds (s) they each took to run 100 m. The data is shown in the following table.

Weight in kg, w	76	64	80	79	67	72	69	74
Time in secs, s	11.4	12.3	13.2	11.8	12.7	11.5	13.8	13.3

Find the product moment correlation coefficient for w and s using the coding $u = w - 60$ and $v = 10(s - 11)$.

Q5 Use a suitable coding to find the product moment correlation coefficient for x and y in the table below.

x	4008	4010	4011	4015	4018	4021
y	100	400	800	300	700	200

Limitations of the PMCC

Correlation is <u>not</u> the same as causation

Correlation and **causation** are often confused, but they're not the same thing at all.

- A high correlation coefficient doesn't necessarily mean that a change in one factor **causes** a change in the other.

  For example, the number of televisions sold in Japan and the number of cars sold in the USA may be correlated, but that doesn't mean that high TV sales in Japan cause high car sales in the USA (or the other way round).

- And the graph on the right shows the number of tooth-fillings a sample of 100 adults have, plotted against their salary. The graph shows that there's a positive correlation between 'fillings' and 'salary'. As the number of fillings goes up, so generally does a person's salary.

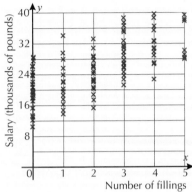

- But... that doesn't mean fillings cause someone to earn more, or that earning more causes fillings.

- The likely explanation is that both the number of fillings and a person's salary are linked to another quantity — age. As people get older, they tend to get paid more, and the number of fillings they have also tends to increase.

- Similarly, the TV sales in Japan and the car sales in the USA are probably both related to the overall strength of the global economy.

The PMCC only shows <u>linear</u> relationships

The product moment correlation coefficient (PMCC) is only a measure of a **linear** relationship between two variables (i.e. how close they'd be to a **straight line** if you plotted a scatter diagram).

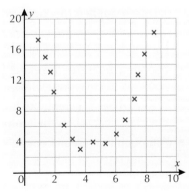

- In the diagram on the right, the PMCC would be pretty low, but the two variables definitely look linked.

- It looks like the points lie close to a parabola (the shape of an x^2 curve) — not a straight line.

2. Linear Regression

Learning Objectives:

- Be able to determine which variable is the explanatory variable and which is the response variable.
- Be able to find the equation of a regression line.
- Be able to use a regression line to predict values of the response variable.
- Be aware of the problems involved with extrapolating beyond the existing data.
- Be able to transform a regression equation relating coded variables to an equation relating the original variables.

Linear regression is all about finding the <u>best</u> line of best fit on a scatter diagram. Lines of best fit are really useful — you can use them to predict how one of the quantities will be affected by a change in the other one.

Explanatory and response variables

When you draw a scatter diagram, you always have **two** variables. For example, this scatter diagram shows the load on a lorry, x (in tonnes), and the fuel efficiency, y (in km per litre).

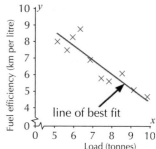

- The two variables are negatively correlated.
- In fact, all the points lie reasonably close to a straight line — the **line of best fit**.
- If you could find the equation of this line, then you could use it as a **model** to describe the relationship between x and y.

Linear regression is a method for finding the equation of a line of best fit on a scatter diagram. Or you can think of it as a method for **modelling** the relationship between two variables.

Before carrying out a linear regression, you first have to decide which variable is the **explanatory variable**, and which is the **response variable**.

- The **explanatory variable** (or **independent variable**) is the variable you can directly control, or the one that you think is **affecting** the other. In the above example, 'load' is the explanatory variable. The explanatory variable is always drawn along the **horizontal axis**.

- The **response variable** (or **dependent variable**) is the variable you think is **being affected**. In the above example, 'fuel efficiency' is the response variable. The response variable is always drawn up the **vertical axis**.

Tip: A place's latitude is an angle showing how far north or south of the equator it lies.

The latitude of the North Pole is 90° north, while the latitude of the South Pole is 90° south.

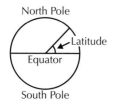

Examples

For each situation below, explain which quantity would be the explanatory variable, and which would be the response variable.

a) **A scientist is investigating the relationship between the amount of fertiliser applied to a tomato plant and the eventual yield.**

- The scientist can directly control the amount of fertiliser she gives each plant — so 'amount of fertiliser' is the explanatory variable.
- She then measures the effect this has on the plant's yield — so 'yield' is the response variable.

b) **A researcher is examining how a town's latitude and the number of days last year when the temperature rose above 10 °C are linked.**

- Although the researcher can't control the latitude of towns, it would be the difference in latitude that **leads to** a difference in temperature, and not the other way around.
- So the explanatory variable is 'the town's latitude', and the response variable is 'the number of days last year when the temperature rose above 10 °C'.

For each situation below, explain which quantity would be the explanatory variable, and which would be the response variable.

Q1 • the time spent practising the piano each week $\in$
   • the number of mistakes made in a test at the end of the week $\imath$

Q2 • the age of a second-hand car $\in$
   • the value of a second-hand car $\imath$

Q3 • the number of phone calls made in a town in a week $\imath$
   • the population of a town $\in$

Q4 • the growth rate of a plant in an experiment $\mathcal{R}$
   • the amount of sunlight falling on a plant in an experiment E

Regression lines

Here's the 'fuel efficiency v load' scatter diagram from the previous page.

■ The **regression line** (which is what I'm going to call the 'line of best fit' from now on) is marked on again. The equation of this regression line is $y = a + bx$, where a and b are numbers to be found.

Tip: b is the **gradient** of the regression line, and a is its **intercept** on the vertical axis.

■ There are also some dotted lines showing the vertical distance between each data value and the regression line.

Each of these small distances is called a **residual** (e_i).

The residuals show the **errors** in the model (the regression line) — they show how the real-life observations differ from what the model predicts.

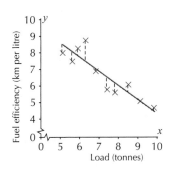

> Residual = Observed y-value – Estimated y-value
> e_i = y_i – $(a + bx_i)$

■ **Linear regression** involves finding the equation of the line that minimises the sum of the squares of the residuals, $\sum e_i^2$.

This will mean the regression line is as close as possible to your points.

Tip: This is why this kind of regression is sometimes called **least-squares regression**.

The formulas below tell you how to find the **regression line of y on x** (the '...of y on x' part means that x is the explanatory variable, and y is the response variable).

The equation of the regression line of y on x is: $\boxed{y = a + bx}$

where: $\boxed{b = \dfrac{S_{xy}}{S_{xx}}}$

and: $\boxed{a = \overline{y} - b\overline{x}}$

Tip: Remember:

$$S_{xy} = \sum xy - \frac{\sum x \sum y}{n}$$

$$S_{xx} = \sum x^2 - \frac{(\sum x)^2}{n}$$

Example 1

The data below shows the load on a lorry, x (in tonnes), and the fuel efficiency, y (in km per litre).

a) Find the equation of the regression line of y on x.

x	5.1	5.6	5.9	6.3	6.8	7.4	7.8	8.5	9.1	9.8
y	8	7.5	8.3	8.8	6.9	5.8	5.6	6.1	5.1	4.7

Tip: This is the data used to draw the graphs on pages 114 and 115.

Tip: Loads of calculators will work out regression lines for you if you type in the pairs of data values (x, y).

But you still need to know this method, since in the exam you might be given just the summations $\sum x$, $\sum y$, $\sum x^2$ and $\sum xy$, rather than the individual data values.

- First, you need to find S_{xy} and S_{xx}:

  Start by working out the four summations $\sum x$, $\sum y$, $\sum x^2$, and $\sum xy$. It's best to draw a table.

x	5.1	5.6	5.9	6.3	6.8	7.4	7.8	8.5	9.1	9.8	$\sum x = 72.3$
y	8	7.5	8.3	8.8	6.9	5.8	5.6	6.1	5.1	4.7	$\sum y = 66.8$
x^2	26.01	31.36	34.81	39.69	46.24	54.76	60.84	72.25	82.81	96.04	$\sum x^2 = 544.81$
xy	40.8	42	48.97	55.44	46.92	42.92	43.68	51.85	46.41	46.06	$\sum xy = 465.05$

- Then: $S_{xy} = \sum xy - \dfrac{\sum x \sum y}{n} = 465.05 - \dfrac{72.3 \times 66.8}{10}$

  $= -17.914$

- And: $S_{xx} = \sum x^2 - \dfrac{\left(\sum x\right)^2}{n} = 544.81 - \dfrac{72.3^2}{10}$

  $= 22.081$

- So the **gradient** of the regression line is b, where:

  $b = \dfrac{S_{xy}}{S_{xx}} = \dfrac{-17.914}{22.081} = -0.81128... = -0.811$ (to 3 sig. fig.)

- And the **intercept** of the regression line is a, where:

  $a = \bar{y} - b\bar{x} = \dfrac{\sum y}{n} - b\dfrac{\sum x}{n} = \dfrac{66.8}{10} - (-0.81128...) \times \dfrac{72.3}{10}$

  $= 12.54559... = 12.5$ (to 3 sig. fig.).

Tip: Remember, $\bar{x} = \dfrac{\sum x}{n}$ and $\bar{y} = \dfrac{\sum y}{n}$.

- This means that the regression line of y on x is: $y = 12.5 - 0.811x$

b) Plot your regression line on a scatter diagram.

- A regression line always goes through the point $(\bar{x}, \bar{y})$.

  Here, $\bar{x} = \dfrac{\sum x}{n} = \dfrac{72.3}{10} = 7.23$ and $\bar{y} = \dfrac{\sum y}{n} = \dfrac{66.8}{10} = 6.68$.

  So the regression line must go through the point $(7.23, 6.68)$.

- By putting $x = 0$ into the equation, you can see the line must also go through the point $(0, 12.5)$.

- So draw the regression line through these two points.

Tip: You don't have to use the point $(\bar{x}, \bar{y})$.

To plot a regression line you can choose any two points to plot. Or you can draw the line using the y-intercept and the gradient.

It's a good idea to make the points you're plotting for the regression line look different from your actual data points.

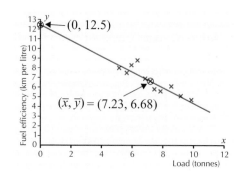

c) Calculate the residuals for: (i) $x = 5.6$, **(ii)** $x = 6.3$.

- (i) When $x = 5.6$, the residual = observed y-value – estimated y-value
  $$= 7.5 - (12.54559... - 0.81128... \times 5.6)$$
  $$= -0.502 \text{ (to 3 sig. fig.)}$$
- (ii) When $x = 6.3$, the residual = observed y-value – estimated y-value
  $$= 8.8 - (12.54559... - 0.81128... \times 6.3)$$
  $$= 1.37 \text{ (to 3 sig. fig.)}$$

Tip: A **positive** residual means the data point is **above** the regression line for that value of x. A **negative** residual means the data point is **below** the regression line.

In the above example, the regression line was $y = 12.5 - 0.811x$, where x was the load (in tonnes) and y was the fuel efficiency (in km per litre).

These values for a (= 12.5) and b (= –0.811) tell you:

- for every extra tonne carried, you'd expect the lorry's fuel efficiency to fall by 0.811 km per litre (since when x increases by 1, y falls by 0.811).
- with no load ($x = 0$), you'd expect the lorry to do 12.5 km per litre of fuel (assuming it was reasonable to use the line down to $x = 0$ — see p118).

Example 2

A taxi company analyses the fares charged by a rival. It looks at 20 different journeys and records the distance (d, in miles) of the journey and the fare charged (f, in pounds). The summary statistics are shown below.

$$\sum d = 210.1, \sum f = 354.8, \sum d^2 = 2953.53, \sum df = 4619.2$$

Tip: Here, d is the explanatory variable, so d 'plays the role of x', while f 'plays the role of y'.

a) Calculate the equation of the regression line of f on d.

- The variables aren't x and y this time, but d and f — so you need to find S_{df} and S_{dd}.
- $S_{df} = \sum df - \dfrac{\sum d \sum f}{n} = 4619.2 - \dfrac{210.1 \times 354.8}{20} = 892.026$
- $S_{dd} = \sum d^2 - \dfrac{(\sum d)^2}{n} = 2953.53 - \dfrac{210.1^2}{20} = 746.4295$
- So the gradient of the regression line is b, where:
  $$b = \frac{S_{df}}{S_{dd}} = \frac{892.026}{746.4295} = 1.1950... = 1.20 \text{ (to 3 sig.fig.)}$$
- And the intercept of the regression line is a, where:
  $$a = \overline{f} - b\overline{d} = \frac{\sum f}{n} - b\frac{\sum d}{n}$$
  $$= \frac{354.8}{20} - (1.1950...) \times \frac{210.1}{20} = 5.19 \text{ (to 3 sig. fig.)}.$$
- So the equation of the regression line is: $f = 5.19 + 1.20d$

b) Interpret your values of a and b in this context.

- The value of **b** tells you that the fare will increase by approximately £1.20 for every extra mile travelled (since when d increases by 1, f increases by 1.20).
- The value of **a** tells you that a journey of 0 miles costs £5.19 — this is a fixed part of the fare that doesn't depend on how far you travel (so the taxi's meter will show approximately £5.19 before you've even gone anywhere).

Tip: Make sure you give your explanations in the context of the question — so here you need to talk about taxis, distances and fares.

Q1   Calculate the equation of the regression line of y on x for the data shown in the table below.

x	2	3	5	7	10	12	15
y	6	9	11	14	20	25	30

(You may use $S_{xx} = 139.4$ and $S_{xy} = 254.9$.)

Q2   The latitude (x, measured in degrees) and the mean annual temperature (y, in °C) were recorded for a number of locations. The data is shown below.

Latitude, x	8	30	19	41	64	12	60	25	52	39
Mean annual temp., y	27	16	24	10	4	27	5	22	9	12

a) Draw a scatter diagram of the data.

b) Calculate the equation of the regression line of y on x.

c) Interpret your values of a and b in this context.

d) Calculate the residuals when: (i) $x = 19$ (ii) $x = 41$

Q3   The HR department of a large company recorded the salary (P, in thousands of pounds) of a sample of 10 of its graduate employees, along with the number of years' experience (e) they had working for the company. The summary statistics are shown below.

$$\sum e = 92, \ \sum P = 264, \ \sum e^2 = 1072, \ \sum P^2 = 7082, \ \sum eP = 2596$$

a) Calculate the equation of the regression line $P = a + be$.

b) Give an interpretation of the values of a and b in this context.

Interpolation and extrapolation

Tip: You can only use a regression line to predict a value of the response variable — **not** the explanatory variable.

You can use a regression line to predict values of your **response variable**. There are two forms of this — **interpolation** and **extrapolation**.

Tip: The data for this example is on page 116.

This scatter diagram shows the data from the lorry example that started on page 114 — with the fuel efficiency of a lorry plotted against different loads.

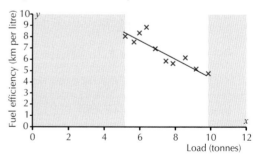

In the original data, the values of x were between 5.1 and 9.8 — the yellow part of the graph.

- When you use values of x within this range (i.e. values of x in the yellow part of the graph) to predict corresponding values of y, this is called **interpolation**. It's okay to do this — the predicted value should be reliable.

- When you use values of x **outside** the range of your original data (i.e. values of x in the grey part of the graph) to predict corresponding values of y, this is called **extrapolation**. It's best **not** to do this, or at least be very **cautious** about it — your prediction may be very unreliable. So here, you'd need to be very careful about using a value of x less than 5.1 or greater than 9.8.

- This is because you don't have any evidence that the relationship described by your regression line is true for values of x less than 5.1 or greater than 9.8 — and if the relationship turns out **not** to hold, then your prediction could be wildly wrong.

Example

The length of a spring (y, in cm) when loaded with different masses (m, in g) is shown in the table below.

Mass, m	200	250	300	400	450	500
Length, y	9.8	10.7	10.8	11.8	12.4	13.2

a) **Calculate the equation of the regression line of y on m.**

- Extend the table to include m^2 and my, so that you can find S_{my} and S_{mm}:

Mass, m	200	250	300	400	450	500	$\sum m = 2100$
Length, y	9.8	10.7	10.8	11.8	12.4	13.2	$\sum y = 68.7$
m^2	40 000	62 500	90 000	160 000	202 500	250 000	$\sum m^2 = 805\,000$
my	1960	2675	3240	4720	5580	6600	$\sum my = 24\,775$

- $S_{my} = \sum my - \dfrac{\sum m \sum y}{n} = 24\,775 - \dfrac{2100 \times 68.7}{6} = 730$

  $S_{mm} = \sum m^2 - \dfrac{(\sum m)^2}{n} = 805\,000 - \dfrac{2100^2}{6} = 70\,000$

- So the gradient of the regression line is b, where:

  $b = \dfrac{S_{my}}{S_{mm}} = \dfrac{730}{70\,000} = 0.010428... = 0.01043$ (to 4 sig. fig.)

- And the intercept of the regression line is a, where:

  $a = \bar{y} - b\bar{m} = \dfrac{\sum y}{n} - b\dfrac{\sum m}{n}$

  $= \dfrac{68.7}{6} - (0.010428...) \times \dfrac{2100}{6} = 7.8$

- So the equation of the regression line is: $y = 7.8 + 0.01043m$

b) **Use your regression line to estimate the length of the spring when loaded with a mass of: (i) 370 g   (ii) 670 g**

- (i) $m = 370$, so $y = 7.8 + 0.01043 \times 370 = $ 11.7 cm (to 1 d.p.).

- (ii) $m = 670$, so $y = 7.8 + 0.01043 \times 670 = $ 14.8 cm (to 1 d.p.).

c) **Comment on the reliability of your estimates in part b).**

- $m = 370$ falls within the range of the original data for m, so this is an interpolation. This means the result should be fairly reliable.

- But $m = 670$ falls outside the range of the original data for m, so this is an extrapolation. This means the regression line may not be valid, and we need to treat this result with caution.

Q1 Hint: For part a), use the fact that this is the regression line **of y on x**. (And see page 115 if necessary.)

Q1 The equation of the regression line of y on x is $y = 1.67 + 0.107x$.

    a) Which variable is the response variable?

    b) Find the predicted value of y corresponding to:

        (i) $x = 5$ (ii) $x = 20$

Q2 The regression line of y on x for a set of data in which x takes values between 2 and 15 is $y = 103 - 4.57x$.

    For each value of x below, estimate the corresponding value of y and comment on your estimate.

    a) $x = 4$ b) $x = 20$ c) $x = 7$

Q3 Data on a large sample of new drivers aged between 17 and 35 was collected. It was found that the number of lessons taken (y) before passing their driving test could be described by the regression equation $y = 1.4x + 7$, where x is the driver's age in years.

    a) Use the equation to estimate the number of lessons a typical 20-year-old could expect to take before they pass their driving test. Comment on your answer.

    b) Use the equation to estimate the number of lessons a typical 50-year-old could expect to take before they pass their driving test. Comment on your answer.

Q4 A pharmaceutical company is testing a product to eliminate acne. A volunteer counted the number of spots (s) on an area of skin after d days of treatment with the product, where d took the values 2, 6, 10, 14, 18 and 22.

    The equation of the regression line of s on d was found to be $s = 58.8 - 2.47d$.

    a) Estimate the number of spots the volunteer had on day 7. Comment on the reliability of your answer.

    b) She forgot to count how many spots she had before starting to use the product. Estimate this number. Comment on your answer.

    c) The volunteer claims that the regression equation must be wrong, because it predicts that after 30 days she should have a negative number of spots. Comment on this claim.

Linear regression with coded data

You could be asked to find a regression line for coded data. Once you've found it, you can easily transform it into a regression line for the original data.

Tip: Remember, the idea behind coding is to make the numbers easier to work with.

Example 1

A company collects data on the age (g) and salary (s) of its senior managers. The data is coded in the following way:

$$x = g - 50 \qquad y = \frac{s - 50\,000}{1000}$$

If the regression line of y on x is given by $y = 1.24x + 5.44$, find the regression line of s on g.

- Substitute the expressions defining x and y into the equation of the regression line for y on x. This gives you an equation involving just s and g.

$$\frac{s - 50\,000}{1000} = 1.24(g - 50) + 5.44$$

- Rearrange this so it is in the form $s = a + bg$, where a and b are constants. This is the regression line of s on g.

$$s - 50\,000 = 1240g - 62\,000 + 5440$$

$$s = 1240g - 6560$$

Example 2

The annual heating bill (h, in £) for 8 office buildings is shown below, along with the total floor area (f, in m²) of each building.

f	600	1000	1500	1800	2400	3400	4400	4900
h	1500	2600	3100	3400	3900	5500	5900	6100

These results were coded in the following way:

$$u = \frac{f - 2500}{100} \qquad v = \frac{h - 4000}{100}$$

Tip: If you work out the means of these variables, you'll find that $\bar{f} = 2500$ and $\bar{h} = 4000$. These are the numbers that have been subtracted in the coding. This will make some of the terms disappear when you do the calculations.

a) **Find the equation of the regression line of v on u.**

- First make a table of the coded data, along with extra rows for u^2 and uv. Include the total for each row as well.

u	−19	−15	−10	−7	−1	9	19	24	$\sum u = 0$
v	−25	−14	−9	−6	−1	15	19	21	$\sum v = 0$
u^2	361	225	100	49	1	81	361	576	$\sum u^2 = 1754$
uv	475	210	90	42	1	135	361	504	$\sum uv = 1818$

Tip: $\sum u = \sum v = 0$

This is a result of subtracting the means of the original variables during the coding.

- $S_{uv} = \sum uv - \dfrac{\sum u \sum v}{n} = 1818 - \dfrac{0 \times 0}{8} = 1818$

$S_{uu} = \sum u^2 - \dfrac{\left(\sum u\right)^2}{n} = 1754 - \dfrac{0^2}{8} = 1754$

- So the gradient of the regression line of v on u is b, where:

$b = \dfrac{S_{uv}}{S_{uu}} = \dfrac{1818}{1754} = 1.036488\ldots = 1.036$ (to 4 sig. fig.)

Tip: a = 0 as a result of subtracting the means of the original variables during coding.

- And the intercept is a, where $a = \bar{v} - b\bar{u} = \dfrac{\sum v}{n} - b\dfrac{\sum u}{n} = 0$

- So the equation of the regression line of v on u is: $v = 1.036u$

b) Hence find the equation of the regression line of h on f.

- Substitute the expressions defining u and v into your regression equation.

$$v = 1.036u$$

$$\frac{h - 4000}{100} = 1.036 \times \frac{f - 2500}{100}$$

- Then rearrange into the form h = c + df.

$$h - 4000 = 1.036f - (1.036 \times 2500)$$

So $h = \boxed{1410 + 1.036f}$

Exercise 2.4

Q1 A set of bivariate data (x, y) has been coded using $p = x - 7$ and $q = y - 50$. The regression line of q on p is given by $q = 40 + 2p$. Find the equation of the regression line of y on x.

Q2 The regression line of q on p is given by the equation $q = -0.9 + 0.1p$. Find the equation of the regression line of y on x if the following coding has been used: $p = \dfrac{x - 20}{2}$ and $q = 10y - 3$.

Q3 An experiment was carried out to see whether people's weight affected how long they could hold their breath for. Each person's weight (w, in kg) was coded using the equation $x = w - 60$. The number of seconds they could hold their breath for (t) was coded using $y = t - 45$.

The regression line for the coded data has equation $y = 17.4 - 0.78x$. Find the equation of the regression line of t on w.

Q4 Mrs Brown put out different amounts of birdseed (s, in grams) each day, and then counted the number of birds (v) in her garden at noon. She coded her data in the following way:

$$x = \frac{s}{100} - 2 \text{ and } y = v - 7$$

The summary statistics for the coded data are as follows:
$$\sum x = 28, \ \sum y = 124, \ \sum x^2 = 140, \ \sum xy = 618 \text{ and } n = 10.$$

a) Find the equation of the regression line of y on x.

b) Hence find the equation of the regression line of v on s.

Q5 The time (t, in hours) that seedlings could survive in water containing different concentrations of salt (s, in mg per litre) was recorded. The results were coded such that $x = \dfrac{s}{10}$ and $y = t - 29$. The coded data is in the table below.

x	1	2	3	5	7	10
y	19	11	9	−1	−14	−24

a) Find the equation of the regression line of y on x.

b) Hence find the equation of the regression line of t on s.

Review Exercise — Chapter 4

Q1 The table below shows the results of some measurements concerning alcoholic cocktails. Here, x = total volume in ml, and y = percentage alcohol concentration by volume.

x	90	100	100	150	160	200	240	250	290	300
y	40	35	25	30	25	25	20	25	15	7

a) Draw a scatter diagram representing this information.

b) Calculate the product moment correlation coefficient (PMCC) of these values.

c) What does the PMCC tell you about these results?

Q2 For each pair of variables below, state which would be the explanatory variable and which would be the response variable.

a) • the annual number of volleyball-related injuries
  • the annual number of sunny days

b) • the annual number of rainy days
  • the annual number of Monopoly-related injuries

c) • a person's disposable income
  • a person's spending on luxuries

d) • the number of trips to the loo per day
  • the number of cups of tea drunk per day

e) • the number of festival tickets sold
  • the number of pairs of Wellington boots bought

Q3 The radius in mm, r, and the weight in grams, w, of 10 randomly selected blueberry pancakes are given in the table below.

r	48.0	51.0	52.0	54.5	55.1	53.6	50.0	52.6	49.4	51.2
w	100	105	108	120	125	118	100	115	98	110

a) Find: (i) $S_{rr} = \sum r^2 - \dfrac{(\sum r)^2}{n}$,   (ii) $S_{rw} = \sum rw - \dfrac{\sum r \sum w}{n}$

The regression line of w on r has equation $w = a + br$.

b) Find b, the gradient of the regression line.

c) Find a, the intercept of the regression line on the w-axis.

d) Write down the equation of the regression line of w on r.

e) Use your regression line to estimate the weight of a blueberry pancake of radius 60 mm.

f) Comment on the reliability of your estimate, giving a reason for your answer.

Q4 The variables P and Q are defined as $P = r - 5$ and $Q = \dfrac{w}{8}$, where r and w are as used in Question 3.

Find the regression line of Q on P.

1   Values of two variables x and y are recorded in the table below.

x	1	2	3	4	5	6	7	8
y	0.50	0.70	0.10	0.82	0.50	0.36	0.16	0.80

a)   Represent this data on a scatter diagram.

(2 marks)

b)   Calculate the product moment correlation coefficient (PMCC) of the two variables.

(4 marks)

c)   What does this value of the PMCC tell you about these variables?

(1 mark)

2   The following times (in seconds) were taken by eight different runners to complete distances of 20 metres and 60 metres.

Runner	A	B	C	D	E	F	G	H
20-metre time (x)	3.39	3.20	3.09	3.32	3.33	3.27	3.44	3.08
60-metre time (y)	8.78	7.73	8.28	8.25	8.91	8.59	8.90	8.05

a)   Plot a scatter diagram to represent the data.

(2 marks)

b)   Find the equation of the regression line of y on x, and plot it on your scatter diagram.

(8 marks)

c)   Use the equation of the regression line to estimate the value of y when:
     (i) $x = 3.15$,   (ii) $x = 3.88$.

Comment on the reliability of your estimates.

(4 marks)

d)   Find the residuals for:
     (i) $x = 3.32$ (ii) $x = 3.27$.

Illustrate them on your scatter diagram.

(4 marks)

3   A journalist at British Biking Monthly recorded the distance in miles, x, cycled by 20 different cyclists in the morning and the number of calories, y, eaten at lunch. The following summary statistics were provided:

$$S_{xx} = 310\ 880 \qquad S_{yy} = 788.95 \qquad S_{xy} = 12\ 666$$

a)   Use these values to calculate the product moment correlation coefficient.

(2 marks)

b)   Give an interpretation of your answer to part (a).

(1 mark)

A Swedish cycling magazine calculated the product moment correlation coefficient of the data after converting the distances to km.

c)   State the value of the product moment correlation coefficient in this case.

(1 mark)

4 The equation of the regression line for a set of data is $y = 211.599 + 9.602x$.

   a) Use the equation of the regression line to estimate the value of y when:
      (i) $x = 12.5$ (ii) $x = 14.7$.

      (2 marks)

   b) Calculate the residuals if the respective observed y-values were $y = 332.5$ and $y = 352.1$.

      (2 marks)

5 Ten athletes all trained for the same 10 000 m race. On the day before the race, they each ran different distances. The distance (d, in km) each athlete ran the day before the race, and the time (t, in seconds) that each athlete recorded in the race itself were recorded.

   The results were then coded using $p = d$ and $q = t - 2367$.
   The values of p and q are shown in the table below.

p	1	2	4	5	6	6	8	8	10	15
q	−219	189	315	105	−141	−333	9	177	−357	255

   a) Calculate S_{pq}, S_{pp} and S_{qq}.
      (You may use $\sum p^2 = 571$, $\sum q^2 = 548\,586$ and $\sum pq = 843$.)

      (6 marks)

   b) Find the product moment correlation coefficient between p and q.

      (2 marks)

   c) Write down the value of the product moment correlation coefficient between d and t. Explain your answer.

      (2 marks)

   d) Use your answer to part (c) to comment on how the length of a run on the day before a race affects the performance of the athletes.

      (2 marks)

6 A scientist is investigating the link between the fat content of different brands of burgers and the price. She measures the amount of fat (x, in grams) in 100 g of each type of burger (when raw), and calculates the price for 100 g of each burger (y, in pence). Her data is shown in this table.

Brand	A	B	C	D	E	F	G	H
x	5	8	10	12	16	19	20	25
y	106	94	82	81	79	42	38	22

   ($\sum x^2 = 1975$, $\sum y^2 = 43\,290$ and $\sum xy = 6446$)

   a) Draw a scatter diagram showing this data.

      (2 marks)

   b) Calculate S_{xy} and S_{xx} for this data.

      (5 marks)

   c) The scientist models the relationship between x and y with the equation $y = a + bx$. Use linear regression to find the values of a and b.

      (4 marks)

   d) Draw the regression line on your scatter diagram.

      (2 marks)

   e) Use the scatter diagram to say which brand of burger appears to be overpriced. Explain your answer.

      (2 marks)

Chapter 5

1. The Normal Distribution

Learning Objectives:

- Know the shape and properties of the normal distribution.
- Know that probabilities are shown by the area under the normal curve.
- Be able to use the correct notation to describe a normal distribution.

In this section you'll be introduced to the normal distribution. Many variables can be modelled by a normal distribution, and this can be very useful, as you'll see later on.

The normal distribution

The shape of a normal distribution

The distributions of lots of quantities in the real world follow a **particular pattern** — with most of the data values falling **somewhere in the middle**, and only a small proportion taking much higher or lower values.

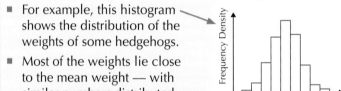

- For example, this histogram shows the distribution of the weights of some hedgehogs.
- Most of the weights lie close to the mean weight — with similar numbers distributed symmetrically above and below.

Tip: Remember, **continuous** variables can take any value within a certain range.

- A quantity like this can often be **modelled** by a **normal distribution**.

- A normal distribution is **continuous**, so can easily model continuous variables — such as height, weight, length, etc.

Tip: It's called a **random** variable because it takes different values with different probabilities. We covered discrete random variables in Chapter 3 — it's a similar idea here, but the variable is continuous.

If X is a **continuous random variable** that follows a **normal** distribution, you can describe the probability distribution of X using just two measures — its **mean**, μ, and **variance**, σ^2.

- Whatever the values of μ and σ^2, the **graph** of a normal distribution always looks like the **curve** below.

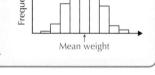

Tip: The vertical axis is labelled f(x) because the equation of the curve is a function of x. It's called the probability density function, but you don't need to know about these in S1.

- The curve is '**bell**-shaped'.
- There's a **peak** at the **mean**, μ.
- It's **symmetrical** about the mean — so values the same distance above and below the mean are equally likely.

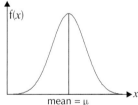

- You can see that the shape of the normal curve **approximately fits** the shape of the hedgehog distribution above. The peak at the mean reflects the fact that values close to the mean are most likely.

Tip: For a normal distribution, mean = median = mode.

- The width and height of the curve depend on the **variance** of the normal distribution. The three graphs on the next page all show normal distributions with the **same mean** (μ), but **different variances** (σ^2).

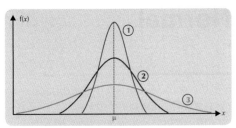

- The **larger** the variance the **wider** the curve, so **graph 3** has the **largest** variance and **graph 1** has the **smallest** variance.
- The **total area** under the curve is always the **same**, so a wider curve needs to have a lower height.

The area under a normal curve

The **area** under a normal curve shows **probabilities**.

- The **total area** under the curve represents the **total probability** of the random variable taking one of its possible values. And since the total probability is 1, the **total area under the curve** must also be **1**.
- The **probability** of the variable taking a value **between two limits** is the **area under the curve** between those limits.

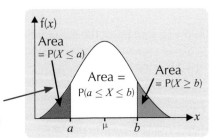

Tip: You'll see how to find and use areas under the normal curve over the next few pages.

There are some **facts** about the **area** under the curve that apply to **all** normal distributions.

- **68%** of the total **area** lies within **±1** standard deviation (±σ) of the mean.
- **95%** of the total **area** lies within **±2** standard deviations (±2σ) of the mean.
- **99.7%** of the total **area** lies within **±3** standard deviations (±3σ) of the mean.

Tip: You don't need to learn these facts, but they should give you an idea of how values close to the mean are **much** more likely than those further away.

So **68%** of **observations** are within ±σ of the mean, **95%** of **observations** are within ±2σ of the mean and **99.7%** of **observations** are within ±3σ of the mean.

Tip: Remember... standard deviation is the square root of the variance — so it's a measure of **dispersion** (how spread out values are from the mean).

Describing a normal distribution

If a continuous random variable X is **normally** distributed with mean μ and variance $σ^2$, it is written like this: $\longrightarrow$ $\boxed{X \sim N(μ, σ^2)}$

'N' stands for '**normal**' and '~' is short for '**is distributed**'.

- So going back to our hedgehog weights on the previous page, we could define a random variable, $W \sim N(μ, σ^2)$, where W represents hedgehog weight.
- Here, μ would represent the mean weight of the hedgehogs and σ would represent the standard deviation of hedgehog weights.

The most **important** normal distribution is the **standard normal distribution Z**, which has a mean of 0 and a variance of 1. There's a lot more about the standard normal distribution on the next few pages.

2. The Standard Normal Distribution, Z

Learning Objectives:

- Be able to use tables to find probabilities for the standard normal distribution, Z.
- Be able to use tables to find values for z, when given probabilities.

The most important normal distribution is the standard normal distribution. The 'special' random variable Z follows a standard normal distribution — Z is called the 'standard normal variable'. In this section you'll see how to use tables to find the probability that Z takes a value in a given range.

The standard normal distribution

The **standard normal distribution, Z,** has **mean 0** and **variance 1**. ⟶ $\boxed{Z \sim N(0, 1)}$

Below is a graph of the standard normal distribution. As you'd expect, the curve is **symmetrical** about the mean, **0**.

Remember that **areas under the curve** show **probabilities**. The **shaded area** here shows the probability that **Z** takes a value that's **less than or equal to** z. So to find this probability, we need to work out the area.

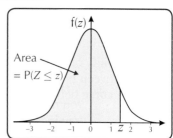

Working out the area under a normal distribution curve is usually difficult. But the reason why **Z** is **so important** is that there are **tables** that list areas under the curve for N(0, 1). The main table you'll use (see page 150) shows values of the normal **cumulative distribution function**, $\Phi(z)$. These are the **areas** under the curve to the **left of** z (the **probability** that $Z \leq z$) for different values of z — i.e. $\Phi(z) = P(Z \leq z)$.

So you can often find $P(Z \leq z)$ by looking up the value of z in the table and reading off the value for $\Phi(z)$. And since Z is a **continuous** distribution, $P(Z = z) = 0$, which means that **$P(Z \leq z)$** and **$P(Z < z)$** are the **same** thing. So you can **interchange** the $\leq$ and $<$ signs — i.e. $\Phi(z) = P(Z < z)$ as well.

Tip: The table only gives $P(Z \leq z)$ for $z \geq 0$.

Tip: For any **continuous** random variable X, $P(X = a) = 0$ for any value of a.

That's because the area under a graph at a single point is zero.

Tip: The table for $\Phi(z)$ is on page 150.

Always write down the full value from the table.

Example 1

Find the following probabilities.

a) **$P(Z \leq 0.64)$**

This is a nice, straightforward one — all you have to do is look up $z = 0.64$ in the table for $\Phi(z)$.

So, $P(Z \leq 0.64) = \boxed{0.7389}$

b) **$P(Z < 0.1)$**

Z is a continuous variable, so $P(Z < 0.1)$ is just the same as $P(Z \leq 0.1)$. So again, you just look up 0.1 in the table for $\Phi(z)$.

So, $P(Z < 0.1) = \boxed{0.5398}$

OK, so finding the probability that Z is **less than** z, where z is **positive**, is easy. And finding the probability that Z takes a value **greater than** (or greater than or equal to) z is only **slightly trickier**.

Using the fact that the **total area** under the curve is **1**, we get this definition. ⟶

$$P(Z > z) = 1 - P(Z \leq z)$$
$$= 1 - \Phi(z)$$

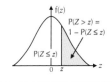
Tip: And we also get:
$P(Z \geq z) = 1 - P(Z < z)$
$= 1 - \Phi(z)$
(since $P(Z < z) = P(Z \leq z)$)

Example 2

Find the following probabilities.

a) **P(Z > 0.23)**

$P(Z > 0.23) = 1 - P(Z \leq 0.23)$
$= 1 - 0.5910$ ⟵ $P(Z \leq 0.23) = 0.5910$
$= 0.4090$

Tip: Drawing a sketch always helps to make things clearer.

b) **P(Z ≥ 1.15)**

$P(Z \geq 1.15) = 1 - P(Z < 1.15)$
$= 1 - 0.8749$ ⟵ $P(Z < 1.15) = 0.8749$
$= 0.1251$

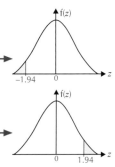

Now then, things start to get a bit **trickier** when z takes a **negative** value. To work these out, you need to use the **symmetry** of the curve. The best thing to do is to start by **drawing a sketch** and **shading** the area you want to find.

Example 3

Find the following probabilities.

a) **P(Z > −0.42)**

- **Shade** the area you want to find. ⟶
- Because z is **negative**, you **can't look it up** in the table — so the method used in Example 2 won't work. Instead, use symmetry to shade an **area of the same size** involving a **positive** value of z.
  This is the area to the **left** of $z = +0.42$. ⟶
- So $P(Z > -0.42) = P(Z < 0.42)$.
  And looking up 0.42 in the $\Phi(z)$ table you get:
  $P(Z > -0.42) = P(Z < 0.42) = 0.6628$

b) **P(Z ≤ −1.94)**

- **Shade** the area you want to find. ⟶
- Again, use symmetry to shade an **area of the same size**, but involving a **positive** value of z instead of a negative one.
  This is the area to the **right** of $z = +1.94$. ⟶
- So $P(Z \leq -1.94) = P(Z \geq 1.94)$.
- You still can't get your answer from the table directly, but using the fact that the area under the curve is 1,
  $P(Z \geq 1.94) = 1 - P(Z < 1.94)$.

Tip: Remember, you're always trying to get to an area that you can look up in the table.

- So, $P(Z \leq -1.94) = P(Z \geq 1.94) = 1 - P(Z < 1.94)$ ⟵ $P(Z < 1.94) = 0.9738$
  $= 1 - 0.9738$
  $= 0.0262$

In the next example, you're asked to find the probability that Z takes a value **between two limits**. You can do this by **subtracting** one area from another.

Example 4

Find the probability that $0.12 < Z \leq 0.82$.

- **Shade** the area you want to find. ⟶
- To find this area, you need to find the area to the left of $z = 0.82$, then **subtract** the area to the left of $z = 0.12$. That will leave you with the area between the two values.

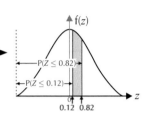

- So, $P(0.12 < Z \leq 0.82) = P(Z \leq 0.82) - P(Z \leq 0.12)$
$$= 0.7939 - 0.5478$$
$$= \boxed{0.2461}$$

Exercise 2.1

Q1 Use the table of the normal cumulative distribution function, $\Phi(z)$, to find the following probabilities.

    a) $P(Z \leq 1.87)$ b) $P(Z \leq 0.39)$ c) $P(Z < 0.99)$ d) $P(Z < 3.15)$

Q2 Use the table of the normal cumulative distribution function, $\Phi(z)$, to find the following probabilities.

    a) $P(Z > 2.48)$ b) $P(Z > 0.85)$ c) $P(Z \geq 1.23)$ d) $P(Z \geq 0.14)$

Q3 By using sketches and the table of the normal cumulative distribution function, $\Phi(z)$, find the following probabilities.

    a) $P(Z > -3.35)$ b) $P(Z > -0.24)$ c) $P(Z > -1.21)$

    d) $P(Z < -0.62)$ e) $P(Z < -1.14)$ f) $P(Z \leq -2.06)$

Q4 Work out the following probabilities.

    a) $P(1.34 < Z < 2.18)$ b) $P(0.76 < Z < 1.92)$

    c) $P(-1.45 < Z < 0.17)$ d) $P(-2.14 < Z < 1.65)$

    e) $P(-1.66 < Z < 1.66)$ f) $P(-0.34 < Z < 0.34)$

    g) $P(-3.25 < Z < -2.48)$ h) $P(-1.11 < Z < -0.17)$

Q4 Hint: For parts g) and h), use symmetry to find an identical area for which both limits are positive.

Using the tables in reverse

So you know how to find **probabilities** using the $\Phi(z)$ table. The other sort of question you need to be able to answer is where you're **given** a **probability**, e.g. $P(Z < z) = 0.5871$, and you have to **find z**. How you go about this depends on the information you're given.

If you're given the probability that Z is **less than** a value of z, $P(Z < z)$, it's usually best to see if you can find what you need in the **table for $\Phi(z)$** (the normal cumulative distribution function). But you need to read the table 'the other way round'.

Example

If $P(Z < z) = 0.9554$, then what is the value of z?

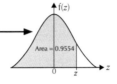

- Start by drawing a **sketch**, showing what you know. ──────→
- OK, so you need to find z for which $\Phi(z) = 0.9554$.
- Using the table, read through the values of $\Phi(z)$ until you find 0.9554. $\Phi(z) = 0.9554$ for $z = 1.70$. ◄──── The table for
  So, if $P(Z < z) = 0.9554$, then $z = 1.70$ $\Phi(z)$ is on p150.

Tip: Always check that the answer seems reasonable. The total probability is 1, so for an area of 0.9554, z will be positive and quite far to the right.

If **$P(Z < z)$** is **less than 0.5**, then z will be **negative**, and these values **aren't listed** in the table. But you can still **use the table** — you just need to do a bit of thinking and sketching to decide what to look up.

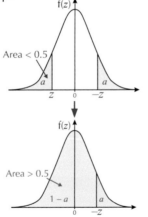

- The area, a, to the **left of z** is less than 0.5. You can see from the graph that there's an area of the same size to the **right** of the value $-z$ (where $-z$ is positive).
- Now you can draw a second graph showing the area to the **left** of $-z$. This is the area $1 - a$.
- The area $1 - a$ is **greater than 0.5**, so you can look it up in the $\Phi(z)$ table to find the value of $-z$.
- Finally, multiply $-z$ by -1 to get z.

Tip: If $P(Z < z) < 0.5$, then z will be negative.

Example

If $P(Z < z) = 0.2611$, then what is the value of z?

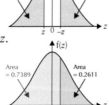

- First, draw a **sketch**, showing what you know, ──────→ and mark on the **equivalent area** to the right of $-z$.
- **Subtract** 0.2611 from 1 to get the area to the **left** of $-z$.
  $1 - 0.2611 = 0.7389$.
- Draw another sketch showing the new area. ──────→
- Look up $\Phi(z) = 0.7389$ in the table.
  $\Phi(z) = 0.7389$ for $z = 0.64$, so $-z = 0.64$.
- So, $z = -1 \times 0.64 = -0.64$. So, if $P(Z < z) = 0.6211$, then $z = -0.64$

Tip: Again, check the answer seems OK. $P(Z < z) < 0.5$, so z should be negative.

If you're given the probability that Z is **greater than** a value of z, $P(Z > z)$, it's usually best to see if you can use the **table of percentage points** of the normal distribution (see page 151).

- The **percentage-points** table gives the value of z for some probabilities, p, where $p = \mathbf{P(Z > z)}$.

- So this time you **start** off with the **probability** that Z is **greater** than a value of z, and look up the value of z in the table.

- However, depending on the **value of p**, you might not be able to find what you want from the percentage-points table. In which case, use the $\Phi(z)$ table and the symmetry of the curve.

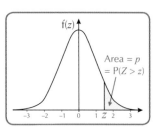

Tip: The values of p in the percentage-points table are all nice, 'round' decimals.

Examples

a) If $P(Z > z) = 0.15$, then what is the value of z?

- Start by drawing a **sketch**, showing what you know. →
- Try looking up $p = \mathbf{0.15}$ in the **percentage-points** table. ← See p151
  From the table, if $p = 0.15$, then $z = 1.0364$.
  So, if $P(Z > z) = 0.15$, then $\boxed{z = 1.0364}$

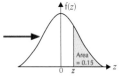

b) Find z if $P(Z \geq z) = 0.01$.

Tip: Remember, $>$ and $\geq$ mean the same for a continuous distribution.

- Start by drawing a **sketch**, showing what you know. →
- Try looking up $p = \mathbf{0.01}$ in the **percentage-points** table.
  From the table, if $p = 0.01$, then $z = 2.3263$.
  So, if $P(Z \geq z) = 0.01$, then $\boxed{z = 2.3263}$

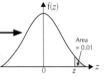

c) If $P(Z > z) = 0.7734$, then what is the value of z?

- Start by drawing a **sketch**, showing what you know. →
- p is a 'horrible' decimal, so the percentage-points table can't help you. And since $p > 0.5$, you know that z is negative.
- So use **symmetry** to shade an area of the **same size** that you can look up in the $\Phi(z)$ table.
  This is the area to the **left of** $-z$. ───────
- From the table, $\Phi(z) = 0.7734$ for $z = 0.75$.
  So, $-z = \mathbf{0.75}$ and $z = -\mathbf{1} \times \mathbf{0.75} = -0.75$. ← See p150
- So, if $P(Z > z) = 0.7734$, then $\boxed{z = -0.75}$

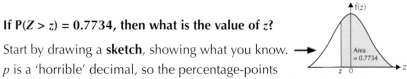

Okay, so the $\Phi(z)$ table contains values for $P(Z \leq z)$ and the **percentage-points** table contains values for $P(Z > z)$. But it really depends on what sort of decimal the **probability** is as to which table you should use to find z.

Examples

a) If P($Z < z$) = 0.9, then what is the value of z?

- Start by drawing a **sketch**, showing what you know.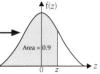
- P($Z < z$) is a nice, 'round' decimal, so you'll probably need to use the percentage-points table in some way.
- If P($Z < z$) = 0.9, then P($Z \geq z$) = 0.1. So try looking up p = **0.1** in the **percentage-points** table.

  From the table, if p = 0.1, then z = 1.2816.

  So, if P($Z < z$) = 0.9, then z = 1.2816

Tip: The $\Phi(z)$ table doesn't contain $\Phi(z) = 0.9$.

And since P($Z < z$) > 0.5, you need to subtract it from 1 before using the percentage-points table.

b) If P($Z < z$) = 0.05, then what is the value of z?

- This is a nice, 'round' probability, so it looks like you're going to need the percentage-points table. But you can't use it directly because you have a probability that $Z < z$ (not $Z > z$).
- Start by drawing a **sketch**, showing what you know.
- This shows that the area to the right of $-z$ is 0.05, so try looking up p = **0.05** in the **percentage-points** table.

  From the table, p = 0.05 for z = 1.6449.
  So, $-z$ = **1.6449** and z = **$-1 \times$ 1.6449** = -1.6449.
- So, if P($Z < z$) = 0.05, then $z = -1.6449$

Tip: You don't always have to do a sketch if you feel you don't need to, but they do help you to avoid mistakes.

c) If P($Z > z$) = 0.0392, then what is the value of z?

- This is a fairly unpleasant decimal, so you'll need to use the table for $\Phi(z)$ this time.
- Start by drawing a **sketch**, showing what you know.
- Since P($Z > z$) = 0.0392, you know that P($Z \leq z$) = 1 − 0.0392 = 0.9608. So look this up in the $\Phi(z)$ **table**.

  From the table, $\Phi(z)$ = 0.9608 for z = 1.76.
- So, if P($Z > z$) = 0.0392, then $z = 1.76$

The final type of example we need to go through is when you're given the **probability** that Z takes a value **between two limits**, and you're asked to **find** the **missing limit**.

Examples

a) If P($0 < Z < z$) = 0.4452, find the value of z.

- Start by drawing a **sketch**, showing what you know.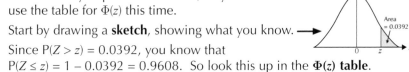
- If you find P($Z < z$), you can use the $\Phi(z)$ table to get z.

  P($Z < z$) = 0.4452 + P($Z \leq 0$) ← P($Z \leq 0$) = P($Z \geq 0$) = 0.5
  $\quad\quad$ = 0.9452
- Using the table, $\Phi(z)$ = 0.9452 for z = 1.60.
- So, if P($0 < Z < z$) = 0.4452, then $z = 1.60$

b) If P(0.8 < Z < z) = 0.20, find the value of z.

- Start by drawing a **sketch**, showing what you know. ⟶
- If you find P(Z < z), you can use the Φ(z) table to get z.

$$P(Z < z) = P(Z \le 0.8) + P(0.8 < Z < z)$$
$$= 0.7881 + 0.20$$
$$= 0.9881 \qquad \text{—Using the Φ(z) table}$$

- Using the table, Φ(z) = 0.9881 for z = 2.26.
- So, if P(0.8 < Z < z) = 0.20, then z = 2.26

Exercise 2.2

Q1 Use the table of the normal cumulative distribution function, Φ(z), to find z, given each of the following probabilities.

a) P(Z < z) = 0.8577   b) P(Z < z) = 0.8264

c) P(Z < z) = 0.3783   d) P(Z < z) = 0.004

e) P(Z > z) = 0.758   f) P(Z > z) = 0.9441

g) P(Z > z) = 0.4801   h) P(Z > z) = 0.0951

Q2 Use the percentage-points table to find z, given each of the following probabilities.

a) P(Z > z) = 0.005   b) P(Z > z) = 0.2

c) P(Z < z) = 0.7   d) P(Z < z) = 0.85

e) P(Z < z) = 0.1   f) P(Z < z) = 0.15

g) P(Z > z) = 0.6   h) P(Z > z) = 0.99

Q3 Hint: If you subtract the given area from 1 and divide by 2, you get the area ≥ z (and ≤ –z). And that means you can easily find P(Z ≤ z).

Q3 Find the value of z, given each of the following probabilities.

a) P(–z < Z < z) = 0.599   b) P(–z < Z < z) = 0.9426

c) P(–z < Z < z) = 0.4   d) P(–z < Z < z) = 0.98

Q4 Hint: Remember, P(Z < 0) and P(Z > 0) both equal 0.5.

Q4 Find the value of z, given each of the following probabilities.

a) P(0 < Z < z) = 0.3869   b) P(0 < Z < z) = 0.4854

Q5 Find the value of z, given each of the following probabilities.

Q5 Hint: One way of doing these is to flip the interval across the line z = 0.

a) P(z < Z < 0) = 0.2422   b) P(z < Z < 0) = 0.1443

Q6 Find the value of z, given each of the following probabilities.

a) P(1.5 < Z < z) = 0.0406   b) P(0.58 < Z < z) = 0.0691

c) P(–1.3 < Z < z) = 0.871   d) P(–0.54 < Z < z) = 0.667

e) P(z < Z < 0.27) = 0.5458   f) P(z < Z < –1.25) = 0.0949

3. Normal Distributions and Z-Tables

All normally distributed variables can be transformed to the standard normal variable, Z. This is really useful, because it means that you can use the Z-tables to find out information about any normal distribution.

Converting to the Z distribution

Any continuous random variable, X, where $X \sim N(\mu, \sigma^2)$, can be **transformed** to the **standard normal variable**, Z, by:

- **subtracting the mean** (μ), and then
- **dividing by the standard deviation** (σ).

Learning Objectives:

- Be able to transform normal variables to the standard normal variable, Z.
- Use Z-tables to find probabilities for normal variables.
- Use simultaneous equations to find the mean and variance of a normal distribution.

$$\text{If } X \sim N(\mu, \sigma^2), \text{ then } \frac{X - \mu}{\sigma} = Z, \text{ where } Z \sim N(0, 1)$$

Once you've transformed a variable like this, you can use the Z-tables.

Tip: Remember, the standard deviation is the square root of the variance.

- Here's a sketch of the distribution of X, where $X \sim N(20, 9)$. $\mu = 20, \sigma = 3$

- To transform X into Z, you need to transform **all values of X** (called x) into **values of Z** (called z), using the formula:

$$z = \frac{x - 20}{3}$$

- For example:
  $x = 23$ becomes $z = \frac{23 - 20}{3} = 1$

- To find a **probability** for X, rewrite it as a probability for Z, then find the corresponding area under the Z curve.

E.g. $P(X < 25) = P\left(Z < \frac{25 - 20}{3}\right) = P(Z < 1.67) = 0.9525$ ← From $\Phi(z)$ table

Tip: Here the z-value has been rounded to 2 decimal places so we can use the $\Phi(z)$ table. This rounding means that the probability we get isn't quite as precise as if we'd been able to use the full value.

Examples

a) If $X \sim N(5, 16)$, find $P(X < 7)$.

- Start by **transforming** X to Z. $\mu = 5, \sigma = \sqrt{16} = 4$

$$P(X < 7) = P\left(Z < \frac{7 - 5}{4}\right) = P(Z < 0.5)$$

- Draw a **sketch** showing the area you need to find. →
- Look up $z = 0.5$ in the table for $\Phi(z)$. ← See p150
$$P(Z < 0.5) = \boxed{0.6915}$$

Tip: You'll usually be given the variance, which means taking the square root to find the standard deviation.

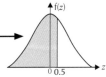

Tip: You might not need a sketch to answer this one, but it's a good habit to get into for the trickier questions.

b) If $X \sim N(5, 16)$, find $P(X > 9)$.

- Start by **transforming** X to Z.
$$P(X > 9) = P\left(Z > \frac{9 - 5}{4}\right) = P(Z > 1)$$

- Draw a **sketch** showing the area you need to find. ⟶

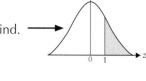

$$P(Z > 1) = 1 - P(Z \le 1)$$
$$= 1 - 0.8413$$
$$= \boxed{0.1587}$$

c) If $X \sim N(5, 16)$, find $P(5 < X < 11)$.

- Start by **transforming** X to Z.
$$P(5 < X < 11) = P\left(\frac{5 - 5}{4} < Z < \frac{11 - 5}{4}\right) = P(0 < Z < 1.5)$$

- Draw a **sketch** showing the area you need to find. ⟶

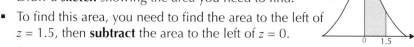

- To find this area, you need to find the area to the left of $z = 1.5$, then **subtract** the area to the left of $z = 0$.
- So, $P(0 < Z < 1.5) = P(Z < 1.5) - P(Z \le 0)$
$$= 0.9332 - 0.5$$
$$= \boxed{0.4332}$$

Tip: See page 129.

As you saw in the previous section, you often need to use the **symmetry** of the curve to answer questions on the normal distribution.

We'll be using the same methods here as in Section 2, but we need to do the **extra step** of transforming X to Z first.

Examples

If $X \sim N(102, 144)$:

a) Find $P(X > 78)$.

- Start by **transforming** X to Z.
$$P(X > 78) = P\left(Z > \frac{78 - 102}{12}\right) = P(Z > -2.0)$$

- Draw a **sketch** showing the area you need to find. ⟶

- Use symmetry to shade an **area of the same size** that you can look up in the $\Phi(z)$ table.
This is the area to the **left** of $z = +2.0$. ⟶

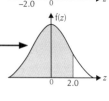

- So $P(Z > -2.0) = P(Z < 2.0)$.
And looking up 2.0 in the $\Phi(z)$ table you get:

$$P(Z > -2.0) = P(Z < 2.0) = \boxed{0.9772}$$ See p150

b) Find P($X \leq 98$).

- Start by **transforming** X to Z.

   To 2 d.p.

   $P(X \leq 98) = P\left(Z \leq \frac{98 - 102}{12}\right) = P(Z \leq -0.33)$

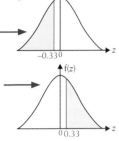

- Draw a **sketch** showing the area you need to find. →

- You can't look up a **negative** value of z in the table, so again, use symmetry to shade an **area of the same size**. This is the area to the **right** of $z = +0.33$. →

- So $P(Z \leq -0.33) = P(Z \geq 0.33)$.

- Now, $P(Z \geq 0.33) = 1 - P(Z < 0.33)$

   $ = 1 - 0.6293$

   $ = \boxed{0.3707}$

Tip: Round z values to 2 decimal places so you can look them up in the table.

c) Find P($84 \leq X \leq 106$).

- Start by **transforming** X to Z.

   $P(84 \leq X \leq 106) = P\left(\frac{84 - 102}{12} \leq Z \leq \frac{106 - 102}{12}\right)$

   $ = P(-1.5 \leq Z \leq 0.33)$

- Draw a **sketch** showing the area you need to find. →

- To find this area, you need to find the area to the left of $z = 0.33$ and **subtract** the area to the left of $z = -1.5$.

- So, $P(-1.5 \leq Z \leq 0.33) = P(Z \leq 0.33) - P(Z < -1.5)$

- You can find $P(Z \leq 0.33)$ directly from the table, but $P(Z < -1.5)$ takes a bit more working out.

   $P(Z < -1.5) = P(Z > 1.5) = 1 - P(Z \leq 1.5)$

   $\phantom{P(Z < -1.5)} = 1 - 0.9332$

   $\phantom{P(Z < -1.5)} = 0.0668$

- So, $P(Z \leq 0.33) - P(Z < -1.5) = 0.6293 - 0.0668 = \boxed{0.5625}$

You also need to be able to **find values**, when you're **given probabilities**.

For example, find a, given that $P(X < a) = 0.6$.

- As usual, the first step is to transform X to Z.

   If $X \sim N(\mu, \sigma^2)$, the equation $P(X < a) = 0.6$ becomes $P\left(Z < \frac{a - \mu}{\sigma}\right) = 0.6$.

- Then you use the same methods as on pages 131-134, and you end up with an equation in a to solve.

Tip: You can look up probabilities in the $\Phi(z)$ table, or the percentage-points table. See p131-134 for a reminder and some examples.

See p131-134

Examples

a) $X \sim N(85, 25)$. If $P(X < a) = 0.9192$, find the value of a.

- Start by **transforming** X to Z.

   $P(X < a) = P\left(Z < \frac{a - 85}{5}\right) = 0.9192$

- Draw a **sketch** to show the information. →

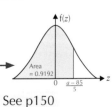

- Use the $\Phi(z)$ table to find z for which $\Phi(z) = 0.9192$.

   $\Phi(z) = 0.9192$ for $z = 1.40$, so $\frac{a - 85}{5} = 1.40$ ← See p150

- Now, just **solve** for a:

   Equation in a.

   $\frac{a - 85}{5} = 1.4 \Rightarrow a - 85 = 7 \Rightarrow \boxed{a = 92}$

b) $X \sim N(85, 25)$. **If** $P(X < b) = 0.0179$, **find the value of** b.

- Start by **transforming** X to Z.

$$P(X < b) = P\left(Z < \frac{b - 85}{5}\right) = 0.0179$$

- Draw a **sketch** to show the information — the area is less than 0.5, so $\frac{b - 85}{5}$ must be negative. Now mark on the **equivalent area** to the right of $-\frac{b - 85}{5}$.

- You can see that $P\left(Z > \frac{85 - b}{5}\right) = 0.0179$.

So $P\left(Z \leq \frac{85 - b}{5}\right) = 1 - 0.0179 = 0.9821$

- Using the $\Phi(z)$ table, $\Phi(z) = 0.9821$ for $z = 2.10$, so $\frac{85 - b}{5} = 2.10$.

- So **solving** for b, $\frac{85 - b}{5} = 2.10 \Rightarrow 85 - b = 10.5 \Rightarrow \boxed{b = 74.5}$

Tip: The equivalent area is to the right of $-\frac{b - 85}{5}$, i.e. to the right of $\frac{85 - b}{5}$.

Exercise 3.1

Q1   If $X \sim N(40, 25)$, find: a) $P(X < 50)$ b) $P(X < 43)$

Q2   If $X \sim N(24, 6)$, find: a) $P(X > 28)$ b) $P(X > 25)$

Q3   If $X \sim N(120, 40)$, find: a) $P(X > 107)$ b) $P(X > 115)$

Q4   If $X \sim N(17, 3^2)$, find: a) $P(X < 15)$ b) $P(X < 12)$

Q5   If $X \sim N(50, 5^2)$, find:
   a) $P(52 < X < 63)$ b) $P(57 < X < 66)$

Q6   If $X \sim N(0.6, 0.04)$, find:
   a) $P(0.45 < X < 0.55)$ b) $P(0.53 < X < 0.58)$

Q7   If $X \sim N(260, 15^2)$, find:
   a) $P(240 < X < 280)$ b) $P(232 < X < 288)$

Q8 $X \sim N(70, 16)$
   a) Find a if $P(X < a) = 0.9938$ b)   Find b if $P(X < b) = 0.7734$

Q9 $X \sim N(95, 25)$
   a) Find m if $P(X > m) = 0.0102$ b)   Find t if $P(X > t) = 0.2296$

Q10 $X \sim N(48, 100)$
   a) Find c if $P(X < c) = 0.1251$ b)   Find d if $P(X < d) = 0.0096$

Q11 $X \sim N(73, 6^2)$
   a) Find w if $P(X > w) = 0.9177$ b) Find k if $P(X > k) = 0.6664$

Q12 $X \sim N(18, 0.25)$. Find a if $P(18 - a < X < 18 + a) = 0.899$.

Q13 $X \sim N(170, 40^2)$. Find t if $P(170 < X < t) = 0.377$.

Q14 $X \sim N(98, 225)$. Find v if $P(107.6 < X < v) = 0.1677$.

Hint: Round z values to 2 d.p. so you can look them up in the table.

Q2 Hint: The standard deviation doesn't have to be a whole number.

Q4 Hint: You'll often see the variance written as a number squared.

The normal distribution in real-life situations

Now it's time to use everything you've learnt about normal distributions to answer questions in **real-life** contexts. These are the kind of questions that usually come up in **exams**.

You always start by **defining** a **normally-distributed random variable** to represent the information you're given. Then you use the usual methods to find out what you need to know.

Tip: The first step is always to define the variable.

Example 1

A machine which fills boxes of cereal is set so that the mass of cereal going into the boxes follows a normal distribution with mean 766 g and standard deviation 8 g.

a) Find the probability that a randomly selected box of cereal contains less than 780 g of cereal.

- First, **define a random variable** to represent the mass of cereal in a box.
  If X represents the mass of cereal in g, then $X \sim N(766, 64)$.
- Next, turn the question into a **probability for X**. $\qquad \overset{8^2}{\curvearrowleft}$
  So you want to find, $P(X < 780)$.
- Now you can **transform** X to Z in the usual way.
  $$P(X < 780) = P\left(Z < \frac{780 - 766}{8}\right)$$
  $$= P(Z < 1.75)$$
- Draw a **sketch** showing the area you need to find. ⟶
- Using the $\Phi(z)$ table, $P(Z < 1.75) = 0.9599$
- So P(a random box of cereal contains less than 780 g) = $\boxed{0.9599}$

Tip: So the variable here is the mass of cereal in a box.

Tip: See p150 for the $\Phi(z)$ table.

Tip: Always check the answer seems sensible. Using the rules on p127, you know that 97.5% of values are less than $2 \times \sigma$ above the mean (and $2 \times 8 + 766 = 782$). So this answer seems about right.

b) Find the probability that a randomly selected box of cereal contains between 780 g and 790 g of cereal.

- Again, turn the question into a **probability for X**.
  So you want to find, $P(780 < X < 790)$.
- Next, **transform** X to Z.
  $$P(780 < X < 790) = P\left(\frac{780 - 766}{8} < Z < \frac{790 - 766}{8}\right)$$
  $$= P(1.75 < Z < 3.0)$$
- Draw a **sketch** to help you see this area. ⟶
  This is the area to the left of 3.0, minus the area to the left of 1.75 (which you found in part a)).
- So, $P(1.75 < Z < 3.0) = P(Z < 3.0) - P(Z \leq 1.75)$
- Using the $\Phi(z)$ table, $P(Z < 3.0) = 0.9987$. ⟵ From part a)
  So, $P(Z < 3.0) - P(Z \leq 1.75) = 0.9987 - 0.9599 = 0.0388$
- This means:
  P(a random box of cereal contains between 780 g and 790 g) = $\boxed{0.0388}$

Here's another example. In part b), we need to use the symmetry of the curve to work out what area to look up in the table.

Example 2

The times taken by a group of people to complete an assault course are normally distributed with a mean of 600 seconds and a variance of 105 seconds. Find the probability that a randomly selected person took:

a) more than 620 seconds

- Start by **defining a random variable** to represent the time taken.
  If X represents the time taken in seconds, then $X \sim N(600, 105)$.
- Next, turn the question into a **probability for X**.
  So you want to find $P(X > 620)$.
- Now you can **transform** X to Z.

$$P(X > 620) = P\left(Z > \frac{620 - 600}{\sqrt{105}}\right)$$

$$= P(Z > 1.95) \longleftarrow \text{To 2 d.p.}$$

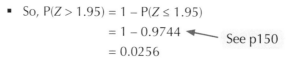

- Draw a **sketch** to show the information.
- So, $P(Z > 1.95) = 1 - P(Z \leq 1.95)$

$$= 1 - 0.9744 \longleftarrow \text{See p150}$$

$$= 0.0256$$

- This means:
  P(a randomly selected person took more than 620 seconds) = $\boxed{0.0256}$

b) fewer than 575 seconds

- Again, turn the question into a **probability for X**.
  So this time you want to find $P(X < 575)$.
- Next **transform** X to Z.

$$P(X < 575) = P\left(Z < \frac{575 - 600}{\sqrt{105}}\right)$$

$$= P(Z < -2.44) \longleftarrow \text{To 2 d.p.}$$

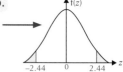

- Draw a **sketch** to show the information. You can't look up a **negative** value of z in the table, so use symmetry to shade an **area of the same size**.
- OK so, $P(Z < -2.44) = P(Z > 2.44)$

$$= 1 - P(Z \leq 2.44)$$

$$= 1 - 0.9927 = 0.0073$$

- This means:
  P(a randomly selected person took fewer than 575 seconds) = $\boxed{0.0073}$

Real-life normal distribution questions also ask you to **find values**, when you're **given probabilities**.

Remember there are **two tables** you can use to look up probabilities — the table of the cumulative distribution function, $\Phi(z)$, and the percentage-points table.

Example

The forces needed to snap lengths of a certain type of elastic are normally distributed with $\mu = 13$ N and $\sigma = 1.8$ N.

a) The probability that a randomly selected length of elastic is snapped by a force of less than a N is 0.7580. Find the value of a.

- Start by **defining a random variable** to represent the force needed.
  If F represents the force needed in N, then $F \sim N(13, 1.8^2)$.

- Next, turn the question into a **probability for F**.
  So you know that $P(F < a) = 0.7580$.

- Next, **transform F to Z**.

  $P(F < a) = P\left(Z < \dfrac{a - 13}{1.8}\right) = 0.7580$

- Draw a **sketch** to show the information.

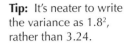

- Use the $\Phi(z)$ table to find z for which $\Phi(z) = 0.7580$.
  $\Phi(z) = 0.7580$ for $z = 0.70$, so $\dfrac{a - 13}{1.8} = 0.70$

- Now, just **solve** for a:

  $\dfrac{a - 13}{1.8} = 0.7 \Rightarrow a - 13 = 1.26 \Rightarrow \boxed{a = 14.26}$

Tip: It's neater to write the variance as 1.8^2, rather than 3.24.

Tip: Use a sensible letter for the variable — it doesn't have to be X.

Tip: $P(Z < z)$ isn't a 'nice' decimal, so you'll need to use the $\Phi(z)$ table.

b) Find the range of values that includes the middle 80% of forces needed.

- It's difficult to know where to start with this one. So it's a good idea to **sketch the distribution of F**, to show the range you need to find.

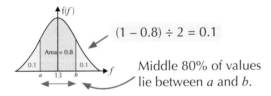

$(1 - 0.8) \div 2 = 0.1$

Middle 80% of values lie between a and b.

- Now you can write **2 probability statements** — 1 for a and 1 for b.
  $P(F < a) = 0.1$ and $P(F > b) = 0.1$.

- Next, **transform F to Z**.

  $P(F < a) = P\left(Z < \dfrac{a - 13}{1.8}\right) = 0.1$ and $P(F > b) = P\left(Z > \dfrac{b - 13}{1.8}\right) = 0.1$

- Draw another **sketch** to show this information.

- So, now you need to use the **tables** to find a and b.
  The easiest one to start with is b, because you can use the **percentage-points** table to find the value of z for which $P(Z > z) = 0.1$.
  From the table, $p = 0.1$ for $z = 1.2816$. ◄── See p151

  So, $\dfrac{b - 13}{1.8} = 1.2816 \Rightarrow b = 15.31$

- And using symmetry, $\dfrac{a - 13}{1.8} = -1.2816 \Rightarrow a = 10.69$

- So the range of values is $\boxed{10.69 \text{ N to } 15.31 \text{ N}}$

Tip: $P(Z > z)$ is a 'nice' decimal, so you'll need to use the percentage-points table.

To 2 d.p.

Tip: The range is symmetrical about $z = 0$, so $\dfrac{a - 13}{1.8} = -\dfrac{b - 13}{1.8}$.

Q1 The lengths of worms in a certain area are found to follow a normal distribution, with mean 8.4 cm and standard deviation 3.1 cm.

  a) What is the probability that a randomly selected worm is shorter than 9.5 cm?

  b) What is the probability that a randomly selected worm is longer than 10 cm?

  c) What is the probability that a randomly selected worm has a length of between 5 cm and 11 cm?

Q2 The lengths of time taken by a group of blood donors to replace their red blood cells are modelled by a normal distribution with a mean of 36 days and a standard deviation of 6 days.

  a) It takes Edward 28 days to replace his red blood cells. Find the probability that a randomly selected donor from the group takes less time than Edward to replace their red blood cells.

  b) 6.3% of the group take longer than Bella to replace their red blood cells. How long does it take Bella?

Q3 The 'personal best' times taken by athletes at a sports club to run 400 m are known to follow a normal distribution with a mean of 51 seconds and a standard deviation of 2.1 seconds.

  a) Gary's 'personal best' time is 49.3 seconds. What percentage of the athletes have a slower 'personal best' time than Gary?

  b) The athletes with 'personal bests' in the top 20% of times are selected for a special training programme. What time do they have to beat to be selected for the programme?

Q4 A particular type of toy car uses two identical batteries. The lifetimes of individual batteries can be modelled by a normal distribution with a mean of 300 hours and a standard deviation of 50 hours.

  a) What is the probability that a battery of this type lasts less than 200 hours?

  b) What is the probability that a battery of this type lasts at least 380 hours?

Q4 Hint: See p68 for a reminder of finding probabilities of multiple events.

  c) Stating any assumptions you make, find the probability that both of the batteries in a car last at least 380 hours.

  d) The probability that a randomly selected battery lasts more than 160 hours, but less than h hours, is 0.9746. Find the value of h.

Q5 The masses of the eggs laid by the hens on farmer Elizabeth's farm are assumed to follow a normal distribution with mean 60 g and standard deviation 3 g.

  a) The probability that a randomly selected egg has a mass of at least $60 - m$ grams is 0.9525. Find the value of m to the nearest gram.

  b) Farmer Elizabeth keeps the lightest 10% of eggs for herself and uses them to make sponge cakes. Find the maximum mass of an egg that could end up in one of farmer Elizabeth's sponge cakes.

Finding the mean and standard deviation of a normal distribution

Remember that any normally distributed variable, $X \sim N(\mu, \sigma^2)$, can be **transformed** to the standard normal variable, Z, by **subtracting the mean**, μ, and **dividing by the standard deviation**, σ.

So X and Z are **linked** by the equation: $Z = \dfrac{X - \mu}{\sigma}$

So far you've used this relationship to find **probability facts** for X, when the mean and standard deviation have been **known**. But you can use exactly the **same approach** to find the **mean** and **standard deviation** when they're **unknown**... as long as you already know some probability facts.

Example 1

If the random variable $X \sim N(\mu, 4)$ and $P(X < 23) = 0.9015$, find μ.

- Okay, start by **transforming the probability** you're given for X into a probability for Z. The mean is unknown, so just leave it as μ for now.

$$P(X < 23) = P\left(Z < \frac{23 - \mu}{2}\right) = 0.9015$$

- Draw a **sketch** to show the information. ───────────▶
- Now, if you use the $\Phi(z)$ table to find z for which $\Phi(z) = 0.9015$, you can form an **equation** in μ.

  From the table, $\Phi(z) = 0.9015$ for $z = 1.29$. See p150

  So, $\dfrac{23 - \mu}{2} = 1.29$ ◀─── Equation in μ.

- Now **solve** this equation for μ.

$$\frac{23 - \mu}{2} = 1.29 \Rightarrow 23 - \mu = 2.58 \Rightarrow \boxed{\mu = 20.42}$$

Tip: As always, check that the answer seems about right. You know it must be a bit lower than 23, so 20.42 seems OK.

Example 2

If the random variable $X \sim N(\mu, 4^2)$ and $P(X > 19.84) = 0.025$, find μ.

- **Transform the probability** you're given for X into a probability for Z.

$$P(X > 19.84) = P\left(Z > \frac{19.84 - \mu}{4}\right) = 0.025$$

- Draw a **sketch** to show the information. ───────────▶
- From the percentage-points table, $p = 0.025$ for $z = 1.96$. See p151

  So, $\dfrac{19.84 - \mu}{4} = 1.96$

- Now **solve** this equation for μ.

$$\frac{19.84 - \mu}{4} = 1.96 \Rightarrow 19.84 - \mu = 7.84 \Rightarrow \boxed{\mu = 12}$$

In the first two examples we found the mean, but you can find the **standard deviation** (s.d.) in exactly the same way.

Example 3

If the random variable $X \sim N(53, \sigma^2)$ and $P(X < 50) = 0.2$, find σ.

- Again, start by **transforming the probability** you're given for X into a probability for Z. The s.d. is unknown, so just leave it as σ for now.

$$P(X < 50) = P\left(Z < \frac{50 - 53}{\sigma}\right) = P\left(Z < -\frac{3}{\sigma}\right) = 0.2$$

- Draw a **sketch** to show the information. The area is less than 0.5, so mark on the **equivalent area** to the right of $-\left(-\frac{3}{\sigma}\right)$. $-(-3/\sigma) = 3/\sigma$

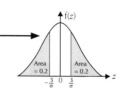

- You can see that $P\left(Z > \frac{3}{\sigma}\right) = 0.2$.

- From the percentage-points table, $p = 0.2$ for $z = 0.8416$.

  So, $\frac{3}{\sigma} = 0.8416$ ⟵ Equation in σ.   See p151

- Now **solve** this equation for σ.

  $\frac{3}{\sigma} = 0.8416 \Rightarrow \sigma = 3.56$ ⟵ To 3 s.f.

Tip: Values of σ should always be positive.

When you're asked to find the mean **and** the standard deviation, the method is a little bit **more complicated**.

You start off as usual, but instead of getting one equation in one unknown to solve, you end up with **two equations** in **two unknowns**, μ and σ. In other words, you have **simultaneous equations**, which you **solve** to find μ and σ.

Tip: Remember, you can solve simultaneous equations by adding or subtracting them to get rid of one unknown.

Example

The random variable $X \sim N(\mu, \sigma^2)$.
If $P(X < 9) = 0.5596$ and $P(X > 14) = 0.0322$, find μ and σ.

- Let's start with the first probability for X, and **transform** it into a probability for Z.

$$P(X < 9) = P\left(Z < \frac{9 - \mu}{\sigma}\right) = 0.5596$$

- Draw a **sketch** to show the information.

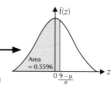

- Now, if you use the $\Phi(z)$ table to find z for which $\Phi(z) = 0.5596$, you can form an **equation** in μ and σ.

  From the table, $\Phi(z) = 0.5596$ for $z = 0.15$.   See p150

  So, $\frac{9 - \mu}{\sigma} = 0.15 \Rightarrow 9 - \mu = 0.15\sigma$ ⟵ 1st equation in μ and σ

- Now do the same thing for the second probability for X. **Transforming** to Z, you get:

$$P(X > 14) = P\left(Z > \frac{14 - \mu}{\sigma}\right) = 0.0322$$

- Draw a **sketch** to show the information. ⟶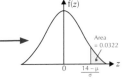

Tip: $p = 0.0322$ isn't in the percentage-points table, so it might help to use a sketch.

- You can see from the graph that:

$$P\left(Z \le \frac{14 - \mu}{\sigma}\right) = 1 - P\left(Z > \frac{14 - \mu}{\sigma}\right) = 1 - 0.0322 = 0.9678$$

- Now use the $\Phi(z)$ table to find z for which $\Phi(z) = 0.9678$. From the table, $\Phi(z) = 0.9678$ for $z = 1.85$.

So, $\dfrac{14 - \mu}{\sigma} = 1.85 \Rightarrow 14 - \mu = 1.85\sigma$ ⟵ 2nd equation in μ and σ

- So now you have your **simultaneous** equations:

$9 - \mu = 0.15\sigma$ ❶
$14 - \mu = 1.85\sigma$ ❷ ⟵ It helps to number the equations, so you can refer to them later.

- Each equation has one 'μ', so you can **subtract** them to get rid of μ, which will leave you with an **equation in σ** to solve.

❷ – ❶ gives $14 - 9 - \mu - (-\mu) = 1.85\sigma - 0.15\sigma$
$\Rightarrow 5 = 1.7\sigma$
$\Rightarrow \sigma = 2.941176... \Rightarrow \sigma = 2.94$ ⟵ To 3 s.f.

- Finally, find μ by **substituting** $\sigma = 2.94...$ back into one of the equations. Using equation ❶,

$9 - \mu = 0.15\sigma \Rightarrow \mu = 9 - 0.15 \times 2.94... \Rightarrow \mu = 8.56$ ⟵ To 3 s.f.

Exercise 3.3

Q1 For each of the following, use the information to find μ.
- a) $X \sim N(\mu, 6^2)$ and $P(X < 23) = 0.9332$.
- b) $X \sim N(\mu, 8^2)$ and $P(X < 57) = 0.9970$.
- c) $X \sim N(\mu, 100^2)$ and $P(X > 528) = 0.1292$.
- d) $X \sim N(\mu, 0.4^2)$ and $P(X < 11.06) = 0.0322$.
- e) $X \sim N(\mu, 0.02^2)$ and $P(X > 1.52) = 0.9938$.

Q2 $X \sim N(\mu, 3.5^2)$. If the middle 95% of the distribution lies between 6.45 and 20.17, find the value of μ.

Q2 Hint: Start by drawing a diagram showing the distribution of X.

Q3   For each of the following, use the information to find σ.
   a) $X \sim N(48, \sigma^2)$ and $P(X < 53) = 0.8944$.
   b) $X \sim N(510, \sigma^2)$ and $P(X < 528) = 0.7734$.
   c) $X \sim N(17, \sigma^2)$ and $P(X > 24) = 0.0367$.
   d) $X \sim N(0.98, \sigma^2)$ and $P(X < 0.95) = 0.3085$.
   e) $X \sim N(5.6, \sigma^2)$ and $P(X > 4.85) = 0.8365$.

Q4 $X \sim N(68, \sigma^2)$. If the middle 70% of the distribution lies between 61 and 75, find the value of σ.

Q5   For each of the following, find μ and σ.
   a) $X \sim N(\mu, \sigma^2)$, $P(X < 30) = 0.9192$ and $P(X < 36) = 0.9953$.
   b) $X \sim N(\mu, \sigma^2)$, $P(X < 4) = 0.9332$ and $P(X < 4.3) = 0.9987$.
   c) $X \sim N(\mu, \sigma^2)$, $P(X < 20) = 0.7881$ and $P(X < 14) = 0.0548$.
   d) $X \sim N(\mu, \sigma^2)$, $P(X < 696) = 0.9713$ and $P(X < 592) = 0.2420$.
   e) $X \sim N(\mu, \sigma^2)$, $P(X > 33) = 0.1056$ and $P(X > 21) = 0.9599$.
   f) $X \sim N(\mu, \sigma^2)$, $P(X > 66) = 0.3632$ and $P(X < 48) = 0.3446$.

> **Q5 Hint:** You need to form and solve simultaneous equations in μ and σ.

Q6   The volume of vinegar contained in bottles of vinegar is modelled by a normal distribution with a standard deviation of 5 ml. Over time, it is found that 71.9% of bottles contain less than 506 ml of vinegar.
   a) Find the mean volume of vinegar contained in the bottles.
   b) The label on each bottle says it contains 500 ml of vinegar. What percentage of bottles contain less than 500 ml?

Q7   The heights of a population of 17-year-old boys are assumed to follow a normal distribution with a mean of 175 cm. 80% of this population of 17-year-old boys are taller than 170 cm.
   a) Find the standard deviation of the heights of the 17-year-old boys in this population.
   b) One 17-year-old boy is selected from the population at random. Find the probability that his height is within 4 cm of the mean height.

Q8   In a particularly wet village, it rains almost continuously. The daily rainfall, in cm, is modelled by a normal distribution. The daily rainfall is less than 4 cm on only 10.2% of days, and it's greater than 7 cm on 64.8% of days.

   Find the mean and standard deviation of the daily rainfall.

Review Exercise — Chapter 5

Q1   Find the probability that:

a) $Z < 0.84$ b) $Z < 2.95$

c) $Z > 0.68$ d) $Z \geq 1.55$

e) $Z < -2.10$ f) $Z \leq -0.01$

g) $Z > 0.10$ h) $Z \leq 0.64$

i) $Z > 0.23$ j) $0.10 < Z \leq 0.50$

k) $-0.62 \leq Z < 1.10$ l) $-0.99 < Z \leq -0.74$

Q2   Find the value of z if:

a) $P(Z < z) = 0.9131$ b) $P(Z < z) = 0.5871$

c) $P(Z > z) = 0.0359$ d) $P(Z > z) = 0.01$

e) $P(Z \leq z) = 0.4013$ f) $P(Z \geq z) = 0.995$

g) $P(-z < Z < z) = 0.5034$ h) $P(0.25 < Z < z) = 0.3917$

Q3   If $X \sim N(50, 16)$ find:

a) $P(X < 55)$ b) $P(X < 42)$ c) $P(X > 56)$ d) $P(47 < X < 57)$

Q4   If $X \sim N(5, 7^2)$ find:

a) $P(X < 0)$ b) $P(X < 1)$ c) $P(X > 7)$ d) $P(2 < X < 4)$

Q5 $X \sim N(80, 15)$

a) If $P(X < a) = 0.99$, find a.

b) If $P(|X - 80| < b) = 0.8$, find b.

Q5 Hint: $|X - 80| < b$ means that X is 'within b' of 80.

Q6   The mass of items produced by a factory is normally distributed with a mean of 55 grams and a standard deviation of 4.4 grams. Find the probability of a randomly chosen item having a mass of:

a) less than 55 grams   b) less than 50 grams   c) more than 60 grams

Q7   The mass of eggs laid by an ostrich is normally distributed with a mean of 1.4 kg and a standard deviation of 300 g. If 88.3% of the eggs laid by this ostrich have a mass of less than a kg, find the value of a.

Q8 $X \sim N(\mu, 10)$ and $P(X < 8) = 0.8925$. Find μ.

Q9 $X \sim N(\mu, 8^2)$ and $P(X > 221) = 0.3085$. Find μ.

Q10 $X \sim N(11, \sigma^2)$ and $P(X < 13) = 0.6$. Find σ.

Q11 $X \sim N(108, \sigma^2)$ and $P(X \leq 110) = 0.9678$. Find σ.

Q12 The random variable $X \sim N(\mu, \sigma^2)$.

If $P(X < 15.2) = 0.9783$ and $P(X > 14.8) = 0.1056$, then find μ and σ.

1   The exam marks for 1000 candidates can be modelled by a normal distribution
     with mean 50 marks and standard deviation 15 marks.

   a)   One candidate is selected at random. Find the probability that they scored less
         than 30 marks on this exam.

                                                                            (3 marks)

   b)   The pass mark is 41.
         Estimate the number of candidates who passed the exam.

                                                                            (3 marks)

   c)   Find the mark needed for a distinction if the top 10% of the candidates achieved
         a distinction.

                                                                            (3 marks)

2   The random variable X follows a normal distribution with mean μ and standard deviation 6.
     The probability that X takes a value of less than 50 is 0.123.

   a)   Find the mean of this distribution.

                                                                            (4 marks)

   b)   Find $P(X > 71)$.

                                                                            (3 marks)

   c)   Find the value of a such that $P(\mu - a < X < \mu + a) = 0.8$.

                                                                            (4 marks)

3   The lifetimes of a particular type of battery are normally distributed with mean μ
     and standard deviation σ. A student using these batteries finds that 40% last less
     than 20 hours and 80% last less than 26 hours.

   a)   Find μ and σ.

                                                                            (7 marks)

   b)   Find the probability that a randomly selected battery of this type has a lifetime
         of at least 15 hours.

                                                                            (3 marks)

4   The random variable X has a normal distribution with mean 120 and standard deviation 25.

    a)   Find $P(X > 145)$.

                                   (3 marks)

    b)   Find the value of j such that $P(120 < X < j) = 0.4641$

                                   (4 marks)

5   The diameters of the pizza bases made at a restaurant are normally distributed.
The mean diameter is 12 inches, and 5% of the bases measure more than 13 inches.

    a)   Write down the median diameter of the pizza bases.

                                     (1 mark)

    b)   Find the standard deviation of the diameters of the pizza bases.

                                   (4 marks)

Any pizza base with a diameter of less than 10.8 inches is
considered too small and is discarded.

    c)   If 100 pizza bases are made in an evening, approximately how many would you
expect to be discarded due to being too small?

                                   (3 marks)

Three pizza bases are selected at random.

    d)   Find the probability that at least one of these bases is too small.

                                   (3 marks)

6   A garden centre sells bags of compost. The volume of compost in the bags is normally
distributed with a mean of 50 litres.

    a)   If the standard deviation of the volume is 0.4 litres, find the probability that a
randomly selected bag will contain less than 49 litres of compost.

                                   (3 marks)

    b)   If 1000 of these bags of compost are bought, find the expected number of bags
containing more than 50.5 litres of compost.

                                   (5 marks)

A different garden centre sells bags of similar compost. The volume of compost, in litres,
in these bags is described by the random variable Y, where $Y \sim N(75, \sigma^2)$. It is found that
10% of the bags from this garden centre contain less than 74 litres of compost.

    c)   Find σ.

                                   (3 marks)

S1 Statistical Tables

The normal distribution function

The cumulative distribution function $\Phi(z)$ is tabulated below.

This is defined as $\Phi(z) = \dfrac{1}{\sqrt{2\pi}} \displaystyle\int_{-\infty}^{z} e^{-\frac{1}{2}t^2} dt$.

z	$\Phi(z)$	z	$\Phi(z)$	z	$\Phi(z)$	z	$\Phi(z)$	z	$\Phi(z)$
0.00	0.5000	0.50	0.6915	1.00	0.8413	1.50	0.9332	2.00	0.9772
0.01	0.5040	0.51	0.6950	1.01	0.8438	1.51	0.9345	2.02	0.9783
0.02	0.5080	0.52	0.6985	1.02	0.8461	1.52	0.9357	2.04	0.9793
0.03	0.5120	0.53	0.7019	1.03	0.8485	1.53	0.9370	2.06	0.9803
0.04	0.5160	0.54	0.7054	1.04	0.8508	1.54	0.9382	2.08	0.9812
0.05	0.5199	0.55	0.7088	1.05	0.8531	1.55	0.9394	2.10	0.9821
0.06	0.5239	0.56	0.7123	1.06	0.8554	1.56	0.9406	2.12	0.9830
0.07	0.5279	0.57	0.7157	1.07	0.8577	1.57	0.9418	2.14	0.9838
0.08	0.5319	0.58	0.7190	1.08	0.8599	1.58	0.9429	2.16	0.9846
0.09	0.5359	0.59	0.7224	1.09	0.8621	1.59	0.9441	2.18	0.9854
0.10	0.5398	0.60	0.7257	1.10	0.8643	1.60	0.9452	2.20	0.9861
0.11	0.5438	0.61	0.7291	1.11	0.8665	1.61	0.9463	2.22	0.9868
0.12	0.5478	0.62	0.7324	1.12	0.8686	1.62	0.9474	2.24	0.9875
0.13	0.5517	0.63	0.7357	1.13	0.8708	1.63	0.9484	2.26	0.9881
0.14	0.5557	0.64	0.7389	1.14	0.8729	1.64	0.9495	2.28	0.9887
0.15	0.5596	0.65	0.7422	1.15	0.8749	1.65	0.9505	2.30	0.9893
0.16	0.5636	0.66	0.7454	1.16	0.8770	1.66	0.9515	2.32	0.9898
0.17	0.5675	0.67	0.7486	1.17	0.8790	1.67	0.9525	2.34	0.9904
0.18	0.5714	0.68	0.7517	1.18	0.8810	1.68	0.9535	2.36	0.9909
0.19	0.5753	0.69	0.7549	1.19	0.8830	1.69	0.9545	2.38	0.9913
0.20	0.5793	0.70	0.7580	1.20	0.8849	1.70	0.9554	2.40	0.9918
0.21	0.5832	0.71	0.7611	1.21	0.8869	1.71	0.9564	2.42	0.9922
0.22	0.5871	0.72	0.7642	1.22	0.8888	1.72	0.9573	2.44	0.9927
0.23	0.5910	0.73	0.7673	1.23	0.8907	1.73	0.9582	2.46	0.9931
0.24	0.5948	0.74	0.7704	1.24	0.8925	1.74	0.9591	2.48	0.9934
0.25	0.5987	0.75	0.7734	1.25	0.8944	1.75	0.9599	2.50	0.9938
0.26	0.6026	0.76	0.7764	1.26	0.8962	1.76	0.9608	2.55	0.9946
0.27	0.6064	0.77	0.7794	1.27	0.8980	1.77	0.9616	2.60	0.9953
0.28	0.6103	0.78	0.7823	1.28	0.8997	1.78	0.9625	2.65	0.9960
0.29	0.6141	0.79	0.7852	1.29	0.9015	1.79	0.9633	2.70	0.9965
0.30	0.6179	0.80	0.7881	1.30	0.9032	1.80	0.9641	2.75	0.9970
0.31	0.6217	0.81	0.7910	1.31	0.9049	1.81	0.9649	2.80	0.9974
0.32	0.6255	0.82	0.7939	1.32	0.9066	1.82	0.9656	2.85	0.9978
0.33	0.6293	0.83	0.7967	1.33	0.9082	1.83	0.9664	2.90	0.9981
0.34	0.6331	0.84	0.7995	1.34	0.9099	1.84	0.9671	2.95	0.9984
0.35	0.6368	0.85	0.8023	1.35	0.9115	1.85	0.9678	3.00	0.9987
0.36	0.6406	0.86	0.8051	1.36	0.9131	1.86	0.9686	3.05	0.9989
0.37	0.6443	0.87	0.8078	1.37	0.9147	1.87	0.9693	3.10	0.9990
0.38	0.6480	0.88	0.8106	1.38	0.9162	1.88	0.9699	3.15	0.9992
0.39	0.6517	0.89	0.8133	1.39	0.9177	1.89	0.9706	3.20	0.9993
0.40	0.6554	0.90	0.8159	1.40	0.9192	1.90	0.9713	3.25	0.9994
0.41	0.6591	0.91	0.8186	1.41	0.9207	1.91	0.9719	3.30	0.9995
0.42	0.6628	0.92	0.8212	1.42	0.9222	1.92	0.9726	3.35	0.9996
0.43	0.6664	0.93	0.8238	1.43	0.9236	1.93	0.9732	3.40	0.9997
0.44	0.6700	0.94	0.8264	1.44	0.9251	1.94	0.9738	3.50	0.9998
0.45	0.6736	0.95	0.8289	1.45	0.9265	1.95	0.9744	3.60	0.9998
0.46	0.6772	0.96	0.8315	1.46	0.9279	1.96	0.9750	3.70	0.9999
0.47	0.6808	0.97	0.8340	1.47	0.9292	1.97	0.9756	3.80	0.9999
0.48	0.6844	0.98	0.8365	1.48	0.9306	1.98	0.9761	3.90	1.0000
0.49	0.6879	0.99	0.8389	1.49	0.9319	1.99	0.9767	4.00	1.0000
0.50	0.6915	1.00	0.8413	1.50	0.9332	2.00	0.9772		

S1 Statistical Tables

Percentage points of the normal distribution

The z-values in the table are those which a random variable

$Z \sim N(0, 1)$ exceeds with probability p, i.e. $P(Z > z) = 1 - \Phi(z) = p$.

p	z	p	z
0.5000	0.0000	0.0500	1.6449
0.4000	0.2533	0.0250	1.9600
0.3000	0.5244	0.0100	2.3263
0.2000	0.8416	0.0050	2.5758
0.1500	1.0364	0.0010	3.0902
0.1000	1.2816	0.0005	3.2905

Answers

Chapter 1: Data

1. Representing Data
Exercise 1.1 — Data basics
Q1 a) Make, Colour

   b) Mileage, Number of doors, Cost of service

Q2 a) Number of medals won last season, Shoe size

   b) Height, Mass

Q3 a) There are no 'gaps' between possible heights.

   b)

Height, h (cm)	No. of members	lower class b'dary (cm)	upper class b'dary (cm)	class width (cm)	class mid-point (cm)
$140 \leq h < 150$	3	140	150	10	145
$150 \leq h < 160$	9	150	160	10	155
$160 \leq h < 170$	17	160	170	10	165
$170 \leq h < 180$	12	170	180	10	175
$180 \leq h < 190$	5	180	190	10	185
$190 \leq h < 200$	1	190	200	10	195

Exercise 1.2 — Histograms
Q1 First add columns to the table to show class boundaries, the class widths and the frequency densities.

Mass (m, in g)	lower class boundary	upper class boundary	class width	Frequency	Frequency density
$100 \leq m < 110$	100	110	10	6	0.6
$110 \leq m < 120$	110	120	10	9	0.9
$120 \leq m < 130$	120	130	10	11	1.1
$130 \leq m < 140$	130	140	10	14	1.4
$140 \leq m < 150$	140	150	10	10	1.0

Then you can plot the histogram:

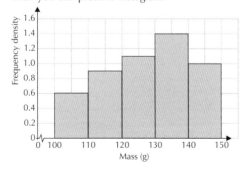

Q2 a) First you need to work out how many people are represented by each square unit on the graph — use the information that the bar for 30-45 seconds represents 54 contestants.

   Bar for 30-45 seconds:
   Width = 45 – 30 = 15 and height = 1.8
   So area = 15 × 1.8 = 27
   — this represents 54 contestants.
   So each square unit represents
   54 ÷ 27 = 2 people.
   Or 'frequency = 2 × area'.

   Bar for 10-30 seconds:
   Width = 30 – 10 = 20 and height = 0.3
   So area = 20 × 0.3 = 6
   — this represents 6 × 2 = 12 contestants

   So 12 contestants' auditions lasted less than 30 seconds.

   b) Now you need to add on the frequencies represented by the other bars as well.
   Area of '45-55' bar = 10 × 2.6 = 26, which represents 26 × 2 = 52 contestants.
   Area of '55-60' bar = 5 × 3.0 = 15, which represents 15 × 2 = 30 contestants.
   Area of '60-75' bar = 15 × 1.0 = 15, which represents 15 × 2 = 30 contestants.
   Area of '75-90' bar = 15 × 0.4 = 6, which represents 6 × 2 = 12 contestants.

   So the total number of contestants who auditioned was:
   12 + 54 + 52 + 30 + 30 + 12 = 190

Q3 a) The area of the bar is 1.5 × 9 = 13.5 cm^2. This represents 12 butterflies.
   So each butterfly is represented by 13.5 ÷ 12 = 1.125 cm^2 on the histogram

   b) 22.5 ÷ 1.125 = 20, so the frequency was 20.

   c) The first bar, representing a class of width 3, was 1.5 cm wide. So the bar representing the class $53.5 \leq w < 58.5$, which has a width of 5, must be <u>2.5 cm wide</u>. And because it needs to represent a frequency of 14, its area must be 14 × 1.125 = 15.75 cm^2. This means it must be 15.75 ÷ 2.5 = <u>6.3 cm high</u>.

Exercise 1.3 — Stem and leaf diagrams
Q1 a) Add up the number of leaves in each row:
   4 + 8 + 5 + 6 + 5 + 0 + 2 = 30 choirs

   b) There are 2 leaves of '5' in the row with stem '4'. So 2 choirs had 45 members.

   c) 5 choirs

   d) 73 members

Q2 **a)** 2 + 5 = 7 towns

b) 10.7 °C

c) 13.7 − 8.2 = 5.5 °C

Q3 **a)**

0	8	(1)
1	2 5 6	(3)
2	1 4 5 6 7 9	(6)
3	5 7	(2)
4	0 3	(2)
5	6	(1)
6	4	(1)

Key: 2 | 1 means 2.1 km

b) **(i)** 6.4 km   **(ii)** 4 children

Q4 **a)** 60 minutes

b) 17

c) 6

2. Location: Mean, Median and Mode

Exercise 2.1 — The mean

Q1 The sum of all 12 prices is £13.92.
So the mean price is £13.92 ÷ 12 = £1.16

Q2 1672 ÷ 20 = 83.6

Q3

Number of goals, x	0	1	2	3	4	**Total**
Frequency, f	5	7	4	3	1	**20**
fx	0	7	8	9	4	**28**

So the mean is 28 ÷ 20 = 1.4 goals

Q4 **a)** 15 × 47.4 = 711 years

b) New total of ages = 711 + 17 = 728
So new mean = 728 ÷ 16 = 45.5 years
Or you could have used the formula with n_1 = 15,
$\overline{x}_1$ = 47.4, n_2 = 1 and $\overline{x}_2$ = 17 to get the same answer.

Exercise 2.2 — The mode and the median

Q1 **a)** First put the amounts in order:
£19, £45, £67, £77, £84, £98, £101, £108, £110,
£123, £140, £185, £187, £194, £216, £250,
£500

There are 17 amounts in total. Since 17 ÷ 2 = 8.5
is not a whole number, round this up to 9 to find
the position of the median.
So the median = £110.

b) All the values occur just once.

Q2 **a)** 6.9%

b) First put the rates in order:
6.2%, 6.2%, 6.3%, 6.4%, 6.4%, 6.5%,
6.9%, 6.9%, 6.9%, 7.4%, 8.8%, 9.9%

There are 12 rates in total. Since 12 ÷ 2 = 6 is a
whole number, the median is halfway between
the 6th and 7th values in the ordered list.
So the median = (6.5% + 6.9%) ÷ 2 = 6.7%.

Q3 **a)** 5

b) There are 176 ratings in total.
176 ÷ 2 = 88, so the median is midway between
the 88th and 89th values.

Add a column to the table to show cumulative
frequencies:

Rating	Number of customers	Cumulative frequency
1	7	7
2	5	12
3	25	37
4	67	104
5	72	176

From the cumulative frequencies, the 88th and
89th values are both 4, so the median = 4.

Q4 **a)** 5 seats

b) There are 35 values altogether.
Since 35 ÷ 2 = 17.5 is not a whole number,
round this up to 18 to find the position of the
median. So the median = 20 seats.

Q5 **a)** **(i)** 4.0 Mbit/s, 5.8 Mbit/s and 6.9 Mbit/s

(ii) 6.2 Mbit/s

b) **(i)** There are 19 values altogether.
Since 19 ÷ 2 = 9.5 is not a whole number,
round this up to 10 to find the position of the
median. So the median = 5.8 Mbit/s.

(ii) There are 22 values altogether.
Since 22 ÷ 2 = 11 is a whole number, the
median is halfway between the 11th and 12th
values in the ordered list.
So the median = (5.5 + 5.9) ÷ 2 = 5.7 Mbit/s.

Exercise 2.3 — Averages of grouped data

Q1 **a)**

Time (t, mins)	Frequency, f	Mid-point, x	fx
$3 \leq t < 4$	7	3.5	24.5
$4 \leq t < 5$	14	4.5	63
$5 \leq t < 6$	24	5.5	132
$6 \leq t < 8$	10	7	70
$8 \leq t < 10$	5	9	45

b) $\sum f = 60$, $\sum fx = 334.5$
So estimate of mean = 334.5 ÷ 60
= 5.6 mins (to 1 d.p.).
You could add an extra row to the table to show the
column totals.

Q2 **a)** 0-2 letters
All the classes are the same width, so you can use
the frequency to find the modal class (instead of the
frequency density).

b) Add some extra columns to the table:

Number of letters	Number of houses, f	Mid-point, x	fx
0-2	20	1	20
3-5	16	4	64
6-8	7	7	49
9-11	5	10	50
12-14	2	13	26

$\sum f = 50$, $\sum fx = 209$

So estimate of mean = 209 ÷ 50 = 4.18 letters

c) Since $\sum f \div 2 = 50 \div 2 = 25$, the median is halfway between the values in this position (25) and the next position (26) in the ordered list. So the median must be in the class 3-5.

Q3 Add a column showing cumulative frequency to the table:

Rainfall (r, mm)	Frequency	Cumulative frequency
$20 \leq r < 40$	5	5
$40 \leq r < 50$	7	12
$50 \leq r < 60$	9	21
$60 \leq r < 80$	15	36
$80 \leq r < 100$	8	44
$100 \leq r < 120$	2	46

So $\frac{n}{2} = \frac{46}{2} = 23$, meaning the median must lie in the class '$60 \leq r < 80$'. Now you need to sketch that class.

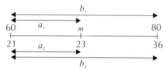

Finally, solve $\frac{a_1}{b_1} = \frac{a_2}{b_2}$. This gives:

$$\frac{m - 60}{80 - 60} = \frac{23 - 21}{36 - 21}$$

or $m = 20 \times \frac{2}{15} + 60 = 62.7\,\text{mm (to 1 d.p.)}$.

Q4 a) Estimated mean = 16 740 ÷ 60 = 279 minutes

b) Add a column showing cumulative frequency to the table:

Time (t, mins)	Frequency, f	Cumulative frequency
$180 \leq t < 240$	8	8
$240 \leq t < 270$	19	27
$270 \leq t < 300$	21	48
$300 \leq t < 360$	9	57
$360 \leq t < 480$	3	60

So $\frac{n}{2} = 30$, meaning the median must lie in the class '$270 \leq t < 300$'. Now you need to sketch that class.

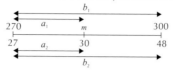

Finally, solve $\frac{a_1}{b_1} = \frac{a_2}{b_2}$. This gives:

$$\frac{m - 270}{300 - 270} = \frac{30 - 27}{48 - 27}$$

or $m = 30 \times \frac{3}{21} + 270 = 274.3\,\text{mins (to 1 d.p.)}$.

Exercise 2.4 — Comparing measures of location

Q1 a) Median — most employees will earn relatively low salaries but a few may earn much higher salaries, so the mean could be heavily affected by a few high salaries.

b) Mean — the data should be reasonably symmetrical so the mean would be a good measure of location. The median would be good as well (for a symmetric data set, it should be roughly equal to the mean).

c) Mode — make of car is qualitative data so the mode is the only average that can be found.

d) Mean — the data should be reasonably symmetrical so the mean would be a good measure of location. The median would be good as well (for a symmetric data set, it should be roughly equal to the mean).

e) Median — most employees will perhaps travel fairly short distances to work but a few employees may live much further away. The median would not be affected by these few high values.
The mode is unlikely to be suitable in b), d) and e) (and possibly a) as well) because all the values may well be different.

Q2 There is a very extreme value of 8 that would affect the mean quite heavily.

3. Dispersion and Skewness

Exercise 3.1 — Range, interquartile range and interpercentile range

Q1 a) Highest value = 88 846 miles
Lowest value = 3032 miles
So range = 88 846 – 3032 = 85 814 miles

b) (i) There are 8 values, and the ordered list is
3032, 4222, 7521, 7926, 30 778, 31 763, 74 898, 88 846

Since $\frac{n}{4} = 2$, the lower quartile (Q_1) is halfway between the values in this position (2) and the next position (3) in the ordered list.
So $Q_1 = (4222 + 7521) \div 2 = 5871.5$ miles.

(ii) Since $\frac{3n}{4} = 6$, the upper quartile (Q_3) is halfway between the values in this position (6) and the next position (7) in the ordered list. So $Q_3 = (31\,763 + 74\,898) \div 2$ = 53\,330.5 miles.

(iii) IQR $= Q_3 - Q_1 = 53\,330.5 - 5871.5$ = 47\,459 miles

Q2 a) and b)

In town at 8:45 am:
The ordered list of 18 values is:
13, 14, 14, 15, 15, 15, 15, 15, 16, 16, 16, 16, 16, 17, 17, 18, 18, 18
So the range = 18 – 13 = 5 mph

Since $\frac{n}{4} = 4.5$, the lower quartile (Q_1) is in position 5 in the ordered list. So $Q_1 = 15$ mph.

Since $\frac{3n}{4} = 13.5$, the upper quartile (Q_3) is in position 14 in the ordered list. So $Q_3 = 17$ mph.

This means IQR $= Q_3 - Q_1 = 17 - 15 = 2$ mph.

In town at 10:45 am:
The ordered list of 18 values is:
25, 29, 29, 29, 30, 30, 31, 31, 31, 32, 33, 34, 34, 35, 36, 36, 38, 39
So the range = 39 – 25 = 14 mph

The lower quartile (Q_1) is in position 5 in the ordered list. So $Q_1 = 30$ mph.

The upper quartile (Q_3) is in position 14 in the ordered list. So $Q_3 = 35$ mph.

This means IQR $= Q_3 - Q_1 = 35 - 30 = 5$ mph.

On the motorway at 1 pm:
The ordered list of 18 values is:
67, 69, 69, 71, 71, 73, 73, 74, 74, 75, 75, 76, 76, 76, 78, 78, 88, 95
So the range = 95 – 67 = 28 mph

The lower quartile (Q_1) is in position 5 in the ordered list. So $Q_1 = 71$ mph.

The upper quartile (Q_3) is in position 14 in the ordered list. So $Q_3 = 76$ mph.

This means IQR $= Q_3 - Q_1 = 76 - 71 = 5$ mph.

Q3 a) Add a column showing cumulative frequency to the table:

Weight of baggage (w)	Number of items	Cumulative frequency
$0 < w < 10$	22	22
$10 \leq w < 14$	75	97
$14 \leq w < 18$	102	199
$18 \leq w < 25$	53	252

So $\frac{n}{4} = 252 \div 4 = 63$, meaning the lower quartile (Q_1) must lie in the class '$10 \leq w < 14$'. Now you need to sketch that class.

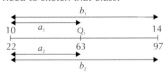

Finally, solve $\frac{a_1}{b_1} = \frac{a_2}{b_2}$. This gives:

$$\frac{Q_1 - 10}{14 - 10} = \frac{63 - 22}{97 - 22}$$

or $Q_1 = 4 \times \frac{41}{75} + 10 = 12.2$ kg (to 1 d.p.).

b) $\frac{3n}{4} = 3 \times 252 \div 4 = 189$, meaning the upper quartile (Q_3) must lie in the class '$14 \leq w < 18$'. Now you need to sketch that class.

Finally, solve $\frac{a_1}{b_1} = \frac{a_2}{b_2}$. This gives:

$$\frac{Q_3 - 14}{18 - 14} = \frac{189 - 97}{199 - 97}$$

or $Q_3 = 4 \times \frac{92}{102} + 14 = 17.6$ kg (to 1 d.p.).

c) So IQR $= Q_3 - Q_1$ = 17.6 – 12.2 = 5.4 kg (to 1 d.p.).

Q4 a) Add a column showing cumulative frequency to the table:

Length (l)	Number of beetles	Cumulative frequency
0-5	82	82
6-10	28	110
11-15	44	154
16-30	30	184
31-50	16	200

The position of the 20th percentile is $\frac{20}{100} \times 200 = 40$, meaning that P_{20} must lie in the class '0-5'. Now you need to sketch that class, taking care to work out the lower and upper class boundaries carefully.

Finally, solve $\frac{a_1}{b_1} = \frac{a_2}{b_2}$. This gives:

$$\frac{P_{20} - 0}{5.5 - 0} = \frac{40 - 0}{82 - 0}$$

or $P_{20} = 5.5 \times \frac{40}{82} = 2.7$ mm (to 1 d.p.).

b) The position of the 80th percentile is
$\frac{80}{100} \times 200 = 160$, meaning that P_{80} must lie in the class '16-30'. Now you need to sketch that class.

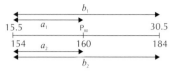

Finally, solve $\frac{a_1}{b_1} = \frac{a_2}{b_2}$. This gives:

$$\frac{P_{80} - 15.5}{30.5 - 15.5} = \frac{160 - 154}{184 - 154}$$

or $P_{80} = 15 \times \frac{6}{30} + 15.5 = 18.5\,\text{mm}$

c) So the 20% to 80% interpercentile range
$= P_{80} - P_{20} = 18.5 - 2.7 = 15.8$ mm (to 1 d.p.).

Exercise 3.2 — Outliers and box plots

Q1 IQR $= Q_3 - Q_1 = 31 - 19 = 12$
Lower fence $= Q_1 - (1.5 \times IQR) = 19 - (1.5 \times 12) = 1$
Upper fence $= Q_3 + (1.5 \times IQR)$
$= 31 + (1.5 \times 12) = 49$

The value 4 is inside the lower fence, so 4 is not an outlier. The value 52 is outside the upper fence, so 52 is an outlier.

Q2 **a)** IQR $= Q_3 - Q_1 = 37 - 16 = 21$

b) Lower fence $= Q_1 - (1.5 \times IQR)$
$= 16 - (1.5 \times 21) = -15.5$
Upper fence $= Q_3 + (1.5 \times IQR)$
$= 37 + (1.5 \times 21) = 68.5$

Since the minimum value and the maximum value both fall inside the fences, there are no outliers in this data set.

c)

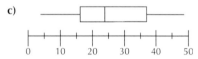

Q3 **a)** **(i)** There are 41 data values altogether, i.e. $n = 41$. Since $41 \div 2 = 20.5$ is not a whole number, round this up to 21 to find the position of the median.
So the median = 46 cars.

(ii) Since $41 \div 4 = 10.25$ is not a whole number, round this up to 11 to find the position of the lower quartile.
So the lower quartile (Q_1) = 35 cars.

(iii) Since $3 \times 41 \div 4 = 30.75$ is not a whole number, round this up to 31 to find the position of the upper quartile.
So the upper quartile (Q_3) = 56 cars.

(iv) IQR $= Q_3 - Q_1 = 56 - 35 = 21$ cars

(v) The lower fence is
$Q_1 - (1.5 \times IQR) = 35 - (1.5 \times 21)$
$= 3.5$ cars

(vi) The upper fence is
$Q_3 + (1.5 \times IQR) = 56 + (1.5 \times 21)$
$= 87.5$ cars

b) The value 1 is outside the lower fence, so that is an outlier. Similarly, the values 91 and 99 are outside the upper fence, so these values are also outliers.

c)

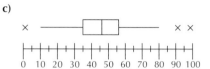

Q4 **a)** **(i)** There are 18 data values for Pigham. Since $18 \div 2 = 9$, the median is halfway between the 9th and 10th data values (which are both 35). So the median = 35.

(ii) Since $18 \div 4 = 4.5$, the lower quartile (Q_1) is the 5th data value.
So the lower quartile = 23.

(iii) Since $3 \times 18 \div 4 = 13.5$, the upper quartile ($Q_3$) is the 14th data value.
So the upper quartile = 46.

(iv) The interquartile range $= Q_3 - Q_1$
$= 46 - 23 = 23$

(v) the lower fence is
$Q_1 - (1.5 \times IQR) = 23 - (1.5 \times 23)$
$= -11.5$

(vi) the upper fence,
$Q_3 + (1.5 \times IQR) = 46 + (1.5 \times 23)$
$= 80.5$

b) No, none of the values fall outside the fences.

c)

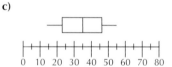

d) There are 18 data values for Goossea, so the median is halfway between the 9th and 10th data values. So the median = 27.5.

The lower quartile (Q_1) is the 5th data value. So the lower quartile = 15.

The upper quartile (Q_3) is the 14th data value. So the upper quartile = 35.

The interquartile range $= Q_3 - Q_1$
$= 35 - 15 = 20$.

The lower fence is
$Q_1 - (1.5 \times IQR) = 15 - (1.5 \times 20)$
$= -15$
This means there are no 'low outliers'.

The upper fence,
$Q_3 + (1.5 \times IQR) = 35 + (1.5 \times 20)$
$= 65$

This means that the value of 75 is an outlier (but the next highest value, 50, is not an outlier).

So the box plot looks like this:

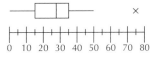

Exercise 3.3 — Variance and standard deviation

Q1 **a)** $\bar{x} = \dfrac{756 + 755 + 764 + 778 + 754 + 759}{6}$

$= \dfrac{4566}{6} = 761$

b) $\sum x^2 = 756^2 + 755^2 + 764^2$
$\qquad\qquad + 778^2 + 754^2 + 759^2$

$\qquad = 3\,475\,138$

c) variance $= \dfrac{\sum x^2}{n} - \bar{x}^2 = \dfrac{3\,475\,138}{6} - 761^2$

$= 68.666... = 68.7$ (to 3 sig. fig.).

d) standard deviation $= \sqrt{\text{variance}} = \sqrt{68.666...}$
$= 8.29$ (to 3 sig. fig.).

e) There are no outliers or extreme values to affect the standard deviation in a way that would make it unrepresentative of the rest of the data set.

Q2 **a)** $\bar{x} = \dfrac{\sum x}{n} = \dfrac{480}{8} = 60$

$\sum x^2 = 35\,292$

variance $= \dfrac{\sum x^2}{n} - \bar{x}^2 = \dfrac{35\,292}{8} - 60^2 = 811.5$

b) standard deviation $= \sqrt{\text{variance}} = \sqrt{811.5}$
$= 28.5$ (to 3 sig. fig.).

Q3 **a)** Start by adding an extra row to the table for fx.

x	1	2	3	4
frequency, f	7	8	4	1
fx	7	16	12	4

Then $\bar{x} = \dfrac{\sum fx}{\sum f} = \dfrac{39}{20} = 1.95$

b) Now add two more rows to the table.

x	1	2	3	4
frequency, f	7	8	4	1
fx	7	16	12	4
x^2	1	4	9	16
fx^2	7	32	36	16

So $\sum fx^2 = 7 + 32 + 36 + 16 = 91$

c) variance $= \dfrac{\sum fx^2}{\sum f} - \bar{x}^2 = \dfrac{91}{20} - 1.95^2 = 0.7475$

d) standard deviation $= \sqrt{\text{variance}} = \sqrt{0.7475}$
$= 0.865$ (to 3 sig. fig.).

Q4 Extend the table to include fx, x^2 and fx^2.

x	7	8	9	10	11	12
frequency, f	2	3	5	7	4	2
fx	14	24	45	70	44	24
x^2	49	64	81	100	121	144
fx^2	98	192	405	700	484	288

So $\sum f = 2 + 3 + 5 + 7 + 4 + 2 = 23$
$\sum fx = 14 + 24 + 45 + 70 + 44 + 24 = 221$
$\sum fx^2 = 98 + 192 + 405 + 700 + 484 + 288 = 2167$

This means $\bar{x} = \dfrac{\sum fx}{f} = \dfrac{221}{23}$.

And so variance $= \dfrac{\sum fx^2}{\sum f} - \bar{x}^2 = \dfrac{2167}{23} - \left(\dfrac{221}{23}\right)^2$

$= 1.8903... = 1.89$ (to 3 sig. fig.)

Q5 **a)**

Pulse rate	56-60	61-65	66-70	71-75	76-80
frequency, f	1	2	4	8	5
(i) mid-point, x	58	63	68	73	78
(ii) fx	58	126	272	584	390
(iii) x^2	3364	3969	4624	5329	6084
(iv) fx^2	3364	7938	18496	42632	30420

b) **(i)** $\sum f = 20$
(ii) $\sum fx = 1430$
(iii) $\sum fx^2 = 102\,850$

c) Variance $= \dfrac{\sum fx^2}{\sum f} - \left(\dfrac{\sum fx}{\sum f}\right)^2$

$= \dfrac{102850}{20} - \left(\dfrac{1430}{20}\right)^2$

$= 30.25$

Q6 **a)** Add some more columns to the table showing the class mid-points (x), as well as fx, x^2 and fx^2.

Yield, w (kg)	f	Mid-point, x	fx	x^2	fx^2
$50 \le w < 60$	23	55	1265	3025	69575
$60 \le w < 70$	12	65	780	4225	50700
$70 \le w < 80$	15	75	1125	5625	84375
$80 \le w < 90$	6	85	510	7225	43350
$90 \le w < 100$	2	95	190	9025	18050

So $\sum f = 58$, $\sum fx = 3870$, $\sum fx^2 = 266\,050$.
Then:

Variance $= \dfrac{\sum fx^2}{\sum f} - \left(\dfrac{\sum fx}{\sum f}\right)^2$

$= \dfrac{266\,050}{58} - \left(\dfrac{3870}{58}\right)^2$

$= 134.95838... = 135\,\text{kg}^2$ (to 3 sig. fig.)

b) Standard deviation $= \sqrt{134.95838...}$
$= 11.6$ kg (to 3 sig. fig.)

Q7 a) Work out the total duration of all the 23 eruptions that Su has timed.

This is $\sum x = n\bar{x} = 23 \times 3.42 = 78.66$ minutes.

Work out the total duration of all the 37 eruptions that Ellen has timed.

This is $\sum y = n\bar{y} = 37 \times 3.92 = 145.04$ minutes

So the total duration of the last 60 eruptions is:

$\sum x + \sum y = 78.66 + 145.04 = 223.7$ minutes

This gives a mean duration of:

$\dfrac{223.7}{60} = 3.72833...$

$= 3.73$ minutes (to 3 sig. fig.).

b) Work out the sum of squares of the durations of all the 23 eruptions that Su has timed — use the formula for variance.

$\text{variance} = \dfrac{\sum x^2}{n} - \bar{x}^2 \Rightarrow 1.07^2 = \dfrac{\sum x^2}{23} - 3.42^2$

So $\sum x^2 = 23 \times (1.07^2 + 3.42^2) = 295.3499$

Do the same for the 37 eruptions that Ellen has timed — use the formula for variance.

$\text{variance} = \dfrac{\sum y^2}{n} - \bar{y}^2 \Rightarrow 0.97^2 = \dfrac{\sum y^2}{37} - 3.92^2$

So $\sum y^2 = 37 \times (0.97^2 + 3.92^2) = 603.3701$

Now you can work out the total sum of squares (for all 60 eruptions):

$\sum x^2 + \sum y^2 = 295.3499 + 603.3701 = 898.72$

So the variance for all 60 eruptions is:

$\text{variance} = \dfrac{898.72}{60} - \left(\dfrac{223.7}{60}\right)^2$

$= 1.0781... = 1.08 \text{ min}^2$ (to 3 sig. fig.)

c) This means the standard deviation of the durations is $\sqrt{1.0781...} = 1.0383...$
$= 1.04$ min (to 3 sig. fig.)

Exercise 3.4 — Coding

Q1 a) Since $y = x - 500$, $\bar{x} = \bar{y} + 500$.
So $\bar{x} = 12 + 500 = 512$.

standard deviation of x = standard deviation of y
$= 4.22$

b) Since $y = 4x$, $\bar{x} = \dfrac{\bar{y}}{4} = \dfrac{6}{4} = 1.5$

stan. dev. of $x = \dfrac{\text{stan. dev. of } y}{4} = \dfrac{2.14}{4} = 0.535$

c) $y = \dfrac{x - 20\,000}{15}$, so $\bar{y} = \dfrac{\bar{x} - 20\,000}{15}$.

This means $\bar{x} = 15 \times 12.4 + 20\,000 = 20\,186$.

stan. dev. of x $= 15 \times$ stan. dev. of y
$= 15 \times 1.34 = 20.1$

Q2 a) The coded data values are 3, 7 and 8.
The mean of these is $\bar{y} = (3 + 7 + 8) \div 3 = 6$.
The standard deviation of the coded values is

$\sqrt{\dfrac{3^2 + 7^2 + 8^2}{3} - 6^2} = 2.16$ (to 3 sig. fig.).

So the mean of the original data values is
$\bar{x} = \bar{y} + 2000 = 6 + 2000 = 2006$.

The standard deviation of the original values is the same as the standard deviation of the coded values — this is 2.16 (to 3 sig. fig.).

b) The coded data values are 2, 17, 3, 11 and 7.
The mean of these is:
$\bar{y} = (2 + 17 + 3 + 11 + 7) \div 5 = 8$.
The standard deviation of the coded values is

$\sqrt{\dfrac{2^2 + 17^2 + 3^2 + 11^2 + 7^2}{5} - 8^2}$

$= 5.51$ (to 3 sig. fig.).

So the mean of the original data values is
$\bar{x} = \bar{y} \div 100 = 8 \div 100 = 0.08$.

The standard deviation of x
$=$ standard deviation of $y \div 100$,
so standard deviation of $x = 5.51 \div 100$
$= 0.0551$ (to 3 sig. fig.).

c) The coded data values are 7, 2, 20 and 15.
The mean of these is:
$\bar{y} = (7 + 2 + 20 + 15) \div 4 = 11$.
The standard deviation of the coded values is

$\sqrt{\dfrac{7^2 + 2^2 + 20^2 + 15^2}{4} - 11^2}$

$= 6.96$ (to 3 sig. fig.).

So the mean of the original data values is
$\bar{x} = \dfrac{\bar{y}}{2} + 350 = \dfrac{11}{2} + 350 = 355.5$.
The standard deviation of x
$=$ standard deviation of $y \div 2$,
so standard deviation of x
$= 6.96 \div 2 = 3.48$ (to 3 sig. fig.).

d) The coded data values are 10, 7, 4, 0 and 6.
The mean of these is:
$\bar{y} = (10 + 7 + 4 + 0 + 6) \div 5 = 5.4$.
The standard deviation of the coded values is

$\sqrt{\dfrac{10^2 + 7^2 + 4^2 + 0^2 + 6^2}{5} - 5.4^2}$

$= 3.32$ (to 3 sig. fig.).

So the mean of the original data values is
$\bar{x} = 10\bar{y} - 8000 = 10 \times 5.4 - 8000 = -7946$.

The standard deviation of x
$=$ standard deviation of $y \times 10$,
so standard deviation of x
$= 3.32 \times 10 = 33.2$ (to 3 sig. fig.).

Q3 a) All the values are of the form '0.6_', and so if you subtract 0.6 from all the values, and then multiply what's left by 100, you'll end up with coded data values between 1 and 10.
So code the data values using $y = 100(x - 0.6)$, where x is an original data value and y is the corresponding coded value.
This gives y-values of: 1, 7, 3, 3, 6, 5, 4, 8, 4, 2

b) $\bar{y} = \dfrac{1 + 7 + 3 + 3 + 6 + 5 + 4 + 8 + 4 + 2}{10}$

$= \dfrac{43}{10} = 4.3$

Find the sum of squares of the coded values, $\sum y^2$. This is $\sum y^2 = 229$.

So variance $= \dfrac{\sum y^2}{n} - \bar{y}^2 = \dfrac{229}{10} - 4.3^2$

$= 4.41$

This gives a standard deviation of $\sqrt{4.41} = 2.1$

c) Since $y = 100(x - 0.6)$, $\bar{y} = 100(\bar{x} - 0.6)$.
This means:

$\bar{x} = \dfrac{\bar{y}}{100} + 0.6 = \dfrac{4.3}{100} + 0.6 = 0.643$ cm

Since $y = 100(x - 0.6)$,
stan. dev. of $y = 100 \times$ stan. dev. of x
So stan. dev. of $x = $ stan. dev. of $y \div 100$
$= 2.1 \div 100 = 0.021$ cm

Q4 Make a new table showing the class mid-points (x) and their corresponding coded values (y), as well as fy, y^2 and fy^2.

Weight (to nearest g)	100-104	105-109	110-114	115-119
Frequency, f	2	6	3	1
Class mid-point, x	102	107	112	117
Coded value, y	0	5	10	15
fy	0	30	30	15
y^2	0	25	100	225
fy^2	0	150	300	225

Then $\bar{y} = \dfrac{\sum fy}{\sum f} = \dfrac{75}{12} = 6.25$

variance of $y = \dfrac{\sum fy^2}{\sum f} - \bar{y}^2 = \dfrac{675}{12} - 6.25^2$

$= 17.1875$

This means standard deviation of $y = \sqrt{17.1875}$
$= 4.15$ (to 3 sig. fig.).

Now you can convert these back to values for x.
Since $y = x - 102$:
$\bar{x} = \bar{y} + 102 = 108.25$ g
stan. dev. of $x = $ stan. dev. of $y = 4.15$ g (to 3 sig. fig.).

Q5 Using the coding $y = x + 2$.
Then $\sum y = 7$ and $\sum y^2 = 80$.

So $\bar{y} = \dfrac{\sum y}{n} = \dfrac{7}{20} = 0.35$

And the variance of y is:

$\dfrac{\sum y^2}{n} - \bar{y}^2 = \dfrac{80}{20} - 0.35^2 = 3.8775$

This gives a standard deviation for y of $\sqrt{3.8775} = 1.97$ (to 3 sig. fig.)
So $\bar{x} = \bar{y} - 2 = 0.35 - 2 = -1.65$.
And standard deviation of x
$= $ standard deviation of $y = 1.97$ (to 3 sig. fig.)

Exercise 3.5 — Skewness

Q1 **a)** symmetrical

b) positively skewed

c) negatively skewed
Here, you can see there's a bit of a tail on the 'left' of the distribution (though you have to imagine rotating the stem and leaf diagram 90° anticlockwise).

Q2 **a)** Pearson's coefficient of skewness
$= \dfrac{\text{mean} - \text{mode}}{\text{standard deviation}} = \dfrac{7 - 5}{1.6} = 1.25$
This is positive, so the distribution is positively skewed.

b) Pearson's coefficient of skewness
$= \dfrac{3(\text{mean} - \text{median})}{\text{standard deviation}} = \dfrac{3 \times (12 - 13.5)}{1.8} = -2.5$
This is negative, so the distribution is negatively skewed.

c) Pearson's coefficient of skewness
$= \dfrac{\text{mean} - \text{mode}}{\text{standard deviation}} = \dfrac{14 - 14}{2.37} = 0$
This is zero, so the distribution is symmetrical.

d) Pearson's coefficient of skewness
$= \dfrac{3(\text{mean} - \text{median})}{\text{standard deviation}} = \dfrac{3 \times (-9 - (-8))}{2.5}$
$= -1.2$
This is negative, so the distribution is negatively skewed.

Q3 **a)** Quartile coefficient of skewness
$= \dfrac{Q_3 - 2Q_2 + Q_1}{Q_3 - Q_1} = \dfrac{15 - 2 \times 8 + 3}{15 - 3}$
$= 0.167$ (to 3 sig. fig.).
This is positive, so the distribution is positively skewed.

b) Quartile coefficient of skewness
$= \dfrac{Q_3 - 2Q_2 + Q_1}{Q_3 - Q_1} = \dfrac{194 - 2 \times 119 + 35}{194 - 35}$
$= -0.0566$ (to 3 sig. fig.).
This is negative, so the distribution is negatively skewed.
Only very slightly skewed, though.

c) Quartile coefficient of skewness $=$
$\dfrac{Q_3 - 2Q_2 + Q_1}{Q_3 - Q_1} = \dfrac{-10 - 2 \times (-23) + (-28)}{-10 - (-28)}$
$= 0.444$ (to 3 sig. fig.).
This is positive, so the distribution is positively skewed.

d) Quartile coefficient of skewness $=$
$\dfrac{Q_3 - 2Q_2 + Q_1}{Q_3 - Q_1} = \dfrac{8.2 - 2 \times 5.3 + 2.4}{8.2 - 2.4} = 0$
This means that the distribution is symmetrical.

Q4 a) mean $= \dfrac{\sum x}{n} = \dfrac{68}{8} = £8.50$

There are 8 values, so the median is halfway between the 4th and 5th values in the ordered list. So the median is £10.

stan. dev. $= \sqrt{\dfrac{\sum x^2}{n} - \bar{x}^2} = \sqrt{\dfrac{660}{8} - 8.5^2}$

$= 3.20156... = £3.20$ (to 3 sig. fig.).

b) Pearson's coefficient of skewness

$= \dfrac{3(\text{mean} - \text{median})}{\text{standard deviation}} = \dfrac{3 \times (8.5 - 10)}{3.20}$

$= -1.41$ (to 3 sig. fig.)

c) This is negative, so the distribution is negatively skewed.

Q5 a) mean $= \dfrac{\sum x}{n} = \dfrac{249}{10} = 24.9$

The mode is 22.

stan. dev. $= \sqrt{\dfrac{\sum x^2}{n} - \bar{x}^2} = \sqrt{\dfrac{7725}{10} - 24.9^2}$

$= 12.3486...$

Pearson's coefficient of skewness

$= \dfrac{\text{mean} - \text{mode}}{\text{standard deviation}} = \dfrac{24.9 - 22}{12.3486...}$

$= 0.235$ (to 3 sig. fig.)

b) This is small but positive, so the distribution is slightly positively skewed.

Exercise 3.6 — Comparing Distributions

Q1 a) The median is higher for Shop B. This shows that the prices in Shop B are generally higher. The median in Shop A is approximately £37 while the median in Shop B is approximately £63, so the difference between the average prices is around £26.

b) Although the ranges in the two shops are quite similar, the interquartile range (IQR) for Shop B is higher than that for Shop A. This shows that the prices of shoes in Shop B are more varied than the prices in Shop A.

c) The distribution of prices in Shop A is approximately symmetrical — this shows that prices are fairly evenly balanced either side of the mean, without a long tail of really high or really low prices. For Shop B, the distribution of prices is negatively skewed, showing that there is a tail on the left of this distribution. This means that the prices of the shoes are generally relatively high, but there were some much cheaper shoes as well.

Q2 a) (i) For Café A:

mean $= \dfrac{\sum x}{n} = \dfrac{1106}{14} = £79$

There are 14 values, so the median is halfway between the 7th and 8th values. So the median is £80.

For Café B:

mean $= \dfrac{\sum x}{n} = \dfrac{1106}{14} = £79$

There are 14 values, so the median is halfway between the 7th and 8th values. So the median is £81.50.

(ii) The mean is the same for both data sets, and the median is only slightly different, so the average daily sales in both cafés are very similar.

b) (i) For Café A:

stan. dev. $= \sqrt{\dfrac{\sum x^2}{n} - \bar{x}^2} = \sqrt{\dfrac{87982}{14} - 79^2}$

$= £6.59$ (to nearest penny)

For Café B:

stan. dev. $= \sqrt{\dfrac{\sum x^2}{n} - \bar{x}^2} = \sqrt{\dfrac{92674}{14} - 79^2}$

$= £19.46$ (to nearest penny)

(ii) The standard deviation is a lot higher for Café B, so sales are a lot more varied there (or sales are a lot more consistent in Café A).

c) (i) For Café A:

There are 14 values, so Q_1 is the 4th value and Q_3 is the 11th value from the ordered list. So $Q_1 = £72$ and $Q_3 = £84$.
This gives:

Quartile coefficient of skewness =

$\dfrac{Q_3 - 2Q_2 + Q_1}{Q_3 - Q_1} = \dfrac{84 - 2 \times 80 + 72}{84 - 72}$

$= -0.333$ (to 3 sig. fig.).

For Café B:

There are 14 values, so Q_1 is the 4th value and Q_3 is the 11th value from the ordered list. So $Q_1 = £61$ and $Q_3 = £90$.
This gives:

Quartile coefficient of skewness =

$\dfrac{Q_3 - 2Q_2 + Q_1}{Q_3 - Q_1} = \dfrac{90 - 2 \times 81.5 + 61}{90 - 61}$

$= -0.414$ (to 3 sig. fig.).

(ii) Both cafés have slightly negative coefficients of skewness, so they both have a 'tail' of relatively quiet days, where sales are relatively low.

Q3 a) (i) For the men:

mean $= \dfrac{\sum x}{n} = \dfrac{73}{10} = 7.3$ hours

There are 10 values, so the median is halfway between the 5th and 6th values in the ordered list. So the median is 7 hours.

Don't forget to sort the list before trying to find the median — it's an easy mistake to make.

For the women:

mean $= \dfrac{\sum x}{n} = \dfrac{85}{10} = 8.5$ hours

Again, there are 10 values, so the median is halfway between the 5th and 6th values. So the median is 8.5 hours.

(ii) The mean and median are both higher for the women, so they get between 1 and 1.5 hours more sleep per night, on average, than the men.

b) (i) <u>For the men:</u>

$$\text{stan. dev.} = \sqrt{\frac{\sum x^2}{n} - \bar{x}^2} = \sqrt{\frac{553}{10} - 7.3^2}$$
$$= 1.42 \text{ hours (to 3 sig. fig.)}$$

<u>For the women:</u>

$$\text{stan. dev.} = \sqrt{\frac{\sum x^2}{n} - \bar{x}^2} = \sqrt{\frac{749}{10} - 8.5^2}$$
$$= 1.63 \text{ hours (to 3 sig. fig.)}$$

(ii) The standard deviation is slightly higher for the women, so the number of hours of sleep for the women varies slightly more from the average than it does for the men.

c) (i) <u>For the men:</u>

Pearson's coefficient of skewness

$$= \frac{3(\text{mean} - \text{median})}{\text{standard deviation}} = \frac{3 \times (7.3 - 7)}{1.42}$$

$$= 0.63 \text{ (to 2 sig. fig.)}.$$

<u>For the women:</u>

Pearson's coefficient of skewness

$$= \frac{3(\text{mean} - \text{median})}{\text{standard deviation}} = \frac{3 \times (8.5 - 8.5)}{1.63} = 0$$

(ii) The distribution for the men is slightly positively skewed, so there are a few relatively high values for the men, while most are relatively low. The distribution for the women, on the other hand, is symmetrical.

Review Exercise — Chapter 1

Q1 12.8, 13.2, 13.5, 14.3, 14.3, 14.6, 14.8, 15.2, 15.9, 16.1, 16.1, 16.2, 16.3, 17.0, 17.2 (all in cm)

Q2 Lots of fiddly details here — a table helps you get them right.

Length of calls	0 - 2	3 - 5	6 - 8	9 - 15
Number of calls	10	6	3	1
Lower class boundary	0	2.5	5.5	8.5
Upper class boundary	2.5	5.5	8.5	15.5
Class width	2.5	3	3	7
Frequency density	4	2	1	0.143

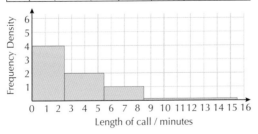

Q3 Add a row to the table showing fx.

x	0	1	2	3	4
f	5	4	4	2	1
fx	0	4	8	6	4

$\sum f = 16$, $\sum fx = 22$, so mean = 22 ÷ 16 = 1.375
Since there are 16 values, the median will be halfway between the 8th and the 9th values (which are both 1), so median = 1
Mode = 0.

Q4 Extend the table to show the class mid-points (x) and the values of fx.

Speed (mph)	30-34	35-39	40-44	45-50
Frequency	12	37	9	2
Class mid-point (x)	32	37	42	47.5
fx	384	1369	378	95

$\sum f = 60$, $\sum fx = 2226$, so estimated mean = 2226 ÷ 60 = 37.1 mph.
Use linear interpolation to find the median. Since there are $n = 60$ values, this means that $n \div 2 = 30$, and so the median will be in the class 35 - 39.

Now draw a diagram of that class showing the cumulative frequencies at either end, as well as the class boundaries.

```
                       b₁
  ◄─────────────────────────────────────►
34.5      a₁          m              39.5
  ├───────┼───────────┼───────────────┤
12        a₂          30               49
  ◄─────────────────────────────────────►
                       b₂
```

So you need to solve: $\dfrac{m - 34.5}{39.5 - 34.5} = \dfrac{30 - 12}{49 - 12}$

This gives $m = 5 \times \dfrac{18}{37} + 34.5$

$$= 36.9 \text{ mph (to 3 sig. fig.)}.$$

The modal class is 35 - 39 mph.
Always work out the class mid-points very carefully.

Q5 Mean $= \dfrac{11 + 12 + 14 + 17 + 21 + 23 + 27}{7}$

$$= \frac{125}{7} = 17.9 \text{ (to 3 sig. fig.)}.$$

Stan. dev. $= \sqrt{\dfrac{\sum x^2}{n} - \bar{x}^2} = \sqrt{\dfrac{2449}{7} - \left(\dfrac{125}{7}\right)^2}$

$$= 5.57 \text{ (to 3 sig. fig.)}.$$

Q6 You need to extend the table here:

Score	100-106	107-113	114-120	121-127	128-134
Frequency, f	6	11	22	9	2
Class mid-point, x	103	110	117	124	131
fx	618	1210	2574	1116	262
x^2	10609	12100	13689	15376	17161
fx^2	63654	133100	301158	138384	34322

$\sum f = 50$, $\sum fx = 5780$, and $\sum fx^2 = 670618$
so mean $= \dfrac{5780}{50} = 115.6$
and variance $= \dfrac{670618}{50} - 115.6^2 = 49$

Q7 Let $y = x - 20$.

Then:

$\bar{y} = \bar{x} - 20$ or $\bar{x} = \bar{y} + 20$

$\sum y = 125$ and $\sum y^2 = 221$

So $\bar{y} = \dfrac{125}{100} = 1.25$ and $\bar{x} = 1.25 + 20 = 21.25$

And:

variance for $y = \dfrac{221}{100} - 1.25^2 = 0.6475$ and so

standard deviation for $y = 0.805$ to 3 sig. fig.

But since $y = x - 20$, this must also equal
the standard deviation for x.

So standard deviation for $x = 0.805$ (to 3 sig. fig.).

Q8

Time to nearest minute	30-33	34-37	38-41	42-45
Frequency, f	3	6	7	4
Class mid-point, x	31.5	35.5	39.5	43.5
Coded value, y	−4	0	4	8
fy	−12	0	28	32
y^2	16	0	16	64
fy^2	48	0	112	256

Then $\sum f = 20$, $\sum fy = 48$, and $\sum fy^2 = 416$

This gives:

$\bar{y} = \dfrac{48}{20} = 2.4$

So $\bar{x} = \bar{y} + 35.5 = 2.4 + 35.5 = 37.9$ minutes

And:

variance for $y = \dfrac{416}{20} - 2.4^2 = 15.04$ and so

standard deviation for $y = 3.88$ to 3 sig. fig.

But since $y = x - 35.5$, this must also equal
the standard deviation for x. So standard deviation
for $x = 3.88$ minutes (to 3 sig. fig.).

Q9 IQR $= 88 - 62 = 26$, so $1.5 \times$ IQR $= 39$.
So upper fence $= 88 + 39 = 127$,
and lower fence $= 62 - 39 = 23$.
This means that:

a) 124 is not an outlier.

b) 131 is an outlier.

c) 28 is not an outlier.

Q10 a) Put the 20 items of data in order:
1, 4, 5, 5, 5, 5, 6, 6, 7, 7, 8, 10, 10, 12, 15, 20,
20, 30, 50
Since $n \div 2 = 20 \div 2 = 10$, the median is halfway
between the values in positions 10 and 11, and
since the 10th and the 11th items are both 7, the
median $= £7$.
Since $n \div 4 = 20 \div 4 = 5$, the lower quartile is
halfway between the values in positions 5 and 6,
and since the 5th and 6th values are both 5, the
lower quartile is £5.

Since $3n \div 4 = 15$, the upper quartile is halfway
between the values in positions 15 and 16.
So upper quartile $= (12 + 15) \div 2 = £13.50$.

b) IQR $= 13.5 - 5 = 8.5$.
So lower fence $= 5 - 1.5 \times 8.5 = -7.75$
and upper fence $= 13.5 + 1.5 \times 8.5 = 26.25$.
So the values 30 and 50 are outliers.

c) This means the box plot looks like this:

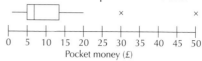

Pocket money (£)

This data is positively skewed. Most of the
15-year-olds earned a relatively small amount of
pocket money. A few got very large amounts.

Q11 Quartile coefficient of skewness $=$

$$\dfrac{Q_3 - 2Q_2 + Q_1}{Q_3 - Q_1} = \dfrac{150 - 2 \times 132 + 86}{150 - 86}$$
$$= -0.4375$$

A possible sketch of the distribution would need to
be negatively skewed — something like this:

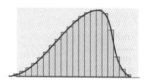

Q12 a) (i) Put the times in order first:
Times $= 2, 3, 4, 4, 5, 5, 5, 7, 10, 12$
Since $n \div 2 = 10 \div 2 = 5$, the median will be
halfway between the 5th and 6th values.
So the median is 5 minutes.

(ii) Since $n \div 4 = 10 \div 4 = 2.5$, the lower quartile
will be the 3rd value.
So the lower quartile is 4 minutes.
The upper quartile is the 8th value, which is
7 minutes.

(iii) IQR $= 7 - 4 = 3$.
So lower fence $= 4 - 1.5 \times 3 = -0.5$
and upper fence $= 7 + 1.5 \times 3 = 11.5$.
So the value 12 is an outlier.

b) For Worker B, the ordered list is:
4, 4, 6, 7, 8, 8, 9, 9, 10, 11
So the median and quartiles are:
$Q_1 = 6$ minutes, $Q_2 = 8$ minutes, $Q_3 = 9$ minutes.
This gives a lower fence of $6 - 1.5 \times 3 = 1.5$,
and an upper fence of $9 + 1.5 \times 3 = 13.5$.

This means there are no outliers for Worker B, so
your box plots should look like this:

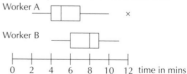

time in mins

c) You could say various things — here, you can choose whether to say something about the location or dispersion or skewness.
E.g. the times for Worker B are 3 minutes longer than those for Worker A, on average.

The IQR for both workers is the same — generally they both work with the same consistency. The range for Worker A is larger than that for Worker B. Worker A had a few items he/she could iron very quickly and a few which took a long time.

Worker A's times are positively skewed, whereas those for Worker B are negatively skewed.

d) Worker A would be better to employ. The median time is less than for Worker B, and the upper quartile is less than the median of Worker B. Worker A would generally iron more items in a given time than worker B.

Exam-Style Questions — Chapter 1

1 a) You need to find the frequency densities, since the classes are not all the same width.

Profit, £x million	Number of businesses	Class width	Frequency density
$4.0 \leqslant x < 5.0$	24	1.0	24
$5.0 \leqslant x < 5.5$	26	0.5	52
$5.5 \leqslant x < 6.0$	21	0.5	42
$6.0 \leqslant x < 6.5$	19	0.5	38
$6.5 \leqslant x < 8.0$	10	1.5	6.67

The frequency densities are the heights of the bars.

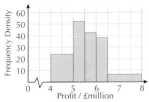

[1 mark for correct axes, plus 2 marks if all bars drawn correctly, or 1 mark for at least 3 bars correct.]

b) The distribution is positively skewed — only a few businesses make a high profit. The modal profit class is between £5 million and £5.5 million.
[1 mark per sensible comment, up to a maximum of 2.]

2 a) Let $y = x - 30$. Then

$\bar{y} = \dfrac{228}{19} = 12$, so $\bar{x} = \bar{y} + 30 = 42$ *[1 mark]*

variance of $y = \dfrac{3040}{19} - 12^2 = 16$ *[1 mark]*,

and so standard deviation of $y = 4$. But standard deviation of x = standard deviation of y and so standard deviation of $x = 4$ *[1 mark]*

b) $\bar{x} = \dfrac{\sum x}{19} = 42$

And so $\sum x = 42 \times 19 = 798$ *[1 mark]*

Variance of $x = \dfrac{\sum x^2}{19} - \bar{x}^2$

$= \dfrac{\sum x^2}{19} - 42^2 = 16$ *[1 mark]*

And so $\sum x^2 = (16 + 42^2) \times 19$
$= 33820$ *[1 mark]*

c) New $\sum x = 798 + 32 = 830$ *[1 mark]*

So new $\bar{x} = \dfrac{830}{20} = 41.5$ *[1 mark]*

New $\sum x^2 = 33820 + 32^2 = 34844$ *[1 mark]*

So new variance $= \dfrac{34844}{20} - 41.5^2 = 19.95$

and new stan. dev. = 4.47 to 3 sig. fig. *[1 mark]*

3 a) $\bar{a} = \dfrac{60.3}{20} = 3.015$ g *[1 mark]*

b) Variance $= \dfrac{219}{20} - 3.015^2$ *[1 mark]*

$= 1.8597...$ g^2 *[1 mark]*

So standard deviation = 1.36 g (to 3 sig. fig.)
[1 mark]

c) Brand A chocolate drops are heavier on average than Brand B. Brand B chocolate drops vary in mass much less than brand A.
[1 mark for each of 2 sensible statements]

d) Combined mean $= \dfrac{\sum a + \sum b}{50}$

$= \dfrac{60.3 + (30 \times 2.95)}{50}$

$= 2.976$ g *[1 mark]*

Standard deviation for B = 1, so $\dfrac{\sum b^2}{30} - 2.95^2 = 1$,

and so $\sum b^2 = 291.075$ *[1 mark]*

Combined variance $= \dfrac{\sum a^2 + \sum b^2}{50} - 2.976^2$

$= \dfrac{219 + 291.075}{50} - 2.976^2$

$= 1.3449...$ *[1 mark]*

So combined standard deviation for all 50 chocolate drops is $\sqrt{1.3449...} = 1.16$ g
[1 mark]

Work through each step carefully so you don't make silly mistakes and lose marks.

4 a) There are 30 males. Since $30 \div 2 = 15$, the median is halfway between the 15th and 16th values in the ordered list. So take the mean of the 15th and 16th readings to get
median $= (62 + 65) \div 2 = 63.5$ *[1 mark]*

b) The female median is halfway between the 8th and 9th readings, so median = 64.5. This means the female median is higher than the male median by 1 mark, so the females scored better than the males on average.
Female range = 79 − 55 = 24.
Male range = 79 − 43 = 36
The female range is less than the male range. Their scores are more consistent than the males'.
[Up to 2 marks available for any sensible comments]
You could also have compared the figures for the mean, interquartile range or skewness.

5 a) Total number of people = 38
So median is halfway between the 19th and 20th values in the ordered list *[1 mark]*.
19th value = 15; 20th value = 16,
so median = 15.5 hits *[1 mark]*.
Mode = 15 hits *[1 mark]*

b) 38 ÷ 4 = 9.5, so lower quartile = 10th value = 14
38 ÷ 4 × 3 = 28.5, so upper quartile = 29th value = 17
[1 mark for both]
So interquartile range = 17 − 14 = 3,
and upper fence = 17 + (1.5 × 3) = 21.5.
This means that 25 is an outlier *[1 mark]*.

c)
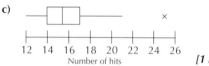
12 14 16 18 20 22 24 26
Number of hits   *[1 mark]*
As $Q_3 - Q_2 > Q_2 - Q_1$, and the line extended from the box is longer on the right-hand side, the distribution seems to be slightly positively skewed. *[1 mark]*
Make sure you can tell positive skew and negative skew apart — from a histogram and from a box plot.

d) If 25 was removed then the distribution would be more symmetrical (but still slightly positively skewed) *[1 mark]*.

6 Find the total area underneath the histogram using the grid squares *[1 mark]*:
2 + 1.5 + 2 + 2 + 1.5 + 4 + 5 + 3 + 4 = 25 *[1 mark]*
So each grid square represents 2 lions *[1 mark]*.
The number of squares for lengths above 220 cm is 7 *[1 mark]*, which represents 7 × 2 = 14 lions *[1 mark]*.

Chapter 2: Probability

1. Elementary Probability

Exercise 1.1 — The sample space

Q1 a) There is 1 outcome corresponding to the 7 of diamonds, and 52 outcomes in total.
So, P(7 of diamonds) = $\frac{1}{52}$

b) There is 1 outcome corresponding to the queen of spades, and 52 outcomes in total.
So, P(queen of spades) = $\frac{1}{52}$

c) There are 4 outcomes corresponding to a '9', and 52 outcomes in total.
So, P(9 of any suit) = $\frac{4}{52} = \frac{1}{13}$

d) There are 26 outcomes corresponding to a heart or a diamond, and 52 outcomes in total.
So, P(heart or diamond) = $\frac{26}{52} = \frac{1}{2}$

Q2 a) 6 of the 36 outcomes are prime numbers.
So, P(product is a prime number) = $\frac{6}{36} = \frac{1}{6}$

b) 14 of the 36 outcomes are less than 7.
So, P(product is less than 7) = $\frac{14}{36} = \frac{7}{18}$

c) 6 of the 36 outcomes are multiples of 10.
So, P(product is a multiple of 10) = $\frac{6}{36} = \frac{1}{6}$

Q3 a) E.g.

```
T  •  •  •  •  •  •  •  •  •  •
H  •  •  •  •  •  •  •  •  •  •
   1  2  3  4  5  6  7  8  9  10
```

b) There are 5 ways of getting an even number and 'tails', and 20 outcomes altogether.
So, P(even number and tails) = $\frac{5}{20} = \frac{1}{4}$

Q4 a) E.g.

−	1	2	3	4	5	6
1	0	1	2	3	4	5
2	1	0	1	2	3	4
3	2	1	0	1	2	3
4	3	2	1	0	1	2
5	4	3	2	1	0	1
6	5	4	3	2	1	0

b) 6 of the 36 outcomes are zero.
So, P(score is zero) = $\frac{6}{36} = \frac{1}{6}$

c) None of the outcomes are greater than 5.
So, P(score is greater than 5) = 0

d) The most likely score is the one corresponding to the most outcomes — so it's 1.
10 of the 36 outcomes give a score of 1, so:
P(1) = $\frac{10}{36} = \frac{5}{18}$

Q5 Start by drawing a sample-space diagram to show all the possible outcomes for the two spins combined. Then circle the ones that correspond to the event 'number on spinner 2 is greater than number on spinner 1'. E.g.

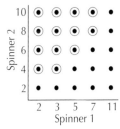

There are 13 outcomes that correspond to the event 'number on spinner 2 is greater than number on spinner 1', and 25 outcomes altogether.

So, P(spinner 2 > spinner 1) = $\frac{13}{25}$

2. Venn Diagrams
Exercise 2.1 — Using Venn diagrams

Q1　**a)**　Label the diagram by starting in the middle with the probability for A ∩ B. Then subtract this probability from P(A) and P(B). And remember to find P(A' ∩ B') by subtracting the other probabilities from 1. So:

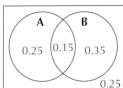

b)　P(A' ∩ B') = 0.25

Q2　**a)**　Let M be 'studies maths' and P be 'studies physics'. Start by labelling the area M ∩ P with 19. Then complete the circles by subtracting 19 from the numbers studying maths and physics. And don't forget to find the number who don't study either subject. So:

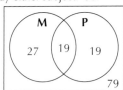

b)　M ∪ P has 27 + 19 + 19 = 65 outcomes.
So P(M ∪ P) = $\frac{65}{144}$

c)　So you're only interested in the 46 students who study maths. 19 students study maths and physics, so P(P, given M) = $\frac{19}{46}$.

Q3　**a)**　P(L ∩ M) = 0.1

b)　P(L ∩ N) = 0

c)　P(L' ∩ N) = 0.25
Since N doesn't overlap with L, L' ∩ N is just N.

d)　P(L' ∩ M' ∩ N') = 1 – (0.25 + 0.1 + 0.15 + 0.25)
= 0.25

e)　P(L ∪ M) = 0.25 + 0.1 + 0.15 = 0.5

f)　P(M') = 0.25 + 0.25 + 0.25 = 0.75
Don't forget to include P(L' ∩ M' ∩ N'). You could also find P(M') by doing 1 – P(M) = 1 – (0.1 + 0.15).

Q4　**a)**　Number of outcomes in S' ∩ F' ∩ G'
= 200 – (17 + 18 + 49 + 28 + 11 + 34 + 6) = 37
So P(S' ∩ F' ∩ G') = $\frac{37}{200}$

b)　You're only interested in those people who have been to France — 49 + 28 + 34 + 11 = 122 people. The number of people who have been to France **and** Germany = 28 + 34 = 62.
So P(G, given F) = $\frac{62}{122} = \frac{31}{61}$

c)　Number of outcomes in S ∩ F' = 17 + 18 = 35.
So P(S ∩ F') = $\frac{35}{200} = \frac{7}{40}$

Q5　**a)**　Start by drawing a Venn diagram to represent the information. If H = 'goes to home league matches', A = 'goes to away league matches' and C = 'goes to cup matches', then:

The people who go to exactly 2 types of match are those in H ∩ A ∩ C', H ∩ C ∩ A' and A ∩ C ∩ H'. That's 200 + 40 + 20 = 260 people.
So P(2 types of match) = $\frac{260}{1000} = \frac{13}{50}$

b)　P(at least 1 type of match) = 1 – P(no matches)
= $1 - \frac{240}{1000} = \frac{760}{1000} = \frac{19}{25}$

3. Laws of Probability
Exercise 3.1 — The addition law

Q1　**a)**　P(A') = 1 – P(A) = 1 – 0.3 = 0.7

b)　P(A ∪ B) = P(A) + P(B) – P(A ∩ B)
= 0.3 + 0.5 – 0.15 = 0.65

c)　P(A' ∩ B') = 1 – P(A ∪ B) = 1 – 0.65 = 0.35
Remember, A' ∩ B' is the complement of A ∪ B.

Q2　**a)**　P(B') = 1 – P(B) = 1 – 0.44 = 0.56

b)　P(A ∪ B) = P(A) + P(B) – P(A ∩ B)
= (1 – 0.36) + 0.44 – 0.27 = 0.81

c)　P(A ∩ B') = P(A) – P(A ∩ B) = 0.64 – 0.27 = 0.37

d)　P(A ∪ B') = P(A) + P(B') – P(A ∩ B')
= 0.64 + 0.56 – 0.37 = 0.83

Q3　Let B = 'car is blue' and E = 'car is an estate'.

a)　P(B') = 1 – P(B) = 1 – 0.25 = 0.75

b)　P(B ∪ E) = P(B) + P(E) – P(B ∩ E)
= 0.25 + 0.15 – 0.08 = 0.32

c)　P(B' ∩ E') = 1 – P(B ∪ E) = 1 – 0.32 = 0.68

Q4 a) $P(Y') = 1 - P(Y) = 1 - 0.56 = 0.44$

b) $P(X \cap Y) = P(X) + P(Y) - P(X \cup Y)$
$= 0.43 + 0.56 - 0.77 = 0.22$

c) $P(X' \cap Y') = 1 - P(X \cup Y) = 1 - 0.77 = 0.23$

d) $P(X' \cup Y') = 1 - P(X \cap Y) = 1 - 0.22 = 0.78$

Q5 a) $P(C' \cap D) = P(C') + P(D) - P(C' \cup D)$
$= (1 - 0.53) + 0.44 - 0.65 = 0.26$

b) $P(C' \cap D') = P(C') - P(C' \cap D)$
$= 0.47 - 0.26 = 0.21$
Just as $C = C \cap D + C \cap D'$,
$C' = C' \cap D + C' \cap D'$.

c) $P(C' \cup D') = P(C') + P(D') - P(C' \cap D')$
$= 0.47 + 0.56 - 0.21 = 0.82$

d) $P(C \cap D) = P(C) + P(D) - P(C \cup D)$
$= P(C) + P(D) - [1 - P(C' \cap D')]$
$= 0.53 + 0.44 - (1 - 0.21) = 0.18$

Q6 Let M = 'has read To Kill a Mockingbird' and A = 'has read Animal Farm'. Then, $P(M) = 0.62$, $P(A') = 0.66$, and $P(M \cup A) = 0.79$.

a) $P(M \cap A) = P(M) + P(A) - P(M \cup A)$
$= 0.62 + (1 - 0.66) - 0.79 = 0.17$

b) $P(M' \cap A) = P(A) - P(M \cap A) = 0.34 - 0.17 = 0.17$

c) $P(M' \cap A') = 1 - P(M \cup A) = 1 - 0.79 = 0.21$

Exercise 3.2 — Mutually exclusive events

Q1 a) $P(X \cap Y) = 0$

b) $P(X \cup Y) = P(X) + P(Y) = 0.48 + 0.37 = 0.85$

c) $P(X' \cap Y') = 1 - P(X \cup Y) = 1 - 0.85 = 0.15$

Q2 a) $P(L \cup M) = P(L) + P(M) = 0.28 + 0.42 = 0.7$

b) $P(L \cup N) = P(L) + P(N) = 0.28 + 0.33 = 0.61$

c) $P(M \cup N) = P(M) + P(N) - P(M \cap N)$
$= 0.42 + 0.33 - 0.16 = 0.59$

d) $P(L \cap M \cap N) = 0$

e) Draw 3 circles to represent events L, M and N, making sure that mutually exclusive events don't overlap. As usual, start the labelling with the intersection and work outwards.

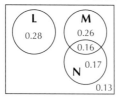

Q3 a) Let B = 'goes bowling', C = 'goes to the cinema', and D = 'goes out for dinner'. All 3 events are mutually exclusive, so:
$P(B \cup C) = P(B) + P(C) = 0.17 + 0.43 = 0.6$

b) P(doesn't do B, C or D) = $P(B' \cap C' \cap D')$
Since either none of B, C and D happen, or at least one of B, C and D happen, $B' \cap C' \cap D'$ and $B \cup C \cup D$ are complementary events. So:
$P(B' \cap C' \cap D') = 1 - P(B \cup C \cup D)$
$= 1 - [P(B) + P(C) + P(D)]$
$= 1 - (0.17 + 0.43 + 0.22)$
$= 1 - 0.82$
$= 0.18$

Q4 a) $P(A \cap B) = P(A) + P(B) - P(A \cup B)$
$= 0.28 + 0.66 - 0.86 = 0.08$
$P(A \cap B) \neq 0$, so A and B are not mutually exclusive.

b) $P(A \cap C) = P(A) + P(C) - P(A \cup C)$
$= 0.28 + 0.49 - 0.77 = 0$
$P(A \cap C) = 0$, so A and C are mutually exclusive.

c) $P(B \cap C) = P(B) + P(C) - P(B \cup C)$
$= 0.66 + 0.49 - 0.92 = 0.23$
$P(B \cap C) \neq 0$, so B and C are not mutually exclusive.

Q5 a) You need to show that $P(C \cap D) = 0$.
$P(C) = 1 - 0.6 = 0.4$.
$P(C \cap D) = P(C) - P(C \cap D') = 0.4 - 0.4 = 0$, so C and D are mutually exclusive.

b) $P(C \cup D) = P(C) + P(D) = 0.4 + 0.25 = 0.65$

Q6 Out of the total of 50 biscuits, 30 are plain, and 20 are chocolate-coated. Half of the biscuits are in wrappers, so 25 biscuits are in wrappers. Since there are more biscuits in wrappers than there are chocolate-coated ones, there must be some biscuits (at least 5) which are plain and in wrappers. So events P and W can happen at the same time (i.e. $P(P \cap W) \neq 0$), which means they are not exclusive.

Exercise 3.3 — The product law — conditional probability

Q1 a) $P(G \mid H) = \dfrac{P(G \cap H)}{P(H)} = \dfrac{0.24}{0.63} = \dfrac{24}{63} = \dfrac{8}{21}$
You could give the answer as a decimal instead, but using a fraction means you can give an exact answer.

b) $P(H \mid G) = \dfrac{P(G \cap H)}{P(G)} = \dfrac{0.24}{0.7} = \dfrac{24}{70} = \dfrac{12}{35}$

Q2 a) $P(B \mid A) = \dfrac{P(A \cap B)}{P(A)} = \dfrac{0.34}{0.68} = 0.5$

b) $P(A \mid C) = \dfrac{P(A \cap C)}{P(C)} = \dfrac{0.16}{0.44} = \dfrac{16}{44} = \dfrac{4}{11}$

c) $P(C' \mid B) = \dfrac{P(B \cap C')}{P(B)} = \dfrac{0.49}{1 - 0.44} = 0.875$

Q3 Let F = 'over 6 feet tall' and G = 'can play in goal'.

a) $P(G \mid F) = \dfrac{P(F \cap G)}{P(F)}$
$P(F \cap G) = \dfrac{2}{11}$ and $P(F) = \dfrac{5}{11}$
So, $P(G \mid F) = \dfrac{P(F \cap G)}{P(F)} = \dfrac{\frac{2}{11}}{\frac{5}{11}} = \dfrac{2}{5}$

b) $P(F \mid G) = \dfrac{P(F \cap G)}{P(G)}$ and $P(G) = \dfrac{3}{11}$. So:
$P(F \mid G) = \dfrac{P(F \cap G)}{P(G)} = \dfrac{\frac{2}{11}}{\frac{3}{11}} = \dfrac{2}{3}$

Q4 a) $P(M \mid A) = \dfrac{P(M \cap A)}{P(A)} = \dfrac{\frac{10}{100}}{\frac{33}{100}} = \dfrac{10}{33}$

b) $P(A \mid E \cap M) = \dfrac{P(A \cap E \cap M)}{P(E \cap M)} = \dfrac{\frac{2}{100}}{\frac{9}{100}} = \dfrac{2}{9}$

c) $P(E \mid M') = \dfrac{P(E \cap M')}{P(M')} = \dfrac{\frac{39}{100}}{\frac{60}{100}} = \dfrac{39}{60} = \dfrac{13}{20}$

d) $P(A \mid E') = \dfrac{P(A \cap E')}{P(E')} = \dfrac{\frac{18}{100}}{\frac{52}{100}} = \dfrac{18}{52} = \dfrac{9}{26}$

e) $P(M \mid A \cap E) = \dfrac{P(M \cap A \cap E)}{P(A \cap E)} = \dfrac{\frac{2}{100}}{\frac{15}{100}} = \dfrac{2}{15}$

Q5 a) $P(Y) = 1 - P(Y') = 1 - 0.72 = 0.28$

b) $P(X \cap Y) = P(X|Y)P(Y) = 0.75 \times 0.28 = 0.21$

c) $P(X \cap Z) = P(Z|X)P(X) = 0.25 \times 0.44 = 0.11$

d) $P(Y \mid Z') = \dfrac{P(Y \cap Z')}{P(Z')} = \dfrac{0.2}{1 - 0.61} = \dfrac{20}{39}$

e) $P(X \cap Y \cap Z) = P(X \cap Y \mid Z)P(Z)$
$$= \dfrac{7}{61} \times \dfrac{61}{100}$$
$$= \dfrac{7}{100} = 0.07$$

There are lots of ways to write an expression for $P(X \cap Y \cap Z)$ — e.g. $P(Z|X \cap Y)P(X \cap Y)$ or $P(X|Y \cap Z)P(Y \cap Z)$. You have to choose the way that makes best use of the information in the question.

Exercise 3.4 — Independent events

Q1 $P(X \cap Y) = P(X)P(Y) = 0.62 \times 0.32 = 0.1984$

Q2 $P(A)P(B) = P(A \cap B)$, so:
$$P(A) = \dfrac{P(A \cap B)}{P(B)} = \dfrac{0.45}{1 - 0.25} = 0.6$$

Q3 a) $P(M \cap N) = P(M)P(N) = 0.4 \times 0.7 = 0.28$

b) $P(M \cup N) = P(M) + P(N) - P(M \cap N)$
$= 0.4 + 0.7 - 0.28 = 0.82$

c) $P(M \cap N') = P(M)P(N') = 0.4 \times 0.3 = 0.12$

Q4 a) Let A = '1st card is hearts' and B = '2nd card is hearts'. Then, since the first card is replaced before the second is picked, A and B are independent events.
So, $P(A \cap B) = P(A) \times P(B)$
There are 13 hearts out of the 52 cards, so P(A) and P(B) both equal $\dfrac{13}{52} = \dfrac{1}{4}$.
So, $P(A \cap B) = \dfrac{1}{4} \times \dfrac{1}{4} = \dfrac{1}{16}$.

b) Let A = '1st card is ace of hearts' and B = '2nd card is ace of hearts'. Then, since the first card is replaced before the second is picked, A and B are independent events.
So, $P(A \cap B) = P(A) \times P(B)$
There is 1 'ace of hearts' out of the 52 cards, so P(A) and P(B) both equal $\dfrac{1}{52}$.
So, $P(A \cap B) = \dfrac{1}{52} \times \dfrac{1}{52} = \dfrac{1}{2704}$.

Q5 A and B:
$P(A) \times P(B) = \dfrac{3}{11} \times \dfrac{1}{3} = \dfrac{3}{33} = \dfrac{1}{11}$
$P(A) \times P(B) = \dfrac{1}{11} = P(A \cap B)$,
so A and B are independent.

A and C:
$P(A) \times P(C) = \dfrac{3}{11} \times \dfrac{15}{28} = \dfrac{45}{308}$
$P(A) \times P(C) = \dfrac{45}{308} \neq P(A \cap C) = \dfrac{2}{15}$,
so A and C are not independent.

B and C:
$P(B) \times P(C) = \dfrac{1}{3} \times \dfrac{15}{28} = \dfrac{15}{84} = \dfrac{5}{28}$
$P(B) \times P(C) = \dfrac{5}{28} = P(B \cap C)$,
so B and C are independent.

Q6 a) $P(X \cap Y) = P(X)P(Y) = 0.84 \times 0.68 = 0.5712$

b) $P(Y' \cap Z') = P(Y')P(Z') = 0.32 \times 0.52 = 0.1664$

c) Since Y and Z are independent,
$P(Y \mid Z) = P(Y) = 0.68$

d) Since Z' and Y' are independent,
$P(Z' \mid Y') = P(Z') = 1 - 0.48 = 0.52$

e) Since Y and X' are independent,
$P(Y \mid X') = P(Y) = 0.68$

Q7 Let J = 'Jess buys a DVD', K = 'Keisha buys a DVD' and L = 'Lucy buys a DVD'.

a) The probability that all 3 buy a DVD is $P(J \cap K \cap L)$. Since the 3 events are independent, you can multiply their probabilities together to get: $P(J) \times P(K) \times P(L) = 0.66 \times 0.5 \times 0.3 = 0.099$

b) The probability that at least 2 of them buy a DVD will be the probability that one of the following happens: $J \cap K \cap L$ or $J \cap K \cap L'$ or $J \cap K' \cap L$ or $J' \cap K \cap L$.
Since these events are mutually exclusive, you can add their probabilities together to give:
$0.099 + (0.66 \times 0.5 \times 0.7) + (0.66 \times 0.5 \times 0.3) + (0.34 \times 0.5 \times 0.3)$
$= 0.099 + 0.231 + 0.099 + 0.051$
$= 0.48$

Exercise 3.5 — Tree diagrams

Q1 a) The events are not independent because the probability that Jake wins his 2nd match depends on whether or not he won his 1st match.

b) (i) P(Win then Win) = $0.6 \times 0.75 = 0.45$

(ii) P(Wins at least 1) = P(Win then Win) + P(Win then Lose) + P(Lose then Win)
$= 0.45 + (0.6 \times 0.25) + (0.4 \times 0.35)$
$= 0.74$
Or you could find 1 − P(Lose then Lose).

Q2 a)

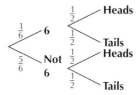

b) P(wins) = P(6 ∩ Tails) = $\frac{1}{6} \times \frac{1}{2} = \frac{1}{12}$

Q3 a) Let D = 'passed driving test' and U = 'intend to go to university'. Since D and U are independent, P(U|D') = P(U|D), and so:

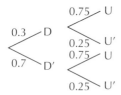

b) P(D' ∩ U') = 0.7 × 0.25 = 0.175

c) P(U') = P(D ∩ U') + P(D' ∩ U')
= (0.3 × 0.25) + 0.175
= 0.25

Or, since the events are independent,
P(U') = P(U'|D) = P(U'|D') = 0.25 (reading from the
tree diagram above).

Q4 Let R = 'orders roast dinner' and let A = 'orders apple pie for pudding'. Then you can draw the following tree diagram:

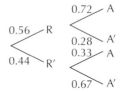

So P(A) = P(R ∩ A) + P(R' ∩ A)
= (0.56 × 0.72) + (0.44 × 0.33)
= 0.5484

Q5 Let S = 'owns smartphone' and let C = 'has contract costing more than £25 a month'. Then you know the following probabilities: P(S) = 0.62, P(C) = 0.539 and P(C'|S) = 0.29, and you want to find P(S|C). Using the conditional probability formula:
$$P(S|C) = \frac{P(S \cap C)}{P(C)}.$$
Use a tree diagram to help you find P(S ∩ C). You don't need to label all the branches, just the ones that help you answer the question:

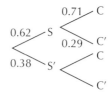

So P(S ∩ C) = 0.62 × 0.71 = 0.4402, and so:
$$P(S|C) = \frac{P(S \cap C)}{P(C)} = \frac{0.4402}{0.539} = 0.817 \text{ (3 s.f.)}.$$

Q6 a) Let R_i = 'ball i is red', Y_i = 'ball i is yellow' and G_i = 'ball i is green', for i = 1 and 2. Since the first ball isn't replaced, the second pick depends on the first pick and you get the following tree diagram:

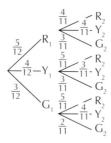

b) P(wins) = P(R₁ ∩ R₂) + P(Y₁ ∩ Y₂) + P(G₁ ∩ G₂)
$$= \left(\frac{5}{12} \times \frac{4}{11}\right) + \left(\frac{4}{12} \times \frac{3}{11}\right) + \left(\frac{3}{12} \times \frac{2}{11}\right)$$
$$= \frac{20}{132} + \frac{12}{132} + \frac{6}{132}$$
$$= \frac{38}{132} = \frac{19}{66}$$

c) If the first ball is replaced, the probability of winning becomes:
$$\left(\frac{5}{12} \times \frac{5}{12}\right) + \left(\frac{4}{12} \times \frac{4}{12}\right) + \left(\frac{3}{12} \times \frac{3}{12}\right)$$
$$= \frac{25}{144} + \frac{16}{144} + \frac{9}{144}$$
$$= \frac{50}{144} = \frac{25}{72}$$

Since $\frac{25}{72} > \frac{19}{66}$, a player is more likely to win now that the game has been changed.

You could also answer this question by explaining that
when a ball of one colour is selected, then replaced, the
proportion of balls of that colour left for the second pick
is higher than if it isn't replaced. So the probability of
picking the colour again is higher.

Review Exercise — Chapter 2

Q1 a) The sample space looks like this:

		1	2	3	4	5	6
				Dice			
Coin	H	2	4	6	8	10	12
	T	5	6	7	8	9	10

b) There are 12 outcomes in total, and 9 are more than 5, so P(score more than 5) = $\frac{9}{12} = \frac{3}{4}$.

c) There are 6 outcomes which have a tail showing, and 3 of these are even, so P(even score given that a tail is thrown) = $\frac{3}{6} = \frac{1}{2}$.

Q2 **a)** 50% of the students eat sausages (S), 20% eat chips (C) and 2% eat sausages and chips, so you get the following Venn diagram:

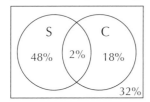

b) Using the Venn diagram, 18% of students eat chips but not sausages.

c) Using the Venn diagram, 18% + 48% = 66% eat chips or sausages, but not both.

Q3 It's best to start by drawing a sample-space diagram:

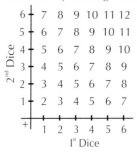

a) 15 of the 36 outcomes are prime (since 2, 3, 5, 7 and 11 are prime), so P(prime) = $\frac{15}{36} = \frac{5}{12}$.

b) 7 of the 36 outcomes are square numbers (since 4 and 9 are square), so P(square) = $\frac{7}{36}$

c) It isn't possible for her score to be both a prime number and a square number, so the events P and S are mutually exclusive.

d) Since P and S are mutually exclusive,
P(P ∪ S) = P(P) + P(S) = $\frac{5}{12} + \frac{7}{36} = \frac{22}{36} = \frac{11}{18}$

e) The score from the second experiment is unaffected by the score from the first experiment, so the events S_1 and S_2 are independent.

f) P($S_1 \cap S_2$) = P(S_1)P(S_2) = $\frac{7}{36} \times \frac{7}{36} = \frac{49}{1296}$

Q4 **a)** Let B = boy, G = girl, U = 'in upper school' and L = 'in lower school', then:

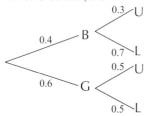

b) **(i)** Reading from the tree diagram, P(L|B) = 0.7.

(ii) P(G ∩ L) = 0.6 × 0.5 = 0.3

(iii) Choosing an upper school pupil means either 'boy and upper' or 'girl and upper'.
P(B ∩ U) = 0.4 × 0.3 = 0.12
P(G ∩ U) = 0.6 × 0.5 = 0.30
So P(U) = 0.12 + 0.30 = 0.42

Exam-Style Questions — Chapter 2

1 **a)** The Venn diagram would look like this:

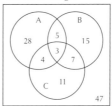

[1 mark for the central figure correct, 2 marks for '5', '7' and '4' correct (get 1 mark for 2 correct), 1 mark for '28', '15' and '11' correct, plus 1 mark for a box with '47' outside the circles.]

b) **(i)** Add up the numbers in all the circles to get 73 people out of 120 buy at least 1 of the soaps *[1 mark]*.
Or you could do 120 − 47 = 73...
So the probability = $\frac{73}{120}$ *[1 mark]*

(ii) Add up the numbers in the intersections to get 5 + 3 + 4 + 7 = 19, meaning that 19 people buy at least two of the soaps *[1 mark]*.
So the probability a person buys at least two of the soaps = $\frac{19}{120}$ *[1 mark]*.

(iii) 28 + 11 + 15 = 54 people buy only 1 of the soaps *[1 mark]*, and of these 15 buy soap B *[1 mark]*.
So the probability of a person who only buys one of the soaps buying type B is $\frac{15}{54} = \frac{5}{18}$ *[1 mark]*.

2 **a)** Let R_1 = '1st red', W_1 = '1st white', G_1 = '1st green', R_2 = '2nd red', W_2 = '2nd white' and G_2 = '2nd green'. Then:

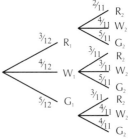

[3 marks available — 1 mark for each set of 3 branches on the right-hand side correct]

b) The second counter is green means one of three results: 'red then green' or 'white then green' or 'green then green'. So P(2nd is green) =
$$\left(\frac{3}{12} \times \frac{5}{11}\right) + \left(\frac{4}{12} \times \frac{5}{11}\right) + \left(\frac{5}{12} \times \frac{4}{11}\right)$$ *[1 mark]*
$$= \frac{15}{132} + \frac{20}{132} + \frac{20}{132} = \frac{55}{132} = \frac{5}{12}$$ *[1 mark]*

c) For both to be red there's only one possibility: 'red then red' *[1 mark]*.
P(both red) $= \frac{3}{12} \times \frac{2}{11} = \frac{6}{132} = \frac{1}{22}$ *[1 mark]*

d) 'Both same colour' is the complementary event of 'not both same colour'. So P(not same colour) $= 1 - $P(both same colour) *[1 mark]*. Both same colour is either R_1 and R_2, or W_1 and W_2, or G_1 and G_2. So P(not same colour)
$$= 1 - \left[\left(\frac{3}{12} \times \frac{2}{11}\right) + \left(\frac{4}{12} \times \frac{3}{11}\right) + \left(\frac{5}{12} \times \frac{4}{11}\right)\right]$$
[1 mark]
$$= 1 - \frac{38}{132} = \frac{94}{132} = \frac{47}{66}$$ *[1 mark]*

(Alternatively, 1 mark for showing $P(R_1W_2$ or R_1G_2 or W_1R_2 or W_1G_2 or G_1R_2 or $G_1W_2)$, 1 mark for adding the 6 correct probabilities and 1 mark for the correct answer.)

3 a) (i) J and K are independent, so
P(J ∩ K) = P(J) × P(K) = 0.7 × 0.1 = 0.07
[1 mark]

(ii) P(J ∪ K) = P(J) + P(K) − P(J ∩ K) *[1 mark]*
= 0.7 + 0.1 − 0.07 = 0.73 *[1 mark]*

b) Drawing a quick Venn Diagram often helps:

P(L|K') = P(L ∩ K') ÷ P(K')
Now L ∩ K' = L — think about it — all of L is contained in K', so L ∩ K' (the 'bits in both L and K') are just the bits in L.
Therefore P(L ∩ K') = P(L)
= 1 − P(K ∪ J) = 1 − 0.73 = 0.27 *[1 mark]*
P(K') = 1 − P(K) = 1 − 0.1 = 0.9 *[1 mark]*
And so P(L|K') = 0.27 ÷ 0.9 = 0.3 *[1 mark]*

4 Start by drawing a tree diagram to make things easier. Let C = 'eats chicken', B = 'eats beef', I = 'eats ice cream' and S = 'eats sponge pudding'.

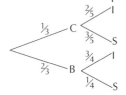

a) P(chicken or ice cream but not both)
= P(C ∩ S) + P(B ∩ I) *[1 mark]*
$$= \left(\frac{1}{3} \times \frac{3}{5}\right) + \left(\frac{2}{3} \times \frac{3}{4}\right)$$ *[1 mark]*
$$= \frac{3}{15} + \frac{6}{12} = \frac{7}{10}$$ *[1 mark]*

b) P(ice cream) = P(C ∩ I) + P(B ∩ I) *[1 mark]*
$$= \left(\frac{1}{3} \times \frac{2}{5}\right) + \left(\frac{2}{3} \times \frac{3}{4}\right)$$ *[1 mark]*
$$= \frac{2}{15} + \frac{6}{12} = \frac{19}{30}$$ *[1 mark]*

c) P(chicken | ice cream)
$$= P(C|I) = \frac{P(C \cap I)}{P(I)}$$ *[1 mark]*
$P(C \cap I) = \frac{2}{15}$ and $P(I) = \frac{19}{30}$ (both from b) above)
So $\frac{P(C \cap I)}{P(I)} = \frac{2}{15} \div \frac{19}{30}$ *[1 mark]*
$$= \frac{4}{19}$$ *[1 mark]*

5 a) Let E = 'goes every week' and R = 'plans to renew membership'. Then $P(E) = \frac{14}{20}$, $P(R) = \frac{13}{20}$ and $P(E|R) = \frac{10}{13}$.
P(R ∩ E) = P(E|R)P(R) *[1 mark]*
$$= \frac{10}{13} \times \frac{13}{20}$$ *[1 mark]*
$$= \frac{10}{20} = \frac{1}{2}$$ *[1 mark]*

b) P(E ∩ R') = P(E) − P(E ∩ R) *[1 mark]*
$$= \frac{14}{20} - \frac{1}{2} = \frac{1}{5}$$ *[1 mark]*

c) $P(E) \times P(R) = \frac{14}{20} \times \frac{13}{20} = \frac{91}{200} \neq P(E \cap R) = \frac{1}{2}$
[1 mark]
So going to the club every week and renewing membership are not independent *[1 mark]*.
Or you could say that $P(E) \neq P(E|R)$.

6 a) P(B') = 1 − 0.2 = 0.8 *[1 mark]*

b) It'll help if you draw a tree diagram before going any further. If F = 'roll a 6 on the fair dice':

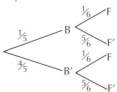

You want to find P(B ∪ F). Now, either at least one of the dice shows a 6 or neither of them do, so these are complementary events.
So P(B ∪ F) = 1 − P(B' ∩ F') *[1 mark]*
$$= 1 - \left(\frac{4}{5} \times \frac{5}{6}\right) = 1 - \frac{20}{30} = \frac{1}{3}$$ *[1 mark]*
Or you can use the addition rule:
P(B ∪ F) = P(B) + P(F) − P(B ∩ F)

c) P(exactly one 6 | at least one 6)

$$= \frac{\text{P(exactly one 6} \cap \text{at least one 6)}}{\text{P(at least one 6)}}$$ *[1 mark]*

The next step might be a bit easier to figure out if you draw a Venn diagram:

'exactly one 6' ∩ 'at least one 6' = 'exactly one 6' (Look at the diagram — 'exactly one 6' is the light grey area, and 'at least one 6' is the light grey area <u>plus</u> the dark grey bit. So the bit in common to both is just the light grey area.)

Now, that means P(exactly one 6 ∩ at least one 6) = P(B ∩ F') + P(B' ∩ F) — this is the light grey area in the Venn diagram,

i.e. P(exactly one 6 ∩ at least one 6)

$$= \left(\frac{1}{5} \times \frac{5}{6}\right) + \left(\frac{4}{5} \times \frac{1}{6}\right) = \frac{9}{30} = \frac{3}{10}$$

[1 mark]

P(at least one 6) = $\frac{1}{3}$ (from b) above).

And all of this means...

P(exactly one 6 | at least one 6)

$$= \frac{3}{10} \div \frac{1}{3} \text{ [1 mark]} = \frac{9}{10} \text{ [1 mark]}$$

Chapter 3: Discrete Random Variables

1. Probability Distributions

Exercise 1.1 — Probability distributions and functions

Q1 a) (i) The discrete random variable X is 'number of tails'.

(ii) x could be 0, 1, 2, 3 or 4.

b) (i) The discrete random variable X is 'number of orange balls selected'.

(ii) x could be 0, 1 or 2.

c) (i) The discrete random variable X is 'sum of the two dice scores'.

(ii) x could be 2, 3, 4, 5, 6, 7 or 8.

Q2 a)

a	1	2	3	4	5	6
P($A = a$)	$\frac{1}{6}$	$\frac{1}{6}$	$\frac{1}{6}$	$\frac{1}{6}$	$\frac{1}{6}$	$\frac{1}{6}$

b) The probability of the score being even is $\frac{3}{6} = \frac{1}{2}$ and the probability of 'otherwise' (the score being odd) is the same. The probability distribution is:

b	0	1
P($B = b$)	$\frac{1}{2}$	$\frac{1}{2}$

c) C can take 6 values, c = 5, 10, 15, 20, 25, 30 (each score × 5) and each one will have probability $\frac{1}{6}$. The probability distribution is:

c	5	10	15	20	25	30
P($C = c$)	$\frac{1}{6}$	$\frac{1}{6}$	$\frac{1}{6}$	$\frac{1}{6}$	$\frac{1}{6}$	$\frac{1}{6}$

Q3 a) (i) $\sum_{\text{all }x} \text{P}(X = x) = 0.2 + 0.4 + 0.1 + a = 1$

So, $a = 1 - 0.2 - 0.4 - 0.1 = 0.3$

(ii) P($X \geq 2$) = P($X = 2$) + P($X = 3$) + P($X = 4$)

$= 0.4 + 0.1 + 0.3 = 0.8$

b) (i) $\sum_{\text{all }x} \text{P}(X = x) = 6k = 1$

So, $k = \frac{1}{6}$.

(ii) P($X \geq 5$)

= P($X = 9$) + P($X = 16$) + P($X = 25$) + P($X = 36$)

$= 4k = \frac{4}{6} = \frac{2}{3}$.

(iii) P($X \geq 10$) = P($X = 16$) + P($X = 25$) + P($X = 36$)

$= 3k = \frac{3}{6} = \frac{1}{2}$.

(iv) P($3 \leq X \leq 15$) = P($X = 4$) + P($X = 9$)

$= 2k = \frac{2}{6} = \frac{1}{3}$.

(v) P(X is divisible by 3) = P(X = 9 or 36)

= P($X = 9$) + P($X = 36$)

$= 2k = \frac{2}{6} = \frac{1}{3}$.

Q4 a) (i) $\sum_{\text{all }x} \text{P}(X = x) = k + 4k + 9k = 14k = 1$

So $k = \frac{1}{14}$.

(ii)

x	1	2	3
P($X = x$)	$\frac{1}{14}$	$\frac{2}{7}$	$\frac{9}{14}$

b) (i) $\sum_{\text{all }x} \text{P}(X = x) = k + \frac{k}{2} + \frac{k}{3} = \frac{11k}{6} = 1$

So $k = \frac{6}{11}$.

(ii)

x	1	2	3
P($X = x$)	$\frac{6}{11}$	$\frac{3}{11}$	$\frac{2}{11}$

c) (i) $\sum_{\text{all }x} \text{P}(X = x) = k + 2k + 3k + 4k + 3k + 2k + k$

$= 1$

So $16k = 1$ so $k = \frac{1}{16}$.

(ii)

x	1	2	3	4	5	6	7
$P(X=x)$	$\frac{1}{16}$	$\frac{1}{8}$	$\frac{3}{16}$	$\frac{1}{4}$	$\frac{3}{16}$	$\frac{1}{8}$	$\frac{1}{16}$

Q5 a) Draw a sample-space diagram to show all the possible outcomes:

Score on dice 1

×	1	2	3	4
1	1	2	3	4
2	2	4	6	8
3	3	6	9	12
4	4	8	12	16

Score on dice 2

So the possible values that X can take are 1, 2, 3, 4, 6, 8, 9, 12 and 16.

To find the probability of X taking each value, count the number of outcomes that give the value and divide by the total number, 16.

$P(X=1) = \frac{1}{16}$, $P(X=2) = \frac{2}{16} = \frac{1}{8}$,

$P(X=3) = \frac{2}{16} = \frac{1}{8}$, $P(X=4) = \frac{3}{16}$,

$P(X=6) = \frac{2}{16} = \frac{1}{8}$, $P(X=8) = \frac{2}{16} = \frac{1}{8}$,

$P(X=9) = \frac{1}{16}$, $P(X=12) = \frac{2}{16} = \frac{1}{8}$,

$P(X=16) = \frac{1}{16}$

So the probability distribution looks like this:

x	1	2	3	4	6	8	9	12	16
$P(X=x)$	$\frac{1}{16}$	$\frac{1}{8}$	$\frac{1}{8}$	$\frac{3}{16}$	$\frac{1}{8}$	$\frac{1}{8}$	$\frac{1}{16}$	$\frac{1}{8}$	$\frac{1}{16}$

b) The probability function is:

$$P(X=x) = \begin{cases} \frac{1}{8} & x = 2, 3, 6, 8, 12 \\ \frac{3}{16} & x = 4 \\ \frac{1}{16} & x = 1, 9, 16 \end{cases}$$

c) $P(3 < X \leq 10)$
$= P(X=4) + P(X=6) + P(X=8) + P(X=9)$
$= \frac{3}{16} + \frac{1}{8} + \frac{1}{8} + \frac{1}{16} = \frac{1}{2}$

Exercise 1.2 — The cumulative distribution function

Q1 a) Add up the probabilities to work out the values of F(x):

$F(1) = P(X \leq 1) = P(X=1) = 0.1$

$F(2) = P(X \leq 2) = P(X=2) + P(X=1)$
$= 0.2 + 0.1 = 0.3$

$F(3) = P(X \leq 3) = P(X=3) + P(X=2) + P(X=1)$
$= 0.3 + 0.2 + 0.1 = 0.6$

$F(4) = P(X \leq 4)$
$= P(X=4) + P(X=3) + P(X=2) + P(X=1)$
$= 0.2 + 0.3 + 0.2 + 0.1 = 0.8$

$F(5) = P(X \leq 5)$
$= P(X=5) + P(X=4) + P(X=3)$
$+ P(X=2) + P(X=1)$
$= 0.2 + 0.2 + 0.3 + 0.2 + 0.1 = 1$

Using all this information, the cumulative distribution function is:

x	1	2	3	4	5
F(x)	0.1	0.3	0.6	0.8	1

b) Add up the probabilities to work out the values of F(x):

$F(-2) = P(X \leq -2) = P(X=-2) = \frac{1}{5}$

$F(-1) = P(X \leq -1) = P(X=-1) + P(X=-2)$
$= \frac{1}{5} + \frac{1}{5} = \frac{2}{5}$

$F(0) = P(X \leq 0) = P(X=0) + P(X=-1) + P(X=-2)$
$= \frac{1}{5} + \frac{1}{5} + \frac{1}{5} = \frac{3}{5}$

$F(1) = P(X \leq 1)$
$= P(X=1) + P(X=0) + P(X=-1) + P(X=-2)$
$= \frac{1}{5} + \frac{1}{5} + \frac{1}{5} + \frac{1}{5} = \frac{4}{5}$

$F(2) = P(X \leq 2)$
$= P(X=2) + P(X=1) + P(X=0)$
$+ P(X=-1) + P(X=-2)$
$= \frac{1}{5} + \frac{1}{5} + \frac{1}{5} + \frac{1}{5} + \frac{1}{5} = 1$

Using all this information, the cumulative distribution function is:

x	−2	−1	0	1	2
F(x)	$\frac{1}{5}$	$\frac{2}{5}$	$\frac{3}{5}$	$\frac{4}{5}$	1

c) Add up the probabilities to work out the values of F(x):

$F(1) = P(X \leq 1) = P(X=1) = 0.3$

$F(2) = P(X \leq 2) = P(X=2) + P(X=1)$
$= 0.2 + 0.3 = 0.5$

$F(3) = P(X \leq 3) = P(X=3) + P(X=2) + P(X=1)$
$= 0.3 + 0.2 + 0.3 = 0.8$

$F(4) = P(X \leq 4)$
$= P(X=4) + P(X=3) + P(X=2) + P(X=1)$
$= 0.2 + 0.3 + 0.2 + 0.3 = 1$

Using all this information, the cumulative distribution function is:

x	1	2	3	4
F(x)	0.3	0.5	0.8	1

d) Add up the probabilities to work out the values of F(x):

$F(2) = P(X \leq 2) = P(X=2) = \frac{1}{2}$

$F(4) = P(X \leq 4) = P(X=4) + P(X=2)$
$= \frac{1}{4} + \frac{1}{2} = \frac{3}{4}$

$F(8) = P(X \le 8) = P(X = 8) + P(X = 4) + P(X = 2)$

$= \frac{1}{8} + \frac{1}{4} + \frac{1}{2} = \frac{7}{8}$

$F(16) = P(X \le 16)$

$= P(X = 16) + P(X = 8) + P(X = 4) + P(X = 2)$

$= \frac{1}{16} + \frac{1}{8} + \frac{1}{4} + \frac{1}{2} = \frac{15}{16}$

$F(32) = P(X \le 32)$

$= P(X = 32) + P(X = 16) + P(X = 8)$

$+ P(X = 4) + P(X = 2)$

$= \frac{1}{32} + \frac{1}{16} + \frac{1}{8} + \frac{1}{4} + \frac{1}{2} = \frac{31}{32}$

$F(64) = P(X \le 64)$

$= P(X = 64) + P(X = 32) + P(X = 16)$

$+ P(X = 8) + P(X = 4) + P(X = 2)$

$= \frac{1}{32} + \frac{1}{32} + \frac{1}{16} + \frac{1}{8} + \frac{1}{4} + \frac{1}{2} = 1$

Using all this information, the cumulative distribution function is:

x	2	4	8	16	32	64
$F(x)$	$\frac{1}{2}$	$\frac{3}{4}$	$\frac{7}{8}$	$\frac{15}{16}$	$\frac{31}{32}$	1

Q2 a) You need to draw up a table showing the cumulative distribution function, so work out the values of $F(x)$:

$F(1) = P(X = 1) = 0.3$

$F(2) = P(X = 2) + P(X = 1) = 0.1 + 0.3 = 0.4$

$F(3) = P(X = 3) + P(X = 2) + P(X = 1)$

$= 0.45 + 0.1 + 0.3 = 0.85$

$F(4) = P(X = 4) + P(X = 3) + P(X = 2) + P(X = 1)$

$= 0.15 + 0.45 + 0.1 + 0.3 = 1$

So the cumulative distribution function looks like this:

x	1	2	3	4
$F(x)$	0.3	0.4	0.85	1

(i) $P(X \le 3) = F(3) = 0.85$

(ii) $P(1 < X \le 3) = P(X \le 3) - P(X \le 1)$

$= 0.85 - 0.3 = 0.55$

b) Again, start by working out the values of $F(x)$:

$F(-2) = P(X = -2) = \frac{1}{10}$

$F(-1) = P(X = -1) + P(X = -2) = \frac{2}{5} + \frac{1}{10} = \frac{1}{2}$

$F(0) = P(X = 0) + P(X = -1) + P(X = -2)$

$= \frac{1}{10} + \frac{2}{5} + \frac{1}{10} = \frac{3}{5}$

$F(1) = P(X = 1) + P(X = 0) + P(X = -1) + P(X = -2)$

$= \frac{1}{5} + \frac{1}{10} + \frac{2}{5} + \frac{1}{10} = \frac{4}{5}$

$F(2) = P(X = 2) + P(X = 1) + P(X = 0)$

$+ P(X = -1) + P(X = -2)$

$= \frac{1}{5} + \frac{1}{5} + \frac{1}{10} + \frac{2}{5} + \frac{1}{10} = 1$

So the cumulative distribution function looks like this:

x	−2	−1	0	1	2
$F(x)$	$\frac{1}{10}$	$\frac{1}{2}$	$\frac{3}{5}$	$\frac{4}{5}$	1

(i) $P(X \le 0) = F(0) = \frac{3}{5}$

(ii) $P(X > 0) = 1 - F(0) = 1 - \frac{3}{5} = \frac{2}{5}$

Here you're just using the fact that $P(X \le O) + P(X > O) = 1$ (all the probabilities add up to 1).

Q3 a) Use the probability function to work out the values of $F(x)$.

$F(1) = P(X = 1) = \frac{1}{8}$

$F(2) = P(X = 2) + P(X = 1) = \frac{1}{8} + \frac{1}{8} = \frac{2}{8} = \frac{1}{4}$

$F(3) = P(X = 3) + P(X = 2) + P(X = 1)$

$= \frac{1}{8} + \frac{1}{8} + \frac{1}{8} = \frac{3}{8}$

Because you are adding on a constant term of $\frac{1}{8}$ each time, the rest are easy to work out:

$F(4) = \frac{4}{8} = \frac{1}{2}$, $F(5) = \frac{5}{8}$, $F(6) = \frac{6}{8} = \frac{3}{4}$,

$F(7) = \frac{7}{8}$, $F(8) = \frac{8}{8} = 1$

So the cumulative distribution function looks like this:

x	1	2	3	4	5	6	7	8
$F(x)$	$\frac{1}{8}$	$\frac{1}{4}$	$\frac{3}{8}$	$\frac{1}{2}$	$\frac{5}{8}$	$\frac{3}{4}$	$\frac{7}{8}$	1

b) (i) $P(X \le 3) = F(3) = \frac{3}{8}$

(ii) $P(3 < X \le 7) = P(X \le 7) - P(X \le 3)$

$= \frac{7}{8} - \frac{3}{8} = \frac{4}{8} = \frac{1}{2}$

Q4 a) $P(X = 5) = P(X \le 5) - P(X \le 4) = 1 - 0.9 = 0.1$

$P(X = 4) = P(X \le 4) - P(X \le 3) = 0.9 - 0.6 = 0.3$

$P(X = 3) = P(X \le 3) - P(X \le 2) = 0.6 - 0.3 = 0.3$

$P(X = 2) = P(X \le 2) - P(X \le 1) = 0.3 - 0.2 = 0.1$

$P(X = 1) = P(X \le 1) = 0.2$

So the probability distribution is:

x	1	2	3	4	5
$p(x)$	0.2	0.1	0.3	0.3	0.1

Always check that the probabilities add up to 1 — if they don't, you know for sure that you've gone wrong.

b) $P(X = 1) = P(X \le 1) - P(X \le 0) = 1 - 0.7 = 0.3$

$P(X = 0) = P(X \le 0) - P(X \le -1) = 0.7 - 0.2 = 0.5$

$P(X = -1) = P(X \le -1) - P(X \le -2) = 0.2 - 0.1 = 0.1$

$P(X = -2) = P(X \le -2) = 0.1$

So the probability distribution is:

x	−2	−1	0	1
$p(x)$	0.1	0.1	0.5	0.3

c) $P(X = 64) = P(X \le 64) - P(X \le 32) = 1 - \frac{3}{4} = \frac{1}{4}$

$P(X = 32) = P(X \le 32) - P(X \le 16) = \frac{3}{4} - \frac{1}{2} = \frac{1}{4}$

$P(X = 16) = P(X \le 16) - P(X \le 8) = \frac{1}{2} - \frac{1}{4} = \frac{1}{4}$

$P(X = 8) = P(X \le 8) - P(X \le 4) = \frac{1}{4} - \frac{1}{8} = \frac{1}{8}$

$P(X = 4) = P(X \le 4) - P(X \le 2) = \frac{1}{8} - \frac{1}{32} = \frac{3}{32}$

$P(X = 2) = P(X \le 2) = \frac{1}{32}$

So the probability distribution is:

x	2	4	8	16	32	64
p(x)	$\frac{1}{32}$	$\frac{3}{32}$	$\frac{1}{8}$	$\frac{1}{4}$	$\frac{1}{4}$	$\frac{1}{4}$

Q5 $P(X = 4) = P(X \le 4) - P(X \le 3) = 1 - 0.8 = 0.2$
$P(X = 3) = P(X \le 3) - P(X \le 2) = 0.8 - a$
$P(X = 2) = P(X \le 2) - P(X \le 1) = a - 0.3$
$P(X = 1) = P(X \le 1) = 0.3$

Now $P(X = 2) = P(X = 3)$ so $0.8 - a = a - 0.3$,
so $2a = 1.1$, so $a = 0.55$.
So $P(X = 2) = P(X = 3) = 0.25$

So the probability distribution is:

x	1	2	3	4
p(x)	0.3	0.25	0.25	0.2

Q6 a) $F(3) = P(X \le 3) = \sum_{\text{all }x} P(X = x) = 1$

So $\frac{(3 + k)^2}{25} = 1 \Rightarrow (3 + k)^2 = 25$

$\Rightarrow 3 + k = 5 \Rightarrow k = 2$

To find the probability distribution, you need to find the probability of each outcome:

$P(X = 3) = P(X \le 3) - P(X \le 2) = F(3) - F(2)$
$= \frac{(3 + 2)^2}{25} - \frac{(2 + 2)^2}{25} = \frac{25}{25} - \frac{16}{25} = \frac{9}{25}$

$P(X = 2) = P(X \le 2) - P(X \le 1) = F(2) - F(1)$
$= \frac{(2 + 2)^2}{25} - \frac{(1 + 2)^2}{25} = \frac{16}{25} - \frac{9}{25} = \frac{7}{25}$

$P(X = 1) = P(X \le 1) = F(1) = \frac{(1 + 2)^2}{25} = \frac{9}{25}$

So the table looks like:

x	1	2	3
$P(X = x)$	$\frac{9}{25}$	$\frac{7}{25}$	$\frac{9}{25}$

b) $F(3) = P(X \le 3) = \sum_{\text{all }x} P(X = x) = 1$

So $\frac{(3 + k)^3}{64} = 1 \Rightarrow (3 + k)^3 = 64$

$\Rightarrow 3 + k = 4 \Rightarrow k = 1$

To find the probability distribution you need to find the probability of each outcome:

$P(X = 3) = P(X \le 3) - P(X \le 2) = F(3) - F(2)$
$= \frac{(3 + 1)^3}{64} - \frac{(2 + 1)^3}{64} = \frac{64}{64} - \frac{27}{64} = \frac{37}{64}$

$P(X = 2) = P(X \le 2) - P(X \le 1) = F(2) - F(1)$
$= \frac{(2 + 1)^3}{64} - \frac{(1 + 1)^3}{64} = \frac{27}{64} - \frac{8}{64} = \frac{19}{64}$

$P(X = 1) = P(X \le 1) = F(1) = \frac{(1 + 1)^3}{64} = \frac{8}{64} = \frac{1}{8}$

So the table looks like:

x	1	2	3
$P(X = x)$	$\frac{1}{8}$	$\frac{19}{64}$	$\frac{37}{64}$

c) $F(3) = P(X \le 3) = \sum_{\text{all }x} P(X = x) = 1$

So $2^{(3 - k)} = 1$.
For 2 to the power of something to be equal to 1, the power must be 0, so $3 - k = 0 \Rightarrow k = 3$.
To find the probability distribution, you need to find the probability of each outcome:

$P(X = 3) = P(X \le 3) - P(X \le 2) = F(3) - F(2)$
$= 2^{(3 - 3)} - 2^{(2 - 3)} = 2^0 - 2^{-1}$
$= 1 - \frac{1}{2} = \frac{1}{2}$

$P(X = 2) = P(X \le 2) - P(X \le 1) = F(2) - F(1)$
$= 2^{(2 - 3)} - 2^{(1 - 3)} = 2^{-1} - 2^{-2}$
$= \frac{1}{2} - \frac{1}{4} = \frac{1}{4}$

$P(X = 1) = P(X \le 1) = F(1) = 2^{(1 - 3)} = 2^{-2} = \frac{1}{4}$

So the table looks like:

x	1	2	3
$P(X = x)$	$\frac{1}{4}$	$\frac{1}{4}$	$\frac{1}{2}$

Q7 a) F(x) means the probability that the larger score on the dice is no larger than x. This means both dice must score no more than x, where $x = 1, 2, 3, 4,$ 5 or 6. The probability that one dice will score no more than x is $\frac{x}{6}$, so the probability that both will score no more than x is $\frac{x}{6} \times \frac{x}{6} = \frac{x^2}{36}$.

Two dice rolls are completely independent, so the probabilities can just be multiplied together.

So $F(x) = \frac{x^2}{36}$, $x = 1, 2, 3, 4, 5, 6$.

b) To find the probability distribution you need to find the probability of each outcome:

$P(X = 6) = P(X \le 6) - P(X \le 5) = \frac{6^2}{36} - \frac{5^2}{36}$
$= \frac{36}{36} - \frac{25}{36} = \frac{11}{36}$

$P(X = 5) = P(X \le 5) - P(X \le 4) = \frac{5^2}{36} - \frac{4^2}{36}$
$= \frac{25}{36} - \frac{16}{36} = \frac{9}{36} = \frac{1}{4}$

$P(X = 4) = P(X \le 4) - P(X \le 3) = \frac{4^2}{36} - \frac{3^2}{36}$
$= \frac{16}{36} - \frac{9}{36} = \frac{7}{36}$

$$P(X = 3) = P(X \le 3) - P(X \le 2) = \frac{3^2}{36} - \frac{2^2}{36}$$
$$= \frac{9}{36} - \frac{4}{36} = \frac{5}{36}$$
$$P(X = 2) = P(X \le 2) - P(X \le 1) = \frac{2^2}{36} - \frac{1^2}{36}$$
$$= \frac{4}{36} - \frac{1}{36} = \frac{3}{36} = \frac{1}{12}$$
$$P(X = 1) = P(X \le 1) = \frac{1^2}{36} = \frac{1}{36}$$

So the table looks like:

x	1	2	3	4	5	6
$P(X = x)$	$\frac{1}{36}$	$\frac{1}{12}$	$\frac{5}{36}$	$\frac{7}{36}$	$\frac{1}{4}$	$\frac{11}{36}$

2. Expected Values, Mean and Variance

Exercise 2.1 — The expected value

Q1 **a)** $E(X) = [0 \times 0.2] + [1 \times 0.2] + [2 \times 0.2]$
$+ [3 \times 0.2] + [4 \times 0.2] = 2$

b) $E(X) = \left[1 \times \frac{1}{14}\right] + \left[2 \times \frac{4}{14}\right] + \left[3 \times \frac{9}{14}\right]$
$= \frac{36}{14} = \frac{18}{7} = 2.57$ to 3 s.f.

c) $E(X) = [2 \times 0.1] + [3 \times 0.4] + [1 \times 0.5] = 1.9$

d) $E(X) = [-2 \times 0.1] + [-1 \times 0.2] + [1 \times 0.2]$
$+ [2 \times 0.2] + [0 \times 0.3] = 0.2$

e) First work out the value of k:
The probabilities add up to 1 so
$3k + 4k + 5k + 6k + 7k = 1$
$25k = 1 \Rightarrow k = \frac{1}{25}$.
Now you can work out $E(X)$:

$E(X) = \left[1 \times \frac{1}{25}(1 + 2)\right] + \left[2 \times \frac{1}{25}(2 + 2)\right]$
$+ \left[3 \times \frac{1}{25}(3 + 2)\right] + \left[4 \times \frac{1}{25}(4 + 2)\right]$
$+ \left[5 \times \frac{1}{25}(5 + 2)\right]$
$= \frac{17}{5} = 3.4$

f) First work out the value of k:
The probabilities add up to 1 so
$\frac{k}{1} + \frac{k}{2} + \frac{k}{3} + \frac{k}{4} + \frac{k}{5} = 1$
$\Rightarrow k\left(\frac{1}{1} + \frac{1}{2} + \frac{1}{3} + \frac{1}{4} + \frac{1}{5}\right) = 1$
$\Rightarrow k\left(\frac{137}{60}\right) = 1$
$\Rightarrow k = \frac{60}{137}$

$$E(X) = \left[1 \times \frac{\left(\frac{60}{137}\right)}{1}\right] + \left[2 \times \frac{\left(\frac{60}{137}\right)}{2}\right]$$
$$+ \left[3 \times \frac{\left(\frac{60}{137}\right)}{3}\right] + \left[4 \times \frac{\left(\frac{60}{137}\right)}{4}\right]$$
$$+ \left[5 \times \frac{\left(\frac{60}{137}\right)}{5}\right]$$
$$= \frac{300}{137} = 2\frac{26}{137} \text{ (or 2.19 to 3 s.f.)}$$

Q2 **a)** $E(X) = [2 \times 0.2] + [5 \times 0.3]$
$+ [6 \times 0.1] + [p \times 0.4]$
$= 2.5 + 0.4p$
So $6.5 = 2.5 + 0.4p \Rightarrow p = 10$.

b) The probabilities add up to 1 so
$0.5 + 0.2 + a + 0.2 = 1 \Rightarrow a = 0.1$
$E(X) = [4 \times 0.5] + [8 \times 0.2]$
$+ [p \times a] + [15 \times 0.2]$
$= 6.6 + 0.1p$
So $7.5 = 6.6 + 0.1p \Rightarrow p = 9$.

Q3 **a)** The sum of the probabilities is 1 so
$0.2 + a + 0.1 + b = 1 \Rightarrow a + b = 0.7$
$E(X)$ is 2.5 so
$0.2 + 2a + 0.3 + 4b = 2.5$
$\Rightarrow 2a + 4b = 2 \Rightarrow a + 2b = 1$
Rearranging the second equation to get $a = 1 - 2b$
and substituting this into the first equation we get:
$(1 - 2b) + b = 0.7 \Rightarrow b = 0.3$
and putting $b = 0.3$ into the first equation we get
$a = 0.4$.

b) The sum of the probabilities is 1 so
$0.1 + a + b + 0.1 = 1 \Rightarrow a + b = 0.8$
$E(X)$ is 7.8 so
$0.3 + 7a + 8b + 1.2 = 7.8 \Rightarrow 7a + 8b = 6.3$
From the first equation, $a = 0.8 - b$, and
substituting this into the second equation, we get:
$7(0.8 - b) + 8b = 6.3$
$\Rightarrow 5.6 - 7b + 8b = 6.3$
$\Rightarrow 5.6 + b = 6.3$
$\Rightarrow b = 0.7$
Now the first equation is $a + b = 0.8$, and
substituting in $b = 0.7$ we get $a = 0.1$.

Q4 **a)** **(i)** $E(X) = [1 \times 0.2] + [2 \times 0.1] + [3 \times 0.25]$
$+ [4 \times 0.25] + [5 \times 0.2]$
$= 3.15$

(ii) $E(X^2) = [1 \times 0.2] + [4 \times 0.1] + [9 \times 0.25]$
$+ [16 \times 0.25] + [25 \times 0.2]$
$= 11.85$

b) **(i)** $E(X) = [-3 \times 0.2] + [-2 \times 0.1] + [-1 \times 0.25]$
$+ [0 \times 0.25] + [1 \times 0.2]$
$= -0.85$

(ii) $E(X^2) = [9 \times 0.2] + [4 \times 0.1] + [1 \times 0.25]$
$+ [0 \times 0.25] + [1 \times 0.2]$
$= 2.65$

c) **(i)** $E(X) = [3 \times 0.1] + [4 \times 0.25] + [5 \times 0.15]$
$+ [7 \times 0.3] + [9 \times 0.2]$
$= 5.95$

(ii) $E(X^2) = [9 \times 0.1] + [16 \times 0.25] + [25 \times 0.15]$
$+ [49 \times 0.3] + [81 \times 0.2]$
$= 39.55$

Exercise 2.2 — Variance

Q1 **a)** $E(X) = [1 \times 0.2] + [2 \times 0.1] + [3 \times 0.2]$
$+ [4 \times 0.1] + [5 \times 0.4] = 3.4$

$E(X^2) = [1 \times 0.2] + [4 \times 0.1] + [9 \times 0.2]$
$+ [16 \times 0.1] + [25 \times 0.4] = 14$

So $\text{Var}(X) = E(X^2) - (E(X))^2 = 14 - 3.4^2 = 2.44$

b) $E(X) = [1 \times \frac{1}{2}] + [3 \times \frac{1}{4}] + [6 \times \frac{1}{8}]$

$+ [8 \times \frac{1}{16}] + [9 \times \frac{1}{32}] + [10 \times \frac{1}{32}]$

$= \frac{99}{32} \ (= 3.09 \text{ to 3 s.f.})$

$E(X^2) = [1 \times \frac{1}{2}] + [9 \times \frac{1}{4}] + [36 \times \frac{1}{8}]$

$+ [64 \times \frac{1}{16}] + [81 \times \frac{1}{32}] + [100 \times \frac{1}{32}]$

$= \frac{541}{32} \ (= 16.9 \text{ to 3 s.f.})$

So $\text{Var}(X) = E(X^2) - (E(X))^2$

$= \frac{541}{32} - \left(\frac{99}{32}\right)^2 = \frac{7511}{1024} \ (= 7.33 \text{ to 3 s.f.})$

c) $E(X) = [-2 \times 0.2] + [-1 \times 0.1] + [0 \times 0.2]$
$+ [1 \times 0.1] + [2 \times 0.4] = 0.4$

$E(X^2) = [4 \times 0.2] + [1 \times 0.1] + [0 \times 0.2]$
$+ [1 \times 0.1] + [4 \times 0.4] = 2.6$

So $\text{Var}(X) = E(X^2) - (E(X))^2 = 2.6 - 0.4^2 = 2.44$

Q2 **a)** $E(X) = [1 \times \frac{1}{5}] + [2 \times \frac{1}{5}] + [3 \times \frac{1}{5}]$
$+ [4 \times \frac{1}{5}] + [5 \times \frac{1}{5}] = 3$

$E(X^2) = [1 \times \frac{1}{5}] + [4 \times \frac{1}{5}] + [9 \times \frac{1}{5}]$
$+ [16 \times \frac{1}{5}] + [25 \times \frac{1}{5}] = 11$

So $\text{Var}(X) = E(X^2) - (E(X))^2 = 11 - 3^2 = 2$

b) $E(X) = [1 \times \frac{1}{30}] + [2 \times \frac{4}{30}] + [3 \times \frac{9}{30}]$
$+ [4 \times \frac{16}{30}] = \frac{10}{3}$

$E(X^2) = [1 \times \frac{1}{30}] + [4 \times \frac{4}{30}] + [9 \times \frac{9}{30}]$
$+ [16 \times \frac{16}{30}] = \frac{59}{5}$

So $\text{Var}(X) = E(X^2) - (E(X))^2 = \frac{59}{5} - \left(\frac{10}{3}\right)^2$

$= \frac{31}{45} \ (= 0.689 \text{ to 3 s.f.})$

Q3 **a)** **(i)** The probabilities must add up to 1:
$0.2 + a + 0.4 + 0.1 = 1 \Rightarrow a = 0.3.$

(ii) $E(X) = [1 \times 0.2] + [2 \times 0.3]$
$+ [3 \times 0.4] + [4 \times 0.1]$
$= 2.4$

$E(X^2) = [1 \times 0.2] + [4 \times 0.3]$
$+ [9 \times 0.4] + [16 \times 0.1]$
$= 6.6$

$\text{Var}(X) = 6.6 - 2.4^2 = 0.84$

b) **(i)** The probabilities must add up to 1:
$a + 0.3 + a + 0.1 = 1 \Rightarrow a = 0.3.$

(ii) $E(X) = [-3 \times 0.3] + [-2 \times 0.3]$
$+ [-1 \times 0.3] + [0 \times 0.1]$
$= -1.8$

$E(X^2) = [9 \times 0.3] + [4 \times 0.3]$
$+ [1 \times 0.3] + [0 \times 0.1]$
$= 4.2$

$\text{Var}(X) = 4.2 - (-1.8)^2 = 0.96$

Q4 **a)** $E(X) = [3 \times 0.2] + [4 \times 0.3] + [6 \times 0.1] + 0.4p$
$= 2.4 + 0.4p$
$5.2 = 2.4 + 0.4p \Rightarrow p = 7.$

$E(X^2) = [9 \times 0.2] + [16 \times 0.3] + [36 \times 0.1]$
$+ [49 \times 0.4]$
$= 29.8$

So $\text{Var}(X) = 29.8 - 5.2^2 = 2.76$

b) The probabilities add up to 1:
$0.2 + a + 0.4 + 0.3 = 1 \Rightarrow a = 0.1$

$E(X) = [1 \times 0.2] + [4 \times 0.1] + 0.4p + [9 \times 0.3]$
$= 3.3 + 0.4p$
$5.7 = 3.3 + 0.4p \Rightarrow p = 6$

$E(X^2) = [1 \times 0.2] + [16 \times 0.1]$
$+ [36 \times 0.4] + [81 \times 0.3]$
$= 40.5$

$\text{Var}(X) = 40.5 - 5.7^2 = 8.01$

Q5 **a)** **(i)** All the probabilities add up to 1:
$9k + 16k + 25k = 1$

$50k = 1 \Rightarrow k = \frac{1}{50}$

(ii) $E(X) = \left[3 \times \frac{1}{50} \times 3^2\right] + \left[4 \times \frac{1}{50} \times 4^2\right]$

$+ \left[5 \times \frac{1}{50} \times 5^2\right]$

$= 4.32$

(iii) $E(X^2) = \left[9 \times \frac{1}{50}3^2\right] + \left[16 \times \frac{1}{50}4^2\right]$

$+ \left[25 \times \frac{1}{50}5^2\right]$

$= 19.24$

So $\text{Var}(X) = 19.24 - 4.32^2 = 0.5776$

b) **(i)** All the probabilities add up to 1:
$\frac{k}{3} + \frac{k}{4} + \frac{k}{5} + \frac{k}{6} = 1$

$\Rightarrow k\left(\frac{1}{3} + \frac{1}{4} + \frac{1}{5} + \frac{1}{6}\right) = 1$

$\Rightarrow \frac{19}{20}k = 1$

$\Rightarrow k = \frac{20}{19}$

(ii) $E(X) = \left[3 \times \frac{\left(\frac{20}{19}\right)}{3}\right] + \left[4 \times \frac{\left(\frac{20}{19}\right)}{4}\right]$

$+ \left[5 \times \frac{\left(\frac{20}{19}\right)}{5}\right] + \left[6 \times \frac{\left(\frac{20}{19}\right)}{6}\right]$

$= \frac{80}{19} = 4.21 \text{ to 3 s.f.}$

Notice that the numbers cancel in each bracket so you're just left to add together four lots of $\frac{20}{19}$.

(iii) $E(X^2) = \left[9 \times \dfrac{\left(\frac{20}{19}\right)}{3}\right] + \left[16 \times \dfrac{\left(\frac{20}{19}\right)}{4}\right]$

$+ \left[25 \times \dfrac{\left(\frac{20}{19}\right)}{5}\right] + \left[36 \times \dfrac{\left(\frac{20}{19}\right)}{6}\right]$

$= \left[\dfrac{20}{19} \times 3\right] + \left[\dfrac{20}{19} \times 4\right]$

$+ \left[\dfrac{20}{19} \times 5\right] + \left[\dfrac{20}{19} \times 6\right]$

$= \dfrac{360}{19}$ (= 18.9 to 3 s.f.)

So $\text{Var}(X) = \dfrac{360}{19} - \left(\dfrac{80}{19}\right)^2 = \dfrac{440}{361}$

(= 1.22 to 3 s.f.)

Exercise 2.3 — Expected value and variance of a function of X

Q1 a) $E(Y) = E(X + 3) = E(X) + 3 = 4 + 3 = 7$
$\text{Var}(Y) = \text{Var}(X + 3) = \text{Var}(X) = 3$

b) $E(Z) = E(5X) = 5E(X) = 5 \times 4 = 20$
$\text{Var}(Z) = \text{Var}(5X) = 25\text{Var}(X) = 25 \times 3 = 75$

c) $E(W) = E(2X - 7) = 2E(X) - 7 = (2 \times 4) - 7 = 1$
$\text{Var}(W) = \text{Var}(2X - 7) = 4\text{Var}(X) = 4 \times 3 = 12$

d) $E(V) = E(7 - 2X) = 7 - 2E(X) = 7 - (2 \times 4) = -1$
$\text{Var}(V) = \text{Var}(7 - 2X) = (-2)^2\text{Var}(X) = 4 \times 3 = 12$

Q2 a) (i) $Y = 3X + 4$

y	7	10	13	16	19
P($Y = y$)	0.1	0.2	0.3	0.2	0.2

(ii) $E(Y) = [7 \times 0.1] + [10 \times 0.2]$
$+ [13 \times 0.3] + [16 \times 0.2] + [19 \times 0.2] = 13.6$

$E(Y^2) = [49 \times 0.1] + [100 \times 0.2]$
$+ [169 \times 0.3] + [256 \times 0.2] + [361 \times 0.2]$
$= 199$

$\text{Var}(Y) = 199 - 13.6^2 = 14.04$

(iii) $E(Y) = E(3X + 4) = 3E(X) + 4 = (3 \times 3.2) + 4$
$= 13.6$
$\text{Var}(Y) = \text{Var}(3X + 4) = 9\text{Var}(X) = 9 \times 1.56$
$= 14.04$

Notice that you get the same values for the mean and variance in parts (ii) and (iii).

b) (i) $Z = 3X - 4$

z	−1	2	5	8	11
P($Z = z$)	0.1	0.2	0.3	0.2	0.2

(ii) $E(Z) = [-1 \times 0.1] + [2 \times 0.2]$
$+ [5 \times 0.3] + [8 \times 0.2] + [11 \times 0.2] = 5.6$

$E(Z^2) = [1 \times 0.1] + [4 \times 0.2]$
$+ [25 \times 0.3] + [64 \times 0.2] + [121 \times 0.2]$
$= 45.4$

$\text{Var}(Z) = 45.4 - 5.6^2 = 14.04$

(iii) $E(Z) = E(3X - 4) = 3E(X) - 4 = (3 \times 3.2) - 4$
$= 5.6$
$\text{Var}(Z) = \text{Var}(3X - 4) = 9\text{Var}(X) = 9 \times 1.56$
$= 14.04$

c) (i) $V = 20 - 3X$

v	17	14	11	8	5
P($V = v$)	0.1	0.2	0.3	0.2	0.2

(ii) $E(V) = [17 \times 0.1] + [14 \times 0.2]$
$+ [11 \times 0.3] + [8 \times 0.2] + [5 \times 0.2] = 10.4$

$E(V^2) = [289 \times 0.1] + [196 \times 0.2]$
$+ [121 \times 0.3] + [64 \times 0.2] + [25 \times 0.2]$
$= 122.2$

$\text{Var}(V) = 122.2 - 10.4^2 = 14.04$

(iii) $E(V) = E(20 - 3X) = 20 - 3E(X) = 20 - (3 \times 3.2)$
$= 10.4$
$\text{Var}(V) = \text{Var}(20 - 3X) = 9\text{Var}(X) = 9 \times 1.56$
$= 14.04$

d) (i) $W = 20 + 3X$

w	23	26	29	32	35
P($W = w$)	0.1	0.2	0.3	0.2	0.2

(ii) $E(W) = [23 \times 0.1] + [26 \times 0.2]$
$+ [29 \times 0.3] + [32 \times 0.2] + [35 \times 0.2] = 29.6$

$E(W^2) = [529 \times 0.1] + [676 \times 0.2]$
$+ [841 \times 0.3] + [1024 \times 0.2]$
$+ [1225 \times 0.2]$
$= 890.2$

$\text{Var}(W) = 890.2 - 29.6^2 = 14.04$

(iii) $E(W) = E(20 + 3X) = 20 + 3E(X)$
$= 20 + (3 \times 3.2) = 29.6$
$\text{Var}(W) = \text{Var}(20 + 3X) = 9\text{Var}(X) = 9 \times 1.56$
$= 14.04$

Q3 a) (i) $E(X) = [8 \times 0.2] + [10 \times 0.3]$
$+ [15 \times 0.1] + [20 \times 0.4]$
$= 14.1$

$E(X^2) = [64 \times 0.2] + [100 \times 0.3]$
$+ [225 \times 0.1] + [400 \times 0.4]$
$= 225.3$

$\text{Var}(X) = 225.3 - 14.1^2 = 26.49$

(ii) $E(Y) = E(4X + 3) = 4E(X) + 3$
$= (4 \times 14.1) + 3 = 59.4$
$\text{Var}(Y) = \text{Var}(4X + 3) = 16\text{Var}(X) = 16 \times 26.49$
$= 423.84$

(iii) $E(Z) = E(50 - 2X) = 50 - 2E(X)$
$= 50 - (2 \times 14.1) = 21.8$
$\text{Var}(Z) = \text{Var}(50 - 2X) = (-2)^2\text{Var}(X)$
$= 4 \times 26.49 = 105.96$

b) (i) $E(X) = \left[-4 \times \frac{1}{2}\right] + \left[-1 \times \frac{1}{4}\right] + \left[0 \times \frac{1}{8}\right]$
$+ \left[2 \times \frac{1}{16}\right] + \left[5 \times \frac{1}{32}\right] + \left[6 \times \frac{1}{32}\right]$

$= -\dfrac{57}{32} = -1.78$ to 3 s.f.

$E(X^2) = \left[16 \times \frac{1}{2}\right] + \left[1 \times \frac{1}{4}\right] + \left[0 \times \frac{1}{8}\right]$
$+ \left[4 \times \frac{1}{16}\right] + \left[25 \times \frac{1}{32}\right] + \left[36 \times \frac{1}{32}\right]$

$= \dfrac{333}{32} = 10.4$ to 3 s.f.

$\text{Var}(X) = \dfrac{333}{32} - \left(-\dfrac{57}{32}\right)^2 = \dfrac{7407}{1024}$

$= 7.23$ to 3 s.f.

(ii) $E(Y) = E(7 - 2X) = 7 - 2E(X) = 7 - (2 \times (-1.78))$
$= 10.56$

$Var(Y) = Var(7 - 2X) = (-2)^2 Var(X) = 4 \times 7.23$
$= 28.9$ to 3 s.f.

(iii) $E(Z) = E(7 + 2X) = 7 + 2E(X)$
$= 7 + (2 \times (-1.78))$
$= 3.44$ to 3 s.f.

$Var(Z) = Var(7 + 2X) = (+2)^2 Var(X) = 4 \times 7.23$
$= 28.9$ to 3 s.f.

Q4 a) $E(X) = [10 \times 0.2] + [12 \times 0.3] + [13 \times 0.1]$
$+ [15 \times 0.3] + [16 \times 0.1] = 13$
$E(X^2) = [100 \times 0.2] + [144 \times 0.3] + [169 \times 0.1]$
$+ [225 \times 0.3] + [256 \times 0.1] = 173.2$
$Var(X) = 173.2 - 13^2 = 4.2$

b) $E(Y) = E(26 - mX) = 26 - mE(X) = 26 - 13m$
So $0 = 26 - 13m \Rightarrow m = 2$.
$Var(Y) = Var(26 - mX) = (-m)^2 Var(X) = 4 \times 4.2$
$= 16.8$

c) $E(Z) = E(3X - c) = 3E(X) - c = (3 \times 13) - c = 39 - c$
So $30 = 39 - c \Rightarrow c = 9$
$Var(Z) = Var(3X - c) = 9Var(X) = 9 \times 4.2 = 37.8$

Exercise 2.4 — The discrete uniform distribution

Q1

x	1	2	3	4	5
$P(X = x)$	$\frac{1}{5}$	$\frac{1}{5}$	$\frac{1}{5}$	$\frac{1}{5}$	$\frac{1}{5}$

$E(X) = \dfrac{a + b}{2} = \dfrac{1 + 5}{2} = 3$

$Var(X) = \dfrac{(b - a + 1)^2 - 1}{12} = \dfrac{(5 - 1 + 1)^2 - 1}{12} = \dfrac{24}{12}$
$= 2$

Q2

y	12	13	14	15
$P(Y = y)$	$\frac{1}{4}$	$\frac{1}{4}$	$\frac{1}{4}$	$\frac{1}{4}$

$E(Y) = \dfrac{a + b}{2} = \dfrac{12 + 15}{2} = 13.5$

$Var(Y) = \dfrac{(b - a + 1)^2 - 1}{12} = \dfrac{(15 - 12 + 1)^2 - 1}{12} = \dfrac{15}{12}$
$= 1.25$

Q3

z	11	12	13	14	15	16	17	18	19	20
$P(Z = z)$	$\frac{1}{10}$	$\frac{1}{10}$	$\frac{1}{10}$	$\frac{1}{10}$	$\frac{1}{10}$	$\frac{1}{10}$	$\frac{1}{10}$	$\frac{1}{10}$	$\frac{1}{10}$	$\frac{1}{10}$

$E(Z) = \dfrac{a + b}{2} = \dfrac{11 + 20}{2} = 15.5$

$Var(Z) = \dfrac{(b - a + 1)^2 - 1}{12} = \dfrac{(20 - 11 + 1)^2 - 1}{12} = \dfrac{99}{12}$
$= 8.25$

So the standard deviation is the square root of the variance, i.e. $\sqrt{8.25} = 2.87$ to 3 s.f.

Q4 a) $E(D) = \left[1 \times \frac{1}{6}\right] + \left[3 \times \frac{1}{6}\right] + \left[5 \times \frac{1}{6}\right]$
$+ \left[7 \times \frac{1}{6}\right] + \left[9 \times \frac{1}{6}\right] + \left[11 \times \frac{1}{6}\right]$
$= 6$

b) $E(D^2) = \left[1 \times \frac{1}{6}\right] + \left[9 \times \frac{1}{6}\right] + \left[25 \times \frac{1}{6}\right]$
$+ \left[49 \times \frac{1}{6}\right] + \left[81 \times \frac{1}{6}\right] + \left[121 \times \frac{1}{6}\right]$
$= \dfrac{143}{3} = 47.7$ to 3 s.f.

$Var(D) = 47.7 - 6^2 = 11.7$ to 3 s.f.

Q5 a) $\mu = E(X) = \dfrac{a + b}{2} = \dfrac{1 + 8}{2} = 4.5$

$\sigma^2 = Var(X) = \dfrac{(b - a + 1)^2 - 1}{12}$

$= \dfrac{(8 - 1 + 1)^2 - 1}{12} = \dfrac{63}{12} = 5.25$

b) Substitute your values for the mean and variance into the inequality and rearrange — then it's just a simple probability question.

$P(|X - \mu| < \sigma) = P(|X - 4.5| < \sqrt{5.25})$
$= P(|X - 4.5| < 2.291)$

If the modulus of $X - 4.5$ is less than 2.291 this means that the size (i.e. ignoring any minus signs) of $X - 4.5$ is less than 2.291. For example, when $X = 3$, $X - 4.5 = -1.5$. The modulus of this is 1.5, which is less than 2.291.

$|X - 4.5| < 2.291$ is satisfied by $X = 3$, 4, 5 and 6.
So $P(|X - \mu| < \sigma) = P(X = 3, 4, 5, 6)$
$= \frac{1}{8} + \frac{1}{8} + \frac{1}{8} + \frac{1}{8} = \frac{1}{2}$

Q6 a) Any single digit number means that Y could take any value between 0 and 9 inclusive.

$\mu = E(Y) = \dfrac{a + b}{2} = \dfrac{0 + 9}{2} = 4.5$

$\sigma^2 = Var(Y) = \dfrac{(b - a + 1)^2 - 1}{12}$

$= \dfrac{(9 - 0 + 1)^2 - 1}{12} = \dfrac{99}{12} = 8.25$

b) $P(|Y - \mu| > \sigma) = P(|Y - 4.5| > \sqrt{8.25})$
$= P(|Y - 4.5| > 2.87)$

$|Y - 4.5| > 2.87$ is satisfied by $Y = 0$, 1, 8 and 9, so $P(|Y - \mu| > \sigma) = P(Y = 0, 1, 8, 9)$
$= \frac{1}{10} + \frac{1}{10} + \frac{1}{10} + \frac{1}{10} = \frac{4}{10} = 0.4$

c) $P(|Y - \mu| > 2\sigma) = P(|Y - 4.5| > 2\sqrt{8.25})$
$= P(|Y - 4.5| > 5.74)$

There are no values that Y can take such that $|Y - 4.5| > 5.74$, so $P(|Y - \mu| > 2\sigma) = 0$.

Q7 a) $E(Z) = \dfrac{a + b}{2} = \dfrac{1 + 7}{2} = 4$

$Var(Z) = \dfrac{(b - a + 1)^2 - 1}{12}$

$= \dfrac{(7 - 1 + 1)^2 - 1}{12} = \dfrac{48}{12} = 4$

b) $E(X) = E(2 - 2Z) = 2 - 2E(Z) = 2 - (2 \times 4) = -6$

$Var(X) = Var(2 - 2Z) = (-2)^2 Var(Z) = 4 \times 4 = 16$

Review Exercise — Chapter 3

Q1 a) All the probabilities have to add up to 1.
So $0.5 + k + k + 3k = 0.5 + 5k = 1$, i.e. $5k = 0.5$,
i.e. $k = 0.1$.

b) $P(Y < 2) = P(Y = 0) + P(Y = 1) = 0.5 + 0.1 = 0.6$.

Q2 $P(W \leq 0.2) = P(W = 0.2) = 0.2$
$P(W \leq 0.3) = P(W = 0.2) + P(W = 0.3) = 0.4$
$P(W \leq 0.4) = P(W = 0.2) + P(W = 0.3)$
$\qquad\qquad + P(W = 0.4) = 0.7$
$P(W \leq 0.5) = P(W = 0.2) + P(W = 0.3)$
$\qquad\qquad + P(W = 0.4) + P(W = 0.5) = 1$

So the cumulative distribution function of W is

w	0.2	0.3	0.4	0.5
$P(W \leq w)$	0.2	0.4	0.7	1

Q3 a) $P(X \leq 1) = P(X = 1) = \frac{3}{25}$
$P(X \leq 2) = P(X = 2) + P(X = 1) = \frac{4}{25} + \frac{3}{25} = \frac{7}{25}$
$P(X \leq 3) = P(X = 3) + P(X = 2) + P(X = 1)$
$\qquad = \frac{5}{25} + \frac{4}{25} + \frac{3}{25} = \frac{12}{25}$
$P(X \leq 4) = P(X = 4) + P(X = 3)$
$\qquad\qquad + P(X = 2) + P(X = 1)$
$\qquad = \frac{6}{25} + \frac{5}{25} + \frac{4}{25} + \frac{3}{25} = \frac{18}{25}$
$P(X \leq 5) = P(X = 5) + P(X = 4) + P(X = 3)$
$\qquad\qquad + P(X = 2) + P(X = 1)$
$\qquad = \frac{7}{25} + \frac{6}{25} + \frac{5}{25} + \frac{4}{25} + \frac{3}{25} = \frac{25}{25} = 1$

So the cumulative distribution function is:

x	1	2	3	4	5
$F(x)$	$\frac{3}{25}$	$\frac{7}{25}$	$\frac{12}{25}$	$\frac{18}{25}$	1

(i) $P(X \leq 3) = F(3) = \frac{12}{25}$
(ii) $P(1 < X \leq 3) = P(X \leq 3) - P(X \leq 1) = F(3) - F(1)$
$\qquad\qquad = \frac{12}{25} - \frac{3}{25} = \frac{9}{25}$

b) $P(X \leq 1) = P(X = 1) = \frac{1}{8}$
$P(X \leq 2) = P(X = 2) + P(X = 1) = \frac{1}{8} + \frac{1}{8} = \frac{2}{8}$
In general, $P(X \leq x) = \frac{x}{8}$.
So the cumulative distribution function is:

x	1	2	3	4	5	6	7	8
$F(x)$	$\frac{1}{8}$	$\frac{1}{4}$	$\frac{3}{8}$	$\frac{1}{2}$	$\frac{5}{8}$	$\frac{3}{4}$	$\frac{7}{8}$	1

(i) $P(X \leq 3) = F(3) = \frac{3}{8}$
(ii) $P(3 < X \leq 7) = P(X \leq 7) - P(X \leq 3) = F(7) - F(3)$
$\qquad\qquad = \frac{7}{8} - \frac{3}{8} = \frac{4}{8} = \frac{1}{2}$

Q4 $P(R = 0) = P(R \leq 0) = 0.1$
$P(R = 1) = P(R \leq 1) - P(R \leq 0) = 0.5 - 0.1 = 0.4$
$P(R = 2) = P(R \leq 2) - P(R \leq 1) = 1 - 0.5 = 0.5$
So the probability distribution of R is:

r	0	1	2
$P(R = r)$	0.1	0.4	0.5

$P(0 \leq R \leq 1) = 0.5$

Q5 There are 5 possible outcomes, and the probability of each of them is k, so $k = 1 \div 5 = 0.2$.
Mean of $X = \frac{0 + 4}{2} = 2$.
Variance of $X = \frac{(4 - 0 + 1)^2 - 1}{12} = \frac{24}{12} = 2$

Q6 a) As always, the probabilities have to add up to 1:
$k = 1 - \left(\frac{1}{6} + \frac{1}{2} + \frac{5}{24}\right) = 1 - \frac{21}{24} = \frac{3}{24} = \frac{1}{8}$

b) $E(X) = \left(1 \times \frac{1}{6}\right) + \left(2 \times \frac{1}{2}\right)$
$\qquad + \left(3 \times \frac{1}{8}\right) + \left(4 \times \frac{5}{24}\right)$
$\qquad = \frac{4 + 24 + 9 + 20}{24} = \frac{57}{24} = \frac{19}{8}$

$E(X^2) = \left(1^2 \times \frac{1}{6}\right) + \left(2^2 \times \frac{1}{2}\right)$
$\qquad + \left(3^2 \times \frac{1}{8}\right) + \left(4^2 \times \frac{5}{24}\right)$
$\qquad = \frac{4 + 48 + 27 + 80}{24} = \frac{159}{24} = \frac{53}{8}$
$Var(X) = E(X^2) - [E(X)]^2 = \frac{53}{8} - \left(\frac{19}{8}\right)^2$
$\qquad = \frac{424 - 361}{64} = \frac{63}{64}$

c) $E(2X - 1) = 2E(X) - 1$
$\qquad\qquad = 2 \times \frac{19}{8} - 1 = \frac{30}{8} = \frac{15}{4}$
$Var(2X - 1) = 2^2 Var(X) = 4 \times \frac{63}{64} = \frac{63}{16}$

Q7 a) $E(X) = (1 \times 0.1) + (2 \times 0.2) + (3 \times 0.25)$
$\qquad + (4 \times 0.2) + (5 \times 0.1) + (6 \times 0.15) = 3.45$

b) $Var(X) = E(X^2) - (E(X))^2$
$E(X^2) = (1 \times 0.1) + (4 \times 0.2) + (9 \times 0.25)$
$\qquad + (16 \times 0.2) + (25 \times 0.1) + (36 \times 0.15) = 14.25$
So $Var(X) = 14.25 - 3.45^2 = 2.3475$

Q8 To find the cumulative distribution function, you need to find $P(X \leq x)$. This is the probability that the highest score rolled is no more than x. So all 3 dice must roll a score no more than x. The individual probability of one dice rolling a score of no more than x is $\frac{x}{6}$ — so the probability that all 3 dice roll a score no more than x is $\left(\frac{x}{6}\right)^3 = \frac{x^3}{216}$ (since the probabilities of the individual dice rolls are independent).

So $F(x) = P(X \leq x) = \frac{x^3}{216}$ $x = 1, 2, 3, 4, 5, 6$

Now to find the probability distribution, you need to work out $P(X = x)$ for each x.

$P(X = 1) = P(X \leq 1) = \frac{1^3}{216} = \frac{1}{216}$

$P(X = 2) = P(X \leq 2) - P(X \leq 1) = \frac{2^3}{216} - \frac{1^3}{216} = \frac{7}{216}$

$P(X = 3) = P(X \leq 3) - P(X \leq 2) = \frac{3^3}{216} - \frac{2^3}{216} = \frac{19}{216}$

$P(X = 4) = P(X \leq 4) - P(X \leq 3) = \frac{4^3}{216} - \frac{3^3}{216} = \frac{37}{216}$

$P(X = 5) = P(X \leq 5) - P(X \leq 4) = \frac{5^3}{216} - \frac{4^3}{216} = \frac{61}{216}$

$P(X = 6) = P(X \leq 6) - P(X \leq 5) = \frac{6^3}{216} - \frac{5^3}{216} = \frac{91}{216}$

So the probability distribution is:

x	1	2	3	4	5	6
$P(X = x)$	$\frac{1}{216}$	$\frac{7}{216}$	$\frac{19}{216}$	$\frac{37}{216}$	$\frac{61}{216}$	$\frac{91}{216}$

Exam-Style Questions — Chapter 3

1 a) The probability of getting 3 heads is:

$\frac{1}{2} \times \frac{1}{2} \times \frac{1}{2} = \frac{1}{8}$ *[1 mark]*

The probability of getting 2 heads is:

$3 \times \frac{1}{2} \times \frac{1}{2} \times \frac{1}{2} = \frac{3}{8}$ (multiply by 3 because any of the three coins could be the tail — the order in which the heads and the tail occur isn't important). *[1 mark]*

Similarly the probability of getting 1 head is:

$3 \times \frac{1}{2} \times \frac{1}{2} \times \frac{1}{2} = \frac{3}{8}$

And the probability of getting no heads is:

$\frac{1}{2} \times \frac{1}{2} \times \frac{1}{2} = \frac{1}{8}$

So the probability of 1 or no heads

$= \frac{3}{8} + \frac{1}{8} = \frac{1}{2}$ *[1 mark]*

Hence the probability distribution of X is:

x	20p	10p	nothing
$P(X = x)$	$\frac{1}{8}$	$\frac{3}{8}$	$\frac{1}{2}$

[1 mark]

b) You need the probability that $X > 10$p *[1 mark]*

This is just $P(X = 20\text{p}) = \frac{1}{8}$ *[1 mark]*

2 a) All the probabilities must add up to 1, so

$2k + 3k + k + k = 1$, i.e. $7k = 1$, and so $k = \frac{1}{7}$.
[1 mark]

b) $P(X \leq 0) = P(X = 0) = \frac{2}{7}$ *[1 mark]*

$P(X \leq 1) = P(X = 0) + P(X = 1) = \frac{5}{7}$ *[1 mark]*

$P(X \leq 2) = P(X = 0) + P(X = 1)$
$\qquad\qquad + P(X = 2) = \frac{6}{7}$ *[1 mark]*

$P(X \leq 3) = P(X = 0) + P(X = 1)$
$\qquad\qquad + P(X = 2) + P(X = 3) = 1$
[1 mark]

So the cumulative distribution function is as in the following table:

x	0	1	2	3
$P(X \leqslant x)$	$\frac{2}{7}$	$\frac{5}{7}$	$\frac{6}{7}$	1

c) $P(X > 2) = 1 - P(X \leq 2)$

$\qquad = 1 - \frac{6}{7} = \frac{1}{7}$ *[1 mark]*

(Or $P(X > 2) = P(X = 3) = \frac{1}{7}$, using part a).)

3 a)

x	0	1	2	3	4	5	6	7	8	9
$p(x)$	$\frac{1}{10}$	$\frac{1}{10}$	$\frac{1}{10}$	$\frac{1}{10}$	$\frac{1}{10}$	$\frac{1}{10}$	$\frac{1}{10}$	$\frac{1}{10}$	$\frac{1}{10}$	$\frac{1}{10}$

[1 mark]

b) Mean $= \frac{0 + 9}{2} = 4.5$ *[1 mark]*

Variance $= \frac{(9 - 0 + 1)^2 - 1}{12}$ *[1 mark]* $= \frac{99}{12}$

$= 8.25$ *[1 mark]*

c) $P(X < 4.5) = P(X = 0) + P(X = 1)$
$+ P(X = 2) + P(X = 3) + P(X = 4)$ *[1 mark]*

$= 0.5$ *[1 mark]*

4 a) $P(X = 1) = a$, $P(X = 2) = 2a$, $P(X = 3) = 3a$.
Therefore the total probability is $3a + 2a + a = 6a$.
This must equal 1, so $a = \frac{1}{6}$. *[1 mark]*

b) $E(X) = \left(1 \times \frac{1}{6}\right) + \left(2 \times \frac{2}{6}\right) + \left(3 \times \frac{3}{6}\right)$

$\qquad = \frac{1 + 4 + 9}{6}$ *[1 mark]*

$\qquad = \frac{7}{3}$ *[1 mark]*

c) $E(X^2) = Var(X) + [E(X)]^2$

$\qquad = \frac{5}{9} + \left(\frac{7}{3}\right)^2 = \frac{5 + 49}{9}$ *[1 mark]*

$\qquad = \frac{54}{9} = 6$ *[1 mark]*

d) $E(3X + 4) = 3E(X) + 4 = 3 \times \frac{7}{3} + 4 = 11$
[1 mark]

$Var(3X + 4) = 3^2 Var(X) = 9 \times \frac{5}{9}$ *[1 mark]*
$= 5$ *[1 mark]*

5 **a)** $E(X) = (0 \times 0.4) + (1 \times 0.3)$
$+ (2 \times 0.2) + (3 \times 0.1)$
$= 0 + 0.3 + 0.4 + 0.3$ *[1 mark]*
$= 1$ *[1 mark]*

b) $E(6X + 8) = 6E(X) + 8 = 6 + 8$ *[1 mark]*
$= 14$ *[1 mark]*

c) The formula for variance is
$Var(X) = E(X^2) - [E(X)]^2$
So first work out $E(X^2)$:
$E(X^2) = (0^2 \times 0.4) + (1^2 \times 0.3)$
$+ (2^2 \times 0.2) + (3^2 \times 0.1)$
$= 0.3 + 0.8 + 0.9$ *[1 mark]*
$= 2$ *[1 mark]*

Then complete the formula by using your answer to part a):
$Var(X) = E(X^2) - [E(X)]^2 = 2 - (1^2)$ *[1 mark]*
$= 1$ *[1 mark]*

d) $Var(aX + b) = a^2 Var(X)$
$Var(5 - 3X)$
$= (-3)^2 Var(X) = 9Var(X)$ *[1 mark]*
$= 9 \times 1$
$= 9$ *[1 mark]*

6 **a)** $E(X) = [0 \times a] + [1 \times 5b] + [2 \times b] + [3 \times 0.2]$
$= 7b + 0.6$ *[1 mark]*
So $1.3 = 7b + 0.6$ *[1 mark]* $\Rightarrow b = 0.1$ *[1 mark]*
All the probabilities must add up to 1 so:
$a + 0.5 + 0.1 + 0.2 = 1$ *[1 mark]*
$\Rightarrow a = 0.2$ *[1 mark]*

b) $E(\frac{10}{13}X + 3) = \frac{10}{13}E(X) + 3$ *[1 mark]*
$= (\frac{10}{13} \times 1.3) + 3 = 4$ *[1 mark]*

c) $E(X^2) = [0^2 \times 0.2] + [1^2 \times 0.5] + [2^2 \times 0.1]$
$+ [3^2 \times 0.2] = 2.7$ *[1 mark]*
$Var(X) = E(X^2) - (E(X))^2$ *[1 mark]*
$= 2.7 - 1.3^2 = 1.01$ *[1 mark]*

d) $Var(4 - X) = (-1)^2 Var(X)$ *[1 mark]*
$= 1.01$ *[1 mark]*

Chapter 4: Correlation and Regression

1. Correlation
Exercise 1.1 — Scatter diagrams and correlation

Q1 **a)**

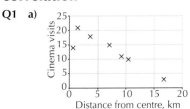

Cinema visits / Distance from centre, km

b) Negative correlation

Q2 **a)**

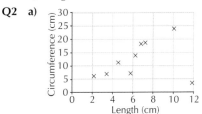

Circumference (cm) / Length (cm)

b) Positive correlation

c) The circumference of 3.5 cm <u>or</u> the length of 11.9 cm.

Exercise 1.2 — S_{xx}, S_{yy} and S_{xy}

Q1 **a)** Add rows to the table for x^2, y^2 and xy. And include a column showing the total of each row.

x	11	6	9	4	8	2	5	45
y	24	13	18	5	19	1	12	92
x^2	121	36	81	16	64	4	25	347
y^2	576	169	324	25	361	1	144	1600
xy	264	78	162	20	152	2	60	738

So $\sum x = 45$, $\sum y = 92$, $\sum x^2 = 347$, $\sum y^2 = 1600$ and $\sum xy = 738$.

b) $S_{xy} = \sum xy - \frac{\sum x \sum y}{n} = 738 - \frac{45 \times 92}{7}$
$= 146.57$ (to 2 d.p.)

$S_{xx} = \sum x^2 - \frac{(\sum x)^2}{n} = 347 - \frac{45^2}{7}$
$= 57.71$ (to 2 d.p.)

$S_{yy} = \sum y^2 - \frac{(\sum y)^2}{n} = 1600 - \frac{92^2}{7}$
$= 390.86$ (to 2 d.p.)

Q2 **a)** $S_{xy} = \sum xy - \frac{\sum x \sum y}{n} = 589 - \frac{29 \times 109}{5}$
$= -43.2$

$S_{xx} = \sum x^2 - \frac{(\sum x)^2}{n} = 167 - \frac{29^2}{5} = -1.2$

$S_{yy} = \sum y^2 - \frac{(\sum y)^2}{n} = 2031 - \frac{109^2}{5} = -345.2$

b) $S_{xy} = \sum xy - \dfrac{\sum x \sum y}{n} = 1013 - \dfrac{206 \times 50}{10} = -17$

$S_{xx} = \sum x^2 - \dfrac{(\sum x)^2}{n} = 4504 - \dfrac{206^2}{10} = 260.4$

$S_{yy} = \sum y^2 - \dfrac{(\sum y)^2}{n} = 326 - \dfrac{50^2}{10} = 76$

Q3 $S_{pq} = \sum pq - \dfrac{\sum p \sum q}{n} = 1880 - \dfrac{115 \times 114}{6} = -305$

$S_{pp} = \sum p^2 - \dfrac{(\sum p)^2}{n} = 2383 - \dfrac{115^2}{6}$

$= 178.83$ (to 2 d.p.)

$S_{qq} = \sum q^2 - \dfrac{(\sum q)^2}{n} = 2762 - \dfrac{114^2}{6} = 596$

Exercise 1.3 — Product moment correlation coefficient

Q1 $S_{xy} = \sum xy - \dfrac{\sum x \sum y}{n} = 1515 - \dfrac{313 \times 75}{15} = -50$

$S_{xx} = \sum x^2 - \dfrac{(\sum x)^2}{n} = 6875 - \dfrac{313^2}{15}$

$= 343.7333...$

$S_{yy} = \sum y^2 - \dfrac{(\sum y)^2}{n} = 473 - \dfrac{75^2}{15} = 98$

This means:

$r = \dfrac{S_{xy}}{\sqrt{S_{xx}S_{yy}}}$

$= \dfrac{-50}{\sqrt{343.7333... \times 98}} = -0.272$ (to 3 sig.fig.)

Q2 a) Make a table including x^2, y^2 and xy. Include a final column showing the total of each row.

x	180	171	182	184	166	180	173	167	1403
y	70	67	66	59	61	75	65	56	519
x^2	32400	29241	33124	33856	27556	32400	29929	27889	246395
y^2	4900	4489	4356	3481	3721	5625	4225	3136	33933
xy	12600	11457	12012	10856	10126	13500	11245	9352	91148

$S_{xy} = \sum xy - \dfrac{\sum x \sum y}{n} = 91148 - \dfrac{1403 \times 519}{8}$

$= 128.375$

$S_{xx} = \sum x^2 - \dfrac{(\sum x)^2}{n} = 246\,395 - \dfrac{1403^2}{8}$

$= 343.875$

$S_{yy} = \sum y^2 - \dfrac{(\sum y)^2}{n} = 33\,933 - \dfrac{519^2}{8} = 262.875$

b) This means:

$r = \dfrac{S_{xy}}{\sqrt{S_{xx}S_{yy}}}$

$= \dfrac{128.375}{\sqrt{343.875 \times 262.875}} = 0.427$ (to 3 sig.fig.)

Q3 a) Make a table including p^2, q^2 and pq. Include a final column showing the total of each row.

p	13	9	15	10	8	11	12	14	92
q	5	7	2	4	3	8	1	2	32
p^2	169	81	225	100	64	121	144	196	1100
q^2	25	49	4	16	9	64	1	4	172
pq	65	63	30	40	24	88	12	28	350

So $\sum p = 92$, $\sum q = 32$, $\sum p^2 = 1100$, $\sum q^2 = 172$, $\sum pq = 350$

b) $S_{pq} = \sum pq - \dfrac{\sum p \sum q}{n} = 350 - \dfrac{92 \times 32}{8} = -18$

$S_{pp} = \sum p^2 - \dfrac{(\sum p)^2}{n} = 1100 - \dfrac{92^2}{8} = 42$

$S_{qq} = \sum q^2 - \dfrac{(\sum q)^2}{n} = 172 - \dfrac{32^2}{8} = 44$

c) This means:

$r = \dfrac{S_{pq}}{\sqrt{S_{pp}S_{qq}}}$

$= \dfrac{-18}{\sqrt{42 \times 44}} = -0.419$ (to 3 sig.fig.)

Q4 a) First find $\sum l = 43$ and $\sum w = 30.4$.

Then:

$S_{lw} = \sum lw - \dfrac{\sum l \sum w}{n} = 181.75 - \dfrac{43 \times 30.4}{8}$

$= 18.35$

$S_{ll} = \sum l^2 - \dfrac{(\sum l)^2}{n} = 258 - \dfrac{43^2}{8} = 26.875$

$S_{ww} = \sum w^2 - \dfrac{(\sum w)^2}{n} = 128.2 - \dfrac{30.4^2}{8} = 12.68$

b) This means:

$r = \dfrac{S_{lw}}{\sqrt{S_{ll}S_{ww}}}$

$= \dfrac{18.35}{\sqrt{26.875 \times 12.68}} = 0.994$ (to 3 sig.fig.)

c) This value for r is very close to 1, which shows that there is a very strong positive correlation between the length of a leaf (l) and its width (w). The longer a leaf is (i.e. the higher the value of l), the wider it tends to be (i.e. the higher the value of w).

Q5 Make a table including a^2, s^2 and as. Include a final column showing the total of each row.

a	57	65	94	88	71	62	79	82	52	650
s	8.9	4.8	5.4	2.8	7.1	7.5	3.1	6.2	8.4	54.2
a^2	3249	4225	8836	7744	5041	3844	6241	6724	2704	48608
s^2	79.21	23.04	29.16	7.84	50.41	56.25	9.61	38.44	70.56	364.52
as	507.3	312	507.6	246.4	504.1	465	244.9	508.4	436.8	3732.5

So $\sum a = 650$, $\sum s = 54.2$, $\sum a^2 = 48\,608$,

$\sum s^2 = 364.52$, $\sum as = 3732.5$

$$S_{as} = \sum as - \frac{\sum a \sum s}{n} = 3732.5 - \frac{650 \times 54.2}{9}$$

$$= -181.9444...$$

$$S_{aa} = \sum a^2 - \frac{(\sum a)^2}{n} = 48\,608 - \frac{650^2}{9}$$

$$= 1663.5555...$$

$$S_{ss} = \sum s^2 - \frac{(\sum s)^2}{n} = 364.52 - \frac{54.2^2}{9}$$

$$= 38.1155....$$

This means:

$$r = \frac{S_{as}}{\sqrt{S_{aa}S_{ss}}}$$

$$= \frac{-181.9444...}{\sqrt{1663.5555... \times 38.1155...}}$$

$$= -0.723 \text{ (to 3 sig.fig.)}$$

This is fairly close to –1, and so there is a fairly strong negative correlation between the age of a patient (a) and their score on the memory test (s). The older a patient is (i.e. the higher the value of a), the lower their score on the memory test tends to be (i.e. the lower the value of s).

Q6 a) Make a table including w^2, k^2 and wk. Include a final column showing the total of each row.

w	66	74	96	83	79	54	64	71	88	675
k	7.9	8.2	2.3	7.1	4.8	9.1	8.4	6.8	3.7	58.3
w^2	4356	5476	9216	6889	6241	2916	4096	5041	7744	51975
k^2	62.41	67.24	5.29	50.41	23.04	82.81	70.56	46.24	13.69	421.69
wk	521.4	606.8	220.8	589.3	379.2	491.4	537.6	482.8	325.6	4154.9

So $\sum w = 675$, $\sum k = 58.3$, $\sum w^2 = 51\,975$,

$\sum k^2 = 421.69$, $\sum wk = 4154.9$

$$S_{wk} = \sum wk - \frac{\sum w \sum k}{n} = 4154.9 - \frac{675 \times 58.3}{9}$$

$$= -217.6$$

$$S_{ww} = \sum w^2 - \frac{(\sum w)^2}{n} = 51975 - \frac{675^2}{9}$$

$$= 1350$$

$$S_{kk} = \sum k^2 - \frac{(\sum k)^2}{n} = 421.69 - \frac{58.3^2}{9}$$

$$= 44.0355...$$

This means:

$$r = \frac{S_{wk}}{\sqrt{S_{ww}S_{kk}}}$$

$$= \frac{-217.6}{\sqrt{1350 \times 44.0355...}} = -0.892 \text{ (to 3 sig.fig.)}$$

b) This is fairly close to –1, and so there is a strong negative correlation between a patient's weight (w) and their kidney function (k). The higher a patient's weight is (i.e. the higher the value of w), the lower their kidney function tends to be (i.e. the lower the value of k).

Exercise 1.4 — Coded data

Q1 Create a new table showing the coded data values u and v. Include extra rows for u^2, v^2 and uv.

u	3	7	2	9	1	5	27
v	4	1	8	7	3	6	29
u^2	9	49	4	81	1	25	169
v^2	16	1	64	49	9	36	175
uv	12	7	16	63	3	30	131

So $\sum u = 27$, $\sum v = 29$, $\sum u^2 = 169$,

$\sum v^2 = 175$, $\sum uv = 131$

Then:

$$S_{uv} = \sum uv - \frac{\sum u \sum v}{n} = 131 - \frac{27 \times 29}{6}$$

$$= 0.5$$

$$S_{uu} = \sum u^2 - \frac{(\sum u)^2}{n} = 169 - \frac{27^2}{6} = 47.5$$

$$S_{vv} = \sum v^2 - \frac{(\sum v)^2}{n} = 175 - \frac{29^2}{6}$$

$$= 34.8333...$$

This means:

$$r = \frac{S_{uv}}{\sqrt{S_{uu}S_{vv}}}$$

$$= \frac{0.5}{\sqrt{47.5 \times 34.8333...}} = 0.012 \text{ (to 3 d.p.)}$$

Because u and v are related by linear transformations to x and y, this means that the PMCC between x and y must also be 0.012 (to 3 d.p.)

Q2 Create a new table showing the coded data values u and v. Include extra rows for u^2, v^2 and uv.

u	4	6	5	3	2	9	11	8	48
v	7	21	9	13	19	15	20	16	120
u^2	16	36	25	9	4	81	121	64	356
v^2	49	441	81	169	361	225	400	256	1982
uv	28	126	45	39	38	135	220	128	759

So $\sum u = 48$, $\sum v = 120$, $\sum u^2 = 356$,

$\sum v^2 = 1982$, $\sum uv = 759$

Then:

$$S_{uv} = \sum uv - \frac{\sum u \sum v}{n} = 759 - \frac{48 \times 120}{8} = 39$$

$$S_{uu} = \sum u^2 - \frac{(\sum u)^2}{n} = 356 - \frac{48^2}{8} = 68$$

$$S_{vv} = \sum v^2 - \frac{(\sum v)^2}{n} = 1982 - \frac{120^2}{8} = 182$$

This means:

$$r = \frac{S_{uv}}{\sqrt{S_{uu}S_{vv}}}$$

$$= \frac{39}{\sqrt{68 \times 182}} = 0.351 \text{(to 3 sig.fig.)}$$

Because u and v are related by linear transformations to x and y, this means that the PMCC between x and y must also be 0.351 (to 3 sig.fig.)

Q3 Create a new table showing the coded data values u and v. Include extra rows for u^2, v^2 and uv.

u	0	1	2	3	4	5	6	7	8	36
v	32	25	21	17	7	12	8	4	2	128
u^2	0	1	4	9	16	25	36	49	64	204
v^2	1024	625	441	289	49	144	64	16	4	2656
uv	0	25	42	51	28	60	48	28	16	298

So $\sum u = 36$, $\sum v = 128$, $\sum u^2 = 204$, $\sum v^2 = 2656$, $\sum uv = 298$

Then:

$$S_{uv} = \sum uv - \frac{\sum u \sum v}{n} = 298 - \frac{36 \times 128}{9} = -214$$

$$S_{uu} = \sum u^2 - \frac{(\sum u)^2}{n} = 204 - \frac{36^2}{9} = 60$$

$$S_{vv} = \sum v^2 - \frac{(\sum v)^2}{n} = 2656 - \frac{128^2}{9}$$
$$= 835.5555...$$

This means:

$$r = \frac{S_{uv}}{\sqrt{S_{uu}S_{uu}}}$$

$$= \frac{-214}{\sqrt{60 \times 835.5555...}} = -0.956 \text{ (to 3 sig.fig.)}$$

Because u and v are related by linear transformations to s and t, this means that the PMCC between s and t must also be −0.956 (to 3 sig.fig.)

Q4 Create a new table showing the coded data values u and v. Include extra rows for u^2, v^2 and uv.

u	16	4	20	19	7	12	9	14	101
v	4	13	22	8	17	5	28	23	120
u^2	256	16	400	361	49	144	81	196	1503
v^2	16	169	484	64	289	25	784	529	2360
uv	64	52	440	152	119	60	252	322	1461

So $\sum u = 101$, $\sum v = 120$, $\sum u^2 = 1503$, $\sum v^2 = 2360$, $\sum uv = 1461$

Then:

$$S_{uv} = \sum uv - \frac{\sum u \sum v}{n} = 1461 - \frac{101 \times 120}{8} = -54$$

$$S_{uu} = \sum u^2 - \frac{(\sum u)^2}{n} = 1503 - \frac{101^2}{8} = 227.875$$

$$S_{vv} = \sum v^2 - \frac{(\sum v)^2}{n} = 2360 - \frac{120^2}{8} = 560$$

This means:

$$r = \frac{S_{uv}}{\sqrt{S_{uu}S_{vv}}}$$

$$= \frac{-54}{\sqrt{227.875 \times 560}} = -0.151 \text{(to 3 sig.fig.)}$$

Because u and v are related by linear transformations to w and s, this means that the PMCC between w and s must also be −0.151 (to 3 sig.fig.)

Q5 Your coding needs to make the numbers easier to use. So use the coding: $u = x - 4000$, and $v = \frac{y}{100}$
Then create a new table showing the coded data values u and v. Include extra rows for u^2, v^2 and uv.

u	8	10	11	15	18	21	83
v	1	4	8	3	7	2	25
u^2	64	100	121	225	324	441	1275
v^2	1	16	64	9	49	4	143
uv	8	40	88	45	126	42	349

So $\sum u = 83$, $\sum v = 25$, $\sum u^2 = 1275$, $\sum v^2 = 143$, $\sum uv = 349$

Then:

$$S_{uv} = \sum uv - \frac{\sum u \sum v}{n} = 349 - \frac{83 \times 25}{6}$$
$$= 3.1666...$$

$$S_{uu} = \sum u^2 - \frac{(\sum u)^2}{n} = 1275 - \frac{83^2}{6}$$
$$= 126.8333...$$

$$S_{vv} = \sum v^2 - \frac{(\sum v)^2}{n} = 143 - \frac{25^2}{6} = 38.8333...$$

This means:

$$r = \frac{S_{uv}}{\sqrt{S_{uu}S_{vv}}}$$

$$= \frac{3.1666...}{\sqrt{126.8333... \times 38.8333...}} = 0.0451 \text{(to 3 sig.fig.)}$$

So the correlation coefficient for x and y is 0.0451 (to 3 sig. fig.).

2. Linear Regression
Exercise 2.1 — Explanatory and response variables

Q1 **Explanatory variable**: the time spent practising the piano each week
Response variable: the number of mistakes made in a test at the end of the week

It is the amount of practice that would determine the performance in the test, not the other way around.

Q2 **Explanatory variable**: the age of a second-hand car
Response variable: the value of a second-hand car

It is the age of the car that would affect its value, not the other way around.

Q3 **Explanatory variable**: the population of a town
Response variable: the number of phone calls made in a town in a week

It is the population that would affect the number of calls, not the other way around.

Q4 **Explanatory variable**: the amount of sunlight falling on a plant in an experiment
Response variable: the growth rate of a plant in an experiment

It is the amount of sunlight that would affect the growth rate, not the other way around.
(Or you could say that the amount of sunlight can be directly controlled, as this is an experiment.)

Exercise 2.2 — Regression lines

Q1 Call the equation of the regression line $y = a + bx$. Then the gradient of the regression line is b, where:
$$b = \frac{S_{xy}}{S_{xx}} = \frac{254.9}{139.4} = 1.82855... = 1.83 \text{ (to 3 sig. fig.)}$$

And the intercept of the regression line is a, where:
$$a = \overline{y} - b\overline{x} = \frac{\sum y}{n} - b\frac{\sum x}{n}$$
$$= \frac{115}{7} - (1.82855...) \times \frac{54}{7}$$
$$= 2.32 \text{ (to 3 sig. fig.)}.$$
So the equation of the regression line of y on x is: $y = 2.32 + 1.83x$

Q2 **a)**

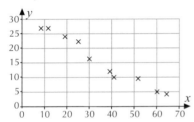

b) Start by working out the four summations $\sum x$, $\sum y$, $\sum x^2$, and $\sum xy$.
It's best to draw a table.

x	8	30	19	41	64	12	60	25	52	39	350
y	27	16	24	10	4	27	5	22	9	12	156
x^2	64	900	361	1681	4096	144	3600	625	2704	1521	15696
xy	216	480	456	410	256	324	300	550	468	468	3928

So $\sum x = 350$, $\sum y = 156$, $\sum x^2 = 15\,696$, $\sum xy = 3928$
Then:
$$S_{xy} = \sum xy - \frac{\sum x \sum y}{n} = 3928 - \frac{350 \times 156}{10}$$
$$= -1532$$
$$S_{xx} = \sum x^2 - \frac{(\sum x)^2}{n} = 15\,696 - \frac{350^2}{10} = 3446$$

Call the equation of the regression line $y = a + bx$. Then the gradient of the regression line is b, where:
$$b = \frac{S_{xy}}{S_{xx}} = \frac{-1532}{3446} = -0.44457...$$
$$= -0.445 \text{ (to 3 sig. fig.)}$$
And the intercept of the regression line is a, where:
$$a = \overline{y} - b\overline{x} = \frac{\sum y}{n} - b\frac{\sum x}{n}$$
$$= \frac{156}{10} - (-0.44457...) \times \frac{350}{10}$$
$$= 31.16006... = 31.2 \text{ (to 3 sig. fig.)}.$$
So the equation of the regression line of y on x is: $y = 31.2 - 0.445x$

c) The value of b tells you that the temperature decreases by approximately 0.445 °C for every extra degree of latitude (since when x increases by 1, y decreases by 0.445).

The value of a suggests that on the equator (when $x = 0$) the mean annual temperature is about 31.2 °C.

d) (i) When $x = 19$, the residual is:
$$e = 24 - (31.16006... - 0.44457... \times 19)$$
$$= 1.29 \text{ (to 3 sig. fig.)}$$
(ii) When $x = 41$, the residual is:
$$e = 10 - (31.16006... - 0.44457... \times 41)$$
$$= -2.93 \text{ (to 3 sig. fig.)}$$

Q3 **a)** You first need to find S_{eP} and S_{ee}.
$$S_{eP} = \sum eP - \frac{\sum e \sum P}{n} = 2596 - \frac{92 \times 264}{10}$$
$$= 167.2$$
$$S_{ee} = \sum e^2 - \frac{(\sum e)^2}{n} = 1072 - \frac{92^2}{10} = 225.6$$

If the equation of the regression line is $P = a + be$, then the gradient of the regression line is b, where:
$$b = \frac{S_{eP}}{S_{ee}} = \frac{167.2}{225.6} = 0.741134...$$
$$= 0.741 \text{ (to 3 sig. fig.)}$$
And the intercept of the regression line is a, where:
$$a = \overline{P} - b\overline{e} = \frac{\sum P}{n} - b\frac{\sum e}{n}$$
$$= \frac{264}{10} - (0.741134...) \times \frac{92}{10}$$
$$= 19.6 \text{ (to 3 sig. fig.)}.$$
So the equation of the regression line of P on e is: $P = 19.6 + 0.741e$

b) The value of b tells you that a graduate employee's salary will generally increase by £741 per year (since when e increases by 1, P increases by 0.741, which is equivalent to £741, as the salaries are given in thousands of pounds).

The value of a tells you that a newly employed graduate (when $e = 0$) typically earns a salary of £19 600.

Exercise 2.3 — Interpolation and extrapolation

Q1 a) y is the response variable (since this is the regression line of y on x).

  b) (i) $1.67 + 0.107 \times 5 = 2.205$

  (ii) $1.67 + 0.107 \times 20 = 3.81$

Q2 a) $103 - 4.57 \times 4 = 84.72$
This is interpolation (since 4 is between 2 and 15). This estimate should be reliable.

  b) $103 - 4.57 \times 20 = 11.6$
This is extrapolation (since 20 is greater than the largest observed value of x, which was 15). This estimate may not be reliable.

  c) $103 - 4.57 \times 7 = 71.01$
This is interpolation (since 7 is between 2 and 15). This estimate should be reliable.

Q3 a) $1.4 \times 20 + 7 = 35$
This is interpolation (since 20 is between 17 and 35, which are the values of x between which data was collected). This estimate should be reliable.

  b) $1.4 \times 50 + 7 = 77$
This is extrapolation (since 50 is greater than the largest value of x for which data was collected). This estimate may not be reliable.

Q4 a) $58.8 - 2.47 \times 7 = 41.51$ — so the volunteer would be predicted to have approximately 42 spots. This is interpolation (since 7 is between 2 and 22, which are the values of x between which data was collected). This estimate should be reliable.

  b) $58.8 - 2.47 \times 0 = 58.8$ — so the volunteer would be predicted to have approximately 59 spots. This is extrapolation (since 0 is less than 2, which was the smallest value of d for which data was collected). This estimate may not be reliable.

  c) Using the formula for $d = 30$ is extrapolation, since 30 is greater than 22, the largest value of d for which data was collected. The model isn't valid for $d = 30$, since you can't have a negative number of spots. But this doesn't mean that the regression equation is wrong.

Exercise 2.4 — Linear regression with coded data

Q1 Substitute the expressions defining p and q into the equation of the regression line for q on p. This gives you an equation involving just x and y.
$q = 40 + 2p$, so $y - 50 = 40 + 2(x - 7)$

Now rearrange this so it is in the form $y = a + bx$, where a and b are constants.
$y = 40 + 2x - 14 + 50 = 76 + 2x$
So the equation of the regression line of y on x is
$y = 76 + 2x$.

Q2 $q = -0.9 + 0.1p$,
and so $10y - 3 = -0.9 + 0.1 \times \dfrac{x - 20}{2}$
Now rearrange this into the form $y = a + bx$.
So $10y = -0.9 + 0.05x - (0.05 \times 20) + 3$
i.e. $10y = 0.05x + 1.1$
Or $y = 0.005x + 0.11$

Q3 $y = 17.4 - 0.78x$, so $t - 45 = 17.4 - 0.78(w - 60)$
Rearrange this to give:
$t = 17.4 - 0.78w + (0.78 \times 60) + 45$,
or $t = -0.78w + 109.2$

Q4 a) $S_{xy} = \sum xy - \dfrac{\sum x \sum y}{n} = 618 - \dfrac{28 \times 124}{10}$
$= 270.8$

$S_{xx} = \sum x^2 - \dfrac{(\sum x)^2}{n} = 140 - \dfrac{28^2}{10} = 61.6$

Call the equation of the regression line $y = a + bx$. Then the gradient of the regression line is b, where:

$b = \dfrac{S_{xy}}{S_{xx}} = \dfrac{270.8}{61.6} = 4.396103...$
$= 4.396$ (to 4 sig. fig.)

And the intercept of the regression line is a, where:

$a = \bar{y} - b\bar{x} = \dfrac{\sum y}{n} - b\dfrac{\sum x}{n}$
$= \dfrac{124}{10} - (4.396103...) \times \dfrac{28}{10}$
$= 0.090909... = 0.09091$ (to 4 sig. fig.).

So the equation of the regression line of y on x is: $y = 0.09091 + 4.396x$

  b) $v - 7 = 0.09091 + 4.396 \times (\dfrac{s}{100} - 2)$
So $v = -1.70 + 0.0440s$

Q5 a) Start by working out the four summations $\sum x$, $\sum y$, $\sum x^2$, and $\sum xy$.
It's best to draw a table.

x	1	2	3	5	7	10	28
y	19	11	9	-1	-14	-24	0
x^2	1	4	9	25	49	100	188
xy	19	22	27	-5	-98	-240	-275

So $\sum x = 28$, $\sum y = 0$, $\sum x^2 = 188$, $\sum xy = -275$
Then:

$S_{xy} = \sum xy - \dfrac{\sum x \sum y}{n} = -275 - \dfrac{28 \times 0}{6}$
$= -275$

$S_{xx} = \sum x^2 - \dfrac{(\sum x)^2}{n} = 188 - \dfrac{28^2}{6} = 57.333...$

Call the equation of the regression line $y = a + bx$. Then the gradient of the regression line is b, where:

$b = \dfrac{S_{xy}}{S_{xx}} = \dfrac{-275}{57.333...} = -4.796511...$
$= -4.80$ (to 3 sig. fig.)

And the intercept of the regression line is a, where:

$$a = \overline{y} - b\overline{x} = \frac{\sum y}{n} - b\frac{\sum x}{n}$$
$$= \frac{0}{6} - (-4.796511\ldots) \times \frac{28}{6}$$
$$= 22.4 \text{ (to 3 sig. fig.).}$$

So the equation of the regression line of y on x is: $y = 22.4 - 4.80x$

b) Substitute expressions for x and y into your regression equation: $t - 29 = 22.4 - 4.80\frac{s}{10}$
This means that: $t = 51.4 - 0.480s$

Review Exercise — Chapter 4

Q1 a)

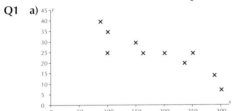

b) First you need to find these values:

$\sum x = 1880$, $\sum y = 247$, $\sum x^2 = 410\,400$,
$\sum y^2 = 6899$ and $\sum xy = 40\,600$.

Then

$$S_{xy} = \sum xy - \frac{\sum x \sum y}{n} = 40\,600 - \frac{1880 \times 247}{10}$$
$$= -5836$$

$$S_{xx} = \sum x^2 - \frac{(\sum x)^2}{n} = 410\,400 - \frac{1880^2}{10}$$
$$= 56\,960$$

$$S_{yy} = \sum y^2 - \frac{(\sum y)^2}{n} = 6899 - \frac{247^2}{10} = 798.1$$

This means:

$$r = \frac{S_{xy}}{\sqrt{S_{xx} S_{yy}}}$$
$$= \frac{-5836}{\sqrt{56\,960 \times 798.1}} = -0.866 \text{ (to 3 sig.fig.)}$$

c) The PMCC tells you that there is a strong negative correlation between drink volume and alcohol concentration — cocktails with smaller volumes tend to have higher concentrations of alcohol.
Don't panic about that PMCC equation — you need to know how to USE it, but they give you the formula in the exam, so you don't need to REMEMBER it.

Q2 a) Explanatory: the annual number of sunny days
Response: the annual number of volleyball-related injuries

b) Explanatory: the annual number of rainy days
Response: the annual number of Monopoly-related injuries

c) Explanatory: a person's disposable income
Response: a person's spending on luxuries

d) Explanatory: the number of cups of tea drunk per day
Response: the number of trips to the loo per day

e) Explanatory: the number of festival tickets sold
Response: the number of pairs of Wellington boots bought

Q3 a) (i) $S_{rr} = 26816.78 - \frac{517.4^2}{10} = 46.504$

(ii) $S_{rw} = 57045.5 - \frac{517.4 \times 1099}{10} = 183.24$

b) $b = \frac{S_{rw}}{S_{rr}} = \frac{183.24}{46.504} = 3.9403\ldots$
$= 3.94$ (to 3 sig. fig.).

c) $a = \overline{w} - b\overline{r}$, where $\overline{w} = \frac{\sum w}{10} = 109.9$
and $\overline{r} = \frac{\sum r}{10} = 51.74$

So $a = 109.9 - 3.9403\ldots \times 51.74$
$= -93.9711\ldots - 94.0$ (to 3 sig. fig.).

d) The equation of the regression line is:
$w = 3.94r - 94.0$

e) When $r = 60$, the regression line gives an estimate for w of: $w = 3.94 \times 60 - 94.0 = 142.4$ g

f) This estimate might not be very reliable because it uses an r-value from outside the range of the original data. It is extrapolation.
You'll be given the equations for finding a regression line — but you still need to know how to use them, otherwise the formula booklet will just be a blur.
And you need to practise USING them of course...

Q4 Rearrange the expressions $P = r - 5$ and $Q = \frac{w}{8}$ to get formulas for r and w. These are $r = P + 5$ and $w = 8Q$.

Substitute these expressions for r and w into the regression line's equation from Question 3.
$w = 3.9403\ldots \times r - 93.9711\ldots,$
and so $8Q = 3.9403\ldots \times (P + 5) - 93.9711\ldots$

Now rearrange to get an equation of the form $Q = a + bP$:
$8Q = 3.9403\ldots \times P + (3.9403\ldots \times 5 - 93.9711\ldots)$
i.e. $Q = 0.493P - 9.28$.

Exam-Style Questions — Chapter 4

1 a)

[2 marks for all points plotted correctly, or 1 mark if at least 3 points are plotted correctly.]

b) You need to work out these sums:

$$\sum x = 36, \sum y = 3.94,$$
$$\sum x^2 = 204, \sum y^2 = 2.4676, \sum xy = 17.66$$

Then:

$$S_{xy} = \sum xy - \frac{\sum x \sum y}{n} = 17.66 - \frac{36 \times 3.94}{8}$$
$$= -0.07$$

$$S_{xx} = \sum x^2 - \frac{(\sum x)^2}{n} = 204 - \frac{36^2}{8} = 42$$

$$S_{yy} = \sum y^2 - \frac{(\sum y)^2}{n} = 2.4676 - \frac{3.94^2}{8} = 0.52715$$

[3 marks available — 1 for each correct term]

This means:

$$r = \frac{S_{xy}}{\sqrt{S_{xx}S_{yy}}} = \frac{-0.07}{\sqrt{42 \times 0.52715}}$$
$$= -0.015 \text{ (to 3 d.p.)}.$$ *[1 mark]*

c) This very small value for the correlation coefficient tells you that there appears to be only a very weak linear relationship between the two variables (or perhaps no linear relationship at all) *[1 mark]*.

2 a)

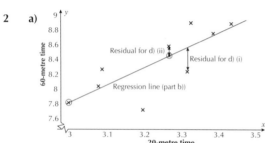

[2 marks for all points plotted correctly, or 1 mark if at least 3 points are plotted correctly.]

b) It's best to make a table like this one first:

	A	B	C	D	E	F	G	H
x	3.39	3.20	3.09	3.32	3.33	3.27	3.44	3.08
y	8.78	7.73	8.28	8.25	8.91	8.59	8.90	8.05
x^2	11.4921	10.24	9.5481	11.0224	11.0889	10.6929	11.8336	9.4864
xy	29.7642	24.736	25.5852	27.39	29.6703	28.0893	30.616	24.794

So $\sum x = 26.12$, $\sum y = 67.49$,
$\sum x^2 = 85.4044$, and $\sum xy = 220.645$.

[2 marks for at least three correct totals, or 1 mark if one total found correctly.]

Then:

$$S_{xy} = 220.645 - \frac{26.12 \times 67.49}{8} = 0.29015$$
[1 mark]
$$S_{xx} = 85.4044 - \frac{26.12^2}{8} = 0.1226$$
[1 mark]

Then the gradient b is given by:

$$b = \frac{S_{xy}}{S_{xx}} = \frac{0.29015}{0.1226} = 2.36663...$$
$$= 2.367 \text{ (to 3 d.p.)}.$$
[1 mark]

And the intercept a is given by:

$$a = \bar{y} - b\bar{x} = \frac{\sum y}{n} - b\frac{\sum x}{n}$$
$$= \frac{67.49}{8} - 2.36663... \times \frac{26.12}{8}$$
$$= 0.709 \text{ (to 3 d.p.)}.$$
[1 mark]

So the regression line has equation:
$$y = 2.367x + 0.709$$
[1 mark]

To plot the line, find two points that the line passes through. A regression line always passes through $(\bar{x}, \bar{y})$, which here is (3.27, 8.44). Then put $x = 3$ (say) to find that the line also passes through (3, 7.81).
Now plot these points (in circles) on your scatter diagram, and draw the regression line through them *[1 mark for plotting the line correctly]*.
Remember, you get marks for method as well as correct answers, so take it step by step and show all your workings.

c) (i) $y = 2.367 \times 3.15 + 0.709$
$= 8.17$ (to 3 sig. fig.),
(or 8.16 if $b = 2.36663...$ used) *[1 mark]*
This should be reliable, since we are using interpolation within the range of x for which we have data *[1 mark]*.

(ii) $y = 2.367 \times 3.88 + 0.709 = 9.89$ (to 3 sig. fig.)
[1 mark]
This could be unreliable, since we are extrapolating beyond the range of the data *[1 mark]*.

d) (i) residual $= 8.25 - (2.367 \times 3.32 + 0.709)$
$= -0.317$ (3 sig. fig.),
(or -0.316 if $b = 2.36663...$ used)
[1 mark for calculation, 1 mark for plotting residual correctly]

(ii) residual $= 8.59 - (2.367 \times 3.27 + 0.709)$
$= 0.141$ (3 sig. fig.),
(or 0.142 if $b = 2.36663...$ used)
[1 mark for calculation, 1 mark for plotting residual correctly]

3 a) Put the values into the PMCC formula:
$$r = \frac{S_{xy}}{\sqrt{S_{xx}S_{yy}}} = \frac{12666}{\sqrt{310880 \times 788.95}}$$
$$= 0.809 \text{ (to 3 sig. fig.)}.$$
[1 mark for correctly substituting the values into the PMCC formula, and 1 mark for the correct final answer.]

b) There is a strong positive correlation between the miles cycled in the morning and calories consumed for lunch. Generally, the further they cycled, the more they ate *[1 mark]*.

c) 0.809 (to 3 sig. fig.) *[1 mark]*
Remember — the PMCC won't be affected if you multiply a set of data values by the same number, so changing the data from miles to km doesn't change it.

4 a) At $x = 12.5$,
$y = 211.599 + (9.602 \times 12.5) = 331.624$

At $x = 14.7$,
$y = 211.599 + (9.602 \times 14.7) = 352.7484$
[1 mark for each value of y correctly calculated]

b) Using the equation:
'Residual = Observed y – Estimated y':
At $x = 12.5$:
Residual $= 332.5 - 331.624 = 0.876$ *[1 mark]*
At $x = 14.7$: Residual $= 352.1 - 352.7484$
$= -0.6484$ *[1 mark]*

5 a) Find the summations $\sum p = 65$ *[1 mark]* and $\sum q$
$= 0$ *[1 mark]*.

Then:
$$S_{pq} = \sum pq - \frac{\sum p \sum q}{n} = 843 - \frac{65 \times 0}{10}$$
[1 mark]

$= 843$ *[1 mark]*
$$S_{pp} = \sum p^2 - \frac{(\sum p)^2}{n} = 571 - \frac{65^2}{10}$$
$= 148.5$ *[1 mark]*
$$S_{qq} = \sum q^2 - \frac{(\sum q)^2}{n} = 548\,586 - \frac{0^2}{10}$$
$= 548\,586$ *[1 mark]*

b) $r = \dfrac{S_{pq}}{\sqrt{S_{pp}S_{qq}}}$

$= \dfrac{843}{\sqrt{148.5 \times 548\,586}}$ *[1 mark]*
$= 0.0934$ (to 3 sig.fig.) *[1 mark]*

c) 0.0934 (to 3 sig. fig.) *[1 mark]*
Because p and q are related by linear transformations to d and t, this means that the PMCC between d and t must be the same as that between p and q *[1 mark]*.

d) The PMCC between d and t is very low *[1 mark]*, which suggests that the length of a run the day before a race has little impact upon the performance of these athletes *[1 mark]*.

6 a)

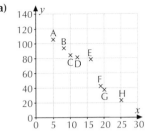

[1 mark for at least 4 points plotted correctly, or 2 marks if all points plotted correctly.]

b) Start by working out the summations
$\sum x = 115$ *[1 mark]* and $\sum y = 544$ *[1 mark]*.
Then:
$$S_{xy} = \sum xy - \frac{\sum x \sum y}{n}$$
$$= 6446 - \frac{115 \times 544}{8}$$ *[1 mark]*
$$= -1374$$ *[1 mark]*
$$S_{xx} = \sum x^2 - \frac{(\sum x)^2}{n}$$
$$= 1975 - \frac{115^2}{8} = 321.875$$ *[1 mark]*

c) The gradient of the regression line is b, where:
$$b = \frac{S_{xy}}{S_{xx}} = \frac{-1374}{321.875}$$ *[1 mark]* $= -4.26873...$
$= -4.27$ (to 3 sig. fig.) *[1 mark]*
And the intercept of the regression line is a, where:
$$a = \bar{y} - b\bar{x} = \frac{\sum y}{n} - b\frac{\sum x}{n}$$
$$= \frac{544}{8} - (-4.26873...) \times \frac{115}{8}$$ *[1 mark]*
$= 129$ (to 3 sig. fig.) *[1 mark]*.

d) The regression line must pass through the point $(\bar{x}, \bar{y}) = (14.375, 68)$. It must also pass through the point $(0, 129)$.

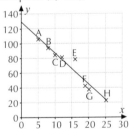

[1 mark if the line passes through one correct point, or 2 marks if line is drawn correctly.]

e) Brand E appears to be overpriced *[1 mark]* — it is much higher than the line, whereas the other points lie very close to it *[1 mark]*.

Chapter 5: The Normal Distribution

2. The Standard Normal Distribution, Z

Exercise 2.1 — The standard normal distribution

Q1 a) Using the $\Phi(z)$ table, $\Phi(1.87) = 0.9693$

   b) Using the $\Phi(z)$ table, $\Phi(0.39) = 0.6517$

   c) Using the $\Phi(z)$ table, $\Phi(0.99) = 0.8389$

   d) Using the $\Phi(z)$ table, $\Phi(3.15) = 0.9992$

Q2 a) $P(Z > 2.48) = 1 - P(Z \leq 2.48)$
$= 1 - 0.9934 = 0.0066$

   b) $P(Z > 0.85) = 1 - P(Z \leq 0.85)$
$= 1 - 0.8023 = 0.1977$

   c) $P(Z \geq 1.23) = 1 - P(Z < 1.23)$
$= 1 - 0.8907 = 0.1093$

   d) $P(Z \geq 0.14) = 1 - P(Z < 0.14)$
$= 1 - 0.5557 = 0.4443$

Q3 a) Use a sketch to find an area you can look up in the table:

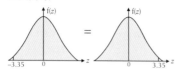

So, $P(Z > -3.35) = P(Z < 3.35) = 0.9996$

   b) Use a sketch to find an area you can look up in the table:

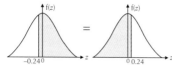

So, $P(Z > -0.24) = P(Z < 0.24) = 0.5948$

   c) Use a sketch to find an area you can look up in the table:

So, $P(Z > -1.21) = P(Z < 1.21) = 0.8869$

   d) The $\Phi(z)$ table doesn't contain negative values of z, so use a sketch to show an equivalent area:

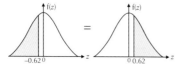

So, $P(Z < -0.62) = P(Z > 0.62)$
$= 1 - P(Z \leq 0.62) = 1 - 0.7324 = 0.2676$

   e) The $\Phi(z)$ table doesn't contain negative values of z, so use a sketch to show an equivalent area:

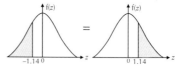

So, $P(Z < -1.14) = P(Z > 1.14)$
$= 1 - P(Z \leq 1.14) = 1 - 0.8729 = 0.1271$

   f) The $\Phi(z)$ table doesn't contain negative values of z, so use a sketch to show an equivalent area:

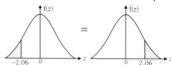

So, $P(Z \leq -2.06) = P(Z \geq 2.06)$
$= 1 - P(Z < 2.06) = 1 - 0.9803 = 0.0197$

We haven't drawn diagrams for the answers to Q4 below, but it often makes it easier to see how to tackle a question if you do a quick sketch.

Q4 a) $P(1.34 < Z < 2.18) = P(Z < 2.18) - P(Z \leq 1.34)$
$= 0.9854 - 0.9099 = 0.0755$

   b) $P(0.76 < Z < 1.92) = P(Z < 1.92) - P(Z \leq 0.76)$
$= 0.9726 - 0.7764 = 0.1962$

   c) $P(-1.45 < Z < 0.17) = P(Z < 0.17) - P(Z \leq -1.45)$
$= P(Z < 0.17) - P(Z \geq 1.45)$
Remember, $P(Z \leq -z) = P(Z \geq z)$.
$= P(Z < 0.17) - [1 - P(Z < 1.45)]$
$= 0.5675 - (1 - 0.9265) = 0.4940$

   d) $P(-2.14 < Z < 1.65) = P(Z < 1.65) - P(Z \leq -2.14)$
$= P(Z < 1.65) - P(Z \geq 2.14)$
$= P(Z < 1.65) - [1 - P(Z < 2.14)]$
$= 0.9505 - (1 - 0.9838) = 0.9343$

   e) $P(-1.66 < Z < 1.66) = P(Z < 1.66) - P(Z \leq -1.66)$
$= P(Z < 1.66) - P(Z \geq 1.66)$
$= P(Z < 1.66) - [1 - P(Z < 1.66)]$
$= 0.9515 - (1 - 0.9515) = 0.9030$

   f) $P(-0.34 < Z < 0.34) = P(Z < 0.34) - P(Z \leq -0.34)$
$= P(Z < 0.34) - P(Z \geq 0.34)$
$= P(Z < 0.34) - [1 - P(Z < 0.34)]$
$= 0.6331 - (1 - 0.6331) = 0.2662$

   g) $P(-3.25 < Z < -2.48) = P(2.48 < Z < 3.25)$
$= P(Z < 3.25) - P(Z \leq 2.48)$
$= 0.9994 - 0.9934 = 0.0060$

   h) $P(-1.11 < Z < -0.17) = P(0.17 < Z < 1.11)$
$= P(Z < 1.11) - P(Z \leq 0.17)$
$= 0.8665 - 0.5675 = 0.2990$

There are different ways of answering some of these, so don't worry if you used a different method to get the same answer.

Exercise 2.2 — Using the tables in reverse

Q1 **a)** Using the $\Phi(z)$ table, $\Phi(z) = 0.8577$ for $z = 1.07$

b) Using the $\Phi(z)$ table, $\Phi(z) = 0.8264$ for $z = 0.94$

c) $P(Z < z) = 0.3783 \Rightarrow P(Z > -z) = 0.3783$
$\Rightarrow P(Z \leq -z) = 0.6217 \Rightarrow -z = 0.31 \Rightarrow z = -0.31$

d) $P(Z < z) = 0.004 \Rightarrow P(Z > -z) = 0.004$
$\Rightarrow P(Z \leq -z) = 0.996 \Rightarrow -z = 2.65 \Rightarrow z = -2.65$

e) $P(Z > z) = 0.758 \Rightarrow P(Z < -z) = 0.758$
$\Rightarrow -z = 0.70 \Rightarrow z = -0.70$

f) $P(Z > z) = 0.9441 \Rightarrow P(Z < -z) = 0.9441$
$\Rightarrow -z = 1.59 \Rightarrow z = -1.59$

g) $P(Z > z) = 0.4801 \Rightarrow P(Z \leq z) = 0.5199$
$\Rightarrow z = 0.05$

h) $P(Z > z) = 0.0951 \Rightarrow P(Z \leq z) = 0.9049$
$\Rightarrow z = 1.31$

Q2 **a)** Using the percentage-points table, $p = 0.005$ for $z = 2.5758$

b) Using the percentage-points table, $p = 0.2$ for $z = 0.8416$

c) $P(Z < z) = 0.7 \Rightarrow P(Z \geq z) = 0.3 \Rightarrow z = 0.5244$

d) $P(Z < z) = 0.85 \Rightarrow P(Z \geq z) = 0.15 \Rightarrow z = 1.0364$

e) $P(Z < z) = 0.1 \Rightarrow P(Z > -z) = 0.1$
$\Rightarrow -z = 1.2816 \Rightarrow z = -1.2816$

f) $P(Z < z) = 0.15 \Rightarrow P(Z > -z) = 0.15$
$\Rightarrow -z = 1.0364 \Rightarrow z = -1.0364$

g) $P(Z > z) = 0.6 \Rightarrow P(Z < -z) = 0.6 \Rightarrow P(Z \geq -z) = 0.4$
$\Rightarrow -z = 0.2533 \Rightarrow z = -0.2533$

h) $P(Z > z) = 0.99 \Rightarrow P(Z < -z) = 0.99$
$\Rightarrow P(Z \geq -z) = 0.01 \Rightarrow -z = 2.3263 \Rightarrow z = -2.3263$

Q3 **a)** $P(-z < Z < z) = 0.599$, so the remaining area is
$1 - 0.599 = 0.401$. Using symmetry,
$P(Z \geq z) = 0.401 \div 2 = 0.2005$
$\Rightarrow P(Z < z) = 0.7995 \Rightarrow z = 0.84$
An alternative way of doing this is to divide 0.599 by 2 to get $P(0 < Z < z) = 0.2995$. Then add 0.5 to get $P(Z < z) = 0.7995$.

b) $P(-z < Z < z) = 0.9426$, so the remaining area is
$1 - 0.9426 = 0.0574$. Using symmetry,
$P(Z \geq z) = 0.0574 \div 2 = 0.0287$
$\Rightarrow P(Z < z) = 0.9713 \Rightarrow z = 1.90$

c) $P(-z < Z < z) = 0.4$, so the remaining area is
$1 - 0.4 = 0.6$. Using symmetry,
$P(Z \geq z) = 0.6 \div 2 = 0.3$. Using the
percentage-points table, $p = 0.3$ for $z = 0.5244$

d) $P(-z < Z < z) = 0.98$, so the remaining area is
$1 - 0.98 = 0.02$. Using symmetry,
$P(Z \geq z) = 0.02 \div 2 = 0.01$. Using the
percentage-points table, $p = 0.01$ for $z = 2.3263$

Q4 **a)** $P(0 < Z < z) = 0.3869$
$\Rightarrow P(Z < z) = 0.3869 + P(Z \leq 0)$
$= 0.3869 + 0.5 = 0.8869$
$\Phi(z) = 0.8869$ for $z = 1.21$

b) $P(0 < Z < z) = 0.4854$
$\Rightarrow P(Z < z) = 0.4854 + P(Z \leq 0)$
$= 0.4854 + 0.5 = 0.9854$
$\Phi(z) = 0.9854$ for $z = 2.18$

Q5 **a)** $P(z < Z < 0) = 0.2422$
$\Rightarrow P(0 < Z < -z) = 0.2422$
$\Rightarrow P(Z < -z) = 0.2422 + 0.5 = 0.7422$
$\Phi(z) = 0.7422$ tells you that $-z = 0.65 \Rightarrow z = -0.65$

b) $P(z < Z < 0) = 0.1443$
$\Rightarrow P(0 < Z < -z) = 0.1443$
$\Rightarrow P(Z < -z) = 0.1443 + 0.5 = 0.6443$
$\Phi(z) = 0.6443$ tells you that $-z = 0.37 \Rightarrow z = -0.37$

Q6 **a)** $P(1.5 < Z < z) = 0.0406$
$\Rightarrow P(Z < z) - P(Z \leq 1.5) = 0.0406$
$\Rightarrow P(Z < z) = 0.0406 + P(Z \leq 1.5)$
$\Rightarrow P(Z < z) = 0.0406 + 0.9332 = 0.9738$
$\Phi(z) = 0.9738$ for $z = 1.94$

b) $P(0.58 < Z < z) = 0.0691$
$\Rightarrow P(Z < z) - P(Z \leq 0.58) = 0.0691$
$\Rightarrow P(Z < z) = 0.0691 + P(Z \leq 0.58)$
$\Rightarrow P(Z < z) = 0.0691 + 0.7190 = 0.7881$
$\Phi(z) = 0.7881$ for $z = 0.80$

c) $P(-1.3 < Z < z) = 0.871$
$\Rightarrow P(Z < z) - P(Z \leq -1.3) = 0.871$
$\Rightarrow P(Z < z) = 0.871 + P(Z \leq -1.3)$
$\Rightarrow P(Z < z) = 0.871 + [1 - P(Z < 1.3)]$
$\Rightarrow P(Z < z) = 0.871 + (1 - 0.9032) = 0.9678$
$\Phi(z) = 0.9678$ for $z = 1.85$

d) $P(-0.54 < Z < z) = 0.667$
$\Rightarrow P(Z < z) - P(Z \leq -0.54) = 0.667$
$\Rightarrow P(Z < z) = 0.667 + P(Z \leq -0.54)$
$\Rightarrow P(Z < z) = 0.667 + [1 - P(Z < 0.54)]$
$\Rightarrow P(Z < z) = 0.667 + (1 - 0.7054) = 0.9616$
$\Phi(z) = 0.9616$ for $z = 1.77$

e) $P(z < Z < 0.27) = 0.5458$
$\Rightarrow P(Z < 0.27) - P(Z \leq z) = 0.5458$
$\Rightarrow P(Z \leq z) = P(Z < 0.27) - 0.5458$
$\Rightarrow P(Z \leq z) = 0.6064 - 0.5458 = 0.0606$
But you can't look up 0.0606 in the table, so there's still some work to do...
$\Rightarrow P(Z \geq -z) = 0.0606 \Rightarrow P(Z < -z) = 0.9394$
$\Phi(z) = 0.9394$ tells you that $-z = 1.55 \Rightarrow z = -1.55$

f) $P(z < Z < -1.25) = 0.0949$
$\Rightarrow P(Z < -1.25) - P(Z \leq z) = 0.0949$
$\Rightarrow P(Z \leq z) = P(Z < -1.25) - 0.0949$
$\Rightarrow P(Z \leq z) = P(Z > 1.25) - 0.0949$
$\Rightarrow P(Z \leq z) = [1 - P(Z \leq 1.25)] - 0.0949$
$\Rightarrow P(Z \leq z) = (1 - 0.8944) - 0.0949 = 0.0107$
$\Rightarrow P(Z \geq -z) = 0.0107 \Rightarrow P(Z < -z) = 0.9893$
$\Phi(z) = 0.9893$ tells you that $-z = 2.30 \Rightarrow z = -2.30$

3. Normal Distributions and Z-Tables

Exercise 3.1 — Converting to the Z distribution

Q1 a) $P(X < 50) = P\left(Z < \dfrac{50 - 40}{5}\right) = P(Z < 2) = 0.9772$

b) $P(X < 43) = P\left(Z < \dfrac{43 - 40}{5}\right)$

$= P(Z < 0.6) = 0.7257$

Q2 a) $P(X > 28) = P\left(Z > \dfrac{28 - 24}{\sqrt{6}}\right) = P(Z > 1.63)$

$= 1 - P(Z \le 1.63) = 1 - 0.9484 = 0.0516$

b) $P(X > 25) = P\left(Z > \dfrac{25 - 24}{\sqrt{6}}\right) = P(Z > 0.41)$

$= 1 - P(Z \le 0.41) = 1 - 0.6591 = 0.3409$

Q3 a) $P(X > 107) = P\left(Z > \dfrac{107 - 120}{\sqrt{40}}\right) = P(Z > -2.06)$

$= P(Z < 2.06) = 0.9803$

b) $P(X > 115) = P\left(Z > \dfrac{115 - 120}{\sqrt{40}}\right) = P(Z > -0.79)$

$= P(Z < 0.79) = 0.7852$

Q4 a) $P(X < 15) = P\left(Z < \dfrac{15 - 17}{3}\right) = P(Z < -0.67)$

$= P(Z > 0.67) = 1 - (Z \le 0.67)$
$= 1 - 0.7486 = 0.2514$

b) $P(X < 12) = P\left(Z < \dfrac{12 - 17}{3}\right) = P(Z < -1.67)$

$= P(Z > 1.67) = 1 - (Z \le 1.67)$
$= 1 - 0.9525 = 0.0475$

Q5 a) $P(52 < X < 63) = P\left(\dfrac{52 - 50}{5} < Z < \dfrac{63 - 50}{5}\right)$

$= P(0.4 < Z < 2.6)$
$= P(Z < 2.6) - P(Z \le 0.4)$
$= 0.9953 - 0.6554 = 0.3399$

b) $P(57 < X < 66) = P\left(\dfrac{57 - 50}{5} < Z < \dfrac{66 - 50}{5}\right)$

$= P(1.4 < Z < 3.2)$
$= P(Z < 3.2) - P(Z \le 1.4)$
$= 0.9993 - 0.9192 = 0.0801$

Q6 a) $P(0.45 < X < 0.55)$

$= P\left(\dfrac{0.45 - 0.6}{0.2} < Z < \dfrac{0.55 - 0.6}{0.2}\right)$
$= P(-0.75 < Z < -0.25)$
$= P(0.25 < Z < 0.75)$
$= P(Z < 0.75) - P(Z \le 0.25)$
$= 0.7734 - 0.5987 = 0.1747$

b) $P(0.53 < X < 0.58)$

$= P\left(\dfrac{0.53 - 0.6}{0.2} < Z < \dfrac{0.58 - 0.6}{0.2}\right)$
$= P(-0.35 < Z < -0.1)$
$= P(0.1 < Z < 0.35)$
$= P(Z < 0.35) - P(Z \le 0.1)$
$= 0.6368 - 0.5398 = 0.097$

Q7 a) $P(240 < X < 280)$

$= P\left(\dfrac{240 - 260}{15} < Z < \dfrac{280 - 260}{15}\right)$
$= P(-1.33 < Z < 1.33)$
$= P(Z < 1.33) - P(Z \le -1.33)$
$= P(Z < 1.33) - P(Z \ge 1.33)$
$= P(Z < 1.33) - [1 - P(Z < 1.33)]$
$= 2 \times P(Z < 1.33) - 1$
$= 2 \times 0.9082 - 1 = 0.8164$

b) $P(232 < X < 288)$

$= P\left(\dfrac{232 - 260}{15} < Z < \dfrac{288 - 260}{15}\right)$
$= P(-1.87 < Z < 1.87)$
$= P(Z < 1.87) - P(Z \le -1.87)$
$= P(Z < 1.87) - P(Z \ge 1.87)$
$= P(Z < 1.87) - [1 - P(Z < 1.87)]$
$= 2 \times P(Z < 1.87) - 1$
$= 2 \times 0.9693 - 1 = 0.9386$

Q8 a) $P(X < a) = 0.9938 \Rightarrow P\left(Z < \dfrac{a - 70}{4}\right) = 0.9938$

Using the $\Phi(z)$ table, $\Phi(z) = 0.9938$ for $z = 2.50$.

So, $\dfrac{a - 70}{4} = 2.5 \Rightarrow a = 2.5 \times 4 + 70 = 80$

b) $P(X < b) = 0.7734 \Rightarrow P\left(Z < \dfrac{b - 70}{4}\right) = 0.7734$

Using the $\Phi(z)$ table, $\Phi(z) = 0.7734$ for $z = 0.75$.

So, $\dfrac{b - 70}{4} = 0.75 \Rightarrow b = 0.75 \times 4 + 70 = 73$

Q9 a) $P(X > m) = 0.0102 \Rightarrow P\left(Z > \dfrac{m - 95}{5}\right) = 0.0102$

$\Rightarrow P\left(Z \le \dfrac{m - 95}{5}\right) = 0.9898$

Using the $\Phi(z)$ table, $\Phi(z) = 0.9898$ for $z = 2.32$.

So, $\dfrac{m - 95}{5} = 2.32 \Rightarrow m = 2.32 \times 5 + 95 = 106.6$

b) $P(X > t) = 0.2296 \Rightarrow P\left(Z > \dfrac{t - 95}{5}\right) = 0.2296$

$\Rightarrow P\left(Z \le \dfrac{t - 95}{5}\right) = 0.7704$

Using the $\Phi(z)$ table, $\Phi(z) = 0.7704$ for $z = 0.74$.

So, $\dfrac{t - 95}{5} = 0.74 \Rightarrow t = 0.74 \times 5 + 95 = 98.7$

Q10 a) $P(X < c) = 0.1251 \Rightarrow P\left(Z < \dfrac{c - 48}{10}\right) = 0.1251$

$\Rightarrow P\left(Z > \dfrac{48 - c}{10}\right) = 0.1251$

Switch c and 48 around to get −z.

$\Rightarrow P\left(Z \le \dfrac{48 - c}{10}\right) = 0.8749$

Using the $\Phi(z)$ table, $\Phi(z) = 0.8749$ for $z = 1.15$.

So, $\dfrac{48 - c}{10} = 1.15 \Rightarrow c = 48 - 1.15 \times 10 = 36.5$

b) $P(X < d) = 0.0096 \Rightarrow P\left(Z < \dfrac{d - 48}{10}\right) = 0.0096$

$\Rightarrow P\left(Z > \dfrac{48 - d}{10}\right) = 0.0096$

$\Rightarrow P\left(Z \le \dfrac{48 - d}{10}\right) = 0.9904$

Using the $\Phi(z)$ table, $\Phi(z) = 0.9904$ for $z = 2.34$.

So, $\dfrac{48 - d}{10} = 2.34 \Rightarrow d = 48 - 2.34 \times 10 = 24.6$

Q11 a) $P(X > w) = 0.9177 \Rightarrow P\left(Z > \frac{w - 73}{6}\right) = 0.9177$

$\Rightarrow P\left(Z < \frac{73 - w}{6}\right) = 0.9177$

Using the $\Phi(z)$ table, $\Phi(z) = 0.9177$ for $z = 1.39$.

So, $\frac{73 - w}{6} = 1.39 \Rightarrow w = 73 - 1.39 \times 6 = 64.66$

b) $P(X > k) = 0.6664 \Rightarrow P\left(Z > \frac{k - 73}{6}\right) = 0.6664$

$\Rightarrow P\left(Z < \frac{73 - k}{6}\right) = 0.6664$

Using the $\Phi(z)$ table, $\Phi(z) = 0.6664$ for $z = 0.43$.

So, $\frac{73 - k}{6} = 0.43 \Rightarrow k = 73 - 0.43 \times 6 = 70.42$

Q12 $P(18 - a < X < 18 + a) = 0.899$

$\Rightarrow P\left(\frac{18 - a - 18}{0.5} < Z < \frac{18 + a - 18}{0.5}\right) = 0.899$

$\Rightarrow P\left(\frac{-a}{0.5} < Z < \frac{a}{0.5}\right) = 0.899$

The remaining area is $1 - 0.899 = 0.101$.

So, $P\left(Z \geq \frac{a}{0.5}\right) = 0.101 \div 2 = 0.0505$.

$\Rightarrow P\left(Z < \frac{a}{0.5}\right) = 0.9495$

Using the $\Phi(z)$ table, $\Phi(z) = 0.9495$ for $z = 1.64$.

So, $\frac{a}{0.5} = 1.64 \Rightarrow a = 1.64 \times 0.5 = 0.82$

Q13 $P(170 < X < t) = 0.377$

$\Rightarrow P\left(\frac{170 - 170}{40} < Z < \frac{t - 170}{40}\right) = 0.377$

$\Rightarrow P\left(0 < Z < \frac{t - 170}{40}\right) = 0.377$

$\Rightarrow P\left(Z < \frac{t - 170}{40}\right) - P(Z \leq 0) = 0.377$

$\Rightarrow P\left(Z < \frac{t - 170}{40}\right) = 0.377 + 0.5 = 0.877$

Using the $\Phi(z)$ table, $\Phi(z) = 0.877$ for $z = 1.16$.

So, $\frac{t - 170}{40} = 1.16 \Rightarrow t = 1.16 \times 40 + 170 = 216.4$

Q14 $P(107.6 < X < v) = 0.1677$

$\Rightarrow P\left(\frac{107.6 - 98}{15} < Z < \frac{v - 98}{15}\right) = 0.1677$

$\Rightarrow P\left(0.64 < Z < \frac{v - 98}{15}\right) = 0.1677$

$\Rightarrow P\left(Z < \frac{v - 98}{15}\right) - P(Z \leq 0.64) = 0.1677$

$\Rightarrow P\left(Z < \frac{v - 98}{15}\right) = 0.1677 + 0.7389 = 0.9066$

Using the $\Phi(z)$ table, $\Phi(z) = 0.9066$ for $z = 1.32$.

So, $\frac{v - 98}{15} = 1.32 \Rightarrow v = 1.32 \times 15 + 98 = 117.8$

Exercise 3.2 — The normal distribution in real-life situations

Q1 a) Let $L \sim N(8.4, 3.1^2)$ represent the length of a worm in cm.

$P(L < 9.5) = P\left(Z < \frac{9.5 - 8.4}{3.1}\right)$

$= P(Z < 0.35) = 0.6368$

b) $P(L > 10) = P\left(Z > \frac{10 - 8.4}{3.1}\right) = P(Z > 0.52)$

$= 1 - P(Z \leq 0.52) = 1 - 0.6985 = 0.3015$

c) $P(5 < L < 11) = P\left(\frac{5 - 8.4}{3.1} < Z < \frac{11 - 8.4}{3.1}\right)$

$= P(-1.10 < Z < 0.84)$
$= P(Z < 0.84) - P(Z \leq -1.10)$
$= P(Z < 0.84) - P(Z \geq 1.10)$
$= P(Z < 0.84) - [1 - P(Z < 1.10)]$
$= 0.7995 - (1 - 0.8643) = 0.6638$

Q2 a) Let $T \sim N(36, 6^2)$ represent the length of time taken to replace red blood cells, in days.

$P(T < 28) = P\left(Z < \frac{28 - 36}{6}\right)$

$= P(Z < -1.33) = P(Z > 1.33) = 1 - P(Z \leq 1.33)$
$= 1 - 0.9082 = 0.0918$

b) Let $b =$ the number of days taken by Bella.
Then, $P(T > b) = 0.063$.

$\Rightarrow P\left(Z > \frac{b - 36}{6}\right) = 0.063$

$\Rightarrow P\left(Z \leq \frac{b - 36}{6}\right) = 0.9370$

Using the $\Phi(z)$ table, $\Phi(z) = 0.9370$ for $z = 1.53$.

So, $\frac{b - 36}{6} = 1.53$

$\Rightarrow b = 1.53 \times 6 + 36 = 45.18$ days

Don't forget to say 'days' in your answer — you need to answer the question in the context it was asked.

Q3 a) Let $T \sim N(51, 2.1^2)$ represent the 'personal best' time taken to run 400 m in seconds.

$P(T > 49.3) = P\left(Z > \frac{49.3 - 51}{2.1}\right)$

$= P(Z > -0.81) = P(Z < 0.81) = 0.7910$
So, 79.1% are slower than Gary.

b) Let $a =$ the time to beat.
Then, $P(T < a) = 0.2$.

$\Rightarrow P\left(Z < \frac{a - 51}{2.1}\right) = 0.2$

$\Rightarrow P\left(Z > \frac{51 - a}{2.1}\right) = 0.2$

Using the percentage-points table,

$p = 0.2$ for $z = 0.8416$

So, $\frac{51 - a}{2.1} = 0.8416$

$\Rightarrow a = 51 - 2.1 \times 0.8416 = 49.2$ s (to 3 s.f.)

Q4 a) Let $L \sim N(300, 50^2)$ represent the lifetime of a battery in hours.

$P(L < 200) = P\left(Z < \frac{200 - 300}{50}\right)$

$= P(Z < -2) = P(Z > 2) = 1 - P(Z \leq 2)$
$= 1 - 0.9772 = 0.0228$

b) $P(L > 380) = P\left(Z > \frac{380 - 300}{50}\right)$

$= P(Z > 1.6) = 1 - P(Z \leq 1.6)$
$= 1 - 0.9452 = 0.0548$

c) Assuming that the lifetimes of the batteries are independent, the probability that both last at least 380 hours $= 0.0548 \times 0.0548 = 0.0030$ (to 2 s.f.).
If two things are independent, it means you can multiply their probabilities together.

d) $P(160 < L < h) = 0.9746$

$\Rightarrow P\left(\dfrac{160 - 300}{50} < Z < \dfrac{h - 300}{50}\right) = 0.9746$

$\Rightarrow P\left(-2.8 < Z < \dfrac{h - 300}{50}\right) = 0.9746$

$\Rightarrow P\left(Z < \dfrac{h - 300}{50}\right) - P(Z \le -2.8) = 0.9746$

$\Rightarrow P\left(Z < \dfrac{h - 300}{50}\right) - P(Z \ge 2.8) = 0.9746$

$\Rightarrow P\left(Z < \dfrac{h - 300}{50}\right) - [1 - P(Z < 2.8)] = 0.9746$

$\Rightarrow P\left(Z < \dfrac{h - 300}{50}\right) = 0.9746 + (1 - 0.9974)$

$\Rightarrow P\left(Z < \dfrac{h - 300}{50}\right) = 0.9772$

Using the $\Phi(z)$ table, $\Phi(z) = 0.9772$ for $z = 2.0$.

So, $\dfrac{h - 300}{50} = 2 \Rightarrow h = 2 \times 50 + 300 = 400$

Q5 a) Let $M \sim N(60, 3^2)$ represent the mass of an egg in grams.

$P(M > 60 - m) = 0.9525$

$\Rightarrow P\left(Z > \dfrac{60 - m - 60}{3}\right) = 0.9525$

$\Rightarrow P\left(Z > \dfrac{-m}{3}\right) = 0.9525$

$\Rightarrow P\left(Z < \dfrac{m}{3}\right) = 0.9525$

Using the $\Phi(z)$ table, $\Phi(z) = 0.9525$ for $z = 1.67$.

So, $\dfrac{m}{3} = 1.67 \Rightarrow m = 1.67 \times 3 = 5.01$

$= 5$ grams to the nearest gram.

b) Let $c =$ the maximum mass of an egg in one of farmer Elizabeth's sponge cakes.

Then, $P(M \le c) = 0.1$.

So, $P\left(Z \le \dfrac{c - 60}{3}\right) = 0.1$

$\Rightarrow P\left(Z \ge \dfrac{60 - c}{3}\right) = 0.1$

Using the percentage-points table, $p = 0.1$ for $z = 1.2816$

$\Rightarrow \dfrac{60 - c}{3} = 1.2816 \Rightarrow c = 60 - 3 \times 1.2816$

$= 56.1552 = 56.2$, to 3 s.f.

So, the maximum mass is 56.2 grams.

Exercise 3.3 — Finding the mean and standard deviation of a normal distribution

Q1 a) $P(X < 23) = 0.9332 \Rightarrow P\left(Z < \dfrac{23 - \mu}{6}\right) = 0.9332$

Using the $\Phi(z)$ table, $\Phi(z) = 0.9332$ for $z = 1.50$.

$\Rightarrow \dfrac{23 - \mu}{6} = 1.5 \Rightarrow \mu = 23 - 1.5 \times 6 = 14$

b) $P(X < 57) = 0.9970 \Rightarrow P\left(Z < \dfrac{57 - \mu}{8}\right) = 0.9970$

Using the $\Phi(z)$ table, $\Phi(z) = 0.9970$ for $z = 2.75$.

$\Rightarrow \dfrac{57 - \mu}{8} = 2.75 \Rightarrow \mu = 57 - 2.75 \times 8 = 35$

c) $P(X > 528) = 0.1292$

$\Rightarrow P\left(Z > \dfrac{528 - \mu}{100}\right) = 0.1292$

$\Rightarrow P\left(Z \le \dfrac{528 - \mu}{100}\right) = 0.8708$

Using the $\Phi(z)$ table, $\Phi(z) = 0.8708$ for $z = 1.13$.

$\Rightarrow \dfrac{528 - \mu}{100} = 1.13$

$\Rightarrow \mu = 528 - 1.13 \times 100 = 415$

d) $P(X < 11.06) = 0.0322$

$\Rightarrow P\left(Z < \dfrac{11.06 - \mu}{0.4}\right) = 0.0322$

$\Rightarrow P\left(Z > \dfrac{\mu - 11.06}{0.4}\right) = 0.0322$

$\Rightarrow P\left(Z \le \dfrac{\mu - 11.06}{0.4}\right) = 0.9678$

Using the $\Phi(z)$ table, $\Phi(z) = 0.9678$ for $z = 1.85$.

$\Rightarrow \dfrac{\mu - 11.06}{0.4} = 1.85$

$\Rightarrow \mu = 1.85 \times 0.4 + 11.06 = 11.8$

e) $P(X > 1.52) = 0.9938$

$\Rightarrow P\left(Z > \dfrac{1.52 - \mu}{0.02}\right) = 0.9938$

$\Rightarrow P\left(Z < \dfrac{\mu - 1.52}{0.02}\right) = 0.9938$

Using the $\Phi(z)$ table, $\Phi(z) = 0.9938$ for $z = 2.50$.

$\Rightarrow \dfrac{\mu - 1.52}{0.02} = 2.5$

$\Rightarrow \mu = 2.5 \times 0.02 + 1.52 = 1.57$

Q2 Start with a sketch showing what you know about X.

So, $P(X < 20.17) = 0.95 + 0.025 = 0.975$

$\Rightarrow P\left(Z < \dfrac{20.17 - \mu}{3.5}\right) = 0.975$

Using the $\Phi(z)$ table, $\Phi(z) = 0.975$ for $z = 1.96$.

$\Rightarrow \dfrac{20.17 - \mu}{3.5} = 1.96$

$\Rightarrow \mu = 20.17 - 1.96 \times 3.5 = 13.31$

There are different ways you could go about this question. For example, you also know that $P(X > 20.17) = 0.025$, so you can look up $p = 0.025$ in the percentage-points table. Or, using the symmetry of the graph, you know that μ is exactly in the middle of 6.45 and 20.17, so you can simply find the average of these 2 values.

Q3 a) $P(X < 53) = 0.8944$

$\Rightarrow P\left(Z < \dfrac{53 - 48}{\sigma}\right) = P\left(Z < \dfrac{5}{\sigma}\right) = 0.8944$

Using the $\Phi(z)$ table, $\Phi(z) = 0.8944$ for $z = 1.25$.

$\Rightarrow \dfrac{5}{\sigma} = 1.25 \Rightarrow \sigma = 5 \div 1.25 = 4$

b) $P(X < 528) = 0.7734$

$\Rightarrow P\left(Z < \frac{528 - 510}{\sigma}\right) = P\left(Z < \frac{18}{\sigma}\right) = 0.7734$

Using the $\Phi(z)$ table, $\Phi(z) = 0.7734$ for $z = 0.75$.

$\Rightarrow \frac{18}{\sigma} = 0.75 \Rightarrow \sigma = 18 \div 0.75 = 24$

c) $P(X > 24) = 0.0367$

$\Rightarrow P\left(Z > \frac{24 - 17}{\sigma}\right) = P\left(Z > \frac{7}{\sigma}\right) = 0.0367$

$\Rightarrow P\left(Z \leq \frac{7}{\sigma}\right) = 0.9633$

Using the $\Phi(z)$ table, $\Phi(z) = 0.9633$ for $z = 1.79$.

$\Rightarrow \frac{7}{\sigma} = 1.79 \Rightarrow \sigma = 7 \div 1.79 = 3.91$ (to 3 s.f.)

d) $P(X < 0.95) = 0.3085$

$\Rightarrow P\left(Z < \frac{0.95 - 0.98}{\sigma}\right) = P\left(Z < -\frac{0.03}{\sigma}\right)$

$= 0.3085$

$\Rightarrow P\left(Z > \frac{0.03}{\sigma}\right) = 0.3085$

$\Rightarrow P\left(Z \leq \frac{0.03}{\sigma}\right) = 0.6915$

Using the $\Phi(z)$ table, $\Phi(z) = 0.6915$ for $z = 0.5$.

$\Rightarrow \frac{0.03}{\sigma} = 0.5 \Rightarrow \sigma = 0.03 \div 0.5 = 0.06$

e) $P(X > 4.85) = 0.8365$

$\Rightarrow P\left(Z > \frac{4.85 - 5.6}{\sigma}\right) = P\left(Z > -\frac{0.75}{\sigma}\right)$

$= 0.8365$

$\Rightarrow P\left(Z < \frac{0.75}{\sigma}\right) = 0.8365$

Using the $\Phi(z)$ table, $\Phi(z) = 0.8365$ for $z = 0.98$.

$\Rightarrow \frac{0.75}{\sigma} = 0.98 \Rightarrow \sigma = 0.75 \div 0.98$

$= 0.765$ (to 3 s.f.)

Q4 Start with a sketch showing what you know about X.

So, $P(X > 75) = 0.15$

$\Rightarrow P\left(Z > \frac{75 - 68}{\sigma}\right) = P\left(Z > \frac{7}{\sigma}\right) = 0.15$

Using the percentage-points table,
$p = 0.15$ for $z = 1.0364$.

$\Rightarrow \frac{7}{\sigma} = 1.0364 \Rightarrow \sigma = 7 \div 1.0364 = 6.75$ (to 3 s.f.)

Q5 a) $P(X < 30) = 0.9192 \Rightarrow P\left(Z < \frac{30 - \mu}{\sigma}\right) = 0.9192$

$\Phi(z) = 0.9192$ for $z = 1.40$

$\Rightarrow \frac{30 - \mu}{\sigma} = 1.4 \Rightarrow 30 - \mu = 1.4\sigma$ *(equation 1)*

$P(X < 36) = 0.9953 \Rightarrow P\left(Z < \frac{36 - \mu}{\sigma}\right) = 0.9953$

$\Phi(z) = 0.9953$ for $z = 2.60$

$\Rightarrow \frac{36 - \mu}{\sigma} = 2.6 \Rightarrow 36 - \mu = 2.6\sigma$ *(equation 2)*

Subtracting equation 1 from equation 2 gives:
$36 - 30 - \mu - (-\mu) = 2.6\sigma - 1.4\sigma$
$\Rightarrow 6 = 1.2\sigma \Rightarrow \sigma = 5$
Putting $\sigma = 5$ into equation 1 gives:
$\mu = 30 - 1.4 \times 5 = 23$
So $\mu = 23$ and $\sigma = 5$

b) $P(X < 4) = 0.9332 \Rightarrow P\left(Z < \frac{4 - \mu}{\sigma}\right) = 0.9332$

$\Phi(z) = 0.9332$ for $z = 1.50$

$\Rightarrow \frac{4 - \mu}{\sigma} = 1.5 \Rightarrow 4 - \mu = 1.5\sigma$ *(equation 1)*

$P(X < 4.3) = 0.9987 \Rightarrow P\left(Z < \frac{4.3 - \mu}{\sigma}\right) = 0.9987$

$\Phi(z) = 0.9987$ for $z = 3.00$

$\Rightarrow \frac{4.3 - \mu}{\sigma} = 3 \Rightarrow 4.3 - \mu = 3\sigma$ *(equation 2)*

Subtracting equation 1 from equation 2 gives:
$4.3 - 4 - \mu - (-\mu) = 3\sigma - 1.5\sigma$
$\Rightarrow 0.3 = 1.5\sigma \Rightarrow \sigma = 0.2$
Putting $\sigma = 0.2$ into equation 1 gives:
$\mu = 4 - 1.5 \times 0.2 = 3.7$
So $\mu = 3.7$ and $\sigma = 0.2$

c) $P(X < 20) = 0.7881 \Rightarrow P\left(Z < \frac{20 - \mu}{\sigma}\right) = 0.7881$

$\Phi(z) = 0.7881$ for $z = 0.80$

$\Rightarrow \frac{20 - \mu}{\sigma} = 0.8 \Rightarrow 20 - \mu = 0.8\sigma$ *(equation 1)*

$P(X < 14) = 0.0548 \Rightarrow P\left(Z < \frac{14 - \mu}{\sigma}\right) = 0.0548$

$\Rightarrow P\left(Z > \frac{\mu - 14}{\sigma}\right) = 0.0548$

$\Rightarrow P\left(Z \leq \frac{\mu - 14}{\sigma}\right) = 0.9452$

$\Phi(z) = 0.9452$ for $z = 1.60$

$\Rightarrow \frac{\mu - 14}{\sigma} = 1.6 \Rightarrow \mu - 14 = 1.6\sigma$ *(equation 2)*

Adding equations 1 and 2 gives:
$20 - 14 - \mu + \mu = 0.8\sigma + 1.6\sigma$
$\Rightarrow 6 = 2.4\sigma \Rightarrow \sigma = 2.5$
Putting $\sigma = 2.5$ into equation 2 gives:
$\mu = 1.6 \times 2.5 + 14 = 18$
So $\mu = 18$ and $\sigma = 2.5$

d) $P(X < 696) = 0.9713$

$\Rightarrow P\left(Z < \frac{696 - \mu}{\sigma}\right) = 0.9713$

$\Phi(z) = 0.9713$ for $z = 1.90$

$\Rightarrow \frac{696 - \mu}{\sigma} = 1.9 \Rightarrow 696 - \mu = 1.9\sigma$ *(equation 1)*

$P(X < 592) = 0.2420$

$\Rightarrow P\left(Z < \frac{592 - \mu}{\sigma}\right) = 0.2420$

$\Rightarrow P\left(Z > \frac{\mu - 592}{\sigma}\right) = 0.2420$

$\Rightarrow P\left(Z \leq \frac{\mu - 592}{\sigma}\right) = 0.7580$

$\Phi(z) = 0.758$ for $z = 0.70$

$\Rightarrow \frac{\mu - 592}{\sigma} = 0.7 \Rightarrow \mu - 592 = 0.7\sigma$ *(equation 2)*

Adding equations 1 and 2 gives:
$696 - 592 - \mu + \mu = 1.9\sigma + 0.7\sigma$
$\Rightarrow 104 = 2.6\sigma \Rightarrow \sigma = 40$
Putting $\sigma = 40$ into equation 2 gives:
$\mu = 0.7 \times 40 + 592 = 620$
So $\mu = 620$ and $\sigma = 40$

e) $P(X > 33) = 0.1056$

$\Rightarrow P\left(Z > \dfrac{33 - \mu}{\sigma}\right) = 0.1056$

$\Rightarrow P\left(Z \leq \dfrac{33 - \mu}{\sigma}\right) = 0.8944$

$\Phi(z) = 0.8944$ for $z = 1.25$

$\Rightarrow \dfrac{33 - \mu}{\sigma} = 1.25 \Rightarrow 33 - \mu = 1.25\sigma$ *(equation 1)*

$P(X > 21) = 0.9599$

$\Rightarrow P\left(Z > \dfrac{21 - \mu}{\sigma}\right) = 0.9599$

$\Rightarrow P\left(Z < \dfrac{\mu - 21}{\sigma}\right) = 0.9599$

$\Phi(z) = 0.9599$ for $z = 1.75$

$\Rightarrow \dfrac{\mu - 21}{\sigma} = 1.75 \Rightarrow \mu - 21 = 1.75\sigma$ *(equation 2)*

Adding equations 1 and 2 gives:
$33 - 21 - \mu + \mu = 1.25\sigma + 1.75\sigma$
$\Rightarrow 12 = 3\sigma \Rightarrow \sigma = 4$
Putting $\sigma = 4$ into equation 2 gives:
$\mu = 1.75 \times 4 + 21 = 28$
So $\mu = 28$ and $\sigma = 4$

f) $P(X > 66) = 0.3632$

$\Rightarrow P\left(Z > \dfrac{66 - \mu}{\sigma}\right) = 0.3632$

$\Rightarrow P\left(Z \leq \dfrac{66 - \mu}{\sigma}\right) = 0.6368$

$\Phi(z) = 0.6368$ for $z = 0.35$

$\Rightarrow \dfrac{66 - \mu}{\sigma} = 0.35 \Rightarrow 66 - \mu = 0.35\sigma$ *(equation 1)*

$P(X < 48) = 0.3446$

$\Rightarrow P\left(Z < \dfrac{48 - \mu}{\sigma}\right) = 0.3446$

$\Rightarrow P\left(Z > \dfrac{\mu - 48}{\sigma}\right) = 0.3446$

$\Rightarrow P\left(Z \leq \dfrac{\mu - 48}{\sigma}\right) = 0.6554$

$\Phi(z) = 0.6554$ for $z = 0.40$

$\Rightarrow \dfrac{\mu - 48}{\sigma} = 0.4 \Rightarrow \mu - 48 = 0.4\sigma$ *(equation 2)*

Adding equations 1 and 2 gives:
$66 - 48 - \mu + \mu = 0.35\sigma + 0.4\sigma$
$\Rightarrow 18 = 0.75\sigma \Rightarrow \sigma = 24$
Putting $\sigma = 24$ into equation 2 gives:
$\mu = 0.4 \times 24 + 48 = 57.6$
So $\mu = 57.6$ and $\sigma = 24$

Q6 a) Let V = volume of vinegar in ml.
Then $V \sim N(\mu, 5^2)$.

$P(V < 506) = 0.719 \Rightarrow P\left(Z < \dfrac{506 - \mu}{5}\right) = 0.719$

$\Phi(z) = 0.719$ for $z = 0.58$

$\Rightarrow \dfrac{506 - \mu}{5} = 0.58$

$\Rightarrow \mu = 506 - 0.58 \times 5 = 503.1$ ml

b) $P(V < 500) = P\left(Z < \dfrac{500 - 503.1}{5}\right)$

$= P(Z < -0.62) = P(Z > 0.62) = 1 - P(Z \leq 0.62)$
$= 1 - 0.7324 = 0.2676$
So, 26.76% of bottles contain less than 500 ml.

Q7 a) Let H = height in cm. Then $H \sim N(175, \sigma^2)$.
$P(H > 170) = 0.8$

$\Rightarrow P\left(Z > \dfrac{170 - 175}{\sigma}\right) = P\left(Z > -\dfrac{5}{\sigma}\right) = 0.8$

$\Rightarrow P\left(Z < \dfrac{5}{\sigma}\right) = 0.8 \Rightarrow P\left(Z \geq \dfrac{5}{\sigma}\right) = 0.2$

$p = 0.2$ for $z = 0.8416 \Rightarrow \dfrac{5}{\sigma} = 0.8416$

$\Rightarrow \sigma = 5 \div 0.8416 = 5.94$ cm (to 3 s.f.)

b) $P(171 < H < 179)$

$= P\left(\dfrac{171 - 175}{5.94} < Z < \dfrac{179 - 175}{5.94}\right)$

$= P(-0.67 < Z < 0.67)$
$= P(Z < 0.67) - P(Z \leq -0.67)$
$= P(Z < 0.67) - [1 - P(Z < 0.67)]$
$= 2 \times 0.7486 - 1$
$= 0.4972$

Q8 Let R = rainfall in cm. Then $R \sim N(\mu, \sigma^2)$.

$P(R < 4) = 0.102 \Rightarrow P\left(Z < \dfrac{4 - \mu}{\sigma}\right) = 0.102$

$\Rightarrow P\left(Z > \dfrac{\mu - 4}{\sigma}\right) = 0.102 \Rightarrow P\left(Z \leq \dfrac{\mu - 4}{\sigma}\right) = 0.898$

$\Phi(z) = 0.898$ for $z = 1.27$

$\Rightarrow \dfrac{\mu - 4}{\sigma} = 1.27 \Rightarrow \mu - 4 = 1.27\sigma$ *(equation 1)*

$P(R > 7) = 0.648 \Rightarrow P\left(Z > \dfrac{7 - \mu}{\sigma}\right) = 0.648$

$\Rightarrow P\left(Z < \dfrac{\mu - 7}{\sigma}\right) = 0.648$

$\Phi(z) = 0.648$ for $z = 0.38$

$\Rightarrow \dfrac{\mu - 7}{\sigma} = 0.38 \Rightarrow \mu - 7 = 0.38\sigma$ *(equation 2)*

Subtracting equation 2 from equation 1 gives:
$\mu - \mu - 4 - (-7) = 1.27\sigma - 0.38\sigma$
$\Rightarrow 3 = 0.89\sigma \Rightarrow \sigma = 3.37$ (to 3 s.f.)
Putting $\sigma = 3.37$ cm into equation 1 gives:
$\mu = 1.27 \times 3.37 + 4 = 8.28$ cm (to 3 s.f.)
So $\mu = 8.28$ cm and $\sigma = 3.37$ cm (to 3 s.f.)

Review Exercise — Chapter 5

Q1 Using the $\Phi(z)$ table:

a) $P(Z < 0.84) = 0.7995$

b) $P(Z < 2.95) = 0.9984$

c) $P(Z > 0.68) = 1 - P(Z \leq 0.68) = 1 - 0.7517$
$= 0.2483$

d) $P(Z \geq 1.55) = 1 - P(Z < 1.55)$
$= 1 - 0.9394 = 0.0606$

e) $P(Z < -2.10) = P(Z > 2.10) = 1 - P(Z \leq 2.10)$
$= 1 - 0.9821 = 0.0179$

f) $P(Z \leq -0.01) = P(Z \geq 0.01)$
$= 1 - P(Z < 0.01) = 1 - 0.5040 = 0.4960$

g) $P(Z > 0.10) = 1 - P(Z \leq 0.10) = 1 - 0.5398$
$= 0.4602$

h) $P(Z \leq 0.64) = 0.7389$

i) $P(Z > 0.23) = 1 - P(Z \leq 0.23) = 1 - 0.5910$
$= 0.4090$

j) $P(0.10 < Z \le 0.50) = P(Z \le 0.50) - P(Z \le 0.10)$
$= 0.6915 - 0.5398 = 0.1517$

k) $P(-0.62 \le Z < 1.10) = P(Z < 1.10) - P(Z < -0.62)$
$= P(Z < 1.10) - P(Z > 0.62)$
$= P(Z < 1.10) - (1 - P(Z \le 0.62))$
$= 0.8643 - (1 - 0.7324) = 0.5967$

l) $P(-0.99 < Z \le -0.74) = P(0.74 \le Z < 0.99)$
$= P(Z < 0.99) - P(Z < 0.74)$
$= 0.8389 - 0.7704 = 0.0685$

Q2 a) If $P(Z < z) = 0.9131$, then from the $\Phi(z)$ table, $z = 1.36$.

b) If $P(Z < z) = 0.5871$, then from the $\Phi(z)$ table, $z = 0.22$.

c) If $P(Z > z) = 0.0359$, then $P(Z \le z) = 0.9641$. From the $\Phi(z)$ table, $z = 1.80$.

d) If $P(Z > z) = 0.01$, then from the percentage-points table, $z = 2.3263$.

e) If $P(Z \le z) = 0.4013$, then z must be negative (and so won't be in the $\Phi(z)$ table).
But this means $P(Z \ge -z) = 0.4013$, and so $P(Z < -z) = 1 - 0.4013 = 0.5987$.
Using the $\Phi(z)$ table, $-z = 0.25$, so $z = -0.25$.
If you need to draw a graph here to make it a bit clearer what's going on, then draw one.

f) If $P(Z \ge z) = 0.995$, then $P(Z \le -z) = 0.995$
$\Rightarrow P(Z > -z) = 1 - 0.995 = 0.005$
From the percentage-points table, $-z = 2.5758$.
So $z = -2.5758$.
When you've answered a question like this, always ask yourself whether your answer looks 'about right'. Here, you need a number that Z is very very likely to be greater than... so your answer is going to be negative, and it's going to be pretty big. So $z = -2.5758$ looks about right.

g) If $P(-z < Z < z) = 0.5034$, then the remaining area $= 1 - 0.5034 = 0.4966$, and $0.4966 \div 2 = 0.2483$.
So, $P(Z < z) = 0.5034 + 0.2483 = 0.7517$.
This is the area between $-z$ and z + the area to the left of $-z$.
Using the $\Phi(z)$ table, $z = 0.68$.
Or you could divide 0.5034 by 2 to get $P(0 < Z < z)$ $= 0.2517$. Then add 0.5 to get $P(Z < z) = 0.7517$.

h) If $P(0.25 < Z < z) = 0.3917$,
$P(Z < z) - P(Z \le 0.25) = 0.3917$
$\Rightarrow P(Z < z) = 0.3917 + P(Z \le 0.25)$
$\Rightarrow P(Z < z) = 0.3917 + 0.5987 = 0.9904$
Using the $\Phi(z)$ table, $z = 2.34$.

Q3 a) $P(X < 55) = P\left(Z < \dfrac{55 - 50}{4}\right)$
$= P(Z < 1.25) = 0.8944$

b) $P(X < 42) = P\left(Z < \dfrac{42 - 50}{4}\right)$
$= P(Z < -2) = P(Z > 2) = 1 - P(Z \le 2)$
$= 1 - 0.9772 = 0.0228$

c) $P(X > 56) = P\left(Z > \dfrac{56 - 50}{4}\right)$
$= P(Z > 1.5) = 1 - P(Z \le 1.5)$
$= 1 - 0.9332 = 0.0668$

d) $P(47 < X < 57) = P\left(\dfrac{47 - 50}{4} < Z < \dfrac{57 - 50}{4}\right)$
$= P(-0.75 < Z < 1.75)$
$= P(Z < 1.75) - P(Z \le -0.75)$
$= P(Z < 1.75) - P(Z \ge 0.75)$
$= P(Z < 1.75) - [1 - P(Z < 0.75)]$
$= 0.9599 - (1 - 0.7734) = 0.7333$

Q4 a) $P(X < 0) = P\left(Z < \dfrac{0 - 5}{7}\right)$
$= P(Z < -0.71) = P(Z > 0.71)$
$= 1 - P(Z \le 0.71) = 1 - 0.7611 = 0.2389$

b) $P(X < 1) = P\left(Z < \dfrac{1 - 5}{7}\right)$
$= P(Z < -0.57) = P(Z > 0.57)$
$= 1 - P(Z \le 0.57) = 1 - 0.7157 = 0.2843$

c) $P(X > 7) = P\left(Z > \dfrac{7 - 5}{7}\right) = P(Z > 0.29)$
$= 1 - P(Z \le 0.29) = 1 - 0.6141 = 0.3859$

d) $P(2 < X < 4) = P\left(\dfrac{2 - 5}{7} < Z < \dfrac{4 - 5}{7}\right)$
$= P(-0.43 < Z < -0.14)$
$= P(0.14 < Z < 0.43)$
$= P(Z < 0.43) - P(Z \le 0.14)$
$= 0.6664 - 0.5557$
$= 0.1107$

Q5 a) Here $X \sim N(80, 15)$.
If $P(X < a) = 0.99$, then $P\left(Z \ge \dfrac{a - 80}{\sqrt{15}}\right) = 0.01$
So $\dfrac{a - 80}{\sqrt{15}} = 2.3263$ (using percentage points).
Rearrange this to get $a = 80 + 2.3263 \times \sqrt{15}$
$= 89.01$ (to 4 s.f.)

b) $|X - 80| < b$ means that X is 'within b' of 80, i.e. $80 - b < X < 80 + b$.
Since 80 is the mean of X, and since a normal distribution is symmetrical,
$P(80 - b < X < 80 + b) = 0.8$ means that
$P(X \ge 80 + b) = 0.1$
$\Rightarrow P\left(Z \ge \dfrac{80 + b - 80}{\sqrt{15}}\right) = P\left(Z \ge \dfrac{b}{\sqrt{15}}\right) = 0.1$
So $\dfrac{b}{\sqrt{15}} = 1.2816$ (using percentage points).
And so $b = 4.964$ (to 4 s.f.)
It's really important you remember that a normal distribution is symmetrical. You often need to use symmetry to work out these sorts of questions.

Q6 If X represents the mass of an item in grams, then $X \sim N(55, 4.4^2)$.

a) $P(X < 55) = P\left(Z < \dfrac{55 - 55}{4.4}\right) = P(Z < 0) = 0.5$

b) $P(X < 50) = P\left(Z < \dfrac{50 - 55}{4.4}\right) = P(Z < -1.14)$
$= P(Z > 1.14) = 1 - P(Z \le 1.14)$
$= 1 - 0.8729 = 0.1271$

c) $P(X > 60) = P\left(Z > \dfrac{60 - 55}{4.4}\right) = P(Z > 1.14)$
$= 1 - P(Z \le 1.14) = 1 - 0.8729 = 0.1271$

Q7 If X represents the mass of an egg in kilograms, then $X \sim N(1.4, 0.3^2)$.

Watch out for the units here — you need to make them the same for both the mean and the variance.

$P(X < a) = 0.8830 \Rightarrow P\left(Z < \frac{a - 1.4}{0.3}\right) = 0.8830$

$\Phi(z) = 0.8830$ for $z = 1.19$

$\Rightarrow \frac{a - 1.4}{0.3} = 1.19 \Rightarrow a = 1.19 \times 0.3 + 1.4 = 1.757$

Q8 $P(X < 8) = 0.8925 \Rightarrow P\left(Z < \frac{8 - \mu}{\sqrt{10}}\right) = 0.8925$

$\Phi(z) = 0.8925$ for $z = 1.24$

$\Rightarrow \frac{8 - \mu}{\sqrt{10}} = 1.24 \Rightarrow \mu = 8 - 1.24 \times \sqrt{10}$

$= 4.08$ (to 3 s.f.)

Q9 $P(X > 221) = 0.3085 \Rightarrow P\left(Z > \frac{221 - \mu}{8}\right) = 0.3085$

$\Rightarrow P\left(Z \leq \frac{221 - \mu}{8}\right) = 1 - 0.3085 = 0.6915$

$\Phi(z) = 0.6915$ for $z = 0.5$

$\Rightarrow \frac{221 - \mu}{8} = 0.5 \Rightarrow \mu = 221 - 0.5 \times 8 = 217$

Q10 $P(X < 13) = 0.6$

$\Rightarrow P\left(Z < \frac{13 - 11}{\sigma}\right) = P\left(Z < \frac{2}{\sigma}\right) = 0.6$

$\Rightarrow P\left(Z \geq \frac{2}{\sigma}\right) = 0.4$

$p = 0.4$ for $z = 0.2533$

$\Rightarrow \frac{2}{\sigma} = 0.2533 \Rightarrow \sigma = 2 \div 0.2533 = 7.90$ (to 3 s.f.)

Q11 $P(X \leq 110) = 0.9678$

$\Rightarrow P\left(Z \leq \frac{110 - 108}{\sigma}\right) = P\left(Z \leq \frac{2}{\sigma}\right) = 0.9678$

$\Phi(z) = 0.9678$ for $z = 1.85$

$\Rightarrow \frac{2}{\sigma} = 1.85 \Rightarrow \sigma = 2 \div 1.85 = 1.08$ (to 3 s.f.)

Q12 $P(X < 15.2) = 0.9783 \Rightarrow P\left(Z < \frac{15.2 - \mu}{\sigma}\right) = 0.9783$

$\Phi(z) = 0.9783$ for $z = 2.02$

$\Rightarrow \frac{15.2 - \mu}{\sigma} = 2.02 \Rightarrow 15.2 - \mu = 2.02\sigma$ *(equation 1)*

$P(X > 14.8) = 0.1056 \Rightarrow P\left(Z > \frac{14.8 - \mu}{\sigma}\right) = 0.1056$

$\Rightarrow P\left(Z \leq \frac{14.8 - \mu}{\sigma}\right) = 1 - 0.1056 = 0.8944$

$\Phi(z) = 0.8944$ for $z = 1.25$

$\Rightarrow \frac{14.8 - \mu}{\sigma} = 1.25 \Rightarrow 14.8 - \mu = 1.25\sigma$ *(equation 2)*

Subtracting equation 2 from equation 1 gives:

$15.2 - 14.8 - \mu - (-\mu) = 2.02\sigma - 1.25\sigma$
$\Rightarrow 0.4 = 0.77\sigma \Rightarrow \sigma = 0.51948... = 0.519$ (to 3 s.f.)
Putting $\sigma = 0.519...$ into equation 1 gives:
$\mu = 15.2 - 2.02 \times 0.519... = 14.2$ (to 3 s.f.)
So $\mu = 14.2$ and $\sigma = 0.519$ (to 3 s.f.)

Exam-Style Questions — Chapter 5

1 Let X represent the exam marks. Then $X \sim N(50, 15^2)$.

a) $P(X < 30) = P\left(Z < \frac{30 - 50}{15}\right) = P(Z < -1.33)$
[1 mark]
$= P(Z > 1.33) = 1 - P(Z \leq 1.33)$ *[1 mark]*
$= 1 - 0.9082 = 0.0918$ *[1 mark]*

b) $P(X \geq 41) = P\left(Z \geq \frac{41 - 50}{15}\right) = P(Z \geq -0.6)$
[1 mark]
$= P(Z \leq 0.6) = 0.7257$ *[1 mark]*
So $0.7257 \times 1000 = 726$ is the expected number who passed the exam *[1 mark]*.

c) If a is the mark needed for a distinction, then:
$P(X \geq a) = 0.1 \Rightarrow P\left(Z \geq \frac{a - 50}{15}\right) = 0.1$ *[1 mark]*
$p = 0.1$ for $z = 1.2816$
$\Rightarrow \frac{a - 50}{15} = 1.2816$ *[1 mark]*
$\Rightarrow a = 69.2$ (to 3 s.f.) *[1 mark]*

2 a) $P(X < 50) = 0.123$
$\Rightarrow P\left(Z < \frac{50 - \mu}{6}\right) = 0.123$ *[1 mark]*
$\Rightarrow P\left(Z > \frac{\mu - 50}{6}\right) = 0.123$
$\Rightarrow P\left(Z \leq \frac{\mu - 50}{6}\right) = 1 - 0.123 = 0.877$ *[1 mark]*
$\Phi(z) = 0.877$ for $z = 1.16$
$\Rightarrow \frac{\mu - 50}{6} = 1.16$ *[1 mark]*
$\Rightarrow \mu = 1.16 \times 6 + 50 = 56.96$ *[1 mark]*

b) $P(X > 71) = P\left(Z > \frac{71 - 56.96}{6}\right)$
$= P(Z > 2.34)$ *[1 mark]*
$= 1 - P(Z \leq 2.34)$ *[1 mark]*
$= 1 - 0.9904 = 0.0096$ *[1 mark]*

c) Since the distribution is symmetrical about μ,
$P(X < \mu + a) = 0.9$ *[1 mark]*
$\Rightarrow P\left(Z < \frac{\mu + a - \mu}{6}\right) = P\left(Z < \frac{a}{6}\right) = 0.9$
[1 mark]
$\Rightarrow P\left(Z \geq \frac{a}{6}\right) = 0.1$
$p = 0.1$ for $z = 1.2816$
$\Rightarrow \frac{a}{6} = 1.2816$ *[1 mark]*
$\Rightarrow a = 7.69$ (to 3 s.f.) *[1 mark]*

3 a) Let X represent the lifetime of a battery in hours.
Then $X \sim N(\mu, \sigma^2)$.
$P(X < 20) = 0.4 \Rightarrow P\left(Z < \frac{20 - \mu}{\sigma}\right) = 0.4$ *[1 mark]*
$\Rightarrow P\left(Z > \frac{\mu - 20}{\sigma}\right) = 0.4$
Using the percentage-points table,
$p = 0.4$ for $z = 0.2533$
$\Rightarrow \frac{\mu - 20}{\sigma} = 0.2533$ *[1 mark]*
$\Rightarrow \mu - 20 = 0.2533\sigma$ *(equation 1)*
$P(X < 26) = 0.8 \Rightarrow P\left(Z < \frac{26 - \mu}{\sigma}\right) = 0.8$ *[1 mark]*
$\Rightarrow P\left(Z \geq \frac{26 - \mu}{\sigma}\right) = 0.2$
Using the percentage-points table,
$p = 0.2$ for $z = 0.8416$
$\Rightarrow \frac{26 - \mu}{\sigma} = 0.8416$ *[1 mark]*
$\Rightarrow 26 - \mu = 0.8416\sigma$ *(equation 2)*
Adding equations 1 and 2 gives:
$\mu - \mu - 20 + 26 = 0.2533\sigma + 0.8416\sigma$ *[1 mark]*
$\Rightarrow 6 = 1.0949\sigma \Rightarrow \sigma = 5.47995... = 5.48$ (to 3 s.f.)
Putting $\sigma = 5.47...$ into equation 1 gives:
$\mu = 0.2533 \times 5.47... + 20 = 21.4$ (to 3 s.f.)
So $\mu = 21.4$ hours *[1 mark]*
and $\sigma = 5.48$ hours *[1 mark]* (to 3 s.f.)

b) From part a), $X \sim N(21.4, 5.48^2)$
So $P(X \geq 15) = P\left(Z \geq \frac{15 - 21.4}{5.48}\right)$ *[1 mark]*
$= P(Z \geq -1.17) = P(Z \leq 1.17)$ *[1 mark]*
$= 0.8790$ *[1 mark]*

4 a) $P(X > 145) = P\left(Z > \frac{145 - 120}{25}\right)$
$= P(Z > 1)$ *[1 mark]*
$= 1 - P(Z \leq 1)$ *[1 mark]*
$= 1 - 0.8413 = 0.1587$ *[1 mark]*

b) $P(120 < X < j) = 0.4641$
$\Rightarrow P\left(\frac{120 - 120}{25} < Z < \frac{j - 120}{25}\right) = 0.4641$
$\Rightarrow P\left(0 < Z < \frac{j - 120}{25}\right) = 0.4641$ *[1 mark]*
$\Rightarrow P\left(Z < \frac{j - 120}{25}\right) - P(Z \leq 0) = 0.4641$
$\Rightarrow P\left(Z < \frac{j - 120}{25}\right) = 0.4641 + 0.5$
$\Rightarrow P\left(Z < \frac{j - 120}{25}\right) = 0.9641$ *[1 mark]*
$\Phi(z) = 0.9641$ for $z = 1.80$
$\Rightarrow \frac{j - 120}{25} = 1.8$ *[1 mark]*
$\Rightarrow j = 1.8 \times 25 + 120 = 165$ *[1 mark]*

5 a) For a normal distribution, mean = median,
so median = 12 inches *[1 mark]*.

b) Let X represent the base diameters.
Then $X \sim N(12, \sigma^2)$. $P(X > 13) = 0.05$ *[1 mark]*,
so $P\left(Z > \frac{13 - 12}{\sigma}\right) = P\left(Z > \frac{1}{\sigma}\right) = 0.05$ *[1 mark]*
Using the percentage-points table,
$p = 0.05$ for $z = 1.6449$
$\Rightarrow \frac{1}{\sigma} = 1.6449$ *[1 mark]*
$\Rightarrow \sigma = 1 \div 1.6449 = 0.608$ (to 3 s.f.) *[1 mark]*

c) $P(X < 10.8) = P\left(Z < \frac{10.8 - 12}{0.608}\right)$
$= P(Z < -1.97)$ *[1 mark]*
$= P(Z > 1.97) = 1 - (Z \leq 1.97)$
$= 1 - 0.9756 = 0.0244$ *[1 mark]*
So you would expect $0.0244 \times 100 \approx 2$ pizza
bases to be discarded *[1 mark]*.

d) P(at least 1 base too small)
= 1 − P(no bases too small).
P(base not too small) = 1 − 0.0244 = 0.9756.
P(no bases too small) = 0.9756^3 = 0.9286
[1 mark]
P(at least 1 base too small) = 1 − 0.9286 *[1 mark]*
= 0.0714 *[1 mark]*.

6 a) Let X represent the volume of compost in a bag.
Then $X \sim N(50, 0.4^2)$.
$P(X < 49) = P\left(Z < \frac{49 - 50}{0.4}\right)$
$= P(Z < -2.5)$ *[1 mark]*
$= P(Z > 2.5) = 1 - P(Z \leq 2.5)$ *[1 mark]*
$= 1 - 0.9938 = 0.0062$ *[1 mark]*

b) $P(X > 50.5) = P\left(Z > \frac{50.5 - 50}{0.4}\right)$
$= P(Z > 1.25)$ *[1 mark]*
$= 1 - P(Z \leq 1.25)$ *[1 mark]*
$= 1 - 0.8944 = 0.1056$ *[1 mark]*
So in 1000 bags, 0.1056×1000 *[1 mark]*
≈ 106 bags *[1 mark]* (approximately) would be
expected to contain more than 50.5 litres of
compost.

c) $P(Y < 74) = 0.1$
$\Rightarrow P\left(Z < \frac{74 - 75}{\sigma}\right) = P\left(Z < -\frac{1}{\sigma}\right) = 0.1$
$\Rightarrow P\left(Z > \frac{1}{\sigma}\right) = 0.1$ *[1 mark]*
Using the percentage-points table,
$p = 0.1$ for $z = 1.2816$
$\Rightarrow \frac{1}{\sigma} = 1.2816$ *[1 mark]*
$\Rightarrow \sigma = 1 \div 1.2816$
$= 0.780$ litres (to 3 s.f.) *[1 mark]*

Glossary

A

Addition law
A formula linking the probability of the **union** and the probability of the **intersection** of events A and B.

B

Bivariate data
Data that comes as an ordered pair of **variables** (x, y).

Boxplot
A diagram showing the **median**, **quartiles** and greatest/least values of a data set, as well as any **outliers**.

C

Coding
Coding means transforming all the readings in a data set to make the numbers easier to work with.

Complement (of an event A)
The group of all **outcomes** corresponding to event A not happening.

Conditional probability
A probability is conditional if it depends on whether or not another **event** happens.

Continuous random variable
A **random variable** which is measured on a continuous scale. It may take any value in a given range (i.e. with no 'gaps' between possible values).

Correlation
A linear relationship between two **variables** showing that they change together to some extent.
(A correlation does not necessarily mean a causal relationship.)

Cumulative distribution function
A function, $F(x)$, which gives the probability that a **random variable**, X, will be less than or equal to a particular value, x.

D

Dependent variable
Another name for the **response variable**.

Discrete random variable
A **random variable** with 'gaps' between its possible values.

Discrete uniform distribution
A **discrete random variable** has a discrete uniform distribution if all the possible values it can take are equally likely.

Dispersion
Measures of dispersion describe how spread out data values are.

E

Event
An event is a 'group' of one or more possible **outcomes**.

Expected value
The expected value of a **random variable** is the 'expected' **mean** of a large number of readings. It's the sum of all possible values multiplied by their probability.

Explanatory variable
In an experiment, the **variable** you can control, or the one that you think is affecting the other.

Extrapolation
Predicting a value of y corresponding to a value of x outside the range for which you have data.

F

Fence
If a data value lies outside a fence, then it is an **outlier**.

Frequency density
The frequency of a class divided by its class width.

H

Histogram
A diagram showing the frequencies with which a continuous variable falls in particular classes — the frequency of a class is proportional to the area of a bar.

I

Independent events
If the probability of an **event** B happening doesn't depend on whether or not an **event** A happens, **events** A and B are independent.

Independent variable
Another name for the **explanatory variable**.

Interpolation
Predicting a value of y corresponding to a value of x within the range for which you have data.

Interquartile range
A measure of **dispersion**. It's the difference between the **upper quartile** and the **lower quartile**.

Intersection (of events A and B)
The set of outcomes corresponding to both **event** A and **event** B happening.

L

Linear regression
A method for finding the equation of a line of best fit on a **scatter diagram**.

Location
Measures of location show where the 'centre' of the data lies.

Lower quartile
The value that 25% of data values in a data set are less than or equal to.

M

Mean
A measure of **location** — it's the sum of a set of data values, divided by the number of data values.

Median
A measure of **location** — it's the value in the middle of the data set when all the data values are in order of size.

Mode
A measure of **location** — it's the most frequently occurring data value.

Mode of a discrete random variable
The value that the random variable is most likely to take — i.e. the one with the highest probability.

Mutually exclusive
Events are mutually exclusive (or just 'exclusive') if they have no **outcomes** in common, and so can't happen at the same time.

Normal distribution
A continuous 'bell-shaped' probability distribution where the further from the mean a value is, the less likely it is to occur.

Outcome
One of the possible results of a **trial** or experiment.

Outlier
A freak piece of data lying a long way from the majority of the values in a data set.

Percentiles
The percentiles (P_1-P_{99}) divide an ordered data set into 100 parts.

Probability distribution for a discrete random variable
A table showing all the possible values that the **random variable** can take, plus the probability that it takes each value.

Probability function
A function that generates the probabilities of a **discrete random variable** taking each of its possible values.

Product law
A formula used to work out the probability of two **events** both happening.

Product moment correlation coefficient
A measure of the strength of the **correlation** between two **variables**.

Qualitative variable
A **variable** that takes non-numerical values.

Quantitative variable
A **variable** that takes numerical values.

Quartiles
The three quartiles Q_1, Q_2 and Q_3 divide an ordered data set into four parts.

Random variable
A **variable** taking different values with different probabilities.

Range
A measure of **dispersion**. It's the difference between the highest value and the lowest value.

Regression line
A line of best fit found using **linear regression**.

Residual
The difference between a real-life observation and what a **regression line** predicts.

Response variable
In an experiment, the **variable** you think is being affected.

Sample space
The set of all possible **outcomes** of a **trial**.

Scatter diagram
Graph showing the two **variables** in a **bivariate** data set plotted against each other.

Skewness
Measures of skewness tell you how symmetrically distributed a data set is.

Standard deviation
A measure of **dispersion** calculated by taking the square root of the **variance.**

Standard normal variable, *Z*
A **random variable** that follows a **normal distribution** with **mean** 0 and **variance** 1.

Stem and leaf diagram
A way of displaying data in which the data values are split into a 'stem' and a 'leaf'. Data values with the same stem are shown in the same row of the diagram.

Tree diagram
Tree diagrams show probabilities for sequences of two or more **events**.

Trial
A process (e.g. an experiment) with different possible **outcomes**.

Union (of events A and B)
The set of **outcomes** corresponding to either **event** A or **event** B (or both) happening.

Upper quartile
The value that 75% of data values in a data set are less than or equal to.

Variable
A quantity that can take a variety of values — its value is not fixed.

Variance
A measure of **dispersion** from the **mean**.

Variance of a discrete random variable
The 'expected' **variance** of a large number of readings.

Venn diagram
A Venn diagram shows how a collection of objects is split up into different groups, where everything in a group has something in common. In probability, the objects are **outcomes**, and the groups are **events**.

Z-tables
Tables relating to the **standard normal variable** (*Z*) — such as the **cumulative distribution function** $\Phi(z)$, and the percentage-points table.

Index

S1 Formula Sheet

These are the formulas you'll be given in the exam, but make sure you know exactly **when you need them** and **how to use them**.

Probability

addition
$$P(A \cup B) = P(A) + P(B) - P(A \cap B)$$

Product $$P(A \cap B) = P(A) \times P(B|A)$$

$$P(A|B) = \frac{P(B|A)P(A)}{P(B|A)P(A) + P(B|A')P(A')}$$

dua-
consecutive

$E(x) = \frac{n+1}{2}$

$Var(x) = \frac{(n+1)(n-1)}{12}$

non-c:
$E(x) = \frac{a+b}{2}$

$Var(x) = \frac{(b-a+1)^2 - 1}{12}$

Discrete Distributions

For a discrete random variable X taking values x_i with probabilities $P(X = x_i)$:

Expectation (mean): $E(X) = \mu = \Sigma x_i P(X = x_i)$

Variance: $Var(X) = \sigma^2 = \Sigma(x_i - \mu)^2 P(X = x_i)$
$$= \Sigma x_i^2 P(X = x_i) - \mu^2$$

For a function g(X): $E(g(X)) = \Sigma g(x_i)P(X = x_i)$

Continuous Distributions

Standard continuous distribution:

Distribution of X	P.D.F.	Mean	Variance
Normal N(μ, σ^2)	$\dfrac{1}{\sigma\sqrt{2\pi}}e^{-\frac{1}{2}\left(\frac{x-\mu}{\sigma}\right)^2}$	μ	σ^2

Correlation and Regression

For a set of n pairs of values (x_i, y_i):

$$S_{xx} = \Sigma(x_i - \bar{x})^2 = \Sigma x_i^2 - \frac{(\Sigma x_i)^2}{n} \qquad S_{yy} = \Sigma(y_i - \bar{y})^2 = \Sigma y_i^2 - \frac{(\Sigma y_i)^2}{n}$$

$$S_{xy} = \Sigma(x_i - \bar{x})(y_i - \bar{y}) = \Sigma x_i y_i - \frac{(\Sigma x_i)(\Sigma y_i)}{n}$$

The **product moment correlation coefficient** is:

$$r = \frac{S_{xy}}{\sqrt{S_{xx}S_{yy}}} = \frac{\Sigma(x_i - \bar{x})(y_i - \bar{y})}{\sqrt{\{\Sigma(x_i - \bar{x})^2\}\{\Sigma(y_i - \bar{y})^2\}}} = \frac{\Sigma x_i y_i - \frac{(\Sigma x_i)(\Sigma y_i)}{n}}{\sqrt{\left(\Sigma x_i^2 - \frac{(\Sigma x_i)^2}{n}\right)\left(\Sigma y_i^2 - \frac{(\Sigma y_i)^2}{n}\right)}}$$

The **regression coefficient** of y on x is b $= \dfrac{S_{xy}}{S_{xx}} = \dfrac{\Sigma(x_i - \bar{x})(y_i - \bar{y})}{\Sigma(x_i - \bar{x})^2}$

Least squares regression line of y on x is $y = a + bx$ where a $= \bar{y} - b\bar{x}$

MES1T51